The 2000 Presidential Campaign

Recent Titles in the
Praeger Series in Political Communication
Robert E. Denton, Jr., *General Editor*

Videostyle in Presidential Campaigns: Style and Content of Televised Political Advertising
Lynda L. Kaid

Political Communication Ethics: An Oxymoron?
Robert E. Denton, Jr., editor

Navigating Boundaries: The Rhetoric of Women Governors
Brenda DeVore Marshall and Molly A. Mayhead, editors

Talk of Power, Power of Talk: The 1994 Health Care Reform Debate and Beyond
Michael W. Shelton

When Congress Debates: A Bakhtinian Paradigm
Theodore F. Scheckels

The Rhetoric of First Lady Hillary Rodham Clinton: Crisis Management Discourse
Colleen Elizabeth Kelley

The Clinton Scandals and the Politics of Image Restoration
Joseph R. Blaney and William L. Benoit

Campaign Craft: The Strategies, Tactics, and Art of Political Campaign Management
Daniel M. Shea and Michael John Burton

The Idea of Political Marketing
Nicholas J. O'Shaughnessy, editor, and Stephan C.M. Henneberg, associate editor

The Primary Decision: A Functional Analysis of Debates in Presidential Primaries
William L. Benoit, P.M. Pier, LeAnn M. Brazeal, John P. McHale, Andrew Klyukovski, and David Airne

Notable Speeches in Contemporary Presidential Campaigns
Robert V. Friedenberg

Global Political Campaigning: A Worldwide Analysis of Campaign Professionals and Their Practices
Fritz Plasser

The 2000 Presidential Campaign

A Communication Perspective

Edited by
Robert E. Denton, Jr.

Praeger Series in Political Communication

Westport, Connecticut
London

Library of Congress Cataloging-in-Publication Data

The 2000 presidential campaign : a communication perspective / edited by Robert E. Denton, Jr.
p. cm.—(Praeger series in political communication, ISSN 1062–5623)
Includes bibliographical references and index.
ISBN 0–275–97107–4 (alk. paper)—ISBN 0–275–97120–1 (pbk. : alk. paper)
1. Presidents—United States—Election—2000. 2. Political campaigns—United States. 3. Communication in politics—United States. 4. Mass media—Political aspects—United States. I. Denton, Robert E., Jr. II. Series.
JK526 2000q
324.973'0929—dc21 2001059151

British Library Cataloguing in Publication Data is available.

Library of Congress Catalog Card Number: 2001059151
ISBN: 0–275–97107–4
0–275–97120–1 (pbk.)
ISSN: 1062–5623

First published in 2002

Praeger Publishers, 88 Post Road West, Westport, CT 06881
An imprint of Greenwood Publishing Group, Inc.
www.praeger.com

Printed in the United States of America

The paper used in this book complies with the Permanent Paper Standard issued by the National Information Standards Organization (Z39.48–1984).

10 9 8 7 6 5 4 3 2 1

This book is dedicated to Herman Doswald, former Dean of the College of Arts and Sciences at Virginia Tech. As a "brash" 34-year-old, Herman gave me an opportunity to come to Virginia Tech and to provide leadership to the Department of Communication Studies. He was the perfect mentor—honest, principled, straightforward, supportive, encouraging, and accessible. Deeds counted more than words, actions more than promises, and reason more than excuses. Such privileged associations define life. With my utmost admiration and appreciation.

Contents

Series Foreword

Those of us from the discipline of communication studies have long believed that communication is prior to all other fields of inquiry. In several other forums I have argued that the essence of politics is "talk" or human interaction.[1] Such interaction may be formal or informal, verbal or nonverbal, public or private, but it is always persuasive, forcing us consciously or subconsciously to interpret, to evaluate, and to act. Communication is the vehicle for human action.

From this perspective, it is not surprising that Aristotle recognized the natural kinship of politics and communication in his writings *Politics* and *Rhetoric*. In the former, he established that human beings are "political beings [who] alone of the animals [are] furnished with the faculty of language."[2] And in the latter, he began his systematic analysis of discourse by proclaiming that "rhetorical study, in its strict sense, is concerned with the modes of persuasion."[3] Thus, it was recognized over 2,300 years ago that politics and communication go hand in hand because they are essential parts of human nature.

Back in 1981, Dan Nimmo and Keith Sanders proclaimed that political communication was an emerging field.[4] Although its origin, as noted, dates back centuries, a "self-consciously cross-disciplinary" focus began in the late 1950s. Thousands of books and articles later, colleges and universities offer a variety of graduate and undergraduate coursework in the area in such diverse departments as communication, mass communication, journalism, political science, and sociology.[5] In Nimmo and Sanders's early assessment, the "key areas of inquiry" included rhetorical analysis, propaganda analysis, attitude change studies, voting studies, government and the news media, functional and systems analyses, technological changes, media technologies, campaign techniques, and research techniques.[6] In a survey of the state of the field in 1983, the same authors and Lynda Kaid found additional, more specific areas of concern such as the presidency, political polls, public opinion, debates, and advertising.[7] Since the first study, they also noted a shift away from the rather strict behavioral approach.

A decade later, Dan Nimmo and David Swanson argued that "political communication has developed some identity as a more or less distinct domain of scholarly work."[8] The scope and concerns of the area have further expanded to include critical theories and cultural studies. While there is no precise definition, method, or disciplinary home of the area of inquiry, its primary domain is the role, processes, and effects of communication within the context of politics broadly defined.

In 1985, the editors of *Political Communication Yearbook: 1984* noted that "more things are happening in the study, teaching, and practice of political communication than can be captured within the space limitations of the relatively few publications available."[9] In addition, they argued that the backgrounds of "those involved in the field [are] so varied and pluralist in outlook and approach . . . it [is] a mistake to adhere slavishly to any set format in shaping the content."[10] More recently, Nimmo and Swanson have called for "ways of overcoming the unhappy consequences of fragmentation within a framework that respects, encourages, and benefits from diverse scholarly commitments, agendas, and approaches."[11]

In agreement with these assessments of the area and with gentle encouragement, in 1988 Praeger established the series entitled "Praeger Series in Political Communication." The series is open to all qualitative and quantitative methodologies as well as contemporary and historical studies. The key to characterizing the studies in the series is the focus on communication variables or activities within a political context or dimension. As of this writing, over 80 volumes have been published and numerous impressive works are forthcoming. Scholars from the disciplines of communication, history, journalism, political science, and sociology have participated in the series.

I am, without shame or modesty, a fan of the series. The joy of serving as its editor is in participating in the dialogue of the field of political communication and in reading the contributors' works. I invite you to join me.

Robert E. Denton, Jr.

NOTES

1. See Robert E. Denton, Jr., *The Symbolic Dimensions of the American Presidency* (Prospect Heights, Ill.: Waveland Press, 1982); Robert E. Denton, Jr., and Gary

Woodward, *Political Communication in America* (New York: Praeger, 1985; 2nd ed., 1990); Robert E. Denton, Jr., and Dan Han, *Presidential Communication* (New York: Praeger, 1986); and Robert E. Denton, Jr., *The Primetime Presidency of Ronald Reagan* (New York: Praeger, 1988).

2. Aristotle, *The Politics of Aristotle*, trans. Ernest Barker (New York: Oxford University Press, 1970), p. 5.

3. Aristotle, *Rhetoric*, trans. W. Rhys Roberts (New York: The Modern Library, 1954), p. 22.

4. Dan Nimmo and Keith Sanders, "Introduction: The Emergence of Political Communication as a Field," in *Handbook of Political Communication*, ed. Dan Nimmo and Keith Sanders (Beverly Hills, Calif.: Sage, 1981), pp. 11–36.

5. Ibid., p. 15.

6. Ibid., pp. 17–27.

7. Keith Sanders, Lynda Kaid, and Dan Nimmo, eds., *Political Communication Yearbook: 1984* (Carbondale: Southern Illinois University Press, 1985), pp. 283–308.

8. Dan Nimmo and David Swanson, "The Field of Political Communication: Beyond the Voter Persuasion Paradigm," in *New Directions in Political Communication*, ed. David Swanson and Dan Nimmo (Beverly Hills, Calif.: Sage, 1990), p. 8.

9. Sanders, Kaid, and Nimmo, *Political Communication Yearbook: 1984*, p. xiv.

10. Ibid.

11. Nimmo and Swanson, "The Field of Political Communication," p. 11.

Preface

> Every four years a gong goes off and a new Presidential campaign surges into the national consciousness: new candidates, new issues, a new season of surprises. But underlying the syncopations of change is a steady, recurrent rhythm from election to election, a pulse of politics, that brings up the same basic themes in order, over and over again.
>
> —James David Barber (1980, 3)

Every presidential campaign is unique and historic. However, the 2000 presidential contest is historic in many ways. Never before in American history have all three of the national elections for president, House, and Senate ended up virtually dead even. There was the virtual tie in the presidential race, even parity in House votes (49 percent for each party), and near-tie in votes in Senate races (Republican advantage 50 percent to 48 percent).

George Bush won the presidency with 47.9 percent of the popular vote, representing just 24.5 percent of the electorate. He is the first president since 1888 to lose the popular vote. In addition, Al Gore wins more popular votes than any presidential candidate except for Ronald Reagan. The campaign was more of a roller-coaster ride than a marathon. There were constant rises and dips for each candidate. A significant number of independent voters changed their minds several times during the general campaign. Much of the support for both candidates was "soft" right up until election day. However, the most volatile of all the voters were women, especially unmarried women who ultimately favored Gore 63 percent to Bush's 32 percent.

Without question, the 2000 presidential campaign was the most expensive in American history. Campaign spending was about 50 percent higher than just four years earlier. Over $3 *billion* was spent, two-thirds raised by candidates and political parties, one-third representing interest group participation. Bush enjoys the distinction of spending the most money by any presidential candidate, well over $160 million. The Republican National Committee raised and spent the most unregulated and "soft money," over $136 million.

Of course, the 2000 presidential campaign will most likely be remembered for what happened after the polls closed on November 7 rather than for the speeches, conventions, issues, debates, or television ads. Traditionally, we think of four phases of a political campaign: preprimary, primary, convention, and general election. With this election, we had an additional phase—some even refer to the period as "the second campaign" of the 2000 presidential election. On election day, no one expected the outcome of the race would take 36 days and more than 50 lawsuits. In addition to just a few hundred votes in Florida determining the next president, it was impossible to anticipate the drama of recounts, challenges, court cases, and the debates over hanging, swinging, or dimpled chads. (The only "Chad" I knew was in high school.) Frozen forever in my mind is the image of judges holding up ballots, examining each one as if it were some freshly mined jewel.

For communication scholars, the essence of politics is "talk" or human interaction. The interaction may be formal or informal, verbal or nonverbal, public or private, but always persuasive, forcing us as individuals to interpret, to evaluate, and to act.

Presidential campaigns are our national conversations. They are highly complex and sophisticated communication events: communication of issues, images, social reality, and personas. They are essentially exercises in the creation, recreation, and transmission of "significant symbols" through human communication. As we attempt to make sense of our environment, "political bits" of communication comprise our voting choices, worldviews, and legislative desires.

The plethora of popular publications about the race seem to take one of three perspectives: It was Al Gore's to lose and he lost it; it was George Bush's to lose and he won it; Gore and/or Bush both tried to "steal" the election.

The purpose of this volume is to review the 2000 presidential campaign from a communication perspective. The analyses go beyond the quantitative facts, electoral counts, and poll results of the election. Each chapter focuses on a specific area of political campaign communication: the early campaign period, the nomination process and conventions, candidate strategies, presidential debates, political advertising, the use of the Internet, and the news coverage of the campaigns.

In the first chapter, Robert E. Denton, Jr. identifies and discusses five pivotal elements that largely explain the ebb and flow of the campaign. Each element altered the dynamics of the campaign and influenced strategies and tactics, public support, media framing, and candidate images. They were critical in the sense that they favored one candidate over another in terms of public support and ultimate victory. The overview provides a macro-analysis of the election season.

In Chapter 2, Judith S. Trent provides an overview of the early campaign period. In addition to identifying the unique elements of the primary and preprimary seasons, Trent argues that it was in the early portions of the 2000 campaign that decisions were made and paths charted that determined the results of the entire election as never before.

In Chapter 3, Henry C. Kenski, from a different perspective, examines the key factors in the Republican and Democratic nominations of 2000. By identifying and analyzing five rather distinct phases, Kenski argues that the nomination contest was a story of two insurgencies that challenged the front-runners and party organization favorites.

In Chapter 4, Craig Allen Smith and Neil Mansharamani analyze the ways George W. Bush and Al Gore enacted the roles of challenger and incumbent in the 2000 election. They contend that situational factors favored Gore; that Gore relinquished significant elements of an incumbent's advantage; that Bush seized upon Gore's error to refocus the contest; and that the campaign concluded as a contest between two challengers, with Bush providing more continuity and the more appealing changes. They conclude by proposing a revised typology of challenger and incumbent styles.

In Chapter 5, Rachel L. Holloway analyzes how the conventions framed the campaigns and positioned the candidates for the fall election. Going beyond traditional analyses of the candidate nomination speeches, Holloway provides a cultural perspective. Rather than viewing the electoral outcome as a divided nation, Bush and Gore actually asked the uncommitted voters in the middle ground to choose between contemporary expressions of progressivism and populism. In the end, Gore and Bush both proposed an egalitarian view of the world, and thus the closeness of the election outcome was more a product of similarity than of difference. The political culture perspective suggests that voters choose those candidates, issue positions, and policies that reinforce their way of life or cultural preferences. Understanding campaign discourse as an expression of political culture allows an explanation of voter preference, absent voter knowledge.

In Chapter 6, Robert V. Friedenberg provides an in-depth analysis of the three presidential debates. George Bush and Al Gore both debated well throughout the three debates. Both men appeared presidential, informed, and knowledgeable about the major issues of concern. They had largely targeted their respective base voters and did nothing to jeopardize that support. However, Bush emerged the "winner." In addition, the debates surfaced the issue of Gore's penchant for exaggeration. Finally, the debates projected an image of Gore that in comparison to Bush was less likable and less favorable.

In Chapter 7, Rita Kirk Whillock and David E. Whillock examine the use of the Internet in the presidential election. Indeed, the role and impact of the Internet upon campaigns continue to evolve. Usage in this presidential campaign was notable for several reasons. Election regulations regarding citizen and campaign use changed, allowing for its legal use while attempting to tame its revolutionary character. Second, campaigns raised an enormous amount of money through campaign Internet Web sites. Finally, all campaigns developed new and better ways to use the Internet as a method of campaign organization and information dissemination.

In Chapter 8, Lynda Lee Kaid explores the effects of political advertising during the general campaign. In analyzing the ads, Kaid focused on verbal components (image or issue, positive or negative tone, type of proof) as well as strategies used by the candidates. Finally, Kaid reviewed some of the more inventive production techniques used in the ads. Although the ads were similar to those of past years, overall they were more positive and issue oriented. Emotional proof was the dominant feature of the ads, with Democrats relying more on fear appeals. Interestingly, candidates were the main presenter or speaker in their ads, a significant change from elections past. Perhaps most troubling for Kaid was the high level of technological distortion present in the ads of both candidates. Kaid concludes with the characterization of each candidate's "videostyle."

In Chapter 9, John C. Tedesco assesses network news presentations of the 2000 campaign focusing on the component of the "public's voice." Using a blend of content analysis and descriptive analysis, he finds that although a wide range of issues were presented by the networks, the concentration of the issue frames for specific issues was not nearly as dense as discussion of candidate ads, political polls, the debates, or voting possibilities. As a result, the media's focus on campaign processes and strategies draws the reporter closer to the campaign strategist and further from the citizens.

In Chapter 10, Henry C. Kenski, Brooks Aylor, and Kate Kenski focus on the final phase of the communication process in the presidential campaign and attempt to explain the ultimate vote. They analyze the messengers and their messages, campaign strategies and the vote in the electoral college, and the demographic base for the presidential vote.

Finally, they examine the role of gender in 2000, issues cited and candidate traits selected by voters as reasons for their vote, and perceptions of presidential job performance and character in the election outcome.

Presidential campaigns communicate and influence, reinforce and convert, motivate as well as educate. Bruce Gronbeck (1984) argues that campaigns "get leaders elected, yes, but ultimately, they also tell us who we as a people are, where we have been and where we are going; in their size and duration they separate our culture from all others, teach us about political life, set our individual and collective priorities, entertain us, and provide bases for social interaction" (496).

In 2000, continuing the trend from four years earlier, too few citizens listened, watched, or cared about the campaign until the drama of Florida's ballot count and vote determination. Less than a quarter of eligible voters selected the leader of the "Free World." And the result of those that did vote was a virtual tie. No clear choice, no clear decision. Once again, too many millions remained silent.

Political communication scholars should remember that *more* communication does not mean *better* communication. More technology does not mean more *effective* communication. For well over 200 years, America has moved toward a more "inclusive" democracy: greater participation of women, minorities, and the young. We have also witness unparalleled advances in communication technologies. Yet during this time of increased opportunity for participation and information, citizen interest, awareness, understanding, and voting have declined.

The central task is how to cultivate an active, democratic citizenry. Civic responsibility and initiative should once again become a keystone of social life. Perhaps by better understanding the role and process of communication in presidential campaigns, we may somehow improve the quality of our "national conversations."

REFERENCES

Barber, James David. 1980. *The Pulse of Politics*. New York: W.W. Norton.

Gronbeck, Bruce. 1984. "Functional and Dramaturgical Theories of Presidential Campaigning." *Presidential Studies Quarterly*, 14 (Fall), 487–498.

Acknowledgments

This is the third edited volume exploring the presidential campaign from a communication perspective. Several of the colleagues participated in past editions. Others join this endeavor for the first time. For many of us, this has become a presidential campaign ritual. I look forward to receiving the chapters and reading analyses of the campaign from a group of such outstanding scholars and colleagues. I learn from their insights, and the chapters inform my classroom instruction. Once again, the contributors made this another most rewarding and enjoyable endeavor. I genuinely appreciate their participation in this volume and their wonderful, insightful contributions. But more important, I value their friendship. Many of us go back further than we may wish to admit.

I want to thank my colleagues in the Department of Communication Studies at Virginia Polytechnic Institute and State University for their continued encouragement and rich environment conducive to thought, reflection, and scholarship. I also want to thank Robert Bates, Dean of the College of Arts and Sciences, and Richard Sorensen, Dean of the Pamplin College of Business, for their continued support of administrative, professional, and scholarly activities. They understand the importance of the "right mix" that makes my job a privilege and pleasure. Special thanks also to Major General (Retired) Jerrold Allen, Commandant of the Corps of Cadets, for his appreciation and encouragement to maximize summertime for writing opportunities. I am fortunate to work for three outstanding administrators who continue to serve as role models, both personally and professionally.

Finally, of course, it is family members who sustain us, encourage us, and provide a sense of belonging and security that frees us to read, write, and pursue projects of interest. Thankfully, they provide the joys of life well beyond academe. Many thanks to my wonderful wife, Rachel, a true blessing and friend in my life. And to my precious sons, Bobby and Chris. Now nearly grown, they have always been tolerant of the countless hours in the study. Together the three enrich every moment of my life.

The 2000 Presidential Campaign

Chapter 1

Five Pivotal Elements of the 2000 Presidential Campaign

Robert E. Denton, Jr.

Every presidential campaign is unique and has those interesting, memorable events that capture media attention and public interest. In the 1988 presidential campaign one recalls the heated interview exchange between George W. Bush and Dan Rather that dispelled Bush's "wimp" image. Remember too the Richmond Presidential Debate during the 1992 presidential campaign when George W. Bush, Sr. casually glanced at his watch; the glance, caught on television during the town hall exchange, came to epitomize the perception of an incumbent being out of touch and distracted. Or Elizabeth Dole's "Oprah-like" introduction of her husband, Bob Dole, at the 1996 Republican convention that enhanced her credibility for her run in 2000.

Among such events or items in the 2000 presidential campaign are:

- Bush's inability to name several foreign leaders during an interview with a reporter
- Gore's hair and clothes makeover with more casual dress and "green suit"
- Bush's referring to *New York Times* correspondent Adam Clymer as a "major league asshole" in front of an open mike
- Gore's verbal and nonverbal mannerisms during the first debate
- Bush's mispronunciation of big words, such as *subliminal*
- The Bush campaign's "RATS" ad
- The networks' retraction of Florida for Gore election night call
- The butterfly ballot
- The multiple definitions of "chad"

The list could contain numerous additional items. But there are those events or elements of a campaign that impact the very nature of the contest. They change the dynamics of the campaign and influence the strategies and tactics and, in some cases, the very outcome of the election. Such events influence public support, alter media framing of the race, or impact candidate image. These events I call "pivotal elements" of a campaign. Of course, in a close campaign everything is important. However, one can identify five pivotal elements of the 2000 presidential campaign. These five elements largely explain the ebb and flow of the contest. They are critical in the sense that they favor one candidate over another in terms of public support and hence ultimate victory. They provide a macro-analysis or frame of the election. Other chapters in this volume provide more detailed analyses of various aspects of the contest.

The five pivotal elements of the 2000 presidential campaign are the structure of the primaries that favored both Bush and Gore; the vice presidential selections that favored Gore; the party conventions that favored Gore; the debates that favored Bush; and the Supreme Court decision that, of course, favored Bush.

I will briefly examine each element and attempt to demonstrate the importance and influence of the event upon the nature of the campaign.

THE FRONT-LOADING OF THE PRESIDENTIAL PRIMARY SEASON

Since the 1970s, the nomination process has consisted of candidates making direct appeals to largely partisan voters in a series of state primary elections. The specific rules of the contests change from election to election. The rules greatly impact who runs and the likelihood of success of party nomination.

Every season since 1980, not only has the number of primaries increased, but the primaries are held closer and closer together. States are motivated to move the date of their primaries in order to have greater influence in the nomination process. As soon as one cycle is complete, states begin the "leap frog" process of moving their contests earlier and earlier in the primary season.

The most important feature of the 2000 primary contests—as was the case in 1996 but even more so this time—was the acceleration of the primaries, or what is known as "front-loading." Front-loading is a contemporary trend where more and more states schedule their primaries and caucuses at an earlier point in the nomination process, resulting in multiple contests in a very short amount of time.

In comparison, in 1976, by the tenth week of the primary season, just 35 percent of the Republican delegates and 43 percent of the Democratic delegates were selected. During this cycle, 78 percent of Republican delegates and 79 percent of Democratic delegates were selected by the tenth week of the primary season (Mayer, 2001, 14).

Most notable for the 2000 season, New York, Ohio, and California moved their primaries from June to Super Tuesday on March 7. Super Tuesday itself has grown in significance. For Democrats, there were 17 contests representing 40 percent of their delegates and 14 contests for Republicans representing 30 percent of their total. Just one week later, another six state primaries delivered another 16 percent of delegates for both parties.

There are several important implications of the front-loading of primaries. Overall, it limits the number of candidates and decreases public deliberation in the decision-making process.

Because of front-loading, the successful candidate needs at least $40 million in the bank well before the first vote is cast. The high "entry fee" places fund-raising as probably the most important element of the primary and preprimary phases. With individual contribution limits of $1,000, candidates are forced to go after the big dollars from political action committees (PACS), corporations, and special interest groups. One suspects such reliance on corporate dollars influences issue positions and the potential to "buy" favors or at least access in the future.

Campaigns that are not well funded make it difficult to challenge all primaries or have the funds available for subsequent contests. Candidates must choose between states and caucases. For less well-funded candidates, the role of the media becomes even more critical. At the very least, large donors, professional fund-raisers, and officeholders control the early nomination process.

Front-loading also forces "campaigns" to begin much earlier. More than a year before the first vote is ever cast, potential candidates must raise money, win endorsements, build minimum organization in key states, and obtain as much "free" media exposure as possible. From a pragmatic perspective, the preprimary, "surfacing" or "invisible primary" phase has become the most critical phase of the nomination process.

Obviously, front-loading favors the well-known candidates and lessens the odds of an underdog prevailing. National polls also play an important role in front-loading. Most citizens are unfocused; thus simple name recognition becomes more important than issue positions. In fact, the short primary season provides less time for candidates to adequately explain issue positions. Likewise, endorsements become important. With less time for issue exploration, key local or statewide endorsements confer instant credibility.

Bush had raised more funds than other candidates from either party since the adoption of the Federal Election Campaign Act amendments of 1974 (Ceaser and Busch, 2001, 67). It is important to note that the Bush campaign declined to accept federal matching funds, freeing him from any restrictions. Of course, the Bush campaign was mindful of the potential of Steve Forbes to spend nearly any amount of funds. They simply could not risk being outspent by any opponent.

By December 1999, heading into the spring primaries, the Bush campaign had $70 million (Ceaser and Busch, 2001, 68). Lamar Alexander noted, upon ending his nomination race, that Bush's war chest allowed him to run a national campaign and "soak up so many donors" that it was difficult for challengers to raise adequate funds. Alexander stated, "The problem is not that Bush has raised too much, it's that nobody else can raise enough to compete" (Ceaser and Busch, 2001, 68). Thus not only did such an impressive war chest allow Bush to run a national campaign and to compete in every primary; it also dried up funds for potential challengers.

From mid-1998, Bush led in all national polls, as well as in head-to-head contests with Gore. In terms of endorsements, Bush had 31 Republican governors and 36 of the 55 Republican senators (Ceaser and Busch, 2001, 68). Recall that the field of 13 Republican candidates was reduced to 6 before the first vote was cast.

As already noted, national media coverage is important in terms of generating positive images and name recognition. Media's "love affair" with John McCain is well known and kept him viable when lesser-known candidates could not maintain the same visibility or viability.

Because of funding, McCain "boycotted" Iowa caucuses and focused on New Hampshire. In public, he claimed the caucuses were not "real" contests, with delegates selected. The importance of McCain's win in New Hampshire cannot be underestimated. Prior to his victory, two out of three Americans did not know enough about McCain to have an opinion of him. However, after his victory, nationally McCain had 80 percent name recognition and a 66 percent favorable rating and was leading in head-to-head contests against Gore by 22 percent (Crotty, 2001, 103).

However, McCain could not adequately maximize his New Hampshire victory because of the general lack of time to build multiple state organizations and the need for fund-raising for the subsequent primaries. While he was successful in generating funds from his Internet site, it was simply not enough. McCain was forced to organize successive states as he went along, hoping to build momentum and funds. He made a strong showing in the following South Carolina primary and won in Michigan, a major victory. However, he could not raise enough funds nor adequately prepare for the multiple primaries in "Super Tuesday" contests.

In the end, the problem with McCain was that his popularity was with the media, the Democrats, and the Independents. Most of McCain's votes were in open primaries, and he stayed competitive only because of the votes of Democrats and Independents. Republicans favored Bush throughout the primaries 57 percent to McCain's 33 percent (Crotty, 2001, 103). It is important to note that McCain did not receive support or endorsements from within his own party. Many colleagues found him difficult to work with. In addition, on several important issues to Republicans, he did not vote along party lines.

It is interesting to note how many potential Democratic candidates declined to run in what was essentially an open race, especially given Gore's poor early poll numbers. Among Democrats who considered a run (given what some label as the public's "Clinton fatigue") were House Minority Leader Richard Gephardt and Senators Paul Wellstone (Minnesota), Bob Kerry (Nebraska), and John Kerry (Massachusetts). Nearly all mentioned the financial burden as decisive in their decisions not to run for the nomination.

By the end of 1999, Gore had locked up 500 of the 716 "Super Delegates," party officials and elected leaders. Interestingly, Gore's poor showing in the polls compared to Bush benefited Bill Bradley as an alternative. The media also enjoyed the growing nomination battle and provided generally positive coverage of Bradley.

Bradley raised $27 million entering the primary season, just $2 million less than Gore (Crotty, 2001, 96). He was at least as financially prepared as Gore. However, he did not have the number and profile of endorsements. Ironically, McCain was viewed as the true "maverick," thus dominating most of the free media. Bradley lost to Gore in New Hampshire by just 4 points. Certainly by any standard, this was a very strong showing. However, within just five weeks, Bradley confronted 14 primaries and caucuses in large and expensive states such as California, New York, and Ohio. Gore's narrow victory in New Hampshire, with superior organization, virtually ended Bradley's campaign. The media was both McCain's and Bradley's best hope for viability in future contests.

It is clear that the early favorites with advantages of money, organization, and elite endorsements are more likely to become the party nominees. However, the current primary system does not enhance voter knowledge, especially this "big bang" approach. For the 2000 primary cycle, several studies show that most Americans did not participate in the primaries—the lowest participation in recent history—and did not pay attention to the contests. The Shorenstein Center's tracking of citizen attention during the primaries is informative: Some 64 percent found the campaigns uninformative, 69 percent, boring; 70 percent, on a weekly basis, paid little or no attention to the campaigns. In fact, 86 percent reported they were not talking about the campaigns, and 76 percent reported not thinking about them.

In the end, the primary process did benefit Gore and Bush. It allowed them to hone their skills and focus their messages. They both became better candidates. But what if the primaries had been more spread out and varied across the nation? Could Bradley and McCain have had time to raise additional funds, campaign in multiple states in order to be competitive in several primaries, and spend more time interacting with the general public via the national media? In summary, according to William Mayer, the front-loading of the primary process resulted in "a surprisingly small number of serious candidates" and compelled "both Bradley and McCain to withdraw much earlier than they would have in a system that started up more slowly" (2001, 42).

THE VICE PRESIDENTIAL SELECTIONS

The vice presidential selections by the candidates fundamentally changed the dynamics of the race. Bush enjoyed a comfortable lead in the polls after the primary season and prior to both conventions. Because of his lead, Bush had more options in terms of vice presidential candidate nominations. However, for Gore, it was a different situation. He was behind, and thus his selection of a running mate needed more traditional political considerations.

Nearly all empirical studies of vice presidential candidate selections reveal that they do not determine votes or elections. However, they do provide a great deal of media coverage for a few days, generate evaluations of "ticket viability," and help shape voter opinion.

Gore's selection of Joe Lieberman jump-started his stalled campaign. Ceaser and Busch (2001) argue that the selection of Senator Joe Lieberman as Gore's vice presidential nominee was the greatest tactical achievement of the Gore campaign (30). They argue that because Gore was behind in the polls, he was under pressure to make a choice that would "shake things up" (137). Being the first Jewish American running for a national office certainly garnered attention and dominated headlines. Lieberman's more traditional and moderate views countered charges of liberalism. The selection was viewed as "bold."

Lieberman at least inoculated Gore against Clinton. He was one of the first to openly condemn Clinton for the Monica Lewinsky affair. Lieberman's strong code of ethics balanced Gore's past campaign finance questions and his overly strong support of Clinton during the impeachment proceedings. The Lieberman selection provided a symbolic break with Clinton.

In addition, Lieberman embraced a "populist style" of campaigning that was energizing. According to Marjorie Hershey (2001), Lieberman was an engaging and warm speaker "frequently invoking images of faith and religious commitment" (54). As some pundits observed, he "brought back God to the democratic party." Some of Lieberman's early campaign statements about the role of religion in public life placed him squarely within the traditional values of most Americans. His candidacy countered many of the Christian Right who long believed Democrats were too sectarian in social issues. As a "New Democrat," Lieberman voted for the Gulf War and was characterized as the "moral conscience" of the Senate.

Simendinger (2000) characterized Lieberman's selection as "a centrist, a moralist, an individualist, a Jew—[it] was probably the closest thing to a qualified, compatible 'wow' running mate Gore was likely to turn up to go *mano a mano* with Bush and Dick Cheney" (2583).

There were some political advantages to the Lieberman selection. First, his selection help solidify support of Jewish voters in New York and Florida. In addition, his more moderate views on such issues as school vouchers, affirmative action, and privatization of part of Social Security balanced Gore's more liberal views. However, Lieberman did have to "revise" or "clarify" some of his issue stances to address criticisms from more liberal members of the Democratic Party.

Gore's choice of Lieberman received a 60 percent approval rating by the public in an ABC poll, and 83 percent said they would vote for a Jewish candidate (Crotty, 2001, 111).

The Dick Cheney selection as vice presidential nominee for Bush strikes one as somewhat arrogant. Bush was well ahead in the polls in July 2000. Cheney brought no geographic area or large electoral-rich state. He did not bring any ideological or issue voting group. It was a safe choice, one that strengthened the personal liabilities of Bush. Cheney's distinguished record of public service helped compensate for Bush's lack of Washington and international experience. If Bush had based his selection upon geographic considerations, for example, Governor Tom Ridge of Pennsylvania or Frank Keating of Oklahoma (a Catholic) would have been strong choices.

As already mentioned, the choice of Lieberman caused quite a media stir. In contrast, Cheney's selection was more puzzling, at first. Few outside of Washington knew Cheney. He came from the same state as Bush. His wife was a controversial conservative. He was not known as a strong campaigner, not to mention his history of heart disease. Richard Cohen and James Kitfield (2000) summarized Cheney's weaknesses as Bush's "daddy's boy," "Big Oil" man, no help on electoral map, charisma gap, and history of heart disease (2456–2459).

However, in all fairness, considering the political context and environment at the time of selection, Cheney did bring some advantages to the ticket. He shored up support of conservatives for Bush. They worked well together. They had very similar views on issues and operating styles. They both were conservative but pragmatists. They both took pride in maintaining cordial relations with members of the opposition party.

"In the end," according to Ceaser and Busch (2001), "both candidates chose individuals who balanced the perceived weaknesses in their own personal qualities and helped them nationally across the board. Bush's selection of Cheney added a dimension of gravitas, while Gore's choice provided a moral prophylactic, helping Gore to separate himself from Clinton by running alongside the first Democratic senator to strongly criticize Clinton's conduct during the Lewinsky scandal" (139). Thus, while both were solid choices, Lieberman was more strategically helpful to Gore. Gore pulled within 2 points of Bush after the Lieberman announcement (Simendinger, 2000, 2583). Jack Germond and Jules Witcover (2000) argued that the major tactical value of selecting Lieberman is that it gave the presidential race a "new look" (2644). The Lieberman selection gave Gore a major advantage in the race. Indeed, as we'll see below, the Lieberman announcement and the Democratic convention speech by Gore totally changed the dynamics of the contest.

THE CONVENTIONS

Since 1984, political conventions have become highly scripted, orchestrated media extravaganzas. Above all else, parties want to present a unified public face to the American people. With the reduction of television coverage, prime time is devoted to speeches, celebrity appearances, and carefully crafted videos. Delegates are reduced to little more than a "studio audience." Today's conventions are "a huge pep rally, replete with ritual, pomp, and entertainment—a made-for-TV production" (Wayne, 2000, 156). Robert Healy, who has run several Democratic conventions, views the role of the convention as "framing devices, mechanisms that help frame the presidential choice. They have one principal task: positioning the presidential candidate for the fall election" (Ceaser and Busch, 2001, 142). However, as Ceaser and Busch note, "As the convention authors have gone to greater and greater lengths to present a media-perfect image of their candidate, there has been a corresponding precipitous drop both in the viewing audience and in the prime-time programming slots allotted the conventions by the traditional major broadcast network" (143).

Republicans wanted to emphasize inclusiveness and diversity in its national convention. Democrats wanted to portray a moderate tone with programmatic solutions to middle-class problems. The composition of the two conventions differed greatly. My focus is on the candidate speeches, their public reception, and ultimately their impact.

Ceaser and Busch (2001) think that the Republican 2000 campaign was the most scripted and orchestrated convention in history (142). The Republican convention presented a friendlier, more inclusive, and moderate convention than in 1992 and 1994. Republicans made direct appeals to those of Democratic leanings. There were speeches by African Americans (most notable, General Colin Powell), Hispanics, Asians, and even a gay member of Congress.

Each evening of the Republican convention had a central theme with an accompanying message delivered by carefully selected individuals. Monday night was "Opportunity with a Purpose: Leave No child Behind," focusing on education and expanding health care. Tuesday night was "Strength and Security with a Purpose: Safe in Our Homes and in the World," focusing on foreign policy issues. Wednesday night was "Prosperity with a Purpose: Keeping America Prosperous and Protecting Retirement Security," and Thursday night was "President with a Purpose: A strong Leader Who Can Unite Our Country and Get Things Done" (Ceaser and Busch, 2001, 144).

Because of Bush's noted lack of oratorical skills, media and pundits created low expectations of Bush's acceptance speech. However, it was a very strong speech, one of Bush's best performances of the entire campaign. He approached it in a more philosophical way. He also mentioned values and integrity. His address sounded more like an inaugural address than a nomination acceptance address. Republicans had a most successful campaign, and Bush enjoyed a 5- to 7-point "bump" in most polls.

A week later was the Democratic convention. James Campbell (2001) argues that the convention "marked a crucial turning point in the campaign of 2000" (128). Although the convention was less scripted, more informal, and in some ways haphazard than the Republican convention, it was clearly successful for Gore. The difference was his acceptance speech. It changed the course of the campaign.

Bush had exceeded expectations partly because of media previews. In contrast, Gore had to exceed expectations, primarily because he was an "accomplished" speaker and slightly behind in the polls. He needed a strong convention bump to remain competitive.

Like Bush, Gore also wanted to address middle America but did so in a very different way. Interestingly, Gore did not provide an incumbent speech, designed to recognize administration accomplishments. Instead, he offered proposals and programs. He provided a laundry list of initiatives for very specific pyschographic and demographic constituent groups. There was literally something for everyone. Gore's address sounded more like a State of the Union address than an acceptance speech.

Marjorie Hershey (2001) characterizes Gore's speech as the high point of his campaign (55). The media's immediate response was negative. But public opinion polling disagreed. The speech was a hit. He came from the convention as "his own man" and reinforced his image as a populist, "old time Democrat" (Ceaser and Busch, 2001, 145). Gore's favorability ratings matched Bush's, and he finally provided a detailed policy agenda for "his" administration. And THAT KISS, the seven-second kiss with his wife, Tipper. It humanized Gore. It demonstrated, especially to women, that their marriage was not like that of Bill and Hillary Clinton. It signaled that he was a family man and a devoted father to lovely children. For whatever reason, women came home to the Democratic Party. One-fourth of subsequent media stories focused on the transformation of Gore establishing himself as his own man.

Depending on the poll reviewed, Gore gained between 11 and 17 points and took the lead over Bush for the first time in the campaign. The real effect was Gore's ability to excite the Democratic base. With his speech more so than the general convention, Gore brought home the Democratic base. In short, while both candidates emphasized their record and encouraged support, Bush emphasized broad, consensus appeals, whereas Gore articulated more narrow, targeted partisan appeals. Bush's speech targeted beyond his base. Gore was more focused toward traditional Democratic constituencies. Perhaps it can be argued that Republicans, overall, had a more perfected and successful convention. But in terms of strategic importance, Gore saved his campaign. Thus, the convention advantage went to Gore.

THE DEBATES

Since 1976, every presidential campaign has had at least one presidential debate. However, not since the 1960 infamous debates between Richard Nixon and John F. Kennedy have debates provided such potential for significant influence. While all debates provide some momentary interest and some memorable exchanges, they seldom dramatically change the dynamics of a campaign. Studies reveal that debates do not change many voters' choice but may impact those who are genuinely undecided. The 2000 presidential debates had a significant impact on candidate persona and images. For the first time in many elections, the debates were very important and played a role in candidate preference, more so than issues. A detailed review of the debates is within this volume by Robert Friedenberg.

Initially there was major disagreement between the two campaigns concerning the debates. Bush preferred face-to-face joint appearances on NBC's *Meet the Press* and CNN's *Larry King Live*. However, Gore insisted on the Commission on Presidential Debates proposal of three 90-minute presidential debates with three different formats and one vice presidential candidate debate. Ultimately, the Gore campaign prevailed.

It was widely held that the debates and formats clearly favored Al Gore. He was well practiced in national debates, doing very well against Dan Quayle in 1992, Jack Kemp in 1996, and in a head-to-head confrontation with Ross Perot on the *Larry King Live* show focusing on the North Atlantic Free Trade Agreement.

The first debate was viewed by 90 million people. Gore was well prepared and aggressive. He was on the offensive throughout the debate. Gore focused on his agenda and a broad set of policy initiatives. In contrast, Bush focused on his personality, character, integrity, and the need for bipartisanship in Washington (Crotty, 2001a, 22). Bush also was more "laid back." In contrast, he appeared more friendly and warm than Gore.

Gore seemed impatient in waiting for his turn to respond to questions to the point of even being perceived as rude. Verbal sighs were noticeable as well as nonverbal gestures of shaking his head and facial frowns. Gore was criticized after the debate not only for his demeanor but also for several "misstatements," "exaggerations," or "lies," depending upon one's perspective. Indeed, *Saturday Night Live* ridiculed Gore for his eagerness to interrupt Bush and to get the last word in, not to mention his overly stated exaggerations. In terms of image, Gore reinforced his overbearing, stiff, even pedantic demeanor.

Charlie Cook (2000) thought the first debate "was a metaphor for the whole race. The strengths and weaknesses of both candidates were on display, and neither candidate exhibited the strength to overpower the other. Likewise, neither candidate disqualified himself by revealing a glaring weakness. Gore came off as smart, knowledgeable, and experienced. Bush came across as comfortable, trustworthy—someone you wouldn't mind having as a next-door neighbor" (3194).

After the first debate, Gallup polls indicated that Gore won 48 percent to 41 percent for Bush (Campbell, 2001, 130). Especially in terms of strategy, the sharing of facts and statistics, and staying on topic, Gore did a better job in the traditional sense of debate. As colleague Robert Friedenberg notes in this volume in his chapter on debates, "Gore was debating well. But as events would prove, he was irritating his audience." However, the fact that Bush did not make a mistake and seemed very comfortable and reasonably knowledgeable, he actually gained ground in the polls. Not only did Bush gain support, but most polls showed that his favorable ratings increased as well. The first debate at least dispelled the notions of Bush not being smart enough to be president.

Ceaser and Busch (2001) argue that the first debate was "probably the most decisive for any presidential candidate since presidential debating began in 1960" (150). In the first debate, Gore was heavily favored. However, he did not score a decisive knockout. Given his "sighs" and "lies," three days after the debate, Gore was perceived the clear political loser. This perception placed even more pressure on him for the second debate.

The format for the second debate was more informal. The candidates were seated at a table with moderator Jim Lehrer of PBS. The focus of this exchange was foreign policy and international affairs. Again, while the format tended to favor Bush, many suspected that Gore's knowledge of international leaders and affairs would be a great advantage. However, as in the first debate, at least for the first 30 minutes, Bush went head-to-head with Gore. He demonstrated knowledge and understanding of foreign affairs and policy implications. Bush was more comfortable and more in control of the information. He was also more confident.

Gore was more restrained than in the first debate. He seemed more hesitant and went out of his way to be less aggressive (and silent). He showed more respect for Bush and even agreed with him several times. Again, from a collegiate perspective, Gore scored more points. However, according to a Gallup poll, the public viewed Bush the "winner" 49 percent to Gore's 36 percent (Campbell, 2001, 130). Ceaser and Busch (2001) think the second debate, on the heels of Cheney's strong performance against Lieberman, was Bush's best showing. From a political perspective, Bush once again "won" the debate.

The third debate was a "town hall meeting" format, once again favoring Gore. Each candidate provided lively exchanges. Gore returned to his more aggressive style and appeals to specific groups of voters with policy initiatives. Although the public viewed this exchange as a draw, Bush again "wins" because of exceeding pundit expectations of performance.

Despite the overwhelming speculation that Gore would have Bush for lunch, Bush not only survived the debates but also enhanced his standing in terms of competency and leadership potential. Over the course of the debates, public preference changed from Gore having an 8-point advantage to Bush pulling out in front by 6 points (Campbell, 2001, 131). In addition, Gore's negatives climbed to their highest level since the beginning of the general campaign season (Frankovic and McDermott, 2001, 85).

Gore came away from the debates with the issue advantage intact. But issues alone seldom determine votes. Style matters. In the end, voters found Bush acceptable and more likable.

The debates were probably the last time Gore had an opportunity to reframe media portrayal of himself and his candidacy. Interestingly, Gary Jacobson (2001) argues that "for the third election in a row, it boiled down to the economy versus character, and for the first time, the economic frame did not clearly prevail" (17).

Bush won the debates from several perspectives. First, his performance demonstrated that he was competent to be president. Second, the debates raised serious questions about Gore's veracity and personality. Third, Bush gained the lead in public opinion polls and, according to Democratic pollster Celinda Lake, Gore lost among voters who made up their minds during the debates (Lake, 2001, 81). Thus, overall the debates helped Bush more than Gore.

THE SUPREME COURT DECISION

It is, of course, the judicial challenges and proceedings that make this an historic election. Many scholars and observers are classifying this postelection period as a separate campaign or phase of the 2000 election. Clearly the drama and spectacle was, at least hopefully from my perspective, a once-in-a-lifetime event.

Of course the Supreme Court vote effectively ended the campaign and the controversy of Florida's electoral vote. It could have gone in many ways, down many paths. For some, the disputes were matters of state legislators. For others, the federal courts. Now, more than a year after the election, several news organizations have confirmed Bush's electoral victory in the state regardless of which ballots were counted or how they could have been counted.

There are a plethora of books claiming each candidate legitimately won the election or stole the election or manipulated the end game. Such titles include Bill Sammon's *At Any Cost: How Al Gore Tried to Steal the Election* (2001), Roger Simon's *Divided We Stand: How Al Gore Beat George Bush and Lost the Presidency* (2001), and Alan M. Dershowitz's *Supreme Injustice: How the High Court Hijacked Election 2000* (2001), to name just a few. The 36 days of indecision, legal strategies, and tactics provided great fodder for journalists, historians, and pundits.

Essential issues included whether recounts should be conducted, standards to be used, and the extent of recanvassing to take place (Crotty 2001b, 75). Two weeks after the final vote, many thought that Florida's Supreme Court's decision would have ended the matter. Little did we know that it would take more than five weeks to determine the outcome. For the candidates, from a strategic perspective, there were legal, political, and public relations concerns (Crotty, 2001b, 59).

We endured counts, recounts, explanations of chads, hearings, and local, state, and national courtroom drama. Although all the attention was on Florida, there where other notable very close votes in such states as New Mexico (366 votes, Gore margin), Wisconsin (5,708 votes, Gore margin), Iowa (4,048 votes, Gore margin), New Hampshire (7,211 votes, Bush margin), and Oregon (6,765 votes, Gore margin).

I am struck by the fact that through it all most Americans were confident in the eventual outcome, although perhaps preferring a different winner. Nearly all citizens indicated support of the new president. Now calls for electoral reform are nonexistent. Cries for reforming the electoral college are silent.

It is beyond the scope of this chapter to explore the "ins" and "outs" of the legal intrigues of the judicial phase of the campaign. It is simply an acknowledgment of the obvious importance of the phase to any analysis or discussion of the campaign. A rather popular joke made the rounds after the Supreme Court decision—that, as a matter of fact, Bush won the presidency by just ONE vote, with the 5-to-4 Court ruling.

CONCLUSION

Although every presidential campaign has some interesting and even dramatic moments, each has what I call one or more "pivotal elements," elements that change the dynamics, nature, direction, or even outcome of the election. Such elements influence candidate support, media framing of the campaign, and candidate image. In addition, each element tends to favor one candidate over others.

There were five pivotal elements to the 2000 presidential campaign. The first is the front-loaded nature of the primaries. The structure and timing of the contests strongly favored Bush and Gore. The second pivotal element was the vice presidential selections. While both Cheney and Lieberman were solid nominations and well received, Lieberman provided more strategic advantage to Gore. The third element of the conventions was perhaps the most decisive. Gore's strong acceptance speech brought home the Democratic base and generated his first lead in the campaign. In contrast, Bush's "political" victories in the debates allowed him to regain, even if ever so slightly, the lead in the polls. The final element, the Supreme Court decision that ended the Florida electoral controversy, is a matter of history.

This brief narrative review of the 2000 presidential election identifies the ebb and flow of the campaign. While certainly not deterministic, one notes that of the pivotal elements each won three. In light of Gore winning the overall popular vote and Bush narrowly the contested electoral vote, perhaps such an analysis captures the "spirit" of the presidential campaign.

REFERENCES

"Americans Take Vacation from Presidential Campaign." 2000. The Vanishing Voter Project, Joan Shorenstein Center for the Press, Politics and Public Policy, June 1. http://www.vanishingvoter.org/releases/06-01-00.shtml.

Campbell, James. 2001. "The Curious and Close Presidential Campaign of 2000." In William Crotty, ed., *America's Choice 2000*. Boulder, CO: Westview Press, 115–37.

Ceaser, James and Andrew Busch. 2001. *The Perfect Tie*. Lanham, MD: Rowman & Littlefield.

Cohen, Richard and James Kitfield. 2000. "Cheney: Pros and Cons." *National Journal*, 32(31) (July 29), 2456–2459.

Cook, Charlie. 2000. "One Wrong Move and It Could Be Over." *National Journal*, 32(41) (October 7), 3194.

Crotty, William. 2001a. "The Election of 2000: Close, Chaotic, and Unforgettable." In William Crotty, ed., *America's Choice*. Boulder, CO: Westview Press, 1–35.

Crotty, William. 2001b. "Elections by Judicial Fiat: The Courts Decide." In William Crotty, ed., *America's Choice*. Boulder, CO: Westview Press, 36–78.

Crotty, William. 2001c. "The Presidential Primaries: Triumph of the Frontrunners." In William Crotty, ed., *America's Choice 2000*. Boulder, CO: Westview Press, 95–114.

Frankovic, Kathleen and Monika McDermott. 2001. "Public Opinion in the 2000 Election: The Ambivalent Electorate." In Gerald Pomper, ed., *The Election of 2000*. New York: Chatham House, 73–91.

Germond, Jack and Jules Witcover. 2000. "Gore's Bold Move." *National Journal*, 33 (August 12), 2644.

Hershey, Marjorie. 2001. "The Campaign and the Media." In Gerald Pomper, ed., *The Election of 2000*. New York: Chatham House, 46–72.

Jacobson, Gary. 2001. *The 2000 Elections and Beyond*. Washington, DC: Congressional Quarterly Press.

Lake, Celinda. 2001. "Issue Kleptomania." *Campaigns and Elections* (December–January), 81.

Mayer, William. 2001. "The Presidential Nominations." In Gerald Pomper, ed., *The Election of 2000*. New York: Chatham House, 12–45.

Simendinger, Alexis. 2000. "On His Own, at Last." *National Journal*, 33 (August 12), 2582–2587.

Wayne, Stephen. 2000. *The Road to the White House 2000*. Boston: Bedford/St. Martin's Press.

Chapter 2

And They All Came Calling: The Early Campaign of Election 2000

Judith S. Trent

January 27 was one of the coldest, most snowy, and sunless mornings of the 2000 New Hampshire presidential primaries. Despite the weather, by 9:00 A.M. former New Jersey Senator Bill Bradley, one of two Democratic presidential contenders, was being introduced by his wife, Ernestine, at a postdebate rally on the site of the Bradley for President Headquarters in Concord. As she began speaking, all of a sudden, the snow stopped, the sun shown brightly, and Ernestine, with a big smile on her face, said she wanted to introduce a man who would bring sunshine into our lives. The senator, standing over at the side of the makeshift platform, let out a big yelp, jumped into the air as though making a hoop shot, ran over to his wife, kissed her, and exclaimed to the assembled supporters and media how great it was to be married to a woman who says that you bring her sunshine. With no question, the moment was vintage "early campaign."

From the outset, it was clear that although much would be traditional, there would be a number of important differences that would set apart campaign 2000 from the one that had taken place just four years earlier. For example, unlike 1996, presidential hopefuls blossomed forth from both the Republican and Democratic Parties as well as the Reform and the Green Parties. And although the 1996 campaign had started earlier than had any presidential contest since 1972, the 2000 race began even earlier, when in May 1997, 31 months before any caucus/primary votes would be counted, four Republicans and two Democrats gave campaign speeches in New Hampshire and began constructing field operations in the early primary states. But not only had everything begun earlier, for all intents and purposes, it ended earlier when as a result of the March

7 primaries (Super Tuesday) it became clear that the two front-runners, Vice President Albert C. Gore and Texas Governor George W. Bush, had each turned back a strong challenge for the presidential nominations from their respective parties.

What also set campaign 2000 apart from any of the earlier such contests was the fact that there were so many "would-be" presidential candidates. At one time or another, 30 individuals (17 Republicans, 8 Democrats, 4 Reform Party, and 1 from the Green Party) let it be known that they were giving some thought to running. And while a number of these potential candidacies never actually materialized, at least 15 of them did for at least some period of time during the earliest periods of the campaign. Not only, however, were there more candidates, but it took a lot more money to run than it had taken in the past. Because so many states had moved their primary or caucus to the beginning of the primary calendar, it was estimated that one of the most important hurdles candidates had to clear was raising $15 million by December 31, 1999, to allow them to run television ads in advance of a state's primary (West, 1999, A9). While this was significantly more money than the early candidates had had to raise in past presidential contests, and while it eventually caused contenders to drop out of the race earlier than it had in the past, in the beginning, there appeared to be a lot more money available, even for those whose candidacies could reasonably be considered a long shot. However, by June 1999, with the first primaries just seven months away, the fund-raising competition became intense with Texas Governor George W. Bush having raised $23 million (and already having determined that he would give up millions of federally matched dollars so that his campaign would not be subjected to government-imposed spending limits during the primaries); Vice President Albert C. Gore, $18.5 million; Senator Bill Bradley, $11.5 million; Arizona Senator John McCain, almost $5 million; and former head of the Family Research Council, Gary Bauer, $10 million (Fournier, 1999a, A7; Salant, 2000, A4; Crowley, 1999, A7).

Just as intriguing as the number of candidates who were running, the front-loaded primary calendar, or the incredible amount of money needed and raised was the fact that early campaign 2000 provided an opportunity to study the campaign of two insurgents who posed serious challenges to the front-runners and a woman who conducted the country's first serious female presidential campaign. Although John McCain was never considered to be the Republican front-runner in 2000, nonetheless, even before officially announcing his candidacy, he appeared to be the media's favorite potential candidate and the one who seemed to spark the interest and imagination of the public. Whether it was his blunt rhetorical style or the fact that he was "not quite running" for president, by summer 1998, and until he dropped out of the race in March 2000, the senator was the "media's main man." Similarly, Bill Bradley, while never considered the front-runner for the Democratic nomination, nonetheless had enough "star power" to capture the attention of the national media and the public as a serious challenger to the presumed nomination of the sitting vice president, Al Gore. Another Republican hopeful, Elizabeth Dole, president of the American Red Cross, also attracted considerable attention when, after public speculation regarding whether or not she would become a candidate for the Republican nomination, she finally announced that she was leaving the Red Cross "because there may be other duties to fill" (Balz and Broder, 1999a, Al) and would likely begin developing an exploratory committee within the next several weeks (Balz and Broder, 1999b, 13–14). If for no other reason than the fact that her candidacy was viewed by some as a chance to continue 1998 Republican inroads into reducing the gender gap by picking up support among married mothers and suburban women, the potential for Dole's unique appeal for many voters in 2000, particularly women, provoked, at least in the beginning, a good deal of media attention (Balz and Broder, 1999b 13–14).

Thus, there were major differences between the early campaign of 2000 and its 1996 counterpart. But 2000, like each of its predecessors, was important, indeed critical to the whole presidential election process. In fact, it was in the early portions of the 2000 campaign that decisions were made and paths were charted for which there could be no turning back. As I will argue, the communication functions performed during the preprimary and primary stages of the 2000 campaign were at least as important in determining the results of the entire election as they have ever been. It is the purpose of this chapter to explore how and why this claim is true.

THE SURFACING STAGE

For a number of years I have argued the wisdom of studying the early campaign, the surfacing and primary periods, not only because it sets the scene for all that comes later but because it has always determined what happens in subsequent stages of the campaign. Since 1972, and with no exceptions thereafter, those presidential hopefuls who have gone on to become viable candidates for the nomination of their parties are those who surfaced earlier than their competition. It has long been the case that presidential contenders who have raised enough money to "go the course" through the primary schedule are those who have understood the necessity of fund-raising much in advance of the Iowa caucus and the New Hampshire primary. Issues discussed during the general election stage are those that are debated by presidential hopefuls in Iowa and New Hampshire. And the candidates' campaign styles, and the resulting labels attached to them by the national media, happen at the beginning of the competition and seldom disappear.

The surfacing or preprimary period of the presidential campaign was first apparent in 1976 when 14 politicians campaigned in the early primary states at least two years in advance of the first contest in an effort to create for themselves enough of a national persona to be considered credible presidential candidates. Since that time, and with extremely little variability in either content or form, the phenomenon known as surfacing has played a significant role in presidential campaigns. It is, in fact, surfacing that accounts for what has become accepted as the permanent or seasonless campaign (Trent and Friedenberg, 2000, 12; Blumenthal, 1982, 23).

Surfacing was defined in 1978 as "the series of predictable and specifically timed rhetorical transactions which serve consummatory and instrumental functions during the preprimary phase of the campaign" (Trent, 1978, 282). No precise timetable can be determined for this first stage of the campaign during any presidential election cycle except that it concludes before the first primary or the first state delegate caucus takes place. In 2000 the surfacing period was over before January 24, the date of the Iowa caucus. When the first stage begins, it is completely candidate specific. In other words, presidential hopefuls give themselves a timetable that is solely dependent on perception of their own national visibility and credibility, fund-raising prowess, and organizational strength as well as the attributes of those they perceive as competitors. Presidential wannabes must assess how long it will take to create a presidential image and interest for themselves in the public imagination and then determine what rhetorical strategies will most help them in achieving that persona.

These are difficult decisions, and in every presidential season there are examples of would-be candidates who have made serious miscalculations in adding up their assets and liabilities and those of their opponents, or who have underestimated the rigor demanded to be successful in the surfacing stage. In campaign 2000, for example, with so many individuals who publicly announced at one time or another that they were interested in running for the nomination of the Republican, Democratic, or Reform Parties, one of the most rhetorically interesting dimensions was who (which hopefuls) got in early and tested the water, stayed in for a while but got out before any votes were cast, and one who came in much too late but stayed for at least one primary anyway.

The major reason that so many individuals made known their interest in running was that the incumbent could not seek a third term. Moreover, although his vice president was clearly the major contender for the Democratic nomination, by March 1997, Al Gore's "Mr. Clean" image was said to be tarnished because of his loyalty to a president plagued with scandals and because during the 1996 reelection campaign he had made phone calls to potential contributors from the White House and had attended and collected money at a Buddhist temple fund-raiser. Thus, Democrats such as Nebraska Senator Bob Kerry, Minnesota Senator Paul Wellstone, Massachusetts Senator John Kerrey, House Minority Leader, Representative Richard Gephardt from Missouri, and the Reverend Jesse Jackson let it be known that they were considering a bid for the nomination. Some had exploratory committees, others had volunteers working and scouting for them in the primary and caucus states, a few had functioning political action committees in significant primary states, and most of them traveled frequently to New Hampshire to be seen and speak at a variety of party functions. Each, however, surfaced and then announced his withdrawal long before the beginning of the primaries as each individually became convinced that even with the impeachment of President Clinton the nomination could not be wrested from the vice president. Bob Kerry was the first to bow out when on December 28, 1998, he announced that his choice was to remain where he was, in the Senate. The senator's decision to drop out of the race was particularly interesting because of all of the early Democratic challengers to the vice president, Kerry was the most organized (unlike his presidential bid in the early stages of the 1992 election), and he had even begun to hire a professional staff and paid field-workers to explore his candidacy. Several weeks later, Paul Wellstone called a press conference and announced that he would not seek a presidential bid in 2000 because he did not believe that he would be able to keep up with the rigorous physical demands of a presidential campaign due to his chronic back pain from a ruptured disk. His advisers assured the media that the senator's decision was not in response to Gore's fund-raising and organizational power. By the end of January 1999, Richard Gephardt had decided to remain in the House of Representatives and help Democrats reclaim it in 2000, and by March 1999, he had officially endorsed the vice president (Fournier, 1999a, A7). At the end of February 1999, John Kerrey announced that he would not run against Al Gore in the 2000 presidential race, and by the end of March 1999, Jesse Jackson announced that he would not make another run for the White House in 2000.

Not having an incumbent who could run was also a factor in the early surfacing of Republicans such as Senators Bob Smith, John Ashcroft, and Fred Thompson and House of Representatives Speaker Newt Gingrich, House of Representatives member John Kasich, former Vice President Dan Quayle, former Tennessee Governor Lamar Alexander, writer and television commentator Patrick Buchanan, and former House of Representatives member and 1996 vice presidential candidate Jack Kemp (clearly, one of their motivations was the fact that for the first time since 1964 there was no Republican heir apparent). Each Republican hopeful let it be known early in the surfacing stage that he was planning on running for the nomination; each engaged in a variety of rhetorical transactions that clearly evidenced his campaign intentions; and each left the race before the first or preprimary stage was over.

By August 1997, Newt Gingrich, Fred Thompson, and Dan Quayle were exploring their viability and visibility within the Republican Party by attending and speaking at party events such as the Midwest Republican Leadership Conference in Indianapolis. By December 1997, Dan Quayle's PAC, Campaign America, had raised $1.9 million, and he had moved to a Phoenix, Arizona, suburb so that he could position himself as the "Western candidate for 2000," and Jack Kemp's PAC had collected $600,000. In February 1998, C-SPAN's "Road to the White House" (Scully, 1998) featured the campaign activities of Dan Quayle, John Ashcroft, and John Kasich. By the end of 1998, John Kasich had spoken in 39 states, and his PAC had gathered more than a million dollars (Wilkinson, 1999, C1). In early May 1998, religious broadcaster Pat Robertson, chairman of the Christian Coalition and founder of the Christian Broadcasting Network, donated $10,000 to John Ashcroft's PAC, Spirit of America, and argued that Ashcroft had far stronger support among Christian and social conservative leaders than other Republican candidates. In the middle of May 1998, Ashcroft beat a field of 22 potential Republican candidates in the first GOP straw poll taken at the South Carolina state party convention. And by the beginning of March 1999, Lamar Alexander had already spent 121 days in Iowa since initiating his quest for the 2000 nomination.

But despite undertaking a variety of the rhetorical transactions typical of surfacing and despite the successes of several of the contenders, by the end of August 1999, five months before the Iowa caucus, these Republican presidential hopefuls had either announced that they would not be seeking the presidency in the 2000 election or, as in the case of Senator Bob Smith, announced that he was leaving the Republican Party.

While it is typical that in the surfacing stage of any presidential election cycle a variety of politicians do all that they can to try and create some public recognition of themselves and in one way or another announce their intentions, in the preprimary period of campaign 2000, surfacing was not limited to politicians. There were the so-called glamour or celebrity contenders, and they added some measure of uniqueness to the process. For example, in August 1999 (after all of the potential Democratic contenders had left the field to Gore and Bradley), Hollywood actor Warren Beatty entered the fray, announced that he might consider running for president, and said that he was offended by the effect that campaign money has had on American politics. Interestingly, immediately after saying that he might consider running, an online ABC news poll showed him at 25 percent, just behind Bradley's 29 percent and

Gore's 45 percent. At the end of August, Beatty had a presidential Web site in which visitors were asked what issues they believed should be discussed in the 2000 campaign, and it was learned that the actor had been in contact with several professional organizers and a media manager. Not to be outdone by a Hollywood actor, in September 1999, billionaire Donald Trump indicated that he was seriously considering a run for the Reform Party's nomination in 2000. Trump said that he was eager to challenge Pat Buchanan (who by that time had almost left the Republican Party to pursue the nomination of the Reform Party) to keep the Party from going to the extreme Right. And finally, although little came of it, actress Cybill Shepherd was said to be considering a run.

While there may be no single way to account for the presence of the celebrity presidential candidates in 2000, it is most likely that the process itself was the motivating factor. In recent presidential elections, as the primary/caucus schedule has become more and more condensed and front-loaded (culminating in 2000, when the bid for delegates started on January 24 and was effectively over on March 7), there has been a major emphasis on what celebrities already have—name recognition, a lot of money, the ability to present themselves well in front of cameras, ready access to television talk shows, and the Internet. Moreover, if you add to it the fact that many Americans were not that excited about the prospect of the two front-runners, Bush and Gore, receiving the nominations, perhaps the attention given to a prospective celebrity candidate becomes less laughable and more understandable.

Not only, however, is the surfacing stage of campaign 2000 rhetorically interesting because of the variety of individuals who got out before any votes were cast, we can also consider the plight of one who came into the process too late but stayed for one of the primaries anyway.

Without much question, campaign 2000's most glaring example of someone who should have known more than he apparently did about the importance of early surfacing was Utah Senator Orrin Hatch. The senator formally entered the competition for the Republican nomination on July 1, 1999, without having done anything to prepare the ground for his candidacy. Unlike most of the other Republican hopefuls who had been actively building their campaigns (surfacing) for at least two years, Hatch had done little. In fact, he acknowledged that he had started late and was therefore way behind when he told a reporter, "Let's face it, most people don't even know I'm in the race. I found that some of my closest friends in California didn't know it" (Rosenbaum, 1999, 25). In August 1999, the senator finished last among nine contestants in the Iowa straw poll and in January 24, 2000 repeated his poor showing with a last-place finish in the Iowa caucuses. Although in announcing his candidacy Hatch had asked 1 million donors to give him $36 each to raise $36 million, by the time he withdrew on January 24, 2000 (two days after the Iowa caucuses), he had received only about $2.5 million from 15,000 contributors (Kelley, 2000, A2).

There were other presidential hopefuls in campaign 2000 who either seriously overestimated their abilities or underestimated the rigor of the challenge that the first stage represents. Although long considered a likely Republican contender, prior to filing for an exploratory committee with the Federal Election Commission on December 30, 1998, John McCain had spent less time in preparing for a presidential run than had other of the Republican contenders. In fact, in July 1998 McCain said that he would not seriously consider running for the presidency until after his reelection campaign for the Senate in November 1998. And despite the fact that he had the full attention of the national media and decisively defeated all of his rivals, first in the New Hampshire primary and later in Michigan, he had not taken the time necessary during the surfacing period to build a campaign organization in the states holding Republican primaries shortly after New Hampshire (Delaware and South Carolina) and in the states holding their primaries on March 7 (Super Tuesday). Because the senator did not have many endorsements from Republican Party officials in the primary states and, therefore, the apparatus of the state parties at his disposal in the post–New Hampshire period, the need for volunteers (Republicans and Independents)—workers who should have been identified and organized during the surfacing period—was critical. When compared to the contender who ultimately defeated him, George W. Bush, McCain, the insurgent, had neither the depth of organization nor the kind of money it took to defeat someone who had raised more than $70 million—although after his win in New Hampshire, the senator's campaign was taking in as much as $200,000 a day via the Internet and large fund-raising events (Mintz, 2000, 15). In a similar vein, on January 4, 1999, when Elizabeth Dole stepped down as president of the American Red Cross and signaled her interest in seeking the Republican presidential nomination, her informal declaration was late (the formation of an exploratory committee came even later and a formal announcement of candidacy never occurred), in that she was seriously behind most of her competitors in fund-raising and organizing a campaign in the early primary states.

Dole, however, began her candidacy with some major advantages—including immediate national name recognition, the fund-raising contacts of her husband (the 1996 Republican presidential nominee), and the mystique of being the first truly viable female presidential candidate (Connolly, 1999b, 12). In fact, none of the other 2000 presidential hopefuls came even close to producing the excitement her appearances generated. Wherever she appeared, big crowds frequently composed of newcomers to presidential politics (middle-aged women) greeted her arrival (Drinkard and Kasindorf, 1999, 6A). But three months after she left her job at the American Red Cross, Dole's campaign was said to be in trouble. Although her name recognition was as high as the front-runner's, her exploratory committee never reached its potential in terms of money raised, endorsements received, and volunteers signed up (Fineman and Cooper, 1999, 33). And although she had received the third largest number of votes in the August 1999 Republican straw poll in Iowa (behind Bush and Forbes), by the first week of October her campaign was clearly in financial and organizational trouble. In comparison, by that time, Governor Bush had already raised more than $60 million (Raasch, 1999b, C1), and Dole, in spite of the fact that her husband, Senator Robert Dole, was contacting his former fund-raisers to argue that it was essential to keep his wife's candidacy alive because it was good for the GOP's image, had raised only $3.5 million (Von Drehle and Balz, 1999, 13). In addition, the campaign appeared dysfunctional with the resignation of two top advisers, repeated cancellations of major policy addresses, and noticeable changes in or sudden silence on previously argued positions on issues such as abortion and gun control (Connolly, 1999c, 11). Thus, on October 20, 1999, Elizabeth Dole withdrew from the race, telling reporters that she "could not see going on against the huge fund-raising advantages" of Bush and Forbes (Raasch, 1999b, C1). She also provided an explanation that related campaign failures to the problems of timing: "The current political calendar and election laws favor those who get an early start, and can tap into huge private fortunes, or who have a pre-existing network of political supporters" (1).

Not surprisingly, the two contenders whose campaigns seemed best to understand the importance of timing during the surfacing stage were the two who went the distance, Al Gore and George Bush. Beginning with the 1996, Clinton/Gore reelection victory, and following the January 1997 inauguration, the vice president was actively pursuing the presidency. Although throughout 1997, with public, media, and the attention of both political parties focused on the Clinton/Gore 1996 fund-raising problems and the Clinton sex scandals, the vice president, nonetheless, continued the organizational and fund-raising transactions important to the surfacing stage. By summer 1998, despite the growing prospect of presidential impeachment proceedings and the inherent difficulties in appearing to be supportive of the president and yet not allowing Clinton's problems to hinder his prospects, the vice president's campaign for the presidency was well under way as he campaigned for Democrats running for election in key states. He traveled across the country speaking on popular policy issues such as literacy, the environment, and law enforcement and attended fund-raisers (80 of them) while his political action committee distributed more than $1 million for Democratic congressional candidates. By election day, he had campaigned for 67 Democrats running for governor or Congress (Connolly, 1998, 12). And in

July 1998 he held the first major gathering of his 2000 presidential campaign fund-raising network, which had already garnered over $1.5 million (Connolly, 1999a, 6).

Similarly, in spite of the fact that George W. Bush consistently deferred discussion of a presidential run until after his 1998 reelection campaign to the Texas governorship, by the summer of 1997 he was the front-runner in the first presidential poll for the 2000 election (Kristof, 2000, 1). It is said that the governor's candidacy "began like a rumor, evanescent and insubstantial but growing on thousands of tongues" (1). Whether sparked by the goal of Republican Party officials to have a candidate early in the season around whom the various branches of the party could coalesce or whether it had been carefully orchestrated by Bush's political strategist, Karl Rove, by early 1997 the governor's bandwagon had begun to roll. Republican governors came to Austin to pay their respects, speaking invitations poured in, Republican Party officials and policy experts endorsed his undeclared candidacy, and Bush became a fairly frequent speaker at Republican gatherings outside of Texas.

Thus, when in early March 1999 the governor officially announced the formation of an exploratory committee because he was seeking the Republican nomination, the "ground had been prepared." For more than two years he and his staff had been engaged in what they termed "reasonable things to keep open the possibility of a presidential run" (Kristof, 2000, 1). For example, Bush undertook a series of tutorials to learn more about federal and foreign policy, he spoke at selected Republican state and regional conferences, and he raised money—a lot of money. In 1997 and 1998 Bush began building a financial network by inviting groups of eight fund-raisers to have lunch with him in Austin. The group was called "the Pioneers," and they consisted of 150 supporters who each agreed to raise $100,000 to help finance the governor's exploratory committee. They raised $13 million, and as noted earlier, long before the primaries began, Bush had raised $23 million, breaking all previous Republican records. Moreover, by September 1999, the governor had collected endorsements from 23 of 31 Republican governors and 169 of 277 Republican members of Congress.

Thus in campaign 2000, timing continued to be an important ingredient to successful surfacing. However, in considering the results of some of the early contests, it might be argued that timing was not so critical a factor in the determination of winners and losers. After all, two of the earliest surfacers, Lamar Alexander and Steve Forbes, did poorly (Alexander dropped out of the race on August 16, 1999, two days after finishing sixth in the Iowa Republican straw poll, and Forbes bowed out on February 10, 1999, after successive losses in Iowa, New Hampshire, and Delaware). Both men had been campaigning for more than five years—indeed, they had never really stopped efforts to win the Republican nomination since their unsuccessful campaigns in 1996. Conversely, John McCain, who surfaced much later than Alexander and Forbes and failed to use the surfacing period to build a strong network of volunteers in most of the primary states, did extraordinarily well in some of the early contests (although he skipped the Iowa caucus, he won New Hampshire, Michigan, and Arizona). Clearly, there were other factors. For example, early as they were, Alexander and Forbes had their negatives. Although he had run in 1996, Alexander was not well known, and neither of his bids for the Republican nomination (1996 or 2000) generated any degree of public or media enthusiasm. In fact, his advisers contended that he had never received a fair break from the media and had never been treated seriously by Beltway pundits. As his media consultant put it, "If you move from the right to the center, the Beltway class will applaud you for your courage and maturity. If you move from the center to the right, they will despise you as a demagogue and opportunist. Lamar is someone who had been moving steadily right for 15 years and paying a price with the cognoscenti" (Balz, 1999a, 11).

In much the same way, Forbes had a credibility problem, and, it was argued, if he had had no money of his own, his candidacy would never have been taken even as seriously as it was (Fournier, 1999c, A3). Although great efforts were made to repackage his image for a second presidential run (all the way from changing his hairstyle and his glasses to extending his discussion of issues beyond the need for a flat tax—in fact, in 2000 he argued that prohibiting abortion is more important than overhauling the tax code), little changed. He had single digits in most early popularity polls, he appeared to have little personal appeal, and even in an editorial in a New Hampshire newspaper that endorsed him voters were quoted as saying that "he looks like a geek" or "he looks like a turtle" (Goldberg, 2000, 20). Neither image, of course, seemed presidential.

McCain, on the other hand, was able to do well—win New Hampshire—because he had high national visibility (in part because of his status as a genuine American military hero; his reputation for "speaking the truth" on issues debated in the Senate, even if in so doing his statements were in opposition to the views of his Republican colleagues; and in part because his "straight talking," "tell it like it is" rhetorical style always drew the attention of the media). But as the primaries went on to the 16 Super Tuesday states in early March, the senator was unable to continue winning because, in addition to not having the organizational base to defeat Bush, he did not have the endorsements of the Republican governors, members of Congress, and the party officials in most of those states. Indeed, McCain was "rather actively disliked by everyone from the Republican leadership in the Senate to the heads of influential groups like the National Right to Life Committee, the Christian Coalition and Americans for Tax Reform" (Berke, 1999b, 4-1).

Although timing was a major variable in the earliest stage of campaign 2000, it was not the only factor. There were, for example (as there always are), two hopefuls who had no chance of winning the nomination even though they may have understood the nuances of timing. The first was Alan Keyes, the host of a radio talk show who had been an ambassador to the United Nations Economic and Social Council during the Reagan administration and a contender in the 1996 presidential contest. While Keyes placed third in the Iowa caucus and was more familiar to the national media covering the 2000 campaign than he had been in 1996, nonetheless his showing in Iowa was the best he did (although he stayed in the race longer than any of the Republican candidates competing with Bush). In short, his campaign was always perceived as a long shot at best or as a "side show" to the main event at worst (Filosa, 2000, B1). And the second was Gary Bauer, who resigned as head of the Family Research Council in January 1999 to run for the Republican nomination. In spite of the fact that Bauer raised $10 million for his campaign and outlasted better-known candidates such as Dan Quayle and Elizabeth Dole, he was never given any chance at all of becoming the Republican nominee because "of his political inexperience and his conservative agenda" (Crowley, 1999, A7).

Not only can the first stage be analyzed in terms of its timing demands on the candidates; it also can be understood with regard to the characteristic *functions* served by *specific* acts of communication. In 2000, three such functions appear to have been particularly important.

The first function for campaign 2000 was that it provided information regarding the *caliber* of those who wanted to be president—their fitness for the job. During the early periods of a campaign, the "public face" of each contender begins to develop as the electorate symbolically draws inferences from campaign actions about how a candidate would perform as president. During early 2000, for example, voters could view for themselves the multipronged, idea-heavy programs proposed by Steve Forbes, the lecturing and sermonizing of Bill Bradley, the heavily scripted and inauthentic rhetorical style of Elizabeth Dole, the constant argument that campaign finance reform is essential for achieving a conservative agenda from John McCain, the new-styled Republican compassionate conservatism of George Bush, and the tenacious and bulldog style of Al Gore and make judgments regarding their presidential qualities.

Bill Bradley, even with his star-studded celebrity status (a three-time all-American basketball player at Princeton University, captain of the U.S. basketball team that won the gold medal at the 1964 Olympics, a New York Knicks basketball player who earned a place in basketball's

Hall of Fame, and an influential former U.S. senator), could sustain neither his image nor a national campaign through the surfacing and primary stages. It was not as if he began his candidacy as an unknown or as someone who was not taken seriously. In fact, from the beginning of his run he generated considerable voter and media attention, perhaps in part because he was taking on a sitting vice president in his own party (about whom there were concerns) but also because of his persona as authentic, a "truth-teller," a person with integrity and honest values, a liberal champion, and an intellectual (Balz, 1999b, 11–12; Hiatt, 1999, 26; Fineman, 1999a, 22–25). He called his insurgency campaign a crusade to show that politics could be done a better way (an obvious reference to the problems of the Clinton/Gore administration), said that he was running against special interests and the corrupting system of campaign finance, and "framed the Democratic contest as a choice between big ideas (his) and small ideas (Gore's)" (Balz, 1999b, 12). And without party backing, he raised large amounts of money within months of announcing his candidacy (in part through adroit use of e-mail and the Internet) and said that he was campaigning against campaigning. The senator clearly excited certain groups of Democratic voters (for example, the college educated and the "new economy" Democrats who worked with technology and were plugged into the digital marketplace), many of whom claimed to be "madly for Bradley" (Allen, 1999a, 15; Fineman, 1999a, 24). Although a stilted and bland public speaker, even in his rumpled suits with his half-glasses sliding down his nose, he had presence—a celebrity status uncommon to presidential contenders who are not incumbents. When he entered the hall—or the room in which he was to give a speech—all talking ceased, little kids were clearly excited and had basketballs ready to throw to him, and adults stood quietly (almost reverently) and applauded. There was a general sense among audience members of being in the presence of a major or famous person.[1] From the beginning, however, there were problems—organizational problems, medical problems, timing and strategy problems. And when solutions were attempted, frequently the solutions were in conflict with the "above the fray" moral crusade that was supposed to be the signature of his campaign.

Bradley insisted that he be his own man, that he not be "handled" or "packaged" by consultants. He was dismissive of outside political advice, followed his own instincts more than he followed the advice of his staff, was frequently prickly and strong-willed, resisted the very advice he paid his advisers to give, and made it clear that no one except his wife could tell him what to do (Allen, 1999b, 12; Dao, 1999, 24; Bai, 2000, 33). Although his campaign used focus groups to test his television commercials, and the senator talked with Madison Avenue advertising executives about shaping his image and message, he had no expert advise on writing speeches, on determining which issues were best for him, or for staging political events (a prerequisite for generating images for television and news magazines). Thus, many times the decisions made were wrong—making speeches that were meant to reach out to labor unions at colleges instead of union halls, giving major speeches on health care in hospital cafeterias where there were only doctors and not photogenic patients, or failing to use a taped endorsement by basketball superstar Michael Jordan in either Iowa or New Hampshire or a joint one by filmmaker Spike Lee and former New York mayor Edward I. Koch until four days before the New York primary (Gellman, Russakoff, and Allen, 2000, 10). His top strategists had no experience running national campaigns and after losing to Gore in Iowa and New Hampshire, no plan for the five weeks of "dead air" between the New Hampshire primary and Super Tuesday (unlike the Republicans who had primaries in Michigan, Arizona, and South Carolina during this time, a Democratic contender had little way to change the subject from early losses). He finally began campaigning for the nonbinding Washington state primary, but not until the last week when Gore's party allies already had the state sewed up for the vice president (Gellman, Russakoff, and Allen, 2000, 11). To add to the senator's problems, in late December 1999, his campaign was forced to announce that in 1996 Bradley had been diagnosed with atrial fibrillation (a treatable irregularity in his heartbeat) after he had had an episode while campaigning in California. In spite of the fact that his condition kept him away from the campaign less than 24 hours, the media had countless questions not only about his medical condition but about truthfulness—why a candidacy that was dedicated to candor, a "different kind of campaign," had not made the disclosure at the beginning of the senator's run (Fineman, 1999b, 30). And in January, just days before New Hampshire voted, in an effort to jolt his slumping presidential bid, Bradley began attacking Gore. He said that the vice president had lied about his (Bradley's) record and then suggested that Gore was not trustworthy enough to be president. The senator called it "a new beginning" (Battenfeld, 2000, 6), but his public image as being "above the fray" and running "a different kind of campaign" was in jeopardy. As some New Hampshire voters put it, Bradley turned out to be "just another politician" (Gellman, Russakoff, and Allen, 2000, 10). On Super Tuesday, Gore so thoroughly dominated the senator in each of the state elections that two days later Bradley officially withdrew.

To an even larger extent, the credibility factor that was a problem for Bradley also plagued Elizabeth Dole. Dole's résumé included two cabinet posts (secretary of labor and secretary of transportation), a seat on the Federal Trade Commission, deputy assistant to President Richard Nixon for consumer affairs, and eight years as president of the American Red Cross. Although in the beginning her candidacy generated a good deal of attention from the media and the electorate (throughout her campaign, she drew large crowds for rallies and other political events), serious problems were soon evident. For one thing, Dole never really had any consistent self-definition. She symbolized so many things to so many people that it was difficult, and maybe impossible, to "merge her competing images into one coherent candidacy" (Raasch, 1999a, A2). With all of the problems attached to being the first viable female presidential candidate, Dole sought to create a political persona that took advantage of her gender but did not rely solely on it to sway voters (Connolly, 1999b, 12). The result, however, was confusion. At times she played down the role of gender in her campaign: "I'm not running because I am a woman, and I don't expect people to vote for me because I am a woman" (12), but most of her speeches were laced with personal reminiscences of how she had always tried to help women fulfill their potential, her efforts to bring more women into management ranks in the government, and that the biggest change she had witnessed during her career was "the role of women" (12). The conflict was apparent, for example, when she advocated equal pay for women who earn $.70 to every $1 earned by men and followed it by a discussion of the positive picture for women today or when she provided a detailed recitation of her own professional résumé and then (although she is childless) followed it with the observation: "I think the most important career a woman can have is that of a mother raising fine young future citizens" (12).

While there is little question that Dole's failure to present a coherent message in regard to the role of gender in her candidacy contributed to the inability of the public (and Republican funding sources) to view her as possessing the stature of a president, she suffered a second credibility problem. Even before she left the Red Cross to pursue her bid for the nomination on a full-time basis, her candidacy was tainted with the perception that she was running for president because her goal was to be vice president ("Never Too Soon to Start," 1998, 4). And even after her strong showing in the August 1999 Iowa straw poll, Dole's advisers had to publicly deny that she had any desire for the vice presidential slot (Connolly, 1999c, 11). Whether or not the perception that she was running for vice president was based on her gender (how could a woman be serious about running for the presidency?), the result was yet another blow to her credibility (believability) as a potential president.

Thus in 2000, as in previous presidential campaign years, the actions of the hopefuls during the early stages of the contest could be seen as representative of their behavior as president. Potential presidents are not supposed to have inconsistencies between what they preach and what they do (as Bradley was perceived when he began attacking his opponent), and they should not present conflicting messages about themselves (as Dole was perceived to have done). Whatever the electorate ultimately decides, it seems clear that one function of the surfacing stage is to provide at least some indication of the caliber of each contender—the fitness for office. And once that first impression is formed it is difficult and sometimes impossible to change.

The functions performed by the 2000 preprimary period were not limited to symbolism. Two of the contributions related to the pragmatic or "instrumental" aspects of the campaign, and each proved important to the success or failure of individual candidates in subsequent stages. The first instrumental function was that the electorate began to have some information about the candidates' potential programs, goals, and initial stands on issues. As the bevy of early presidential hopefuls found multiple events that gave them excuses to be in Iowa and New Hampshire, they were able to determine what issues appeared to be on voters' minds, and then they could formulate specific responses to or positions on those issues. They were, in other words, able to begin building a "stock" campaign speech that resonated with their interpretation of the issues important to the electorate. The earliest of the contenders (obviously in response to the Clinton scandals and the impending congressional presidential impeachment proceedings) attached themselves to issues of morality and character. Gary Bauer said that the most important issue was the need for a moral center in politics. Pat Buchanan called for a renewal in moral leadership in the White House. Dan Quayle, Lamar Alexander, John Ashcroft, and Gary Bauer called for President Clinton's resignation. Bush promised that he would restore integrity and dignity to the White House. And the vice president, who to this point in time had been one of Clinton's most vocal and visible supporters, said in his announcement speech that he intended to rebuild the morals and values of the country.

As the surfacing stage proceeded, however, those contenders who had not dropped out expanded their discussion beyond issues of morality. Thus, voters began to learn what Steve Forbes meant by "freedom from fear" of the Internal Revenue Service, why Alan Keyes called abortion the "slavery issue of our time," what Gary Bauer meant when he talked about "faith-based politics," and how John McCain would institute campaign finance reform. Although such information gathering has been important to the preprimary stage in every presidential race, in 2000 its importance increased because the surfacing period was so long (beginning for some hopefuls as early as May 1997) and the eventful part of the primary stage was so brief—just 44 days (beginning with the Iowa caucus on January 24 and, in effect, concluding after the 16-state March 7 primaries because a large number of delegates pledged to Bush and Gore had already been determined).

One of the most unique characteristics about 2000 was that the campaign actually revolved around the discussion of issues, including issues related to character. While clearly there was, at least, media attention to others matters (e.g., Gore's change in the color and style of his clothing and Bush's mangled syntax), the fact is that in the early campaign (and beyond through the general election) the contenders were discussing those issues they had discovered were important to the electorate, identifying themselves with specific issues, and presenting their plan or program for solving problems. Indeed, several weeks after the general election a Pew Center poll found not only that the public recognized that substantive issues affecting their lives were being discussed by the candidates but that they felt they had the information they needed to make informed decisions (Broder, 2000, 4). And the discussion of those issues began during the surfacing stage when "policy wonks" Gore and Forbes presented their plans for dealing with issues such as education, Social Security, health insurance, prescription drugs, and tax relief; in so doing, they and the media forced Bush and McCain to provide more of the "specifics" than the governor and the senator had been doing in the early days of their campaigns. For example, Forbes, who argued that he "had more substance than all the other candidates put together" (Powell, 1999, 6), had opinions and a step-by-step plan for ending abortions, a flat 17 percent federal income tax, school choice, improved benefit distribution to veterans, a health care system that would permit the selection of doctors and other health care professionals, and a plan for allowing all Americans to manipulate their own Social Security retirement fund (Goldberg, 2000, 20).

And Gore, long known for his "mastery of substance" (Shapiro, 1999, 15A) and his expertise in policy matters but who was also said to be "too caught in policy gobbledygook to excite voters" (Weisman, 2000, 16), presented proposals on everything from a plan for the public financing of campaigns to network economics—how decision making could be distributed in the network world. In California, for example, he talked about "salmon as an indicator species," forestry, water issues, and clean air and, as some in the audience suggested, "was more informed than some of the enviros" (Janofsky, 1999, 16). He also generated headlines in July 1998 when he explained the new federal rules on computer privacy, which pollsters said was "near the top of the [voters'] list," giving the vice president "a great hit on a very substantive issue" (Connolly, 1998, 12). And in January 1999, in New York, Gore began discussing a series of proposals designed to boost the economy, such as a doubling of the economic empowerment zones to revitalize inner-city neighborhoods (Dugan, 1999, 12). In short, Gore, like Forbes, lived up to his reputation as a policy wonk during the surfacing stage.

No one, however, mistook either George W. Bush or John McCain as candidates with a heavy reliance on detailed policy proposals—at least not in the beginning. Bush, for example, although he had positions on issues, was accused of speaking in "vague terms with versatile words" and, at least in the opinion of one journalist, used imprecise language on issues from "abortion to Kosovo to gun control, hate crimes, affirmative action and the environment" (Fournier, 1999b, A21). In July 1999, after he had been on the campaign trail for a month and had traveled to 12 states and the District of Columbia, it was argued that "the real substance of a presidential platform was missing" (Balz, 1999b, 11). It was also reported that the candidate looked liked he was trying to remember his cue cards, that the campaign seemed ponderous, and that Bush was not willing to "sweat the nitty-gritty of policy" (11). In fact, during the surfacing period Bush did need to form policies on a range of federal issues he had not had to contemplate as governor, and he claimed not to be embarrassed when he told reporters and voters that he did not know the answers to some of their questions. His advisers maintained that in the fall the governor intended to "roll out a series of policy speeches." In November 1999 a Boston television reporter apparently surprised Bush with a "pop quiz" on foreign policy. He was asked to name the leaders of Taiwan, India, Pakistan, and Chechnya but knew only Taiwan's in spite of the fact that the coup in Pakistan had been in the news for several weeks. The governor said: "The new Pakistani general, he's just been elected—not elected, this guy took over office. It appears this guy is going to bring stability to the country and I think that's good news for the subcontinent" (Dowd, 1999, A20). And even by the time of the New Hampshire primary, although his campaign had by then been pushed into specificity on the governor's tax relief proposal, his support of private accounts for Social Security, and his education proposals, Bush continued to be short on policy details on other issues, spending more than twice as much time on personal interaction with voters who came to his campaign appearances as he did on his formal speeches.[2]

In a similar manner, John McCain's style did not always include specifics on issues other than campaign finance reform and tax relief. Before January 2000, when McCain began making "major policy speeches" on budget policy, health care, Social Security, rebuilding the military, and the environment (largely because the press wanted fresh material), the senator had not prepared carefully on areas outside of his legislative focus and said that he felt more comfortable with "issues I grew up with" (Mitchell, 2000, 15). Sometimes he told questioners at his town hall meetings that he did not have an answer to a question on a specific social issue and said that he would "be glad to educate myself" (15). It is not that the senator failed to take stands on issues. Like Bush, McCain had a position—an initial response—to all issues. It was simply that neither the governor nor McCain campaigned as a policy wonk with a fulsome plan for every problem. Bush campaigned as a new-style Republican, one with "greater sensitivity" to the problems of all Americans than other Republicans appeared to have had. While he did not use the word *character*, nonetheless the governor had as one of his "sure-fire" winning issues the pledge that when he had his right hand raised, he would swear to uphold not only the Constitution but also "the dignity of the office" of the president (Balz, 1999b, 11). And McCain, whose most important issue was his own authenticity (Cohen, 1999, 27), excited voters not because of his stand on policy issues but, as most exit polls revealed, because of character and personal qualities (Kohut, 2000, 15). Thus, whether contenders Forbes, Gore, Bush, and McCain used the surfacing stage to provide information about issues of character or to provide information about issues of policy, they were successful. As the Pew Center study discussed earlier indicated, American voters believed that they had the information necessary to make informed decisions about the candidates. Such information gathering begins in the preprimary period.

The second instrumental function evident in the preprimary period of campaign 2000 was also important in that the *themes*—much of the rhetorical agenda for later stages of the campaign—were established.

For the most part, the surfacing stage of the 2000 contest was like most others in that as the contenders traveled the primary/caucus states, they began to develop some sensitivity to the problems that were on voters' minds and began formulating " 'solutions' to problems that seem to be compatible with popular perception" (Trent and Friedenberg, 2000, 26). Themes that related to education, "saving" Social Security, prescription drugs, and health insurance were foremost among the topics tested by those contenders who stuck around for at least one primary. From the beginning, for example, George W. Bush had two themes, tax relief for all Americans and the need for higher standards in education—"rewarding" those school systems achieving them and "punishing" those who do not. Forbes expanded his 1996 tax reform theme to include Christian conservative issues—anti-abortion and prayer in schools. Bill Bradley focused on health care, impoverished children, and the working family's life, whereas Al Gore centered on education (from providing high-quality preschool for all children to tax-free tuition for college), health care (enacting a patient's bill of rights and helping seniors pay for prescription drugs), and the economy (keeping it growing).

The most rhetorically interesting, however, was John McCain's theme, campaign finance reform. McCain argued that the soft money collected by and contributed to the political parties and to candidates' PACS had to be eliminated to take the greed and corruption out of politics. Although the issue was received enthusiastically in the senator's spirited town hall meetings (Lawrence, 2000, 6A), it had not been a problem on the minds of voters—McCain "gave" voters the issue; it did not originate with the electorate. Moreover, as noted earlier, exit data from the primaries revealed that the voters who were McCain supporters really just liked McCain. They did not necessarily, as a group, share the same values nor care strongly about the same issues, including campaign finance reform. What they had in common was that they were drawn to all of the things they believed the senator personally represented. Campaign finance reform was just one of them (Kohut, 2000, 15). Once introduced, the issue lived on in subsequent stages to become part of the rhetorical agenda of campaign 2000, even after its sponsor dropped from the race.

These, then, were the communication functions of the surfacing stage of the 2000 campaign. As in other contemporary presidential elections they provided information regarding the caliber of those who sought the presidency. They also gave voters some idea of the candidates' goals, potential programs, and positions on issues. Finally, the surfacing period was important because much of the rhetorical agenda for the entire campaign was established before the primaries and caucuses even began.

THE PRIMARY STAGE

The primaries, the second stage of the early presidential campaign, are one of the most controversial of election events. That is not surprising since the primary elections, not the national nominating conventions, have determined the identity of the Democratic Party's nominee since 1972 and the Republican Party's nominee since 1980.

While primaries have been referred to as "America's most original contribution to the art of democracy" (Miller, Wattenberg, and Malanchuk, 1986, 533), there is less and less agreement each presidential election cycle that they represent the *best* way to select presidential candidates. As a matter of fact, the 2000 primaries may have been criticized even more than those of other years because the problems they have generated since 1972 were exacerbated in 2000 by having so many of them, a more compressed calendar than had ever existed in the past, greater expense, and no surprises at the end. There is truth to each charge. For example, in 1980 (the first year that both parties had the vast majority of their delegates to the national nominating conventions selected as a result of state elections) there were 37 caucuses and primaries. In 2000, excluding all of the straw polls and all of the primaries held in American territories, there was a grand total of 89 (counting the caucuses and primaries of both Republican and Democratic Parties), and they stretched from January 24 through June 6. One of the most frequently voiced complaints, however, regarded the extreme front-loading of the schedule, which in 2000, for the first time, included most of the states with the greatest number of delegates. The problem was that in spite of the fact that primaries were conducted through June 6, the 16-state Super Tuesday contests on March 7 accounted for nearly a third of the 2,066 delegates to the Republican convention and the 4,338 delegates to the

Democratic convention. And when the two front-runners, Gore and Bush, won decisively on Super Tuesday, the race for the nomination of both parties was effectively over—in spite of the fact that the process lingered for another three months. The front-loaded primary schedule that culminated in early March also irritated voters and the governors of the Interior West—eight states that account for nearly a quarter of the country's land mass but only 40 of its electoral votes. All, except Arizona, which had had a Republican-only primary before March 7, were virtually ignored. Their primaries occurred after Super Tuesday, and thus issues important to them (land management, water rights, nuclear waste cleanup, or endangered species) had not been part of the dialogue of the presidential contenders (Janofsky, 2000, 14).

There were other concerns with the 2000 primaries. Although the record-setting amount of money raised and spent by the 2000 hopefuls has been discussed earlier, the fact is that in spite of the huge resources expended the race ended as it had begun—the two contenders who had been the front-runners all the way through, Vice President Gore and Texas Governor George W. Bush, became the nominees of their parties. Nothing had really changed. Moreover, despite the fact that voters had participated in record number in those few primaries that really matter (i.e., Carolina, and Michigan) (Ceasar and Busch, 2001, 103), interest in the overall campaign dropped sharply in the months following Super Tuesday when the nominations of the two parties had been decided. In a mid-March poll of voters by the Joan Shorenstein Center on the Press, Politics and Public Policy, 49 percent of those surveyed indicated their interest in the primaries and said they had discussed the campaign that day. In mid-May, only 15 percent of those questioned said that they had talked about the campaign in the previous day (Clymer, 2000, 1).

Although the 2000 primaries generated some criticism, they did uphold a couple of political traditions that had been broken in the 1996 contest. After much interparty debate and after frequent changes (the New Hampshire legislature, for example, invoked their 1975 law that demands that they hold their presidential primary one week earlier than any other), the primary schedule was finally set. And although some states continued to try and move their election before Iowa's precinct caucuses and New Hampshire's primary, in the end, tradition prevailed—first Iowa and then New Hampshire. Of course, to be first, Iowa had to move to January 24 and New Hampshire to February 1—a week earlier than had been originally scheduled. There was, however, one tradition that did not hold true in 2000. Beginning with the first preferential presidential primary in 1952, and extending until 1992, New Hampshire citizens had voted for the candidate who eventually won the general election. They were "wrong in '92" (New Hampshire Democrats selected Paul Tsongas and Republicans selected George Bush, and Bill Clinton won the presidency) and "wrong" again in 2000, when Democrats selected Gore and Republicans selected McCain.

In spite of the problems created and the traditions broken or reconstituted during the primary stage of the 2000 presidential campaign, the communication acts and symbols of the period provided three functions that were important to the entire electoral process.

The first function is that the primaries and caucuses serve as a *valuable source of information* to the political parties before they bestow their nomination on a single individual. It is in the primary campaigns where the parties can learn which of their contenders can craft coherent messages and deliver them effectively in a wide variety of formats. They are also able to distinguish from among their presidential hopefuls who has the ability to organize a competent national campaign staff and who is able to raise money from a variety of national constituencies. They are also able to see who among their candidates is flexible and able to adjust to and sustain the physical and emotional stress of a prolonged campaign and who is not or cannot. It is useful information. Indeed, in 2000 it was critical to both the Republican and Democratic Parties. The Republican Party, for example, reaffirmed that Steve Forbes, despite unlimited money, a well-organized and professional staff, and policy-rich speeches, had little or no appeal to voters and did not win any state before he withdrew. They also learned that John McCain, despite not having the endorsement of any part of the party, was able to wage a credible and serious challenge by raising a lot of money and attracting citizens who had never before been interested in or participated in the Republican primaries. In fact, McCain energized and attracted Independents and Democrats who participated in record numbers in the New Hampshire, Michigan, and South Carolina primaries. Finally, Republicans learned, after Bush defeated McCain in South Carolina and won decisively on Super Tuesday, that they had made the "correct" call when early in the surfacing period they had determined that the Texas governor could give them back the White House. To some extent Republican unification around Bush had been a leap of faith in that although the governor had a famous name, he also had "a spotty business record and a fairly blank political slate—and yet practically the entire party had rallied around him—indeed, come beseeching him to run" (Thomas and Brant, 2000, 36). His coalition "was a big-tent alliance of practically everybody who mattered—fat cats, officeholders, K Street lobbyists, the Christian right, the George I government in exile, the Gingrich Revolution remnants—everybody" (36). But it was the governor's defeat of McCain in South Carolina that gave the party the feedback they wanted. They had "picked" a winner.

The Democratic Party also received critical information during the primaries. They learned, for example, that both of their contenders were successful fund-raisers but stilted, ponderous public speakers who did not generally excite voters. They also learned that each had the unfortunate tendency to believe that he better understood the nuances of running a national campaign and therefore had more confidence in his own knowledge than he had in his campaign staff. Finally, Democrats learned that Bradley was unable to make the necessary changes in campaign strategy and style—was, in fact, not flexible enough to adapt to prevailing campaign conditions. Indeed, the changes or repositioning that occurred and did not occur in the campaigns of the Democratic contenders directly relate to the second function—that the primaries and caucuses serve as a *valuable source of feedback to the candidates* about the campaign they are conducting—the organization they have put together, their message, the competence of their staffs, their fund-raising efforts, their own emotional and physical stamina—in other words, what they do well and what they do not, what has "worked" and what has not, and what mistakes can be repaired and which cannot. During the surfacing period, the only way candidates are able to measure how they are doing is through the media, the amount of money that is coming in, an occasional straw poll of party leaders, or from polls, either their own or those commissioned by the various media outlets. The primaries, however, provide direct feedback from the voters and, thus, an opportunity to learn from any mistakes that have been made. And there was much for the candidates of 2000 to learn.

George Bush, for example, learned after a resounding defeat to John McCain in New Hampshire that there was no longer "a sense of inevitability about his candidacy"—that he might no longer be the candidate best positioned to win the nomination and the presidency. Accordingly, the candidate and his staff made some changes. First, they made Bush more accessible to the media. The governor had spent much of the surfacing and early primary season aloof from the media. But following the New Hampshire loss, Bush was, all of a sudden, a regular fixture in the back of his campaign plane, giving impromptu press conferences, joking with reporters, and assigning "nicknames" to some of them (Thomas and Brant, 2000, 31–37). Moreover, following New Hampshire, Bush's speeches became more conservative, he began attacking McCain, and his staff either worked with or allowed the Christian Right to run a smear campaign against McCain in South Carolina and Michigan (31–37).

Although Al Gore had made numerous changes in his campaign and in his own rhetorical style during the surfacing period, once the primaries began and he was regularly defeating his rival, there was little reason to reposition. The feedback he received from voters was that he would be the Democratic nominee. The only change, and it was temporary, was eliminating some of his attacks on Bill Bradley. Before the primaries had begun, Gore began the onslaught against the former senator. At a

Jefferson-Jackson Day political dinner in Iowa in early October, Gore charged that Bradley was a quitter for leaving the Senate during the tough times in the mid-1990s, called Bradley's health care plan "risky" because it would replace Medicaid with "vouchers," and charged (inaccurately) that Bradley had voted against flood relief for farmers (Thomas and Brant, 2000, 31–37). But after defeating Bradley in Iowa, the vice president came into New Hampshire as the front-runner—above the fray—taking pains not to attack Bradley. In fact, Gore said that he hoped that "Bradley's attacks will only tarnish the image the New Jersey Senator cultivated all year—of a politician who wouldn't stoop to 'politics as usual' " (Zuckman and Hohler, 2000, A1).

Bill Bradley, on the other hand, after losing to the vice president in Iowa and New Hampshire, did attempt to do some repositioning. The problem is that he waited too long, and as noted earlier, the changes he made were at odds with why he had said he was running for president. From the beginning through the end of his campaign in Iowa, Bradley steadfastly refused to respond in kind to Gore's attacks on him. In fact, at one point he said that political attacks were what he called "dartboard politics." "Throw a little dart and hope that it will be a poison dart. I think people are fed up with that . . . I'm not in the business of responding to every one of their darts" (Balz, 1999c, 13). However, in the final days before New Hampshire voters went to the polls, Bradley began to attack the vice president, questioning whether or not he was honest enough to be president. In justification of his change in strategy the senator said that "after absorbing months of misleading statements and misrepresentations . . . I decided, well, it's my turn and I threw a little elbow" (Battenfeld, 2000, 6). Bradley's repositioning had no visible success. On February 1, he lost his second contest when New Hampshire Democrats voted for the vice president. Following New Hampshire, the senator made another futile attempt to recast himself. He pretty much stopped attacking Gore (although they had a spirited debate in New York in late February over the depth of their commitment to racial justice) and attempted to reposition himself as the "true heir to Clinton's Democratic base" (Bai, 2000, 33). The problem was that while many voters liked Bradley, they were not sure just who he was. Throughout the campaign, he had rarely talked with the media and would not provide any information about himself to anyone—even in terms of what books he enjoyed reading (Collins, 1999, 16). It was argued, for example, that "he talks passionately to black audiences about racial injustice but rarely discusses his own experiences as a white man in a black sport" (Bai, 2000, 33). In short, he did not give voters much of himself and seemed not to understand that the American electorate feel the need "to know" politicians to whom they give their votes. Once again his attempt to reposition himself and his campaign was unsuccessful. He lost every primary he entered.

The final function served by communication acts and symbols of the primary stage of the 2000 campaign is closely related to the other two; it gave both voters and candidates *a chance to frame questions and evaluate responses* to those questions. Despite the compression of the primary calendar (particularly for the Republican candidates), contenders still had the opportunity to answer voter doubts about their candidacy, and voters still had the chance to evaluate the responses. For example, after placing second in Iowa, Steve Forbes, buoyed by his success, could go into New Hampshire (a state with a long tradition of opposing taxation and refusing to adopt either a state income tax or a sales tax) and trumpet his antitax plan while ridiculing what he called the "convoluted tax-cut proposals of Governor Bush and Senator McCain" (Rosenbaum, 2000, A16). It gave Al Gore time to move from an attack mode to a more presidential "above the fray" posture and then back to attack again and George Bush time to change his rhetorical posture as a compassionate Republican in Iowa and New Hampshire to a highly conservative Republican in South Carolina and then back to the "compassionate center" by Super Tuesday. It could have given Bill Bradley time to learn how to respond to Gore's attacks on him and how to attack and sustain his criticisms of the vice president. And it provided countless opportunities for each of the candidates to better frame their answer to "why I should be president" and each voter countless opportunities for evaluation.

These, then, were the communication functions of the primary stage of the 2000 campaign. As in other presidential elections since 1972, they were important because they were a source of feedback to the candidates and to the political parties, and they allowed the people—not the media, not the political parties—to determine who the candidates would be. But for Democrats and Republicans alike, there were no surprises. Voters overwhelmingly confirmed conventional wisdom by declaring that the front-runners would be the nominees.

ACKNOWLEDGMENTS

Thanks to Lisa A. Connelly, a graduate student in the Department of Communication at the University of Cincinnati, for her outstanding help in preparing the manuscript.

Thanks also to former Cincinnati graduate students Andrew K. Nusz, Amy M. Schmisseur, and Lene C. Taylor for the excellent campaign chronologies they developed for the 2000 presidential election.

NOTES

1. These are my personal observations after traveling with the candidates and the media in New Hampshire and observing Bradley in the final week of the New Hampshire primary.

2. These are my personal observations after traveling with the candidates and the media in New Hampshire and observing Bush in the final week of the New Hampshire primary.

REFERENCES

Allen, Mike. 1999a. "Will the Shining Armor Get Tarnished?" *Washington Post*, November 29, 15.

Allen, Mike. 1999b. "Bradley Goes It Alone." *Washington Post*, December 20–27, 12.

Ayres, Drummond, Jr. 1999. "Political Briefing." *New York Times*, September 5, 18.

Bai, Matt. 2000. "Bill Bradley's Last Stand." *Newsweek*, March 26, 33.

Balz, Dan. 1999a. "This Time, He's Not Lamar." *Washington Post*, March 15, 11.

Balz, Dan. 1999b. "A Surprise Fast Break for the Underdog." *Washington Post*, May 10, 11–12.

Balz, Dan. 1999c. "Keeping His Darts to Himself." *Washington Post*, October 18, 13–14.

Balz, Dan and David S. Broder. 1999a. "Elizabeth Dole Hints at Presidential Bid." *Washington Post*, January 5, A1.

Balz, Dan and David S. Broder. 1999b. "Reshaping the Republican Race in 2000?" *Washington Post*, January 11, 13–14.

Battenfeld, Joe. 2000. "Bradley Says It's No More Mr. Nice Guy." *Boston Herald*, January 28, 6.

Berke, Richard L. 1999a. "Conservatives Backing Bush's Abortion Strategy." *New York Times*, November 7, 1.

Berke, Richard L. 1999b. "What If McCain Gains the World, But Loses the Party?" *New York Times*, December 12, 4-1.

Blumenthal, Sidney. 1982. *The Permanent Campaign*. New York: Simon and Schuster.

Broder, David S. 2000. "Don't Laugh Just Yet." *Washington Post*, May 19, 4.

Ceaser, James and Andrew Busch. 2001. *The Perfect Tie*. Lanham, MD: Rowman & Littlefield.

Clymer, Adam. 2000. "Poll Finds Voters Skeptical about Role in Nomination." *New York Times*, May 18, 1–4.

Cohen, Richard. 1999. "McCain Is Who He Is." *Washington Post*, November 22, 27.

Collins, Gail. 1999. "So, Exactly When Is Bill Bradley Going to Enter the Charisma Phase?" *New York Times*, May 16, 16.

Connolly, Ceci. 1998. "Alter Ego—Up to a Point." *Washington Post*, October 19, 12. Connolly, Ceci. 1999a. "The $55 Million Man." *Washington Post*, April 12, 6.

Connolly, Ceci. 1999b. "The Dole Mystique." *Washington Post*, April 26, 12.

Connolly, Ceci. 1999c. "Can Elizabeth Dole Become the Anti-Bush?" *Washington Post*, September 20, 11.

Crowley, Patrick. 1999. "Newport Native Mulls Run at GOP Nomination." *Cincinnati Enquirer*, January 15, A7.

Dao, James. 1999. "Bradley Is in Full Control and Some Friends Fret." *New York Times*, November 21, 24.

Dowd, Maureen. 1999. "Pop Quiz Puts Bush in Jeopardy." *Cincinnati Enquirer*, November 10, A20.

Drinkard, Jim and Martin Kasindorf. 1999. "Dole Campaign Trying to Build on Momentum from Iowa." *USA Today*, August 23, 6A.

Dugan, Ianthe Jeanne. 1999. "Al Gore's Wooing Wall Street." *Washington Post*, January 18, 12.

Filosa, Gwen. 2000. "Slim Chances Can't Quiet Keyes." *Concord Monitor*, January 28, B1.

Finemen, Howard. 1999a. "Bradley's Shot." *Newsweek*, September 13, 22–28.

Fineman, Howard. 1999b. "Bradley's Episodes of the Heart." *Newsweek*, December 20, 30–31.

Fineman, Howard and Matthew Cooper. 1999. "Back in the Amen Corner." *Newsweek*, March 22, 33.

Fournier, Ron. 1999a. "Democrats Gather Around Gore, Though Some Warily." *Cincinnati Enquirer*, March 21, A7.

Fournier, Ron. 1999b. "Bush Rivals Clinton in Obfuscation." *Cincinnati Enquirer*, May 30, A21.

Fournier, Ron. 1999c. "Forbes Launches Ads for 2000 Bid." *Cincinnati Enquirer*, May 30, A3.

Gellman, Barton, Dale Russakoff, and Mike Allen. 2000. "What Happened to Bill Bradley?" *Washington Post*, March 13, 10–11.

Goldberg, Carey. 2000. "Remember Homely Abe, Forbes Says." *New York Times*, January 30, 20.

Hiatt, Fred. 1999. "Bradley's Dilemma." *Washington Post*, May 24, 26.

Janofsky, Michael. 1999. "Gore Building Network in California." *New York Times*, January 24, 16.

Janofsky, Michael. 2000. "Amid Campaign Hoopla, One Region Feels Left Out." *New York Times*, February 13, 14.

Kelley, Matt. 2000. "Orrin Hatch Throws in the Towel." *Union Leader*, January 26, A2.

Kohut, Andrew. 2000. "What 'McCain Voter'?" *New York Times*, March 12, 15.

Kristof, Nicholas D. 2000. "For Bush, His Toughest Call Was the Choice to Run at All." *New York Times*, October 29, 1.

Lawrence, Jill. 2000. "McCain Tries to Ignore Pothole on Campaign Road." *USA Today*, January 10, 6A.

Milibank, Dana. 2000. "McCain's 'No-Brain' Trust." *Washington Post*, March 6, 10.

Miller, A.H., M.P. Wattenberg, and O. Malanchuk. 1986. "Schematic Assessments of Presidential Candidates." *American Political Science Review* 8, 521–540.

Mintz, John. 2000. "McCain's Net Advantage." *Washington Post*, February 21, 15.

Mitchell, Alison. 2000. "Conservative with a Populist Streak." *New York Times*, January 16, 15.

"Never Too Soon to Start." 1998. *Newsweek*, March 9, 4.

Powell, Michael. 1999. "In Search of Steve Forbes." *Washington Post*, November 22, 6.

Raasch, Chuck. 1999a. " 'Quiet Revolutionary' Aims High." *Cincinnati Enquirer*, June 11, A2.

Raasch, Chuck. 1999b. "Cash Runs Short; Dole Run Ends." *Cincinnati Enquirer*, October 21, C1.

Rosenbaum, David E. 1999. "Hatch Is the Latest to Dream a Senator's Dream." *New York Times*, October 3, 25.

Rosenbaum, David E. 2000. "Forbes Buoyed by Success in Iowa." *New York Times*, January 26, A16.

Salant, Jonathan D. 2000. "McCain Closing Money Gap." *Cincinnati Enquirer*, February 15, A4.

Scully, Steve (Executive Producer). 1998. "Road to the White House." Washington, DC: C-SPAN.

Shapiro, Walter. 1999. "Repackaged Al Gore Shows His Many Faces in N.H." *USA Today*, October 29, 15A.

Thomas, Evan and Martha Brant. 2000. "The Fight of His Life." *Newsweek*, February 28, 31–37.

Trent J.S. 1978. "Presidential Surfacing: The Ritualistic and Crucial First Act." *Communication Monographs*, 45 (November), 282.

Trent, Judith S. and Robert V. Friedenberg. 2000. *Political Campaign Communication: Principles and Practices* (4th ed.). Westport, CT: Praeger.

Van Natta, Don, Jr. 1999. "Bush Is Hardly a Passive Fund-Raiser." *New York Times*, May 16, 20.

Von Drehle, David and Dan Balz. 1999. "Cashing in on Connections." *Washington Post*, October 4, 13.

Weisman, Steven R. 2000. "Trotting Out the Latest Reinvention of Al Gore." *New York Times*, June 11, 16.

West, Paul. 1999. "Bush Gets Crucial Jump-Start in Presidential Race." *Cincinnati Enquirer*, April 1, A9.

Wilkinson, Howard. 1999. "Is GOP Ready for Kasich?" *Cincinnati Enquirer*, February 21, C1.

Zuckman, Jill and Bob Hohler. 2000. "Bradley Steps Up as Gore Plays the Front-Runner." *Boston Globe*, January 29, A1.

Chapter 3

The Rebels Revolt and the Empires Strike Back: A Tale of Two Insurgencies in the Presidential Nominations of 2000

Henry C. Kenski

> There are four parts to any campaign: the candidate, the issues of the candidate, the campaign organization, and the money to run the campaign with. Without money, you can forget the other three.
>
> —Democratic House Speaker Tip O'Neill (Jacobson, 1980, 33)

> The danger for Bush of an insurgency campaign is that McCain has a brush fire that he's going to turn into a wildfire. If Governor Bush had beaten Senator McCain decisively it would have crippled, if not mortally wounded his campaign.
>
> —Statement after the New Hampshire primary by Steve Duprey, chairman of the New Hampshire Republican Party, on February 2, 2000 (Berke, 2000, A17)

The 2000 presidential nomination contests offered sharp and spirited clashes in both major parties. The party establishment favorites, Republican Governor George Bush of Texas and Democratic Vice President Al Gore, prevailed only after extinguishing feisty insurgent campaigns that threatened their nominations. The biggest surprise was the impressive GOP challenge of Senator John McCain, who captured both media and public attention, although being outspent and outgunned decisively by the Bush campaign. Former Democratic New Jersey Senator Bill Bradley had a window of opportunity in late 1999 to January 2000, when he raised expectations early in the contest before wilting amid a strong attack campaign by Al Gore.

The study of political campaign communication focuses on the messengers, the messages, the channels of communication (print, radio, television etc.), the audience, and the effects. The candidates or political messengers and their issues, their individual traits and qualifications, and past political performances are at the heart of campaign communication. Although some analysts draw a distinction between issues and personality/character in campaigns, I contend that American elections have always been image oriented/issue involved. The two concepts are like overlapping concentric circles. Candidates use issues to demonstrate personal qualities like knowledge, experience, competence, leadership, vision, trust, and empathy. Popkin (1994) argues that voters may lack detailed knowledge of issues but can easily observe campaign behavior and assess how candidates fare on important traits. Kendall (2000) notes that candidates within the same party are often not that different on issues so that the critical distinguishing factors are personal qualities like being a fighter or more electable than your opponents. How a candidate uses issues provides the context to portray a candidate's strongest traits like knowledge, empathy, or standing up for one's beliefs.

The nominations of 2000 were like past nomination contests as candidates used traits and issues to convey messages to earn voter support as their party's nominee. This author had the opportunity to attend the University of Pennsylvania Annenberg School of Communication Election Debriefing on February 10, 2001, featuring the top personnel from both the Bush and Gore campaigns.[1] This meeting focused more on the general election, but some time was given to the nomination contests also. The comments and discussion provided insights as to why both the Bush and Gore campaigns were successful in presenting a credible messenger, delivering messages, targeting states, and targeting demographic groups that resulted in their nomination victories. I draw upon this and other material to explain the 2000 nomination outcomes.

The purpose of this chapter is to look at key factors in the Republican and Democratic nominations of 2000. It does so by examining both contests in terms of phases. They are: the preliminaries (the rules, standing in the polls, money, endorsements, media, and for Republicans, the Iowa straw poll); Round I (Iowa caucus, New Hampshire and Delaware primaries); Round II (South Carolina to Super Tuesday); Round III (Super Tuesday); Round IV (post–Super Tuesday to the convention); and Round V (the convention). The presidential nomination contests of 2000 were a story of two insurgencies that challenged the front-runners and party organization favorites. I turn now to the insurgent challenge in the Republican race.

THE REPUBLICANS: THE PRELIMINARIES

Kathleen Kendall (2000) argues persuasively that to understand the nomination process, particularly the role of presidential primaries, one must look at the rules and their impact on political communication. The effects of the McGovern-Fraser Commission Democratic Party presidential reforms before the 1972 presidential election and the subsequent revisions of these rules have had an impact on the way the nomination game is played in both political parties. State legislatures have changed the rules so that most states now hold primaries to allocate convention delegates. Many more candidates run if there is no incumbent. Moreover, those running must excel at building a campaign organization, using mass media, and raising money (Coleman, Cantor, and Neale, 2000). The extensive use of primaries, Kendall (2000) argues, promotes a candidate-based system rather than a party-based system.

One of the newer changes in the rules, particularly since 1992, is the trend toward "front-loading" of the primaries and caucuses in the nomination schedule. This is the name given to the behavior of the states that move their primaries or caucuses up at the start of the campaign season to increase their influence and political leverage (Kendall, 2000). The nomination time frame in past elections has run from some point in February to early June. The two political parties have given special recognition to two states, Iowa and New Hampshire. The nomination season, therefore, will start with the Iowa caucus and be followed by the New Hampshire primary. Other states vied to start first, and the subsequent conflict led to earlier starting dates for both events in 2000, with January 24 for the Iowa caucus and February 1 for the New Hampshire primary. Democratic Party rules forbid any states except Iowa and New Hampshire from holding delegate selection before the first Tuesday in March. Republican Party rules are more permissive, however, and a number of states scheduled events in February, following the New Hampshire primary. Moreover, the front-loading trend continued, and a number of states, including the large delegate states of California, New York, and Ohio, moved from the end of the nomination season to earlier dates in 2000 (Bacon, 2000a).

Another important aspect of the rule changes in recent years has been the nature of the primaries. Congressional Research analyst Kevin Coleman (2000) compiled a report that summarized the state rules on voter participation in primaries and noted that at present 12 states have open primaries, and 38 states and the District of Columbia have closed primaries. He notes further, however, that closed primaries can be divided into three categories. They are: (1) "those that register voters by party and limit primary voting to party members (independent voters forfeit the opportunity to participate in the primary); (2) those that register voters by party but allow them to choose the other party's ballot on primary day (independents may participate in primaries); and (3) those that do not have party registration but require voters to ask for one party's ballot on primary election day" (2). The last two closed primaries in reality are "semi-open" primaries because of increased voter choice. In recent presidential nominations, open primaries and the type of closed primaries have been critical. In 2000, for example, they were important to Republican John McCain, who attracted Independent voters and some crossover Democrats. His campaign would have collapsed much earlier, save for the primary rules in early states like New Hampshire, South Carolina, and Michigan. Still, however, the front-loading meant that the Republican nominee was chosen for all practical purposes after 11 states held primaries and 2 states held caucuses on March 7, 2000 (Bacon, 2000a), despite the fact that 27 states and D.C. had not yet held their Republican primaries or caucuses.

These preliminary activities have been called "the invisible primary" (Hadley, 1976; Buell, 1996). Today, however, these political activities are so public and attract media stories that they are scarcely invisible any more and hence are more accurately considered preliminaries designed to maximize a candidate's visibility and strategic advantages. Matthew Dowd (2001), Bush's campaign director of polling and media planning, contends that the nomination process is part of the overall general election strategy to achieve victory in the fall. He likened the nomination battle to competition in hockey, where you have to establish a record over the regular season to get into the playoffs and the real season. The first stage of the process consists of preprimary events or the preliminaries. Dowd includes standing in polls, money, endorsements, media coverage, and the Iowa straw poll as events that need to be dominated and won to build momentum and put the other candidates on the defensive. He says it is also important to prepare for the key challenger who constitutes the major obstacle to your candidate's nomination. He observed that the Bush camp thought that at the start of the preliminaries their key opponent would be Steve Forbes and not John McCain. There is no automatic cutoff for the preliminaries, but they tend to conclude by the end of December in the year before the official election nomination kickoff with the Iowa caucus.

In the preliminaries, the standing in the polls of the respective candidates was an important factor. In 2000, George Bush was the dominant figure in national trial heats against Gore and Bradley and in the few early state Republican primary preference polls ("General Election: National Polls," 2000; "General Election: State Polls," 2000; Milbank, 2001). About 35 sources ranging from professional pollsters like Gallup and Zogby, news media polling organizations like ABC News and the *Washington Post*, political party sources like the Republican Leadership Council and the Republican National Committee, and special interest groups like Emily's List conducted national trial heat polls. Bush led in these polls, often with double-digit advantages over both Gore and Bradley. Elizabeth Dole also did well against both Gore and Bradley, but usually by single-digit margins. Millionaire Steve Forbes, the other visible Republican during most of 1999, did not fare well. A Fox News/Dynamic poll on August 25–26, 1999, shortly after the Iowa straw poll, for example, showed Bush ahead of Gore 52 percent to 34 percent, while Forbes lost to Gore 49 percent to 31 percent. A slightly earlier Fox News/Dynamic poll on August 11–12, 1999, registered Bush 56 percent to Gore 29 percent, and Dole 51 percent to Gore's 32 percent. It also had Bush ahead of Bradley 56 percent to 25 percent ("General Election: National Polls," 2000).

McCain was not on the national political radar screen at this point in time. Diligent and extensive campaigning and a concentrated focus on New Hampshire resulted in political dividends for McCain. By November 1999 he pulled ahead in a New Hampshire Republican primary preference poll. The CNN/*Time* poll reported that McCain had a narrow 37 percent to 35 percent lead over Bush, while Bush led by a commanding margin in their GOP South Carolina preference poll (Holland, 1999). By October Elizabeth Dole had dropped out of the race (Milbank, 2001), and McCain was stronger than Forbes in poll standing and was emerging as Bush's leading challenger. This showed up in the end of the year national trial heats. A CNN/Gallup/*USA Today* December 20–21, 1999, poll revealed Bush with a smaller but 53 percent to 42 percent lead over Gore, and with a narrower 50 percent to 45 percent edge over Bradley. The same poll registered McCain as even with Gore at 47 percent. Throughout the preliminaries, Bush led in poll standing, but his very impressive double-digit lead over Gore had declined to the 11 percent range, with an even smaller 5 percent lead over Bradley. By the end of the preliminaries, McCain emerged as Bush's main challenger.

One of the realities of American politics is money. It is truly the mother's milk of politics and is essential to establish the credibility of the messenger or candidate as well as broadcast his or her messages to voters. Insufficient money has sunk many promising campaigns, and the nomination election of 2000 would not be an exception. The late famous Democratic Speaker of the House Tip O'Neill once observed: "There are four parts to any campaign. There is the candidate, the issues of the candidate, the campaign organization, and money. Without money, you can forget the other three" (Jacobson, 1980, 33). This statement is more than Irish hyperbole and summarizes one of the important truths of American politics. Money is a necessary but not sufficient condition for success. Republican presidential candidates John Connally in 1980, Phil Gramm in 1996, and millionaire Steve Forbes in 1996 all surpassed their opponents in fund-raising but ended up running weak campaigns and dropping out early.

Since the nomination contests of 1976, the finance system for presidential nomination has been a mixed system. The candidates must raise private money subject to individual contribution limits of $1,000 per person and $5,000 per political action committee (PAC). The federal government then matches individual contributions up to $250, dollar for dollar. Thus for a $1,000 individual contribution the match will only be for the first $250. In order to receive the match, candidates must adhere to a total spending limit for the campaign as well as how much money they can spend in each individual state. The law allows an extra 20 percent for campaign fund-raising expenses, and the total ceiling for participants in 2000 was $40.54 million (Cantor, 2001). Under the Supreme Court's interpretation of the law, individuals need not participate and if they did not, they would not be subject to the total ceiling. The money, of course, still had to be raised in amounts of no more than $1,000 per person and $5,000 per PAC. Most candidates have participated in the mixed finance system since its initial use in 1976, with Connally, Gramm, and Forbes being the notable exceptions. A front-loaded campaign schedule with the nomination likely to be decided by March suggested that a candidate who opted out would have a tremendous spending advantage over his competitors in the early important contests, especially without the individual state spending limit restrictions.

George Bush opted out of the matching system in 1999 and 2000. His campaign felt the need for great sums of money in the early contests. His advisers also feared the deep pockets of millionaire candidate Steve Forbes, who was free to spend his personal fortune under existing law, as he had in the 1996 campaign (Dowd, 2001). George Bush was the king of the hill in the realm of money, and his fund-raising literally drove candidates from the race. The Federal Election Commission for the April 15, 2000, reporting period showed that Bush had collected a record $68.7 million for the nomination contest. His nearest money competitor, Steve Forbes, had spent $34.1 million before dropping out after the Delaware primary on February 5. John McCain fought a valiant insurgency but had raised only $15.7 million. Alan Keyes, the only candidate to stay in the race to the end, raised $4.5 million. Bauer and Hatch, who dropped out after the New Hampshire primary, had raised $9.7 million and $2.3 million, respectively ("Campaign 2000 Fund-raising," 2001). The resource disparity in money had already had a major impact by August 1999. Representative John Kasich and Senator Bob Smith had already dropped out, citing money problems (Milbank, 2001), and four others would shortly follow.

A critical event was the nonscientific Republican straw poll in Iowa, which has a poor record in predicting party nominees but "is widely seen as a measure of the candidate's organizational skill" (Kendall, 2000, 213). Nearly 25,000 Iowans took part and paid $25 to participate, paid largely by candidate organizations. Forbes spent $2 million on the event; Bush, $750,00 and Dole, $250,000. After it was over, Bush came in first in a crowded field with an unimpressive 31 percent, with Forbes second at 20 percent, and Dole third. Shortly after the event, Lamar Alexander, who had run well in 1996, and Vice President Dan Quayle both dropped out, citing insufficient money to be competitive. Pat Buchanan, who no longer dominated the conservative field, would leave the GOP in October to seek the nomination of the Reform Party. Elizabeth Dole, who had fared better than most, would drop out of the race in October. "The bottom line remains money," she noted. She said that she had done 108 fund-raisers in 1999, but even then Bush and Steve Forbes "would enjoy a 75- or 80-to-1 cash advantage. Perhaps I could handle 2-to-1 or 10-to-1, but not 80-to-1" (Milbank, 2001, 97). She ended up raising $5.3 million ("Campaign 2000 Fund-raising," 2000). Bush had triumphed in the money game and would have ample resources to establish his credentials as a messenger as well as communicate messages to targeted voters.

In addition to poll standing and money, endorsements play an important in the preliminaries. Candidates work to demonstrate broad-based and influential support. In this realm, Bush again dominated the field, and his campaign excelled at demonstrations of institutional support from House and Senate members, fellow governors, state and local officials, and Republican Party officials (Milbank, 2001). It was a trademark throughout his campaign, and political analyst Charlie Cook would note in February that of the 54 Republican senators, 37 supported Bush and only 4 McCain. Of the 223 House Republicans 174 endorsed Bush, as did 26 of his fellow 29 Republican governors (Cook, 2000b, A27). One important endorsement for Governor Bush in the preliminaries and Round I was from popular Iowa Senator Charles Grassley. He appeared in a Bush ad in the battle for the Iowa caucus urging voters to vote Bush and to ignore negative campaigns ("Ad Spotlight," January 21, 2000). Bush also received the endorsement of New Hampshire Senator Judd Gregg and used him in a political ad ("Ad Spotlight," January 24, 2000). Steve Forbes had more difficulty acquiring endorsements but did receive one from prominent conservative activist Paul Weyrich. Forbes used Weyrich in a 1999 ad to say: "Steve Forbes is the only conservative who can win" ("Ad Spotlight," August 12, 1999). At the time Forbes was contending with Bauer, Buchanan, Keyes, and Quayle to be the front-runner for the conservative vote, McCain and his supporters played down endorsements as largely a pro-establishment tactic. McCain "can tout it as a badge of honor that he doesn't have everyone's endorsement," said a fellow senator and McCain supporter. "It pretty much fits what his message is" (Barnes, Victor, Cohen, and Stone, 2000, 458). Still, McCain did not rule out selective endorsements like his use of Representative Lindsay Graham in South Carolina (Barnes et al., 2000). Bush won the battle for endorsements both in the preliminaries and throughout the campaign.

Another important factor in all stages of the campaign is media, both the professional media and paid advertising by candidates. Leading media scholars like Thomas Patterson (1994) and Kathleen Hall Jamieson (1992) have established that modern media campaign coverage tends to focus heavily on the game or horse race and gives little attention to issues or past performances of candidates in political offices. Election 2000 was no different, and the major networks gave only half as much time in 1999 to presidential campaign stories compared to their coverage in 1995. The ABC, CBS, and NBC total time on the air from January to November in 1999 was only six hours and 42 minutes. The front-runners Gore and Bush received the most coverage, and their challengers received very little. The Media Monitor research group measured the desirability of candidates, or their positive and negative assessments. It also measured the viability of candidates or their likelihood of winning. From January to November 1999 Bush and McCain received mainly positive assessments (Bush 63 percent and McCain 58 percent), while evaluations of Bush's electoral viability were 91 percent and McCain's a surprising 58 percent ("Campaign 2000—Early Returns: Network News Coverage of the Campaign Preseason," 1999). Electability, as Kendall (2000) has emphasized, is a major campaign message. In the six-candidate GOP field, Bush and McCain proved dominant on professional media coverage.

All of the candidates except for Allan Keyes began political advertising at some point in 1999, but the buys for Hatch and Bauer were minimal ("Ad Spotlight," 1999). The biggest spender by far was Steve Forbes. He committed the use of his personal fortune to the pursuit of the nomination and launched a national ad buy of seven TV spots for cable in June ("Ad Spotlight," June 2, 1999). In them he identified his views on Social Security, the flat tax, and the need for a leader with a "moral compass." He also bought radio spots with the same themes. The buys and other spots to come were to cost $10 million by the end of the summer. He followed with a new batch of ads in July that emphasized his personal qualities as family man, and so on, and featured his wife and daughters. These were targeted for Iowa and New Hampshire and were designed to soften his image as a slash-and-burn candidate ("Ad Spotlight," July 27, 1999). In 1996 many regarded Forbes as a single-issue candidate, with the issue being the flat tax. This time he sought not only economic conservatives but social conservatives as well. Religious conservatives were 35 percent of the 1996 GOP Iowa electorate (Solomon, 2000). Forbes cultivated these voters in 2000. A July radio ad, for example, said: "As President, I will have the authority to appoint judges to the federal bench. Their appointment will be for life. Therefore, any judge I appoint for life will be pro-life" ("Ad Spotlight," July 27, 1999). He continued to produce more ads along these lines for the remainder of 1999 and in early 2000. In November, for example, he called for Social Security reform ("Ad Spotlight," November 17, 1999). He also ran some attack ads against Bush on his Texas tax record and on his position on Social Security ("Ad Spotlight," December 2, 1999, and January 10, 2000). Forbes was not as attack oriented as he was in 1996, but he did more attacking before the Iowa caucus than the other major candidates did. He got into an ad exchange with a group called the Republican Leadership Council, which pleaded with him not to go negative ("Ad Spotlight," November 17, 1999), and he ran a rebuttal spot calling them Bush's liberal friends ("Ad Spotlight," November 30, 1999). The Republican Leadership Council responded to the Forbes rebuttal by running an ad that informed voters that Forbes used to be one of their board members ("Ad Spotlight," December 1, 1999). Forbes lost in this advertising exchange as it reminded voters of his reputation to go negative.

McCain from the outset ran an unconventional and exciting campaign that ignored participation in the Iowa caucus and concentrated on Iowa, South Carolina, and California. His chief strategist was John Weaver, the field director for Phil Gramm's disastrous 1996 campaign. From that campaign, Weaver felt he had learned 15 lessons. "Those conclusions—skip the straw polls, create a crusade, downplay organization and emphasize media—would in time become the blueprint for McCain's insurgency against George Bush" (Milbank, 2001, 69). McCain would run quite unscripted, and professional media probably never had as much access to a major contender for the nomination. He traveled by a bus called "The Straight Talk Express" and campaigned many days in New Hampshire. McCain would feature his strong biography and run as a reform candidate against the establishment. His TV buys were select but effective and maximized his persona and reform message. In June 1999, for example, he opened with an exploratory California TV spot urging voters to join the fight to oppose special interests and promote Social Security and military reform ("Ad Spotlight," June 29, 1999). In October McCain unveiled three Reaganesque radio spots that utilized personal disclosure and featured his wife, Cindy, former New Hampshire Senator Warren Rudman, and former Naval Academy classmate Frank Gamboa. These spots hit the New Hampshire radio and underscored McCain's "convictions and principles" ("Ad Spotlight," October 20, 1999).

He launched his first major television ad in New Hampshire in October, and it combined his bio as a prisoner of war (POW) and reform and emphasized McCain's "convictions and principles" ("Ad Spotlight," October 20, 1999). He revised this ad slightly due to criticism of using the Arlington Cemetery on federal property in the footage and took some visuals out. The revision still promoted his military service and POW stint in Vietnam with a strong tag line that said: "Today John McCain is ready to lead America into the new century" ("Ad Spotlight," November 15, 1999). In December, McCain released his second major TV ad that targeted New Hampshire, and in it he enunciated his commitment to reduce pork barrel spending. As with his campaign speeches, the language used in the ad made him sound presidential. In one statement he says: "If Congress overrides my veto and tries to force me to waste your money, I'll make sure you know who they are" ("Ad Spotlight," December 7, 1999). He later released radio ads in South Carolina that related a Christmas story in a Vietnam prison ("Ad Spotlight," December 16, 1999). McCain underscored his image as a reformer and joined hands with Democrat Bill Bradley in Claremont, New Hampshire, to call for a "temporary truce in partisan politicking and sign a pledge to turn down huge sums from their parties if either becomes the presidential nominee" (Allen, 1999, A11). It was the same site in 1995 where Newt Gingrich and Bill Clinton made a similar pledge and then quickly abandoned it. McCain's political ads stressed his candidate qualities and moved him in the direction of scoring big on the character issue, especially when contrasted to Clinton. Unlike the other candidates, his decision to skip the Iowa caucus allowed for more concentrated targeting in New Hampshire and South Carolina, two very important early primaries.

The Bush campaign was concerned about the messenger as well as the message. Matthew Dowd (2001), Bush's campaign director of polling and media planning, has noted that issues and personality traits are not mutually exclusive. Personality, he contends, signals broader values and traits like leadership and empathy. Mark McKinnon (2001), Bush's media director, has suggested that Bush never should have won the general election, given the historic models that underscore the near impossibility of defeating an incumbent or the incumbent party candidate if the country was experiencing economic prosperity and was at peace. Overcoming these two factors was a tough hill to climb that was made even more difficult by the fact that issues like education, health care, and Social Security favored the Democrats. The Bush strategy and approach beginning in the nomination contest was to stress leadership, shared values, honesty, and trust and to contend that now was the time to do hard things. The campaign and Bush's political advertising had to show Bush as a leader and as a different kind of Republican who would offer his own proposals on education, health care, and Social Security. The advertising strategy in the preliminaries was broad based and somewhat low-key, with Bush appearing as the inevitable winner and placing himself somewhat above the campaign fray. McCain's success in the New Hampshire polls in late 1999 and early 2000 would force Bush's strategists to adapt and include attack advertising as part of their media package in the next phase, Round I.

Bush's advertising in the preliminaries was launched in October 1999, as McKinnon produced a radio spot and four TV commercials for the New Hampshire market. The radio spot was in Spanish and proclaimed a new day for Latinos and urged Iowans to elect a president so that no one be left behind. The four TV spots featured Bush speaking on his issue agenda, education, Social Security, Medicare, tax cuts, positive campaigning, and his "compassionate conservatism" ("Ad Spotlight," October 26, 1999). Conscious of the fact that McCain was campaigning almost exclusively in New Hampshire and South Carolina, and the latter was a patriotic state with many veterans, a November TV ad was produced for South Carolina. It discussed Bush's foreign policy goal of rebuilding the military. In it Bush says: "As president, I will have a foreign policy with a touch of iron, driven by American interests and American values" ("Ad Spotlight," November 17, 1999). Shortly, thereafter, two radio ads were made for New Hampshire. In one, Bush calls for character education in schools, and in the other he cites his tax-cut policies in Texas and calls for federal tax cuts "as an insurance policy against economic downturn" ("Ad Spotlight," November 22, 1999). In the week before Thanksgiving, he released a TV ad in New Hampshire that discusses the need for morality in the White House and the need for a moral compass. It was rotated with an ad entitled "Every Child" that stressed the importance of education and leaving no child behind ("Ad Spotlight," November 30, 1999). The preliminaries allowed Bush to present himself as a leader and frame the policy focus that would portray him as a different kind of Republican. His media concluded in December with what his campaign called "crash ads," which are produced in less than 24 hours and tap local settings in Iowa and New Hampshire. They featured Bush talking to high school students and local residents about his education and tax plans ("Ad Spotlight," January 3, 2000).

The final resource applies only to the Republican Party. It is the traditional Iowa straw poll that took place on August 14, 1999. As noted earlier, it is nonscientific and is designed to raise money for the Iowa Republican Party. Participation costs $25 and is paid for by the various campaigns, and they bring their supporters to the event. Kendall notes that it "is widely seen as a measure of the candidates' organizational skill" (Kendall, 2000, 213). I would add it also taps the money skills of candidates. Some 25,000 people participated, and Bush won but did not dominate the field. As noted earlier, shortly after this event, Lamar Alexander and Dan Quayle dropped out. Buchanan was disillusioned and eventually left the Republican Party in October to pursue the Reform Party nomination. Elizabeth Dole finished third but also became disillusioned about the amount of money necessary to get her messages out, and she dropped out in October (Milbank, 2001). McCain chose to ignore the straw poll and Iowa to focus on New Hampshire.

THE REBELS REVOLT: ROUND I (IOWA CAUCUS, NEW HAMPSHIRE AND DELAWARE PRIMARIES)

Table 3.1 outlines the campaign schedule for events most critical for the nomination. Round I starts with the Iowa caucus, then moves on to

Table 3.1
Republican Presidential Primary (P) and Caucus/Convention (C/C) Results in Percentages for 2000 from Iowa Caucus (1/24) to Super Tuesday (3/7)

State	Date	Delegates	Method	Bush	McCain	Other	Winner
Iowa	1/24	25	C/C	41	5	54	Bush
N.H.	2/1	17	P	31	49	21	McCain
Del.	2/8	12	P	51	25	24	Bush
Hawaii[1]	2/7-13	14	C/C				Bush
S.C	2/19	37	P	53	42	5	Bush
Ariz.	2/22	30	P	36	60	4	McCain
Mich.	2/22	58	P	43	50	6	McCain
Puerto Rico	2/27	14	P	94	6	0	Bush
N.D.	2/29	19	C/C	76	19	5	Bush
Va.	2/29	56	P	53	44	3	Bush
Wash.[2]	2/29	12	P	58	38	3	Bush
Calif.	3/7	162	P	60	35	5	Bush
Conn.	3/7	25	P	46	49	3	McCain
Ga.	3/7	54	P	67	28	5	Bush
Maine	3/7	14	P	53	43	3	Bush
Md.	3/7	31	P	56	36	8	Bush
Mass.	3/7	37	P	32	65	3	McCain
Minn.	3/7	34	C/C	63	17	20	Bush
Mo.	3/7	35	P	58	35	6	Bush
N.Y.	3/7	101	P	51	43	6	Bush
Ohio	3/7	69	P	58	37	5	Bush
R.I.	3/7	14	P	36	61	3	McCain
Vt.	3/7	12	P	35	61	4	McCain
Wash.	3/7	25	C/C	80	15	5	Bush

[1] Hawaii did not hold a caucus but pledged all of its delegates to Bush at a May convention.
[2] Washington has a split system with 12 delegates allocated in a primary and 25 delegates allocated in GOP caucuses.

Source: Bacon, 2000a, 2502.

the New Hampshire and Delaware primaries. Round II begins with a primary in South Carolina and is followed by primaries in Arizona, Michigan, Puerto Rico, Virginia, and Washington, as well as a caucus in North Dakota. Round III is Super Tuesday, with 11 primaries and two caucuses, including such large delegate states like California, New York, and Ohio. Most political analysts assumed that the winners of both party nominations would be known after the March 7 Super Tuesday results. Success in early events is necessary for all candidates, but particularly insurgents. The compressed and front-loaded schedule requires extensive political support, organizational skills, and financial resources to wage a 50-state campaign and certainly a 23-state campaign by Super Tuesday. Steve Forbes focused on Iowa and New Hampshire, and John McCain concentrated on New Hampshire and South Carolina. Political analyst Charlie Cook observed in January 2000: "The Bush campaign has put together a 50-state effort, giving him a tremendous advantage once the campaign moves beyond the handful of states cherry-picked for attention by his rivals" (Cook, 2000a, 345).

In Round I, the campaigns in Iowa, New Hampshire, and to a lesser extent Delaware had been launched in 1999 but intensified in January 2000. Despite the strong base of Republican Party support for Texas Governor George Bush, five candidates sought to derail his nomination. Senators Orrin Hatch and Gary Bauer were unable to generate much support and would drop out after the New Hampshire primary. Alan Keyes attracted a very minuscule segment of the social conservatives but would stay the course for the campaign. This meant that the two top insurgents were Steve Forbes and Arizona Senator John McCain. Forbes attempted to build a coalition of economic and social conservatives and felt that Bush was too liberal. Senator McCain, on the other hand, ran as a reform candidate who sought to attract new voters to make the Republican Party more inclusive (Schneider, 2000a). Forbes believed that the contests in Round I required extensive retail and wholesale campaigning. A travel log from March 15, 1999, to January 5, 2000, shows that he spent more time in Iowa than any candidate with 49 visits, followed by 47, Bauer; 30, Hatch; 24, Bush; 17, Keyes; and only 2 for McCain. McCain, on the other hand, led with 49 visits to New Hampshire, followed by 37, Bauer; 36, Forbes; 24, Bush; 19, Keyes; and 15, Hatch (Fenoglio, 2000, 116). If one combined Iowa and New Hampshire visits, Forbes led in time allocated to retail campaigning. He continued his mass media advertising, enunciating his conservative themes ("Ad Spotlight," January 3, 2000; January 4, 2000; January 12, 2000; February 1, 2000), attacking Bush ("Ad Spotlight," January 10, 2000), and using average citizens to testify to his personal qualities and character ("Ad Spotlight," January 20, 2000).

With limited money and believing Iowa to be unwinnable, McCain focused exclusively on New Hampshire with extensive personal campaigning and mass advertising. By the time of the New Hampshire primary, McCain held 114 of his freewheeling, unscripted town halls and logged nearly 20,000 miles in his campaign bus, the "Straight Talk Express" (Mitchell, 2000a, A17). His mass advertising continued to push his bio and reform themes. In January, his issue messages focused more on Social Security, and his tax-cut plan, which was half the size of Bush's tax cut. McCain vowed to protect Social Security ("Ad Spotlight," January 3, 2000). He claimed that he opposed "tax cuts that mostly benefit the wealthy" and that his would benefit working families. Moreover, a smaller tax cut would "use the bulk of the surplus to secure Social Security far into the future" ("Ad Spotlight," January 20, 2000). McCain later used an endorsement ad both on TV and radio by former New Hampshire Senator Warren Rudman that strongly supported the McCain tax plan. It did so by linking it to the Social Security issue and attacking Bush. Rudman says: "What Bush isn't telling you is how his own tax plan fails to set aside one dime for Social Security or the national debt" ("Ad Spotlight," January 25, 2000). One McCain ad complained about Bush's negativity for breaking a January 10, 2000, Michigan debate pledge not to use negative ads. He was upset about an ad where Bush said: "My opponent trusts the people of Washington to spend money" ("Ad Spotlight," January 24, 2000). McCain finished the New Hampshire primary with a strong reform ad promising to return government to the people and to oppose the special interests. His opening line in the ad said: "New Hampshire can send a powerful message to America" ("Ad Spotlight," February 1, 2000).

The Bush campaign allocated some time for personal campaigning in both Iowa and New Hampshire, but they were not willing to devote as much time as either Forbes or McCain. Their strategy from the outset was that Bush would win if they could use their resources to wage a national campaign in all 50 states if necessary (Cook, 2000a). In January, Bush's mass advertising had to adapt to some of the campaign attacks put forth by his opponents. One adaptation was a January ad that promised a tax cut while protecting Social Security ("Ad Spotlight," January 12, 2000). Bush suggested that they were not mutually exclusive, while his Republican and Democratic attackers argued that too large a tax cut threatened Social Security. He followed this with a response ad defending his tax-cut plan and urging people to express their views in the Iowa caucus and the New Hampshire primary ("Ad Spotlight," January 19, 2000). Two high-profile endorsement ads were used featuring Iowa Senator Charles Grassley and New Hampshire Senator Judd Gregg ("Ad Spotlight," January 21, 2000, and January 24, 2000). Bush still had comfortable leads in the national polls but trailed McCain, often by double-digit percentages in most New Hampshire primary polls ("Republican Primary: State Polls," 2000). He, therefore, used an attack spot that attempted to portray McCain as a big spender. It was filmed in New Hampshire on January 18, 2000, and in it Bush says: "My opponent trusts the people of Washington to spend the money. I trust the people of New Hampshire to make the right decisions for their families" ("Ad Spotlight," January 26, 2000). It was too little and too late as McCain had already established a strong appeal to the electorate, especially the In-

Table 3.2
Proportion of Republican Presidential Primary and Iowa Caucus Participants and Candidate Preferences by Party Identification by Percent from Iowa Caucus to Super Tuesday

	Republicans			Independents			Democrats		
State	All	Bush	McCain	All	Bush	McCain	All	Bush	McCain
Iowa	83	44	3	15	29	10	2	0	0
N.H.	53	41	38	41	19	62	4	13	78
Del.	80	56	21	18	26	45	2	0	0
S.C.	61	69	26	30	34	60	9	18	79
Ariz.	80	41	56	18	20	72	2	0	0
Mich.	48	66	29	35	26	67	17	10	82
Va.	63	69	28	29	31	64	8	11	87
Calif.	82	63	32	16	41	50	2	0	0
Conn.	72	56	39	26	25	69	3	0	0
Ga.	62	77	19	29	52	41	8	45	54
Maine	66	63	33	31	33	62	3	0	0
Md.	69	66	27	28	33	59	3	0	0
Mass.	37	54	43	54	21	75	8	8	88
Mo.	67	72	21	29	43	49	10	21	76
N.Y.	74	57	38	23	33	58	3	0	0
Ohio	69	68	28	24	37	56	7	30	66
R.I.	40	57	42	53	24	72	6	0	0
Vt.	50	51	44	42	23	74	8	19	81

Source: Data collected from various state polls (December 2000) at www.cnn.com/ELECTION/2000/primaries.html.

dependents who were eligible to vote in the GOP primary. Bush ended his Round I advertising with a spot on values saying that he'll "restore values" and "pride in the presidency" ("Ad Spotlight," January 27, 2000) and another that looked ahead to target Delaware and South Carolina. The latter was an inoculation effort to sell his tax cut by promising he would both lower taxes and "protect and strengthen Social Security and pay down the debt" ("Ad Spotlight," January 27, 2000).

Table 3.2 presents data on the results for the Iowa caucus and all the Republican primaries from January 24 to March 7, 2000, for George Bush and his major challenger, John McCain. The proportion of voters participating who identify as Republican, Independents, or Democrats are identified, followed by the respective Bush and McCain percentages for each partisan group. This was done in order to examine the McCain appeal to Independents and Democrats, who registered high percentages in some primaries, depending on state primary rules. The three events in Round I saw Bush win the Iowa caucus with 44 percent, with Forbes second at 30 percent and Allan Keyes third with 14 percent (Schneider, 2000b). McCain did not contest Iowa and received 5 percent of the vote. McCain won a stunning 49 percent to 31 percent victory in New Hampshire, while Bush rebounded to win Delaware 51 percent to 25 percent (Bacon, 2000a). McCain did not campaign actively in Delaware. Steve Forbes fared poorly in both the New Hampshire primary and the Delaware primary that he won in 1996 and dropped out of the race.

An examination of the exit surveys is revealing. Political analyst Charlie Cook analyzed the Iowa exit poll findings and noted that "Bush carried most demographic groups, but he did best among older and wealthier Republicans. Forbes prevailed among caucus-goers with household incomes between $30,000 and $50,000, and among Independents" (Cook, 2000a, 344). Bush also ran up big leads with those voters who were concerned with education, Social Security, and world affairs. Forbes had the advantage with those most concerned with taxes and abortion. Cook noted that Bush spent considerable time in every stump speech in Iowa defending his tax cut and yet lost the vote 55 percent to 38 percent to Forbes with the one-quarter or 25 percent of voters who identified taxes as the most important issue. On personal qualities, Bush scored well on "can win in November," strong leadership, and experience (Cook, 2000a). It was basically a race between Bush and Forbes, with Bush prevailing by a respectable but not overwhelming margin of victory. As the data in Table 3.2 indicate, this a partisan caucus as 83 percent of those who participated identified themselves as Republican. Forbes won the Independent vote, but only 15 percent of Iowa GOP caucus participants viewed themselves as Independent.

The New Hampshire primary was a horse of a different color. As the data in Table 3.2 illustrate, only 53 percent of the participants in the New Hampshire primary identified themselves as Republican, with a sizable 41 percent seeing themselves as Independent and 4 percent as Democratic. "Independent participation in the Republican primary was 10 percentage points higher than in 1988, the last time Granite State Independents had the opportunity to choose between two meaningful primaries." This was crucial for McCain's victory, as a full one-quarter of the 2000 GOP primary participants considered voting in the Democratic primary, and most would have voted for Bill Bradley (Pew Research Center for the People and the Press, 2000a). The Pew analysis suggests that candidate qualities were more important than issues in McCain's victory, as he "benefited from his background as a war hero and was regarded as more authentic than George W. Bush, while many voters had doubts about Bush's depth." He bested Bush by a large mar-

Table 3.3
Proportion of Republican Presidential Primary and Iowa Caucus Participants and Candidate Preferences by Gender and for Seniors (60 Years or Older) by Percentage from Iowa Caucus to Super Tuesday

	Men			Women			Seniors		
State	All	Bush	McCain	All	Bush	McCain	All	Bush	McCain
Iowa	54	41	6	46	41	3	32	50	5
N.H.	57	28	50	43	32	49	24	30	52
Del.	54	47	27	46	52	24	44	53	28
S.C.	50	51	43	50	55	41	35	51	47
Ariz.	47	33	61	53	39	58	44	38	59
Mich.	51	41	52	49	45	49	25	44	53
Va.	52	49	47	48	57	41	30	60	38
Calif.	48	57	38	52	61	33	36	57	40
Conn.	53	47	47	47	45	50	32	46	50
Ga.	51	68	25	49	67	30	28	72	27
Maine	53	47	48	47	55	39	35	53	45
Md.	51	55	38	49	58	35	26	56	37
Mass.	50	31	66	50	31	65	33	39	59
Mo.	53	55	37	47	60	33	34	63	32
N.Y.	55	47	46	45	55	40	39	50	47
Ohio	53	56	38	47	59	36	25	60	38
R.I.	53	36	62	47	38	58	30	46	53
Vt.	54	36	59	46	37	60	27	38	58

Source: Data collected from various state polls (December 2000) at www.cnn.com/ELECTION/2000/primaries.html.

gin among voters as a candidate who stands up for his beliefs and who is a strong leader (Pew, 2000a).

The data in Tables 3.2 and 3.3 underscore the demographics of the McCain victory. He contested Bush for the 53 percent identifying as Republican, losing only 41 percent to 38 percent to the Texas governor. Then he dominated the 41 percent who saw themselves as Independent by 62 percent to 19 percent over Bush, and the 4 percent Democrats by a 78 percent to 13 percent margin. There was no gender gap, as McCain won the 57 percent of voters who were men by 50 percent to 28 percent and the 43 percent who were women by 49 percent to 32 percent. He also won the 24 percent of seniors (60 years old or more) 52 percent to 32 percent. A further examination of the New Hampshire exit poll ("GOP Primary: New Hampshire," 2000) shows that New Hampshire was not only different from Iowa in the large percentage of Independents but also in the smaller percentage of those identifying with the Religious Right. Only 16 percent of voters identified themselves as such in New Hampshire compared to 37 percent in Iowa ("Demo and GOP Caucuses: Iowa," 2000). The New Hampshire poll demonstrated that Steve Forbes was viewed as a weak messenger, with favorability ratings of 44 percent favorable to 42 percent unfavorable, compared to McCain with 75 percent favorable and only 14 percent unfavorable and Bush at 60 percent favorable and 29 percent unfavorable. The single most important issue was moral values, and those 28 percent of voters selecting it favored McCain 47 percent to 32 percent over Bush and only 4 percent for social conservative Steve Forbes. The single most important quality was standing up for your beliefs, and the 35 percent of voters choosing it favored McCain decisively with 61 percent, compared to 13 percent for Bush and 14 percent for Forbes. Given a dichotomous choice as to which issue should be given higher priority, Social Security or tax cuts resulted in parity, with 46 percent favoring both ("GOP Primary: New Hampshire," 2000). Only 9 percent chose campaign reform, McCain's signature issue, as the most important issue to address. There is little doubt that McCain's strength was simply himself. Although campaign reform did not score well as an issue, it may have allowed McCain to be seen as a reformer and helped him to make inroads on the candidate quality that New Hampshire Republican primary participants most admired, namely, "stands up for what he believes in."

The Delaware primary on February 8, 2000, concluded Round I. It pitted Bush against Steve Forbes, who won it in 1996. McCain did not contest it and went on to South Carolina for Round II. Bush won it by a 51 percent to 25 percent margin for McCain. As the data in Table 3.2 indicate, it was definitely a partisan primary with 80 percent Republican, only 18 percent Independent, and 2 percent Democrat. Bush had a decisive edge among Republicans, 56 percent to 21 percent, while McCain had a 45 percent to 25 percent edge among Independents. Table 3.3 shows Bush winning the 54 percent of participants who were male, 47 percent to 27 percent, and the 46 percent who were female, 52 percent to 24 percent. Bush also carried the sizable 44 percent of voters who were seniors by a 53 percent to 28 percent margin. The single most important issue was moral values, selected by 27 percent, and those choosing it favored Bush 58 percent to 23 percent for McCain and only 11 percent for social conservative Steve Forbes. The issue of taxes was the second most important issue, chosen by 24 percent, and they gave Bush 45 percent, Forbes 46 percent, and McCain only 8 percent. The top candidate quality was stand up for your beliefs, selected by 26 percent, who favored McCain with 38 percent over Bush and Forbes with 27 percent each. The second most important quality was conservative values, and the 18 percent who chose it favored Bush decisively with 61 percent to 21 percent for Forbes and only 10 percent for McCain. Given a dichotomous choice as to which issue should be given higher priority, tax cut or Social Security, tax cut received 49 percent and Social Security 44 percent. The good news for Bush was that those desiring tax cuts favored him with 54 percent, compared to 25 percent for Forbes, and 14 percent for McCain, as did those choosing Social Security, with 46 percent Bush, 38 percent McCain, and 13 percent Forbes. Matthew Dowd (2001), Bush's pollster, has argued that the Delaware primary was important, after the lopsided loss in New Hampshire, to show that Bush could win and to communicate to a media infatuated with McCain that the race was far from over.

THE EMPIRE STRIKES BACK: ROUND II (SOUTH CAROLINA TO SUPER TUESDAY)

The next round took a dramatic turn, as Bush mobilized help from Republican activists in various states to confront the McCain insurgency. He gave them a strong rationale for doing so as he now framed the situation as "a clear race between a more-moderate-to-liberal candidate vs. a conservative candidate" (Schneider, 2000c, 438). He no longer had the aura of political invincibility. South Carolina was the next primary, and it was to be his political firewall, meaning an impregnable fallback position. It had performed that function for his father in 1992 and for Bob Dole in 1996 (Germond and Witcover, 2000d). The risk in his strategy, according to analyst Bill Schneider (2000d), was that South Carolina had a primary that was open to all voters. If the proportion of Independents and Democrats increased substantially, there could be a repeat of New Hampshire. It was a risk, however, that the campaign had to take. Matthew Dowd (2001), Bush's pollster, said that New Hampshire had really hurt them as Bush was behind McCain by 5 percent when they resumed the campaign in South Carolina. Bush had to go one on one and do extensive personal campaigning throughout South Carolina to match up with McCain on the ground. The Bush air war strategy also changed to include considerable attack advertising.

Bush struck quickly in a post–New Hampshire South Carolina TV ad to claim that McCain misrepresented Bush's tax plan and that one of McCain's own economic advisers would support the Bush plan. The adviser, former Congressman Vin Weber, released a statement denying that he supported the Bush plan ("Ad Spotlight," February 7, 2000). Bush then followed with an effort to identify himself as a real reformer with results. Given his maverick style, McCain did not get along with many of his congressional colleagues and did not have an extensive list of legislative accomplishments. Bush, on the other hand, felt he had been successful in achieving tax reform, educational reform, tort reform, and welfare reform in Texas and produced ads to sell his case ("Ad Spotlight," February 9, 2000). He contested McCain for the reform mantle.

Another advertising gambit led to the creation of two radio ads, one that attacked McCain's tax plan and the other his campaign finance reform plan. The thematic in both was that McCain's plans were "not South Carolina values." In one ad the announcer said: "No wonder Al Gore said he prefers the McCain plan to the Bush plan." The second was a testimonial featuring the South Carolina Attorney General Charlie Condon, who focused on both the exemption for labor unions and the free speech restrictions, weaknesses in the McCain campaign reform proposal. In perhaps one of the best attack formulations on campaign reform, Condon said that McCain's campaign plan would allow labor unions to take "mandatory dues from working people to elect liberal Democrats" while "curtailing free speech rights of individuals and citizens' groups" ("Ad Spotlight," February 15, 2000). Another facet to the Bush attack on campaign reform came in ads and speeches where he called McCain the insider and himself the outsider. He noted that he resided in Austin, but McCain had been in Washington and in Congress the past 17 years. "He's Mr. Chairman," Bush argued. "He's been there a long time, so long that he's chairman of a very important committee. He preaches reform yet solicits money" (Schneider, 2000e, 586).

Finally, the Bush campaign produced three response ads to McCain's earlier attack spots that the senator finally suspended. Shortly before the South Carolina primary, a TV ad called "Comprehensive" was made accusing McCain of making false statements about Bush and his campaign reform proposals on the February 13 broadcast of NBC's *Face the Nation*. A modified version was also produced for the upcoming primaries in Washington, Virginia, and Maryland, as well as for the North Dakota caucus. The third TV spot, "Integrity," complained that McCain was over the line when he attacked Bush's integrity and compared him to Bill Clinton ("Ad Spotlight," February 18, 2000). These ads were exempletive of the Bush approach in Round II, as they really opted for attack politics and enlisted many Republicans to join them in their effort to extinguish the McCain insurgency. The Michigan primary presented a difficult challenge as Bush really lined up extensive support from Governor Engler and the state party, with 250 party leaders in 83 counties with volunteers phoning and dropping Bush leaflets at GOP households. The problem was that Engler had political enemies in Detroit and in the labor union movement who were committed to countermobilization for McCain. Michigan was an open primary, with the prospect of not only a high Independent vote but also a significant Democratic turnout as well (Germond and Witcover, 2000e). The situation appeared more promising in Virginia and Washington, but the Independent vote was a wild card favoring McCain.

McCain campaigned extensively in South Carolina and was encouraged by the change in the polls, the open primary format, and the large percentage of veterans in the state. He immediately sold himself and his reform image while invoking conservative credentials. Early on, however, he opted for two attack TV spots. In one he speaks to the camera and says Bush "twists the truth like Clinton. As president, I'll be conservative and always tell you the truth, no matter what." In the other, he suggests that Bush's advertisements have been breaking a pledge not to use advertising ("Ad Spotlight," February 9, 2000). With the attacks escalating, McCain announced that he would not use them and would return to positive ads. He challenged Bush to do the same, but the governor refused, saying that McCain was doing so after running his negative spots for two weeks, McCain's new spots used biographical material touting his war hero experience and maverick reputation. His new positive spot said in Vietnam he "stood up to his communist captors" and in Washington he's a "leader attacking big government waste." The announcer says that McCain can beat Gore with his "character" and "courage" ("Ad Spotlight," February 15, 2000). He remained upbeat in three radio ads that had people praise him for running a positive campaign, for being a pro-life Reagan conservative, and for his courage in Vietnam and in attacking the special interests in Washington ("Ad Spotlight," February 17, 2000). A later TV ad compared himself to Ronald Reagan and has McCain saying he can "beat Al Gore like a drum" ("Ad Spotlight," February 18, 2000).

There was much persuasive material in the McCain ads to establish his impressive bio, his heroism, maverick style, conservative positions on government waste and spending, his identification with Reagan, his long-standing pro-life voting record, and his electability when matched with Al Gore. To the McCain campaign, it was particularly unfair and difficult to be bashed repeatedly in radio ads by both national and South Carolina pro-life groups. He was attacked because of his refusal to support a blanket repeal of *Roe v. Wade* and for his vote in favor of the use of fetal tissue for medical research ("Ad Spotlight," February 10, 2000, and February 18, 2000), despite having one of the best pro-life voting records in Congress for 17 years. He would continue his insurgency, however, throughout the second round and continued to make an effort to reach out to a Republican base, by running ads proclaiming that he is a "proud Reagan Republican" ("Ad Spotlight," February 25, 2000).

In his frustration with some of the criticism and negative campaigning directed against him, McCain made a controversial move when he gave a much-publicized speech right before the Virginia and Washington primaries on February 28, 2000. In it he criticized Pat Robertson and Jerry

Falwell, prominent leaders of the conservative Christian Right, as "agents of intolerance" and then followed it up the next day in California by describing Falwell and Robertson as "forces of evil" (Barnes, 2000b, 722). Although he took care to praise other conservative Christian leaders and activists, the speech did not help him, especially in Virginia. The Pew Research Center for the People and the Press suggested in a March 1, 2000, release that McCain probably hurt himself in southern states as well as certain midwestern and western states, where white evangelicals make up the largest religious bloc of voters. "This group comprises 46% of Republicans in Southern Super Tuesday states and 30% in Midwestern and Western states that will hold primaries in the next two weeks" (Pew, 2000b).

Table 3.1 summarizes the results of this round, characterized by vigorous campaign exchange. The Empire had struck back, but McCain and the Jedi knights were still able to inflict a few wounds of their own and survived to advance to Round III. Bush won South Carolina 53 percent to 42 percent, only to see McCain rebound and win Michigan 50 percent to 43 percent and his home state Arizona 60 percent to 36 percent. Bush then won Puerto Rico 94 percent to 6 percent, the North Dakota caucus 76 percent to 19 percent, the Virginia primary 53 percent to 44 percent, and the Washington primary 58 percent to 38 percent. Table 3.2 contains the results from exit surveys for the South Carolina, Michigan, Arizona, and Virginia primaries by party identification and identifies the proportions of Republicans, Independents, and Democrats in each state. The broad picture is clear, with Bush receiving solid support from Republicans, and McCain dominating Independents and Democrats. The only state in which McCain won a majority of Republicans was his home state of Arizona. South Carolina, Bush's firewall, held as Republicans constituted 61 percent of the vote and Republicans favored Bush 69 percent to 26 percent. Independents were 30 percent, considerably less than New Hampshire's 41 percent, with McCain favored 60 percent to 34 percent, as he was by the 9 percent identifying as Democrats who went 79 percent to 18 percent for him. The much acclaimed McCain victory in Michigan occurred because Republicans lost control of their party and were not even a majority of the vote (48 percent), although they were solidly for Bush, 66 percent to 29 percent. Two-thirds of the 35 percent of Independents voted for McCain, as did the sizable one-sixth (17 percent) who were Democrats and registered 82 percent to 10 percent for McCain. McCain won both Republicans and Independents in Arizona by sizable margins, and only a minuscule 2 percent of the participants identified as Democrats. Bush's success in Virginia, like South Carolina, was due to the fact that a respectable 63 percent of the voters were Republican and supported him 69 percent to 28 percent. The Independent proportion was 29 percent and captured by McCain 64 percent to 31 percent, as were the 8 percent identifying as Democrats who went 87 percent to 11 percent for the Arizona senator.

Table 3.3 reveals no consistent pattern by gender or for seniors. Males, females, and seniors in South Carolina and Virginia favored Bush. Alternately, males, females, and seniors in Michigan and Arizona chose McCain. Political communication campaigns are about persuasion, and the exit polls provide us with information as to what moved voters. Time and parsimony preclude a detailed analysis of them, but illustrations from a key primary like South Carolina will illustrate some of the points ("GOP Primary: South Carolina," 2000). In South Carolina, 34 percent identified with the Religious Right and voted 68 percent to 24 percent for Bush. Keyes was still in the race and drew single-digit support, in this case 8 percent from Religious Right identifiers. Non–Religious Right identifiers voted 52 percent to 46 percent for McCain. South Carolinians gave slightly higher favorability ratings to Bush (73 percent to 26 percent), but McCain did well too (67 percent to 30 percent), despite the extensive attack advertising by both campaigns. Some 35 percent said they thought Bush attacked unfairly, while 43 percent thought that McCain attacked unfairly. Bush was seen by 59 percent as a reformer and edged McCain, who was seen by 53 percent as a reformer. Bush won the air war.

Asked to choose between which issue should be given higher priority, tax cut or Social Security, voters favored Social Security 52 percent to 44 percent. The single most important issue was moral values, selected by 37 percent who favored Bush 55 percent to 36 percent. The second most important issue was Social Security, chosen by 19 percent who favored McCain 58 percent to 40 percent. The single most important quality was stand up for your beliefs, selected by 31 percent who endorsed McCain 54 percent to 38 percent. The second most important quality was strong leader, and the 20 percent who chose it voted for Bush 60 percent to 39 percent. The data show that Bush was successful in establishing his image as a reformer and that McCain recorded a higher percentage for unfair attacks, despite the fact that he changed in midstream and went to positive advertising. It may well be that his earlier attack comparing Bush to Bill Clinton had a more lasting impact on Republican identifiers than other Bush or McCain attacks. Despite the attacks, both candidates have quite respectable favorability ratings, suggesting that voters may process and weigh different items of information differently than the professional media.

Round II came to an end with the Virginia and Washington primaries on February 29, 2000. In a front-loaded and very compressed schedule, the candidate only had one week before 11 states would hold GOP primaries and 2 states would have GOP caucuses in Round III. There would be little time for personal or retail campaigning, and now the importance of political support, money, and media would prove dominant. Political analyst Charlie Cook noted that Bush would be a strong favorite on Super Tuesday despite his shortcomings as candidate because he "is running a national campaign for a national office. McCain isn't, but should be" (Cook, 2000c, 648). Germond and Witcover (2000f) pointed out that on Super Tuesday only 4 of the 11 primary states—Georgia, Missouri, Ohio, and Vermont—allow participation as open as New Hampshire and Michigan, both won by McCain. With the Democrats holding their first primaries since New Hampshire, there would be little crossover to the Republican primaries. In short, Bush would prevail.

THE EMPIRE CONSOLIDATES AS YOU CANNOT WIN THE REPUBLICAN NOMINATION WITHOUT REPUBLICANS: ROUND III (SUPER TUESDAY)

The single week before Tuesday went by quickly, and the massive resources Bush had accumulated proved essential. Both candidates had to compete in 11 primaries and two caucuses, and there was little time to do so. This compressed and front-loaded calendar was not like past calendars in the 1970s and 1980s where a handful of states held events over the 12- to 13-week period for the nomination. The old schedules allowed Jerry Brown and Frank Church to slow down Jimmy Carter's drive for the nomination in 1976, and for Ronald Reagan to take incumbent Gerald Ford down to the wire the same year. It also allowed Gary Hart to give front-runner Walter Mondale a fight to the finish in the Democratic nomination race in 1984. John McCain had proven to be a strong personal campaigner, but he no longer had the time he had in New Hampshire and South Carolina to battle Bush one-on-one. This was wholesale politics week, and by Super Tuesday it would be all over.

The advertising was basically the same with a few new wrinkles. In big states like California, Ohio, and New York, Bush TV ads described him as a "once in a generation leader" who as Texas governor reformed education, wrote a patient's bill of rights, and wrote a "Reaganesque" tax proposal. He also used an attack radio spot in New York that used a woman who claimed that McCain opposed breast cancer research. The *New York Times* reported that the ad's claim that McCain "singled out these particular programs" is a "dubious proposition given the long list of projects he promises to cut" ("Ad Spotlight," March 6, 2000). A few days before the primaries in New York and California, the two biggest delegate prizes in the country, Bush ended with a radio attack spot hitting McCain on education. In it the announcer said: "If John McCain has never made education a priority as senator, why would he as president?" ("Ad Spotlight," March 8, 2000). Also, in the week before Super Tuesday, a group calling itself Republicans for Clean Air ran a $2.5 million ad campaign attacking McCain on the clean air issue. The *New York Times* reported that there are flaws in every claim in the ads and that the sponsor was Dallas businessman Sam Wyly and his family. It was an enormous buy and one that is allowed under independent expenditures. The McCain campaign filed a Federal Election Commission (FEC) complaint as Wyly had already donated $1,000, the individual maxim to the Bush campaign, and FEC regulations treat expenditures by an authorized campaign fund-raiser as contributions to the campaign ("Ad Spotlight," March 7, 2000).

McCain lacked the money to match Bush, and he used his scarce resources to advertise in the three largest states, California, New York, and Ohio. He reprised an older ad that claimed that McCain is a "Republican like Ronald Reagan who can win." It was the ad originally used in South Carolina. His last ad buy promoted his newspaper endorsements in California, New York, and Ohio ("Ad Spotlight," March 7, 2000).

Table 3.1 summarizes the Super Tuesday outcomes, with Bush winning seven primaries, including those in the three largest states, and both caucuses. McCain fought valiantly to the end and won four primaries in New England states. Table 3.2 captures why he lost, as he failed to win a majority of Republicans in any of the 11 primaries and two caucuses, including the four New England states that he won. The bottom line is that you cannot win the Republican nomination without Republicans. It may well be that McCain started too late in his message strategy stressing his conservative voting record and Reagan association. For whatever reason his messages on these themes did not persuade many Republicans. In fact, for the 19 states for which we have exit polls from the Iowa caucus to Super Tuesday, the only state giving McCain a Republican majority was his own Arizona. On the other hand, he demonstrated a tremendous appeal for Independents and won a majority or more of them in every Super Tuesday primary except Georgia. Democratic participation in Republican primaries was not significant on Super Tuesday. For the five states where the subsamples were large enough to offer estimates, McCain won a majority or more of Democrats from a low of 54 percent in Georgia to a high of 88 percent in Massachusetts.

Table 3.3 presents the Super Tuesday results by gender and for seniors. Bush won a majority of men in the seven primaries he won and tied McCain in Connecticut, where the senator won. McCain carried males in the other three New England primaries he won. Bush captured a majority of females in the seven primaries he won, as did McCain in the four primaries he won. McCain made a strong effort to use the Social Security issue to reach seniors, by arguing that the program would be jeopardized by Bush's large tax cuts. The data in Table 3.3 demonstrate, however, that seniors followed the voting trend in their states. Hence

Bush won a majority of seniors in the seven primaries he won, and McCain captured them in the four primaries he won.

Again time and parsimony preclude a detailed examination of the exit polls, but two observations are necessary. The first observation deals with the primary audience to which the candidates have to make their appeal. California had a nonpartisan presidential primary but counted only Republicans for purposes of delegate allocation. This meant that of California's registered Republicans, 82 percent identified as Republicans, 16 percent as Independents, and 2 percent as Democrats. This meant that there was a more partisan Republican audience for Bush to make his appeal. On the other hand, in the Massachusetts GOP primary, only 37 percent identified as Republicans, and in the Rhode Island GOP primary only 40 percent saw themselves as Republicans. McCain ran strongest where the Republican identification base was low. The second observation has to do with McCain's attack on some leaders of the Religious Right. Overall, it hurt him politically. In the large state of Ohio, for example, in which he hoped to be competitive, respondents were asked about the effect of McCain's view of the Religious Right. Some 19 percent said it had a great effect and voted 80 percent to 12 percent for Bush. Another 22 percent claimed it had some effect and favored Bush 73 percent to 23 percent. About 20 percent said not much effect and favored Bush by a lower margin of 57 percent to 40 percent. Approximately 37 percent reported that it had no effect at all, and they cast a decisive 57 percent to 38 percent margin for McCain ("GOP Presidential Primary: Ohio," 2000). As Alison Mitchell of the *New York Times* observed, South Carolina began the pattern that McCain could never escape, and despite victories in Michigan and Arizona, he could never get enough support within his own party. "Any hope of doing so was dashed when he delivered an extraordinary speech in Virginia Beach" that attacked leaders of the Christian Right (Mitchell, 2000c, A8). The Super Tuesday outcomes in Ohio and in other states would support this claim. Still, it was a hell of a ride with the birth and death of the "Straight Talk Express" and a fascinating political high wire act.

Table 3.4 presents trial heat data from July 1999 to April 2000, with trial heats matching Bush versus Gore and McCain versus Gore. Keep in mind, of course, that McCain did not appear on the national political radar screen until December 1999. Both Bush and McCain topped Gore in the trial heats. By February 2000, however, McCain ran better than Gore in all four trial heats in February but was unable to convert this advantage to convince Republican primary voters that he was more electable than Bush. In the final February 27 CNN/Gallup/*USA Today* trial heats Bush defeated Gore 52 percent to 43 percent, while McCain beat him 59 percent to 35 percent. It may well be that some of the Independents and most of the Democratic crossover voters may have dropped off

Table 3.4
Presidential General Election Preferences in Percentages for Registered Voters in 1999 and Likely Voters in 2000 by Percent from July 18, 1999, to April 2, 2000

Date Completed	Bush	Gore	McCain	Gore	Bush	Bradley
2000						
4/2	46	45				
3/12	49	43				
2/27	52	43	59	35		
2/21	50	45	59	35	55	41
2/15	50	45	55	39		
2/6	53	44	58	36		
1/19	53	42			49	45
1/16	57	38	52	42	53	42
1/10	52	43	54	41	49	47
1/7	52	43			49	47
1999						
12/21	53	42	47	47	50	45
12/12	55	42	52	44	51	45
11/21	56	40			55	40
11/7	55	40			53	42
10/24	52	43			54	39
10/10	56	40			54	42
9/26	55	37				
9/14	56	39			55	41
8/18	55	41			55	40
7/18	55	38				

Source: CNN/Gallup/*USA Today* 1999 and 2000 polls (December 2000) at http://nationaljournal/00/races/whitehouse/wh2000gen2.htm. (The 1999 polls were based on samples of registered voters and the 2000 polls on samples of likely voters.)

as Gore bounced back, as he eventually did in August. Still, with limited resources, McCain proved to be a strong insurgent.

THE WRAP-UP: ROUND IV (POST–SUPER TUESDAY TO THE CONVENTION) AND ROUND V (THE CONVENTION)

The final two phases will be dealt with briefly and only to focus on the effects of the insurgency on Governor Bush's nomination. On March

9, 2000, Senator John McCain dropped out of the race but stopped short of endorsing Bush (Mitchell, 2000b). McCain had always said that Super Tuesday would decide it all. If he had chosen to continue, his prospects looked dim as the next set of primaries would be held in southern states like Florida, Oklahoma, Mississippi, and Texas where the polls had him far behind (Firestone, 2000, A16). Matthew Dowd, Bush's pollster, points out that after Super Tuesday the campaign had been hurt by the bruising intraparty battle with McCain, and Bush was pushed more to the Right than they originally planned. Bush used the next six weeks to get back to his broader policy agenda on education, health care reform, Social Security, and the like, and went from even to 6 points up. This was an advantage in the polls that he would maintain until the convention. Bush's success, he noted, stopped a lot of media chatter about the alleged weaknesses of the Bush campaign and speculation about who would be fired (Dowd, 2001). By July, McCain had endorsed Bush, and the Texas governor was successful in overcoming any lingering negative effects of the nomination battle in July. As Marshall Wittmann of the Heritage Foundation put it: "It's very clear the crossroads we're at. Bush has won the post-primary period. Now the question is, can Gore regroup?" (Balz, 2000a). Round IV went to Bush.

The national convention that was held in Philadelphia in late July/early August provided four days to build political interest, select the vice president, and energize the Republican base. The Bush advisers felt they were successful in their goal. Mark McKinnon, Bush's media director, observed that there are three events where campaigns can have an impact. They are the debates, the selection of the vice president, and the convention. He felt the Bush campaign was successful with all three. The vice presidential selection and the convention were definite pluses, with Bush ending the convention with an 11 percent lead in the polls. Bush looked like a leader by giving a good convention speech. He made the Republican Party more inclusive. McKinnon notes that Bush was able to use the convention not only to establish that he was a leader but also to show that he was a different kind of Republican, willing to tackle issues that Republicans were inclined to ignore (McKinnon, 2001). Karl Rove, Bush's chief campaign strategist, felt that they had accomplished what they had set out to do. He said: "We leave the convention as a united and energized party that's able to spend a lot of its time and energy reaching out to independents and Democrats and swing voters" (Balz, 2000b). He was right. Bush had a good Round V. Al Gore, however, would rebound and have an even better convention later in August.

THE DEMOCRATS: THE PRELIMINARIES

In times of economic prosperity and peace, incumbent presidents or their heir apparents are strongly favored to win and are often unopposed or receive only token opposition for their party's nomination. Vice President Al Gore was a strong favorite and the front-runner for the Democratic nomination. A number of Democrats looked at the race and thought it impossible to defeat Gore. The lone exception was former New Jersey senator and professional basketball player Bill Bradley. He was willing to challenge the Democratic establishment because of his commitment to liberal policy views and his belief in the need to offer a new kind of politics.

Both Gore and Bradley tapped resources in the preliminaries during 1999. Standing in the polls is the first important resource. Gore had name recognition and dominated in national polls, although he trailed George Bush and Elizabeth Dole in trial heats, as did Bradley ("General Election: National Polls," 2000; "General Election: State Polls, 2000) in most trial heats. After Elizabeth Dole dropped out in October, Bradley began to draw more media attention when he fared better in trial heats against Bush than did Gore. Thus the December 20–21 CNN/Gallup/*USA Today* trial heat showed Gore losing to Bush 53 percent to 42 percent, or by an 11 percent margin, with newcomer Bradley only losing by 50 percent to 45 percent, or a 5 percent margin. Individual state polls usually had Gore leading as the preferred Democratic candidate, but Bradley struck political gold when some polls had him ahead in New Hampshire, the first primary state ("Democratic Primary: State Polls," 2000). The December 1999 ABC News/*Washington Post* likely voter poll had Bradley ahead of Gore 48 percent to 45 percent. A December Reuters/WHDH-TV likely voter poll by Zogby International also had Bradley ahead of Gore 48 percent to 42 percent. Although not on the radar screen in many states, Bradley conducted himself well enough in the preliminaries to be a little more competitive than Gore in the national polls against Bush and to run slightly ahead of Gore in New Hampshire. Gore led decisively, however, in the polls in Iowa.

As noted earlier, most candidates end up dropping out because they are unable to raise enough money to challenge the incumbent. This was not a problem for Bradley. Bradley's war chest would total $20 million by the end of 1999. He was able to tap a network of donors outside the traditional base of major Democratic contributors and had tremendous success as a fund-raising insurgent. "His celebrity status as a former basketball star—he captained the 1964 Olympic basketball team and played for the New York Knicks—attracted dollars from professional team owners. He has also received support from Wall Street and Silicon Valley" (Barnes, 2000a, 380). Bradley raised more money than Gore in the final three months of 1999 (Glasser, 2000, A4). In the April 15, 2000, Federal Election filing, Bradley reported raising $27.8 million and Gore $29 million ("Campaign 2000 Fund-raising," 2001). It was extraordinary that an insurgent would be close to parity in money with a sitting vice presidential incumbent.

Both solicited endorsements, although Gore had a tremendous advantage as the incumbent. During the preliminaries Gore lined up some critical endorsements from individuals who were later used in timely political ads in the battle for Iowa and New Hampshire. Among the individuals Gore attracted included the popular Iowa Senator Tom Harkin ("Ad Spotlight," January 18, 2000), Senator Ted Kennedy ("Ad Spotlight," January 20, 2000), Robert Kennedy, Jr. ("Ad Spotlight," January 25, 2000), and popular New Hampshire Governor Jeanne Shaheen ("Ad Spotlight," January 28, 2000). Harkin and Shaheen were especially valuable in the early contests in their home states. Both Kennedys help invoke their liberal Democratic family tradition, and the senator is a credible source to use in debating the health care issue.

Bill Bradley won the endorsements of retiring New York Senator Daniel Patrick Moynihan and former Nebraska Senator Bob Kerrey, as well as a woman, Maureen Drumm, who claimed that Bradley's work in health care saved one of her children ("Ad Spotlight," November 17, 2000). Bradley received the endorsement and active support of former Boston Celtics star Bill Russell ("Ad Spotlight," January 21, 2000). Later down the campaign road in February, Bradley would attract a high-profile endorsement from the famous Chicago Bull basketball star Michael Jordan ("Ad Spotlight," February 11, 2000). Both candidates did well in attracting high-profile supporters, but the edge goes to Gore for more timely and credible sources in the early state matchups.

Media was an important source in the preliminaries. As noted earlier, coverage of the nomination by the three major television networks was cut in half in 1999 when compared to 1995. Gore as the Democratic front-runner received more stories than did Bradley (73 to 40). The Media Monitor research team found that Gore received more favorable evaluations on desirability (positive and negative assessments of the candidates by news sources) than Bradley. Gore registered 66 percent positive to 51 percent positive for the insurgent. Bradley, however, did well as a challenger because he received much higher evaluations on viability or the prospects of winning. Here he had a stunning 86 percent positive to only 35 percent for Gore ("Campaign 2000—The Primaries: TV News Coverage of the Democratic and GOP Primaries," 1999).

Both Bradley and Gore both used extensive paid political advertising in the final phase of the preliminaries. Bradley was idealistic when he announced his candidacy in September 1999, and "his hope was that he could compete against Gore in a campaign free of ad hominem personal attacks, and deliberate distortion of an opponent's record was short-lived" (Cannon, 2000, 321). As soon as Bradley appeared, Gore honed in. In October he labeled Bradley a quitter for retiring from politics in 1996 after the Republicans took control of Congress in 1994. The attack was deliberate and tactical (Cannon, 2000, 321).

Through the first half of 1999 Gore had campaigned as the incumbent and as the vice president and barely acknowledged Bradley's challenge. When Bradley began to make inroads, Gore changed direction and moved his campaign from Washington to Nashville in October and with the move adopted a new philosophy. His focus group research showed that people liked him in town meetings when he appeared fighting. This led to the thematic of Al Gore fighting for you (Barnes, 2000a, 379). It also led to the adoption of an attack philosophy against Bradley for tactical reasons. It had three specific aims. One was "to inoculate Gore against being seen as a career politician. Another was to taunt Bradley into dropping his high-minded intentions. The third was to lay the groundwork for the rhetorical gimmick that Gore has made his virtual battle cry in Iowa and New Hampshire—that he's a fighter" (Cannon, 2000, 322). It was a strategy that would bear political fruit in Round I in January 2000, when Bradley would take the bait.

Gore's paid political advertising was largely directed at Iowa and New Hampshire. In October 1999 his first spot consisted of an ad bashing the Republican Senate for opposing the Comprehensive Test Ban Treaty ("Ad Spotlight," October 14, 1999). His second was a bio ad to introduce himself to the voters ("Ad Spotlight," October 19, 1999). The third was a spot announcing his support for a ban on new offshore oil and gas drilling ("Ad Spotlight," October 25, 1999). In November, Gore aired an ad calling for health insurance "for millions and millions of children who have none" ("Ad Spotlight," November 11, 1999) and an ad stressing his efforts to save Medicare and Medicaid. This ad does not mention Bradley by name, but it is a criticism of Bradley's health care plan ("Ad Spotlight," November 24, 2000). In December he begins with a bio ad on his experience in Vietnam and as a reporter and an ad that attacks vouchers as an educational solution. The latter is a criticism of Bradley ("Ad Spotlight," December 6, 1999). He aired a later ad on health care that proclaimed that he is "the only candidate to take on the big drug companies" and is "the only candidate who protects Medicare and preserves Medicaid" ("Ad Spotlight," December 13, 1999). Gore courted black voters with radio ads on how he has fought for them ("Ad Spotlight," December 14, 1999). He concluded with an ad that highlighted his insider experience ("Ad Spotlight," January 3, 2000). His paid advertising really stayed on message, portraying him as a fighter, and attacked Bradley's positions and not by name. In debates and speeches he made direct attacks on Bradley. He hammered away with the quitter accusation, and in October in California and in Maryland in December he asserted that Bradley's health plan would hurt minorities. Bradley responded by saying, "I think we've reached a sad day in political life in this country when the sitting Vice-President distorts a fellow Democrat's record because he thinks he can score a few political points" (Cannon, 2000, 322).

Bob Shrum (2001), a top Gore campaign strategist from the firm of Shrum, Devine, and Dolan, said at the Annenberg Debriefing on February 10, 2001, that Gore had two favorite messages during the election. They were both put in ads early in the nomination fight. The first ad was a very spontaneous commentary by Gore to a group of citizens on his thoughts on the job of the president. The other, with many variations, was his theme of "he's fighting for us," which portrayed him as saving Medicare, Medicaid, and Social Security and protecting seniors and working families. Shrum said that the vice president believed that they captured the real Al Gore.

Bradley launched his first television ads in Iowa and New Hampshire about a month after Gore had aired his. The first was an endorsement ad that featured Senator Daniel Patrick Moynihan and former Senator Bob Kerrey talking about Bradley in the Senate. Also featured was Maureen Drumm, who credits Bradley's 1996 bill to keep pregnant women in the hospital longer as the reason her daughter "is alive today" ("Ad Spotlight," November 17, 1999). Bradley's campaign would highlight health care, and he cut ads from town meetings in both Iowa and New Hampshire in which he tells local residents about his health care plan ("Ad Spotlight," December 8, 1999). In December Bradley put out a response ad to Gore's criticism on his health care plan. It was cut for Iowa and again features a scene from a town meeting in which Bradley says as a senator he "successfully protected Medicare from premium increases or cuts" and that as president he would "expand Medicare" ("Ad Spotlight," December 21, 1999).

In the preliminaries the candidates already began to debate, and the first debate in New Hampshire on October 27, 1999, set out the central themes of the two campaigns, and it would pit a problem-solver against a fighter. In that debate Bradley said: "You ought to have big solutions to big problems. Because that's what America is all about. It's about dreaming and being able to fulfill those dreams." Bradley depicted himself as an outsider who could rise above partisanship and "engender trust on both sides of the aisle," Gore also used the debate to outline his message: "I would like to have your support for me because I want to fight for you as President and fight for all the people." Gore portrayed himself as someone who would get down in the trenches. He said, "For 23 years, I have been a fighter for working men and women" (Schneider, 2000a, 282). The preliminaries ended with a basic contrast between a problem-solver versus a fighter. The two would fight hard in Round I.

THE INSURGENT REBELLION AND THE EMPIRE STRIKES BACK: ROUND I FOR THE DEMOCRATS (IOWA CAUCUS, NEW HAMPSHIRE, DELAWARE)

Both candidates spent considerable time in Iowa and New Hampshire, although Bradley spent more than Gore. Between March 15, 1999, and January 5, 2000, Bradley had spent 45 days in Iowa and 37 days in New Hampshire, while Gores's visits totaled 30 for Iowa and 32 for New Hampshire (Fenoglio, 2000). Table 3.5 summarizes the Democratic nomination campaign schedule from the Iowa caucus to Super Tuesday. As the data indicate, Gore was very dominant and won every single event. Bradley had a window of opportunity in December 1999 and January 2000, as he led in New Hampshire until the middle of the month ("Democratic Primary: State Polls," 2000). He was defeated decisively in Iowa by a 63 percent to 35 percent margin and lost a close 52 percent to 48 percent race New Hampshire. This was followed by a 57 percent to 40 percent loss in Delaware. The table underscores Bradley's fundamental problem, which was that Democratic reform rules precluded any more primaries until the first Tuesday in March. This meant that the media would focus on the Republican race and would give little coverage to the Democratic contest. Bradley advisers felt after the senator conceded after the Super Tuesday results were announced that Bradley "was unfairly written off by the news media after he lost the New Hampshire primary on Feb. 1" (Dao, 2000a, A16). Bradley, in short, was hurt by the calendar since he lost all three races in Round I and could not get the traction to rebound.

Bradley's campaign really was an impossible dream, and his fundamental premise that he could "rebuild the ambitiously liberal and steadfastly multiracial coalition of the 1960s" would be questioned by many Democrats (Edsall, 2000a, A8). Democratic pollster Peter Hart suggested that while Bradley was a good person, he was out of touch with the mood of the country. The year 2000, he said, was more like 1956 than 1968, and there was economic contentment. A major difficulty with Bradley strategy, he further noted, is that "you are not going against LBJ and the war. There is no 'anti' feeling here" (Edsall, 2000, A8).

Another important feature in Round I was Gore's success with an attack strategy that took the momentum away from Bradley and put him on the defensive. Bradley and various media sources flat out accused Gore of blatant distortions of Bradley's positions. Germond and Witcover (2000a) contend that in his stump speeches and in the debates Gore distorted Bradley's positions and that Bradley either did not answer them or gave ineffective answers. Faced with Gore attacks, they said, Bradley was "like an indolent hound flicking off fleas" (196). Among other things, Gore continually charged that Bradley's health care reform package

Table 3.5
Democratic Presidential Primary (P) and Caucus/Convention (C/C) Results in Percentages for 2000 from Iowa Caucus (1/24) to Super Tuesday (3/7)

State	Date	Delegates Pledged	Delegates Unpledged	Method	Gore	Bradley	Winner
Iowa	1/24	47	9	C/C	63	35	Gore
N.H.	2/1	22	7	P	52	48	Gore
Del.[1]	2/5	15	7	P	57	40	Gore
Am. Samoa	3/7	3	3	C/C	84	16	Gore
Calif.	3/7	367	68	P	81	18	Gore
Conn.	3/7	54	13	P	55	42	Gore
Ga.	3/7	77	15	P	84	16	Gore
Hawaii	3/7	22	11	C/C	80	17	Gore
Idaho	3/7	18	5	C/C	63	33	Gore
Maine	3/7	23	9	P	54	41	Gore
Md.	3/7	68	25	P	67	29	Gore
Mass.	3/7	93	25	P	60	38	Gore
Minn.	3/7	74	17	C/C	73	14	Gore
Mo.	3/7	75	17	P	65	34	Gore
N.Y.	3/7	243	51	P	65	34	Gore
N.D.	3/7	14	8	C/C	78	22	Gore
Ohio	3/7	146	24	P	73	25	Gore
R.I.	3/7	22	11	P	57	41	Gore
Vt.	3/7	15	7	P	55	44	Gore
Wash.	3/7	75	19	C/C	68	32	Gore

[1] Delaware delegates allocated on 3/27 by caucus convention.

Source: Bacon, 2000b, 2630.

would harm Medicaid but "ignored Bradley's plan to replace Medicaid with improved coverage for the elderly." Gore also repeatedly accused Bradley of supporting vouchers and undermining public schools, but Bradley stated over and over that he supported public schools and only endorsed vouchers as an experimental and supplemental program (Germond and Witcover, 2000a).

In an Iowa debate, Gore ambushed Bradley by planting a farmer in the audience who had experienced flooding in 1993 who spoke up and claimed that Bradley voted against flood assistance for Iowa. Bradley sidestepped the question and said that this was about the past and the more critical concern was to change agriculture in the future. Bradley was clearly not prepared as he announced the next day that he had voted for flood assistance and that the negative vote mentioned by the farmer was on a minor amendment. This episode hurt Bradley on farm policy in an agricultural state, as did Gore's continual assaults on Bradley's big health care plan and his other so-called big ideas (Germond and Witcover, 2000b, 272). In assessing the attacks that were made in January, a *New York Times* editorial said: "Mr. Gore's charge that Mr. Bradley's proposal for universal health care would mean abandoning the people on Medicaid is a willful misrepresentation. Mr. Bradley's plan to replace Medicaid with other insurance programs is similar to the approach used in the Clinton-Gore health plan in 1993" ("The Uses of Negative Campaigns," 2000, A24).

Despite being ineffective through a good part of January, Bradley opted to attack at the end on the character issue and as effective. Paul Gigot observed that Bradley connected the dots between Gore's distortions and the ability of Democrats to win in November. Bradley finally said at the close of the New Hampshire primary: "If we don't clean our own House, the Republicans will clean it for us" (Gigot, 2000). Gore realized the significance of the late Bradley surge and invoked the power of the Democratic empire by having House Minority Leader Richard Gephardt and Senate Minority Leader Thomas Daschle put out a press release claiming that the Bradley campaign "has taken a sharp negative turn and veered into the kind of negative personal attacks he repeatedly denounced" (Barnes, 2000a, 376).

The messages for both campaigns were extensive in Round I, but time and parsimony preclude a detailed analysis. They are available on "Ad Spotlight," which can be found at http://nationaljournal.com. The final closing ads for both candidates before the New Hampshire primary indicate what was most important to them. Gore closed with an ad that claimed he would support universal health care, protect Medicare, save Social Security, and pay down the debt. It also said he is pro education, pro environment, and pro choice. It ended with his tag line: "Al Gore—fighting for us" ("Ad Spotlight," February 1, 2000). Bradley ended with three ads, and two were recycles of the Bill Russell endorsement, and the Drumm personal endorsement on hospital stays for pregnant women. Bradley focused on the female vote by stressing his strong pro-choice voting record to a more mixed record for Gore when the latter served in the Congress. His ad stressed that the abortion problem is "the kind of issue that you can't straddle" ("Ad Spotlight," February 1, 2000).

The Democrats did not have a problem with a Republican crossover. After New Hampshire, there was a relatively uncontested primary in Delaware. After that, the Democrats had no official delegate allocation contests until March 7. At that time Republicans also had primaries and caucuses, which reduced the GOP incentives to crossover and participate in Democratic primaries. Table 3.6 summarizes the results for Democrats,

Table 3.6
Proportion of Democratic Presidential Primary and Iowa Caucus Participants and Candidate Preferences by Party of Identification (Democrat and Independent) and Labor Union Household Membership in Percent from Iowa Caucus to Super Tuesday

	Democrats			Independents			Labor Union Households		
State	All	Gore	Bradley	All	Gore	Bradley	All	Gore	Bradley
Iowa	82	66	29	17	39	42	33	69	24
N.H.	56	59	41	40	41	56	23	60	38
Del.	75	60	37	23	51	45	30	68	30
Calif.	85	82	17	13	64	35	26	83	16
Conn.	77	60	38	20	39	54	35	57	38
Ga.	81	88	12	17	68	32	22	90	10
Maine	69	60	36	29	43	53	27	55	42
Md.	80	74	23	16	42	48	29	73	22
Mass.	67	65	33	29	53	43	29	63	33
Mo.	78	70	28	16	44	51	26	65	33
N.Y.	80	70	29	18	46	50	40	70	30
Ohio	77	80	19	21	52	43	46	74	22
R.I.	60	65	33	38	43	55	33	62	34
Vt.	58	60	39	39	49	50	20	54	45

Source: Data collected from various state polls (December 2000) at www.cnn.com/ELECTION/2000/primaries.html.

Independents, and labor union household membership, a key Democratic constituency. As the data demonstrate, Gore won the Democratic identifiers overwhelmingly in Iowa, New Hampshire, and Delaware. His weakest showing was New Hampshire, where he nevertheless received 59 percent of the Democratic vote. Bradley won Independents narrowly in Iowa (42 percent to 39 percent) and by a substantial margin in New Hampshire (56 percent to 41 percent). Although Independents were 40 percent of the Democratic vote, he may have done better and won had McCain not attracted so many Independents to the GOP primary (41 percent). Gore did win the 23 percent of voters who were Independents in Delaware by a slim 51 percent to 45 percent margin. Despite running from the Left, the data in Table 3.6 show that Bradley lost the labor vote overwhelmingly, with his highest percentage being 38 percent in New Hampshire.

Table 3.7 contains data on gender and seniors. In contrast to the Republicans, women are often a higher proportion of voters in Democratic primaries. Some 57 percent of Iowa caucus participants were women, as

Table 3.7
Proportion of Democratic Presidential Primary and Iowa Caucus Participants and Candidate Preferences by Gender and for Seniors (60 Years or Older) from Iowa Caucus to Super Tuesday

	Men			Women			Seniors		
State	All	Gore	Bradley	All	Gore	Bradley	All	Gore	Bradley
Iowa	43	60	32	57	61	32	39	73	24
N.H.	38	47	51	62	50	48	23	51	48
Del.	49	56	41	51	58	39	40	64	35
Calif.	44	81	19	56	80	19	29	84	16
Conn.	43	50	47	57	59	38	34	58	39
Ga.	41	80	20	59	87	13	28	81	19
Maine	43	55	42	57	54	42	31	60	33
Md.	43	59	35	57	73	25	33	66	29
Mass.	42	59	37	58	61	37	32	66	31
Mo.	41	60	37	59	68	31	38	68	30
N.Y.	42	57	42	58	70	29	36	71	28
Ohio	40	65	34	60	78	19	30	77	23
R.I.	47	50	48	53	55	43	32	63	34
Vt.	40	49	50	60	59	40	23	69	30

Source: Data collected from various state polls (December 2000) at www.cnn.com/ELECTION/2000/primaries.html.

were 62 percent of New Hampshire Democrats and 51 percent of Delaware Democrats. Gore won 60 percent of men in Iowa and 56 percent of men in Delaware. Bradley had a narrow 51 percent to 47 percent advantage with men in New Hampshire. Bradley targeted women with his health care plan and his emphasis on abortion rights. It was a disappointment for him that Gore carried women in all three primaries, with 61 percent in Iowa, 50 percent in New Hampshire, and 58 percent in Delaware. Gore's 2 percent edge with women in New Hampshire was the determining factor, as over three-fifths of all Granite State voters were women. Despite Bradley's health care plan, seniors in all three primaries favored Gore. He won 73 percent of Iowa seniors and 64 percent of Delaware seniors. Bradley's best showing with seniors was a narrow 51 percent to 48 percent loss in New Hampshire.

An examination of the Iowa caucus exit poll shows Gore dominating most demographic categories. The few groups according Bradley a majority included Independents, Democrats making over $75,000 a year, those disapproving of Clinton's job performance, and those indicating that the most important quality was having new ideas ("Demo and GOP Caucuses: Iowa," 2000). For Iowa voters the single most important issue was Social Security, selected by 26 percent, and they favored Gore 75 percent to 21 percent, followed by education, chosen by 22 percent, supporting Gore, 56 percent to 33 percent. Health care, Bradley's signature issue and picked by 16 percent, also ended up in the Gore column, 60 percent to 37 percent. The two most important candidate qualities were standing up for your beliefs and experience, chosen by 26 percent and 21 percent, respectively, and Democrats selecting both went for Gore, respectively, by 50 percent to 41 percent and 92 percent to 6 percent margins ("Demo and GOP Caucuses: Iowa," 2000). Gore was clearly effective with his fighter image, as well as with insider status and his emphasis on experience.

Bradley's best hope and swan song was his close loss in New Hampshire. Had he won, there might have been a "Bradley phenomenon" along with a McCain phenomenon. Despite the attack advertising, New Hampshire voters gave high favorability ratings to both Gore (70 percent to 29 percent) and Bradley (78 percent to 18 percent). Some 28 percent felt that Gore attacked unfairly, while 25 percent believed Bradley attacked unfairly. The single most important issue for New Hampshire Democrats was education, selected by 22 percent, and they favored Gore 55 percent to 44 percent. Health care was the second most important issue, and here Bradley dominated 61 percent to 39 percent. The New Jersey senator also won a majority of the 30 percent who picked "stands up for his beliefs" as the most important candidate quality by a dramatic 70 percent to 27 percent margin. The second most important quality, picked by 20 percent, was experience, and those choosing it went heavily for Gore (92 percent to 8 percent). In a close race, any one of a number of factors might have been the main reason for the loss. In New Hampshire, one such factor could have been voter concern over Bradley's health (heart problems). Some 21 percent of Democratic primary participants expressed concern about Bradley's health, and they voted 84 percent to 14 percent for Gore. The 77 percent, on the other hand, who were not concerned favored Bradley 58 percent to 40 percent ("Dem. Primary: New Hampshire," 2000).

Bradley's close loss concealed Gore's vulnerability on the character issue. Some 81 percent of New Hampshire Democratic participants approved the job Clinton was doing, but only 42 percent gave him a favorable rating as a person. A highly significant factor is that 55 percent gave Clinton an unfavorable rating as a person. Those doing so supported Bradley 60 percent to 38 percent. Although losing his lead to Gore, Bradley's decision to attack Gore on character at the end in New Hampshire resulted in a Bradley surge (Gigot, 2000). Those Democratic primary participants who decided their vote the previous year, about 18 percent of all voters, favored Gore 63 percent to 35 percent, as did the 34 percent who decided early in 2000, by a 52 percent to to 47 percent margin. The 21 percent deciding the last week went for Bradley 52 percent to 47 percent, as did the 11 percent decided the last three days, with 63 percent Bradley and 36 percent Gore. The 15 percent who finally decided the day of the primary also favored Bradley, 57 percent to 41 percent ("Dem. Primary: New Hampshire," 2000). Bradley discovered the right issue, character and ethics, and the right tactic, attack messages, but did so a little too late.

ROUND III (SUPER TUESDAY) AND ROUND IV (POST–SUPER TUESDAY TO THE CONVENTION)

Round III was frustrating for Bradley. The calendar gave him no place to go, and the media gave little coverage (Germond and Witcover, 2000c). The Media Monitor data for the five weeks following New Hampshire gave McCain five times as much coverage as Bradley or Gore ("Campaign 2000—The Primaries: TV News Coverage of the Democratic and GOP Primaries," 2000). Both sides continued their message strategy both on the stump and in their advertising. To build his coalition, Bradley had to reach the core Democratic constituencies, namely, members of labor union households, women, seniors, and blacks. He attempted to break through with four message strategies, all of which failed. First, he called for big ideas and portrayed Gore as small-minded (Schneider, 2000f). He forgot that Clinton became more successful when he abandoned his big health care program and opted for smaller or the so-called small-bore programs (Morris, 1997). Gore, too, had absorbed the lesson. Second, Bradley cast the Clinton-Gore administration as ethically compromised. This was certainly persuasive for Independents in New Hampshire and made it a close race. Democratic Party identifiers did not as well receive the charge, and Bill Schneider claims that Democrats resented it because "Bradley seemed to be handing ammunition to Republicans" (Schneider, 2000f, 826). His third message strategy was to portray Gore as a loser and to suggest that he was more electable. Bush, however, would lose the New Hampshire, Michigan, and Arizona primaries in Round III and no longer looked unbeatable. Most trial heat national polls in February had Bush slipping, although still ahead of Gore. Moreover, Gore's trial heat percentages against Bush were better than Bradley's ("General Election: National Polls," 2000). Bradley's final message, used in February, was to call Al Gore a conservative and to refer to old congressional votes on abortion and gun control to prove his point. Schneider points out that the votes on these issues were a long time ago and that it was difficult to label conservative a candidate endorsed by both

Ted Kennedy and Jesse Jackson, two of the party's more prominent liberals (Schneider, 2000f, 826).

Gore's rebuttal ads on the conservative charge were absolutely devastating. For African-American voters, Gore matched Bradley's marquee Michael Jordan endorsement with one from Jesse Jackson. On the gun control criticism, Gore produced a Jim Brady TV ad endorsement ("Ad Spotlight," February 28, 2000). On abortion, he released an ad touting his support from the National Abortion and Reproductive Rights Action League (NARAL), the top national abortion rights group ("Ad Spotlight," February 28, 2000). He also received a high-profile TV ad endorsement from Kristina Kiehl, who cofounded Voters for Choice with Gloria Steinem. Previously Kiehl had endorsed Bradley but says in the ad: "I no longer support Bradley because his unfair tactics divide us at the very moment we should stand together against the Republicans" ("Ad Spotlight," February 25, 2000).

Round III ended at the end of February, and then there was only a week in Round IV for Super Tuesday. Bradley began to get media coverage again, but it was a little late. The data in Table 3.5 outline the Democratic calendar on March 7, 2000, including 11 primaries and 6 caucuses. Bradley lost all 17 contests. Table 3.6 summarizes the candidate percentages for 11 state primaries for Democrats, Independents, and members of labor union households. Gore won Democratic identifiers in all 11 primaries, while Bradley continued to show Independent strength, as he won this group in 7 of the 11 primaries. Gore, on the other hand, captured the labor union vote in all 11 primaries. Data are presented in Table 3.7 for gender and seniors. Gore won all three demographic groups—men, women, and seniors, with the exception of Vermont males—in all 11 primaries and often by decisive margins. Gore defeated Bradley by a 3-to-1 ratio with labor union household members and captured the black vote overall by a lopsided 83 percent to 15 percent spread (Schneider, 2000f, 826). Round IV turned out to be a rout.

ROUND V (POST–SUPER TUESDAY TO THE CONVENTION) AND ROUND VI (CONVENTION)

The spirited nomination clash between Gore and Bradley did not hurt Gore as much as some speculated. Exit survey data show that the attitude of Bradley voters toward Al Gore was 58 percent to 35 percent favorable but 71 percent to 25 percent unfavorable for Bush. As Schneider notes: "Big difference. They like Gore. They don't like Bush. There's not likely to be much competition for the Bradley vote" (2000g, 914). For reasons that had nothing to do with his nomination performance and the Bradley insurgency, the Gore campaign got off-message from March to the August convention, and Bush had a much better postnomination period. Gore's spring season was marked by indecision, lack of focus, strategic mistakes, Bush's control of the campaign agenda, negative ratings, failure to consolidate the Democratic base, and a failure to soften his image (Balz, 2000a). He began Round VI and the convention behind by 11 percent. Gore, however, would have an even stronger convention and made a remarkable comeback. Kathleen Frankovic, director of Surveys and producer of CBS News, observed that Al Gore had the largest Democratic bounce in history, moving from a −11 percent to a +1 percent and the lead (Frankovic, 2001). After an exhaustive fight for their respective parties' nomination, Al Gore and George Bush were at parity and posed for a yet more difficult struggle in the general election.

CONCLUDING OBSERVATIONS

First, the trend toward front-loading has compressed the political calendar and time necessary to win so that the role of political parties has been revitalized. The candidate who can attract party activists like party state and county chairmen and precinct activists will have an organizational advantage in a short campaign season. Front-loading makes it even harder for insurgents to win. This was the case in 2000, as both Bush and Gore had strong party backing that allowed the respective party empires to help the front-runners put down the revolt.

Second, the role of money, particularly the lack of money, is important. It was not a factor in the Democratic contest, but it was critical in the Republican race. Six Republican candidates were forced to drop out of the race before the Iowa caucus in large part because of money. Three, Alexander, Dole, and Quayle, were serious contenders based on qualifications. Two other GOP candidates were forced out after the New Hampshire primary, and another, Alan Keyes, never had enough money to make a serious race. Money, however, is a necessary but not sufficient condition to win. Money could not buy Steve Forbes the necessary positive favorability ratings to make him a serious candidate.

Third, as political communication research has repeatedly indicated, you cannot win unless you have source credibility as a messenger. McCain waged a serious insurgent challenge by his compelling personality and biography. It was McCain the candidate and not his issue stances that led to his primary successes, where voters admired him because he stood up for his beliefs. Bradley, on the other hand, proved to be a weak messenger, especially for a candidate running from the Left and attempting to build a liberal, multiracial coalition. Emory political scientist Merle Black observed that to appeal to white, blue-collar workers you have to be a populist. "What they want to see is someone who fights when challenged, not all this talk about new politics. That's more like Common Cause [a group that advocates government reform], very elitist." Black felt that Bradley had used the Common Cause style, and "it doesn't work" (Edsall, 2000, A8).

Fourth, the message is important, too. Elsewhere, Michael Pfau and I have analyzed the importance of attack messages, which have the advantage of grabbing voter attention and being remembered more than positive messages (Pfau and Kenski, 1990). To work, however, attack messages have to be credible. What is striking about the nomination contests in 2000 is that attack messages were critical to the outcome. Gore's attack message strategy that hammered Bradley on both issues and qualifications proved effective. Bradley's brief countersurge during the week before the critical New Hampshire vote was due to the fact that Bradley took off the white gloves and attacked Gore, especially on character. McCain ran strong in Round I with a reformist and attack message on the establishment and special interests. Bush rebounded with very strong attack messages after New Hampshire that portrayed McCain as moderate to liberal and more like the Democrats on policy. He also hit hard that McCain was part of the Washington establishment who took big campaign contributions while preaching reform. Bush energized and reinforced his Republican base with these attack messages. McCain needed to inoculate more effectively in Round I to establish his conservative Republican credentials and preempt the Bush attacks. Hindsight also suggests that he may have erred in returning to a positive message strategy instead of rebutting Bush's charges in Round II during the battle for South Carolina.

Finally, the final phase in the political communication process is the audience. The most creative message strategies in the world will prove ineffective if they fail to persuade voters. It was the audience that decided the fates of Bradley and McCain. The former could not crack the core Democratic constituencies of blacks, labor, seniors, and women. McCain, on the other hand, could not persuade enough Republicans. The candidacies of Bradley and McCain demonstrate that appealing to Independents is not enough. You cannot win the Democratic nomination without Democrats, and you cannot win the GOP nomination without Republicans.

NOTE

1. I express my appreciation to Dean Kathleen Jamieson of the Annenberg School of Communication for inviting me to be an observer at the Presidential Election Debriefing 2000 at the Annenberg Public Policy Center in Philadelphia, Pennsylvania, on February 10, 2001. My use of comments is based on my notes of the debriefing. A video has been made of some of the proceedings and is available by contacting the Annenberg Public Policy Center at the University of Pennsylvania, 3620 Walnut Street, Philadelphia, PA 19104 or by calling (215) 898–

7041. The University of Pennsylvania will publish a book form of the debriefing, *Electing the President* (expected to be published in 2002).

REFERENCES

"Ad Spotlight." 2000. A submenu at http://nationaljournal.com. All the 1999 and 2000 ads cited by date in this chapter are available here.

Allen, Mike. 1999. "Bradley, McCain Vow to Reject 'Soft Money' Help If Nominated." *Washington Post*, December 17, A11.

Bacon, Perry, Jr. 2000a. "Republican Presidential Primary Results." *National Journal*, 32(31) (July 29), 2502.

Bacon, Perry, Jr. 2000b. "Democratic Presidential Primary Results." *National Journal*, 32(33) (August 12), 2630.

Balz, Dan. 2000a. "Surplus Is Gore Team's New Focus." *Washington Post*, July 2. http://www.washingtonpost.com

Balz, Dan. 2000b. "Gore's Task Is to Show He's Different." *Washington Post*, August 6. http://www.washingtonpost.com

Barnes, James A. 2000a. "Primary Numbers." *National Journal*, 32(6) (February 5), 376–380.

Barnes, James A. 2000b. "McCain's Controversial Calculus." *National Journal*, 32(10) (March 4), 722–723.

Barnes, James A., Kirk Victor, Richard E. Cohen, and Peter H. Stone. 2000. "Battle Stations." *National Journal*, 32(7) (February 12), 454–459.

Berke, Richard. 2000. "McCain Romps in First Primary; Gore Wins, Edging Out Bradley: Voters Stun Bush." *New York Times*, February 2, A1, A17.

Buell, Emmett. 1996. "The Invisible Primary." In William G. Mayer, ed., *In the Pursuit of the White House: How We Choose Our Presidential Nominees*. Chatham, NJ: Chatham House, 1–43.

"Campaign 2000—Early Returns: Network News Coverage of the Campaign Preseason." 1999. *Media Monitor*, 13 (November–December). http://www.cmpa.com/Mediamon/mm111299.htm

"Campaign 2000 Fund-raising." 2001. http://cnn.com/ELECTION/resources/fec.reports/

"Campaign 2000—The Primaries: TV News Coverage of the Democratic and GOP Primaries." 2001. *Media Monitor*, 14 (March–April). http://www.cmpa.com/Mediamon/mm1112999.htm

Cannon, Carl M. 2000. "A Rough Ride for Reform." *National Journal*, 32(5) (January 29), 320–323.

Cantor, Joseph. 2001. "Campaign Finance in the 2000 Federal Elections: Overview and the Estimate of the Money Flow." *Congressional Research Service Long Report for Congress*, RL30884 (March 16), 1–18.

Coleman, Kevin. 2001. "Voting in Primary Elections: State Rules on Participation." *Congressional Research Service Long Report for Congress*, RL30441 (July 11), 1–11.

Coleman, Kevin, Joseph Cantor, and Thomas H. Neale. 2000. "Presidential Elections in the United States: A Primer." *Congressional Research Service Long Report for Congress*, RL30527 (April 17), 1–48.

Cook, Charlie. 2000a. "Don't Bet on Any Landslides in November." *National Journal* 32(5) (January 29), 344–345.

Cook, Charles E., Jr. 2000b. "Bush's Secret Weapon: Congress." *New York Times*, February 24, A27.

Cook, Charlie. 2000c. "When Will McCain Run a National Campaign?" *National Journal*, 32(9) (February 26), 648.

Dao, James. 2000. "Saying It Is 'Time for Unity,' Bradley Steps Aside." *New York Times*, March 10, A16.

"Demo and GOP Caucuses: Iowa." 2000. www.cnn.com/ELECTION/2000/primaries/IA/poll.html

"Democratic Primary: State Polls." 2000. http://nationaljournal.com. Turn to the Poll Track submenu for data on Democratic nomination preferences by states for 1999 and 2000.

"Dem. Primary: New Hampshire." 2000. www.cnn.com/ELECTION/2000/primaries/WH.dem.html

Dowd, Matthew. 2001. "Comments at the Annenberg School of Communication Election Debriefing, University of Pennsylvania, February 10.

Edsall, Matthew. 2000. "Times May Be Wrong for Bradley's Liberal, Multiracial Strategy." *Washington Post*, February 9, A8.

Fenoglio, Gia. 2000. "At the Races." *National Journal*, 32(2) (January 8), 116–117.

Firestone, David. 2000. "Campaign Briefing: The South." *New York Times*, March 10, A16.

Frankovic, Kathleen. 2001. "Comments at the Annenberg School of Communication Election Debriefing, University of Pennsylvania, February 10.

"General Election: National Polls." 2000. http://nationaljournal.com. Turn to Poll Track submenu for the national trial heat polls for both 1999 and 2000.

"General Election: State Polls. 2000. http://nationaljournal.com. Turn to Poll Track submenu. This source covers the trial heat polls for the various states for 1999.

Germond, Jack and Jules Witcover. 2000a. "Will Distortions Win for Al?" *National Journal*, 32(3) (January 15), 196.

Germond, Jack and Jules Witcover. 2000b. "Granite State, Ho!" *National Journal*, 32(4) (January 22), 272.

Germond, Jack and Jules Witcover. 2000c. "The Politics of the Calendar." *National Journal*, 32(6) (February 5), 432.

Germond, Jack and Jules Witcover. 2000d. "The Maginot Line Looked Impregnable Too." *National Journal*, 32(7) (February 12), 501.

Germond, Jack and Jules Witcover. 2000e. "Why South Carolina Isn't the End of It." *National Journal*, 32(8) (February 19), 580.

Germond, Jack and Jules Witcover. 2000f. "Now Comes the Hard Part." *National Journal*, 32(9) (February 26), 649.

Germond, Jack and Jules Witcover. 2000g. "And For the Losers . . ." *National Journal*, 32(11) 816.

Gigot, Paul. 2000. "A Vote for Character." *Wall Street Journal*, February 3. www.opinionjournal.com

Glasser, Susan B. 2000. "Bush Raised $69 Million, Spent $37 Million in '99." *Washington Post*, February 1, A4.

"GOP Presidential Primary: Ohio." 2000. www.cnn.com/ELECTION/primaries/OH/poll.rep.html

"GOP Primary: New Hampshire." 2000. www.cnn.com/ELECTION/2000/primaries/NH/poll.rep.html

"GOP Primary: South Carolina." 2000. www.cnn.com/ELECTION/2000/primaries/SC/poll.rep.html

Hadley, Arthur. 1976. *The Invisible Primary*. Englewood Cliffs, NJ: Prentice-Hall.

Holland, Keating. 1999. "Polls: Tight Race in New Hampshire; Bush Well Ahead in South Carolina." November 26. www.cnn.com/AllPolitics/stories/1999/11126/polls/index.html

Jacobson, Gary C. 1980. *Money in Congressional Elections*. New Haven, CT: Yale University Press.

Jamieson, Kathleen Hall. 1992. *Dirty Politics: Deception, Distraction, and Democracy*. New York: Oxford University Press.

Kendall, Kathleen E. 2000. *Communication in the Presidential Primaries: Candidates and the Media, 1912–2000*. Westport, CT: Praeger.

McKinnon, Mark. 2001. "Comments at the Annenberg School of Communication Election Debriefing," University of Pennsylvania, February 10.

Milbank, Dana. 2001. *Smashmouth*. New York: Basic Books.

Mitchell, Alison. 2000a. "Concentrating on One State Was the Key for McCain." *New York Times*, February 2, A17.

Mitchell, Alison. 2000b. "McCain Quits Race But Stops Short of Endorsing Bush." *New York Times*, March 10, A1, A17.

Mitchell, Alison. 2000c. "Birth and Death of the 'Straight Talk Express,' from Gamble to Gamble." *New York Times*, March 11, A8.

Morris, Dick. 1997. *Behind the Oval Office: Winning the Presidency in the Nineties*. New York: Random House.

Patterson, Thomas E. 1994. *Out of Order*. New York: Vintage Books.

Pew Research Center for the People and the Press. 2000a. "Notes from the New Hampshire Exit Polls: Bush Faces Stature Gap, Bradley a Gender Gap." February 2, 1–3. http://www.people-press.org/00watch2htm

Pew Research Center for the People and the Press. 2000b. "The Religious Landscape in Up-Coming GOP Primary States." March 1, 1–2. http://www.people-press.org/00watch3.htm

Pfau, Michael and Henry C. Kenski. 1990. *Attack Politics: Strategy and Defense*. New York: Praeger.

Popkin, Samuel L. 1994. *The Reasoning Voter: Communication and Persuasion in Presidential Campaigns*. Chicago: University of Chicago Press.

"Republican Primary: State Polls." 2000. http://nationaljournal.com. Turn to the Poll Track submenu for Republican nomination preferences by states for 1999 and 2000.

Schneider, William. 2000a. "The New Hampshire Wild Card." *National Journal*, 32(4) (January 22), 282.

Schneider, William. 2000b. "Why Al Pulverized Bill in Iowa." *National Journal*, 32(5) (January 29), 354.

Schneider, William. 2000c. "Riding to George W.'s Rescue." *National Journal*, 32(6) (February 5), 438.

Schneider, William. 2000d. "A Bounce off the Richter Scale." *National Journal*, 32(7) (February 12), 506.

Schneider, William. 2000e. "The Down Side of Riding a Wave." *National Journal*, 32(8) (February 19), 586.

Schneider, William. 2000f. "A Not-So-Super Tuesday for the GOP." *National Journal*, 32(11) (March 11), 826.

Schneider, William. 2000g. "Why the Gore-Bush Race Is Close." *National Journal*, 32(12) (March 18), 914.

Shrum, Bob. 2001. "Comments at the Annenberg School of Communication Election Debriefing," University of Pennsylvania, February 10.

Solomon, Burt. 2000. "Where's the Flock?" *National Journal*, 32(4) (January 22), 250–254.

State Exit Polls. 2000. www.cnn.com/ELECTION/primaries.html

"The Uses of Negative Campaigns" (editorial). 2000. *New York Times*, February 1, A24.

Chapter 4

Challenger and Incumbent Reversal in the 2000 Election

Craig Allen Smith and Neil Mansharamani

Years from now Americans will recall the 2000 presidential election as one of the closest in history, that it all came down to Florida, that thousands of ballots were recounted, that the courts decided the outcome, and that—for only the second time—the popular vote winner lost the presidency. But a focus on the postelection campaign diverts attention from the preelection factors that made the election so close—factors likely to recur in future elections.

This chapter analyzes the ways George W. Bush and Al Gore enacted the roles of challenger and incumbent in the 2000 campaign. It contends that situational factors favored a Gore victory on the basis of policy continuity, that Gore relinquished significant elements of the incumbent's advantage, that Bush seized upon Gore's error to refocus the contest, and that the campaign concluded as a contest between two challengers, with Bush providing more continuity and the more appealing changes. We conclude by proposing a revised typology of challenger and incumbent styles.

PREVAILING CONDITIONS FAVORED GORE

The 2000 campaign occurred amidst prevailing conditions that affected both candidates. In the eighth year of Bill Clinton's reign it was technically an open-seat election. America was at peace in 2000, and the administration had worked toward significant Middle East, Irish, and Balkan peace agreements. Equally important, the nation was experiencing an unprecedented period of sustained economic prosperity. Quinn (2000) points out "Jobs are easy to get [and] poverty stands at its lowest rate in 20 years. Homeownership is at record highs. Median, real household income has risen for five years straight, to a record $40,816 . . . [and] real wages have risen sharply since the mid-1990s" (57). Not surprisingly, the Clinton administration claimed credit for this economic progress, and Republicans claimed that they had achieved it despite Clinton. But their war of words was viewed against the backdrop of Clinton's legendary 1992 headquarters sign "It's the economy, stupid" and the popular support he received during his impeachment trial. Clearly, the Clinton-Gore administration had the benefit of presumption on the issue of economic progress. In addition to peace and prosperity the Clinton administration claimed as significant achievements the turn from deficit to debt reduction, reduced crime, and welfare reform. So although this was technically an open-seat election, Democrats sought continuity in the face of a Republican challenge.

The political conditions of peace, prosperity, reduced crime, and reduced debt normally favor candidates seeking continuity, and 2000 did not shape up as an election to "throw the bums out." Public satisfaction with "the way things are going in the United States at this time" stood at 69 percent in January of 2000 as the primaries began and at 62 percent just before the general election and fell no lower than 55 percent (Gallup, 2001a). Berke and Elder (2000) cite a *New York Times*/CBS News Poll showing that voters "like the direction the country is moving and are not eager to change course." Frolik (2000) found that in Ohio, a key battleground state, a Zogby poll found that three out of five likely primary voters said the country was "on the right track." In national polls, 60 percent of the public still approved of President Clinton's job performance, and 73 percent approved of his management of the economy (Berke and Elder, 2000). In short, the Clinton-Gore administration's record provided a generally favorable basis for Al Gore's candidacy (Gallup, 2001b).

If peace and economic progress favored Gore's candidacy, they presented a challenge for George W. Bush, who had to convince voters to change leaders. Bush's best opportunity was "Clinton Fatigue." Although Clinton's *job approval* ratings were high, his *personal* ratings revealed a much different picture. A poll in early November 2000 showed that three-fifths of likely voters in the states of Michigan, Pennsylvania, and Florida disliked Clinton as a person. Most Americans had grown tired of Clinton's character problems as well as the constant denying, defending, and spinning from his administration (Brownstein, 2000b). Moreover, in the years leading up to the 2000 election, congressional gridlock had become commonplace, and the partisan bickering over the Clinton-Lewinsky scandal and impeachment had left many Americans disgusted with the declining civility of politics in Washington. Public disgust with "old style Washington politics" offered an opportunity for a candidate distanced from the Washington culture and thus distanced from these problems. Familiarity with Washington thus became a disadvantage, and a candidate able to parlay familiarity with the hinterland into a source of change could have a significant resource.

Thus the prevailing political climate offered both opportunities and challenges for candidates Bush and Gore. Americans wanted a continuation of the good economy and many Clinton policies, but they wanted a president with better character and a change of tone in Washington. Thus, the candidate who could continue peace and prosperity with a more pleasing public persona would be well positioned for the campaign.

ANALYZING CHALLENGER AND INCUMBENT CAMPAIGN STYLES

The challenger and incumbent campaign styles have long been a staple of campaign analysis. The distinction is a natural one because most races pit an elected official interested in continuity against a bevy of contenders—some from within the party and some from other parties—who seek either innovative or restorative change. Trent and Friedenberg were among the first to realize that one's status as incumbent or challenger carried with it implicit rhetorical potentialities, and the first edition of their classic text *Political Campaign Communication* (1983) introduced their notion of challenger and incumbent campaign styles. Thus Trent and Friedenberg transformed the simple political roles of incumbent and challenger into rhetorical personae. A generation of students cut their analytical teeth on this distinction, with the result that practitioners have used it to strategize, scholars have used it to explain, and citizens have used it to understand five presidential elections.

This chapter uses the challenger and incumbent campaign styles to explain the peculiarities of the 2000 presidential campaign. Like Trent and Friedenberg, we will assume that any candidate can run a challenger or incumbent style campaign and that the styles can be mixed. In their second edition (1991) they wrote, "The incumbent and challenger categories are not absolute categories. Those candidates who are incumbents are not restricted to a specific set of incumbency strategies any more than challengers are confined to a specific set of challenger strategies" (85). The key to their hybrid style is "the abandonment of the essential purpose or thrust of incumbent or challenger rhetoric and abandonment of the responsibilities each has" (85–86). They base this new position primarily on Ronald Reagan's 1984 reelection campaign, in which the incumbent envisioned a future and used incumbent strategies only to support his campaign of challenge. Table 4.1 summarizes Trent and Frie-

Table 4.1
Trent and Friedenberg's Incumbent and Challenger Styles

Incumbent	Challenger
• Use the symbolic trappings of the office • Borrow the legitimacy of the office • Draw on the sense of competency associated with the office • Use the charisma of the office • Create pseudo events to attract media • Make appointments to office • Create task forces • Appropriate funds and grants • Consult or negotiate with world leaders • Manipulate the economy or issues • Get endorsements • Emphasize accomplishments • Create and maintain an "above the political trenches" posture • Use surrogates to advantage • Interpret and intensify a foreign policy situation in a crisis	• Attack the record of opponents • Take the offensive on issues • Call for change • Emphasize optimism • Speak to traditional values rather than changing values • Appear to represent the philosophical center of the party • Delegate personal or harsh attacks

Source: Trent and Friedenberg, 1995.

denberg's most recent (1995) typology of the strategic moves associated with the incumbent and challenger styles.

This study sought examples of the challenger and incumbent strategies in the Gore and Bush speeches, debates, and ads as well as in news commentary about them. Web sites for the candidates, the Commission on Presidential Debates, and news organizations were major sources of primary documents, as was the Stanford Mediaworks Ebook *In Their Own Words*. Four questions guided analysis. The first two questions were intuitive:

- Which incumbent strategies did incumbent Gore emphasize and which did he minimize?
- Which challenger strategies did challenger Bush emphasize and which did he minimize?

The other two questions were counterintuitive:

- Which challenger strategies did incumbent Gore emphasize and which did he minimize?
- Which incumbent strategies did challenger Bush emphasize and which did he minimize?

Although we anticipated that each candidate would use the strategies appropriate to his political role, the results permit analysis of the personae set forth by the two campaigns.

GORE RELINQUISHES INCUMBENCY

Trent and Friedenberg quoted political scientist R.F. Fenno to the effect that "incumbency is 'a resource to be employed, [and] an opportunity to be exploited' " (1983, 85). But our analysis suggests that Al Gore did not fully "exploit" this resource. The most obvious incumbent strategy that Gore failed to employ was the Clinton-Gore administration's record of accomplishment. Trent and Friedenberg argue:

> One of the strategies that form the core of the incumbency style is emphasizing accomplishments. Candidates must be able to demonstrate tangible accomplishments either in their first term of office if they are incumbent or in some related aspect of public service if they only assume the style. This is, of course, the reason that incumbents go to great lengths to list for voters all that they have done while in office. Thus the strategy is simple as long as the deeds exist. (97)

Gore had those deeds.

Gore was part of a twice-elected administration with successes previously discussed. Moreover, he had been at the center of most of the activity in the Clinton-Gore administration (Broder and Hennenberger, 2000). Stephen Hess of the Brookings Institution notes that "in the history of the vice presidency, Al Gore has a unique and remarkable record" (Broder and Hennenberger, 2000). But Gore minimized his record.

Although Gore mentioned the administration's achievements, he did not highlight them. Broder and Hennenberger (2000) wrote, "Gore has failed to capitalize on his significant record of accomplishment to make the case for election." Gore's failure was fourfold: He credited Bill Clinton and Bill Bradley rather than himself, he minimized the economic progress, he framed the election around future progress, and he did not link that future to Clinton-Gore's accomplishments. Let us examine each of those errors.

The first problem was that Gore failed to fully associate himself with accomplishments. This trend began during his primary contest with former New Jersey Senator Bill Bradley. Although Bradley was never the front-runner, he nevertheless forced Gore to expend resources—money, arguments, time, and perceived legitimacy—to win the nomination. Because Bradley challenged Clinton-Gore policies, Gore developed the habit of trying to preempt Bradley's criticisms. The result was that Gore began to reposition himself away from the Clinton policies he needed to invoke. By the time he had won the nomination, Gore was saying things like the following in Green Bay, Wisconsin:

> There is no more passionate voice for justice and equality in all of American than Senator Bill Bradley. . . . No one has done more to put campaign finance reform at the top of our national agenda. . . . Bill Bradley called our party and our nation to the cause of health care reform. . . . Nobody has spoken more eloquently about the need for our country to address the problem of child poverty. . . . I pledge to translate his plans and his words on child poverty into the deeds of this great nation in confronting the problem of child poverty in our country. I treasure Bill Bradley's support. He is a good Democrat, who speaks and stands for principles we all believe in. (Gore, 2000b)

Ideally, *Bradley* would have used those words to characterize *Gore*, who was, after all, their party's candidate. Alternatively, Gore could have similarly committed himself to *Clinton's* agenda even without mentioning his name. But by doing neither, Gore made Bradley the kind of internal problem that Democrats had avoided in 1996 (Smith, 1998). Gore beat Bradley but then elevated his stature. While many observers questioned the sincerity of Bradley's support for Gore, the point here is that Gore pledged himself to Bradley's leadership.

Similarly, Gore credited President Clinton with their current progress rather than stressing his own role. At the Democratic National Convention he personalized Clinton's role in the administration's economic record, saying: "For almost eight years now, I've been the partner of a leader who moved us out of the valley of recession and into the longest period of prosperity in American history. I say to you tonight: millions of Americans will live better lives for a long time to come because of the job that's been done by President Clinton" (Gore, 2000c, 1). Clearly, this was an opportunity to discuss their partnership, to use collective pronouns of which he was a part, or to associate himself with the accomplishment of these goals. Instead, he gave the lion's share of the credit to Bill Clinton. In effect, he invited voters to see him as a fresh candidate, lacking a record of personal policy achievement.

Second, Gore minimized the administration's accomplishments. In a June 13 address to the New York Historical Society, he said:

> No serious person can question the achievements of the 1990's. Now we must ask: Will we be better off still—in terms of our affluence and in terms of our spirit—four years from this day? I intend to win this election on behalf of the American people to see to it that the answer is yes. I intend to build even higher

on the foundation of the Clinton years. Because this is a turning point for America. (Gore, 2000a)

In his acceptance speech he said, "Crime has fallen in every major category for seven years in a row. But there's still too much danger and there's still too much fear" (Gore, 2000c, 9). He said during the first debate that "22 million new jobs, the greatest prosperity ever. But it's not good enough. My attitude is you ain't seen nothing yet. We need to do more and better" (Commission on Presidential Debates, 2000a, 19). These three examples illustrate Gore's insistence that the progress of their eight-year administration was insufficient to warrant his election.

The third problem was that Gore reframed the campaign around future progress rather than past accomplishments. In 1984 President Reagan asked, "Are you better off than you were four years ago?" and voters overwhelmingly reelected him. His question became a powerful way for both incumbents and challengers to frame elections as a contest between change and continuity. Gore was favorably positioned to ask Reagan's question. For example, Baker (2000) wrote, "The incumbent's advantage in times of economic abundance has been demonstrated repeatedly throughout US history, and, given that this is the longest expansion on record, Mr. Gore should have an unusually powerful story to tell" (12). But Gore told a different story. Rewording Reagan's question, he said, "The question is, will we be better off four years from now than we are today?" (Commission on Presidential Debates, 2000a) Gore's question refocuses the campaign around whether voters will believe Gore is the right person to create a better future—a much more challenging task than if Gore had argued that present economic success is sufficient to warrant voting for him, as Reagan had done.

Finally, Gore failed to adequately connect his proposals to the administration's successes. In his acceptance speech, for example, he used the metaphor of chapters in a book to link past and future:

Our progress on the economy is a good chapter in our history. But now we turn the page and write a new chapter. And that's what I want to speak about tonight. This election is not an award for past performance. I'm not asking you to vote for me on the basis of the economy we have. Tonight, I ask for your support on the basis of the better, fairer, more prosperous America we can build together. (Gore, 2000c, 2)

But pages and chapters do not occur in isolation; they are parts of a book. Gore's metaphor would have been apt, had it been encompassed in the larger metaphor of a book. Of course, such a book was available to him: *Putting People First* (Clinton and Gore, 1992). But his campaign rhetoric was less suggestive of a progression of new chapters than an anthology of short stories with a fresh start after each one.

In short, Gore gave credit to Clinton and Bradley while minimizing his own role, minimized the administration's accomplishments, emphasized the future as opposed to accomplishments, and failed to adequately link his proposals to the administration's success. This disadvantaged Gore. Trent and Friedenberg (1995) say that the strategy of emphasizing accomplishments is so powerful that incumbents go to "great lengths" to inform voters about their record (97). But Gore seemed to go to "great lengths" to avoid running on his record, either because his priorities were unlike Clinton's or because he could not differentiate between fatigue with Clinton and fatigue with Clinton's policies. Gore should have clearly and consistently argued that we had made historic progress during the last seven years and that we still needed to do more but that we cannot risk a return to policies that failed us. For example, Gore could have said something like this:

> Are we better off than we were eight years ago? You bet. In the last seven years we have made incredible progress. Crime, welfare, and teen pregnancy are down. Instead of budget deficits we have budget surpluses. I cast the tie-breaking vote that put our economy on the right track and led us to the greatest prosperity ever. And while I did not invent the Internet, I did sponsor important legislation that led to the development of the Internet, which many experts credit as part of the key to our amazing economic growth. This is what happens when government and business focus on the future and work together to benefit America. Now we must write the next chapter in our country's progress. We are finally in a position to invest in education, health care, and the economic and medical security of our senior citizens. We all need to ask the question, "Do we really want to go back to deficits, debt, a weak economy, and failure? Or shall we stay with surplus, less debt, a booming economy, and success?

Gore should have established continuity with the country's progress, argued for incremental change, and warned voters that going back to the same old policies would be disastrous.

Gore also mishandled four other strategies available to incumbents: endorsements by leaders, an "above the political trenches" posture, consulting with foreign leaders, and acting presidential. These failures are illustrated in the examples below. The Gore campaign did not highlight the endorsements of key leaders. Gore's decision to distance himself from Bill Clinton—a president who had vowed to campaign ceaselessly on behalf of his vice president—was much discussed during the final weeks of the campaign. This decision is understandable in light of Clinton's low personal approval ratings and Clinton fatigue. But Gore's only rival in the primaries, Senator Bill Bradley, was rarely seen campaigning with him. The campaign was well represented by the Gore and Lieberman families, but other Democratic officials were conspicuously absent. By failing to associate himself with other leaders, Gore lost an opportunity to legitimate his role as a leader.

Second, Gore took an unusual approach to maintaining an "above the political trenches" posture (Trent and Friedenberg, 1995). Trent and Friedenberg point out that statesmen do not directly attack their opponents, and Gore did refuse to attack Bush and Cheney on the basis of personal character. And his was not a narrow definition of character. The first debate began with moderator Jim Lehrer asking Gore about his attacks on Governor Bush's experience. One would expect an incumbent-style campaign to use that opportunity to remind viewers of Gore's 24 years of public service (8 as vice president) and to contrast that record with Bush's 6 years as governor, possibly even quoting Vice President Bush's 1992 comments about the irrelevance of Clinton's gubernatorial experience to the presidency. Instead, Gore said simply, "I have actually not questioned Governor Bush's experience. I have questioned his proposals" (Commission on Presidential Debates, 2000c). It is one thing to take the high road by attacking one's opponent with dignity and quite another to ignore the importance of experience.

In addition, Gore's decision to break from the Clinton administration and join Republicans and Cuban Americans who sought citizenship and asylum for six-year-old Elian Gonzales looked to some like pandering for votes from the influential Cuban American community in south Florida. Jordan (2000, E4) asserts that Gore "will have a hard time overcoming the damage done by the Elian issue, because it gave some credence to critics' arguments that Gore will do or say virtually anything to get elected." Gore's perceived pandering ran counter to the strategy of developing an image of someone who was "above" politics.

Third, Gore failed to interpret or intensify a foreign policy crisis. In 1988 Vice President George Bush used this strategy in a television ad that showed him shaking hands with Soviet President Mikhail Gorbachev while the announcer said, "There is no time for retraining." This advertisement implied that his opponent, Governor Michael Dukakis, would need retraining in the area of diplomacy. Gore could have used this strategy in 2000. For example, he might have used problems in the Middle East as an opportunity to say that he and Clinton had contributed to groundbreaking progress in the Arab-Israeli peace process, including the historic ceremony on the White House Lawn in 1993 (Stephanopoulos, 1999). He might have argued that the world could not risk changing policy at that time. And considering Bush's foreign policy inexperience, this strategy should have benefited Gore. But he did not use it.

Gore also missed an opportunity to establish his foreign policy experience during the first debate. Consider the following question and answer:

Moderator: Vice President Gore, if President Milosevic of Yugoslavia refuses to leave office, what action, if any, should the United States take to get him out of there?

Gore: I think we should support the people of Serbia and Yugoslavia, as they call the Serbia plus Montenegro, and put pressure in every way possible to recognize the lawful outcome of the election. The people of Serbia have acted very bravely in kicking this guy out of office. Now he is trying to not release the votes and then go straight to a so-called runoff election without even announcing the results of the first vote. Now, we've made it clear, along with our allies, that when Milosevic leaves, then Serbia will be able to have a more normal relationship with the rest of the world. That is a very strong incentive that we've given them to do the right thing. Bear in mind also, Milosevic has been indicted as a war criminal and he should be held accountable for his actions. Now, we have to take measured steps because the sentiment within Serbia is, for understandable reasons, against the United States because their nationalism—even if they don't like Milosevic, they still have some feelings lingering from the NATO action there. So we have to be intelligent in the way we go about it. But make no mistake about it, we should do everything we can to see that the will of the Serbian people expressed in this extraordinary election is done. And I hope that he'll be out of office very shortly. (Commission on Presidential Debates, 2000c)

There is no mistake in Gore's foreign policy answer; instead, his mistake was answering the question. By providing a solution he stepped out of the administration and put himself on level ground with the governor. A better incumbent answer would have been something such as:

Jim, this is a serious situation, and I'd like very much to state my position. But as part of the National Security Team I am engaged in sensitive discussion within the administration and with our allies, and it would be inappropriate for me to comment publicly. I'll yield my time on this question to Governor Bush.

Such an answer would have reinforced Gore's incumbency and demonstrated his ability to be discreet while reminding viewers of Governor Bush's freedom to propose actions for which he would not be accountable.

Fourth, Gore failed to use his consultations with foreign leaders to bolster his image as a world leader. When Gore did meet with Mexican President Vicente Fox he did not highlight it for campaign purposes. Nor did Gore make any foreign trips as vice president to meet with other leaders. Although Gore briefly mentioned having a phone call with the former prime minister of Russia during the second presidential debate, Gore significantly underutilized this strategy. He could have mentioned his work with Viktor Chernomyrdin to develop arms control agreements between the United States and Russia. Precisely because Governor Bush's foreign policy credentials were minimal, Gore should have used this opportunity to position himself as a world leader. By failing to employ these strategies, Gore failed to maximize his image as a credible and legitimate world leader.

Finally, an incumbent wants to seem presidential. This strategy requires the candidate to appear more a "statesman" than a political candidate. But in an effort to warm his image as a cold technocrat and to connect with voters in his town hall meetings, Gore began to dress casually. Night after night television news viewers saw one candidate in a suit and the other in a golf shirt and slacks. This not only allowed the governor of Texas to look the more presidential; it also invited viewers to wonder why Gore was wearing warm weather clothing for winter visits to Iowa, New Hampshire, Michigan, and other cold weather venues (after all, Dan Rather had worn a sweater under his sport coat to achieve the same effect on the *CBS Evening News*). As a result, Gore looked more like an average person than a statesman and potential president. After securing the Democratic nomination, Gore declared that he would no longer speak as the vice president but as himself. This disadvantaged him by relinquishing the legitimacy that the office provides, and he became just another aspiring politician.

Additionally, problems with Gore's veracity undermined his statesmanship. His claiming credit for the invention of the Internet, his penchant for details and stories (such as the girl who had to stand because of overcrowded classrooms or his claim that his mother's medication cost more than that for his dog) combined to invite reporters and Republicans to pursue verification. When several of those claims proved to be "exaggerated," Gore looked less than presidential. Moreover, Gore's frequent sighs and interruptions during the first presidential debate made him appear rude and possibly untrustworthy. These problems also supported Bush's implication that electing Gore would mean four more years of what people were most tired of—a president who lacked character and integrity.

This section has described a variety of ways in which Vice President Gore relinquished the role of incumbent by ignoring, underutilizing, or executing poorly the strategic potential of the incumbent style. As Gore rejected the strategies typically used by incumbents, he instead used the strategies of a challenger.

TWO CHALLENGERS SQUARE OFF

Gore as Challenger

As Vice President Gore became simply Al Gore, he employed three key challenger strategies: calling for change, taking the offensive position on the issues, and attacking the record of his opponent. He clearly stated that despite the country's progress he would focus on bringing change. As he said at the Democratic National Convention:

> And for all of our good times, I am not satisfied [2]. . . . We're entering a new time. We're electing a new President. And I stand here tonight as my own man, and I want you to know me for who I truly am [3]. . . . Let others try to restore the old guard. We come to this convention as the change we wish to see in America. (Gore, 2000c, 6)

Gore proceeded to call for change in three areas: He vowed to fight the powerful special interests, he outlined new goals with specific plans toward their attainment, and he called for changes in our culture. The important point is that he characterized all three as changes—apparently away from the Clinton-Gore agenda.

Gore's first key theme for change was that he would fight for "the people" against powerful "special interests." Gore said :

> To all the families in America who have to struggle to afford the right education and the skyrocketing cost of prescription drugs—I want you to know this: I've taken on the powerful forces. And as president, I'll stand up to them, and I'll stand up for you. . . . This is not just an election between my opponent and me. It's about our people, our families, and our future—and whether forces standing in your way will keep you from having a better life. . . . We will fight for affordable health care for all—so patients and ordinary people are not left powerless and broke . . . big tobacco, big oil, the big polluters, the pharmaceutical companies, the HMO's. Sometimes you have to be willing to stand up and say no—so families can have a better life. (Gore, 2000c)

This is good old-fashioned populist rhetoric, and it is a staple of American political campaigns. But it sounds almost surreal coming from the incumbent vice president—especially one who grew up the son of a senator and served in the House, the Senate, and the White House. Gore uses the word "fight" 19 times in his acceptance speech, establishing the theme of him "fighting" for the American people as a challenger against the established order. His position invites people to ask why he has been unable to do so as vice president. His "fight" rhetoric also supported Bush's argument that there was too much partisan "fighting" in Washington. Further, Gore framed the election around the "people versus the powerful" rather than "staying the course against those who would pull us off course" as would a candidate using the incumbency-style strategies.

Second, Gore called for change by outlining new goals and specific plans for their attainment. He makes it clear that he wants to present specific plans for many issues. It is important to bear in mind that Clinton ran in 1992 on the basis of a plan and a series of multipoint plans.

But Clinton framed his plans with a political jeremiad (Smith, 1994), the essence of which was that America had always been the greatest nation in the world because we believed in two things: Tomorrow will be better than today. And, Each American has a personal moral responsibility to make it so. America was in trouble in 1992, said Clinton, because the Reagan-Bush administration was afraid to change in a world that was changing fast. A Clinton-Gore administration would restore America's greatness by making change, by putting people first, and by implementing a series of multipoint programs. But in 2000 Gore offered no comparable framework for his proposals.

Unlike Clinton, Gore often seemed to offer specifics for the sake of offering specifics. In the process he seemed to invite critics, opponents, and voters to check his specifics. He said at the Democratic National Convention: "I'm here to talk seriously about the issues. I believe people deserve to know specifically what a candidate proposes to do. I intend to tell you tonight. You ought to be able to know, and then judge for yourself" (Gore, 2000c). This created a difficult situation for Gore. His audience could find him (1) more specific than Bush (who had set no such standard) but less specific than promised, (2) specific but inaccurate or impractical, or (3) specific and accurate. The odds were against him.

Gore announced goals for his administration that could not meet the test of specificity he set for them. He supported "revers[ing] the silent tide of global warming" (Gore, 2000c, 4) by moving beyond "the current technologies to have a whole new generation of more efficient, cleaner, energy technology" (Commission on Presidential Debates, 2000a, 6). He supported making "every school in America . . . a good place to get a good education" (Commission on Presidential Debates, 2000c), passing a "strong Patients' Bill of Rights" (Commission on Presidential Debates, 2000c 7), making "high-quality universal pre-school—available to every child, in every family, all across this country," and "cut[ting] the crime rate year after year—every single year throughout this decade" (Gore 2000c, 9). Where Clinton's jeremiad would have framed those goals as ways to put people first and to make change, Gore asked us to assess them with respect to the insatiable monster of specificity.

Finally, Gore called for change in American culture. Gore told us, "We must challenge a culture with too much meanness, and not enough meaning." He goes on to pledge that as president he "will stand with you for a goal that we share: to give more power back to parents, to choose what your own children are exposed to, so you can pass on your family's basic lessons of responsibility and decency" (Gore, 2000c, 2). Gore's message is that of an outsider. Gore is arguing that conditions in America are not what they should be and that we as a nation need to do better.

The second challenger strategy that Gore used was taking the offensive position on the issues. Rather than protecting the incumbents' fortress, Gore attacked Bush's policies. Gore charged that Bush would "take taxpayer money away from public schools" (Commission on Presidential Debates, 2000a), "wreck our good economy" by giving a "huge tax cut for the wealthy at the expense of everyone else," and "strip one out of every six dollars from the Social Security trust fund" (Gore, 2000c). He also charged that Bush would "destroy precious parts of America's environment" and "appoint justices [that would] overturn a woman's right to choose" (Commission on Presidential Debates, 2000a, 6). This was perhaps Gore's most effective strategy of the campaign because of the unpopularity of several of Bush's proposals.

Finally, Gore attacked Bush's Texas record. Gore relished his command of the facts and treated the Texas experience as a predictor of presidential performance:

> Texas ranks 49th out of 50 states in health care—in children with health care. 49th for women with health care, and 50th for families with health care. . . . Governor [Bush] opposed a measure to expand the number of children that would be covered. And instead directed the money toward a tax cut, a significant part of which went to wealthy interests. I believe there are 1.4 million children in Texas who do not have health insurance. (Commission on Presidential Debates, 2000b)

Gore also attacked Bush's environmental record: "Houston has just become the smoggiest city in the country. And Texas is number one in industrial pollution" (Commission on Presidential Debates, 2000b). By attacking Bush's record, Gore hoped to gain the public's favor that he was the better presidential candidate, but he did so at the cost of enhancing Bush's experience. Importantly, attacking the Texas record acknowledged Bush's executive experience even as he was relinquishing his vice presidential credentials, thus leveling the playing field.

While Gore employed these challenger strategies he employed but mishandled three others: appearing to represent the party's philosophical center, speaking to the current values of the electorate, and "emphasizing optimism for the future" (Trent and Friedenberg, 1995). Many of Gore's policy positions had popular support and were consistent with the centrist New Democrat approach that the party used in 1992 and 1996, such as middle-class tax cuts, free trade, and the support of the death penalty. However, Gore's very anticorporate "champion the little guy" rhetoric, his almost enthusiastic and unconditional support for abortion rights, and large spending proposals did little to negate Bush's characterization of him as a big-government liberal. Gore's development of a more centrist theme would have better executed the challenger strategy while demonstrating continuity with the New Democrat approach of the previous seven years.

Gore failed to speak to the current values of the electorate by misperceiving voters' self-conceptions. According to Trent and Friedenberg (1995), a successful challenger "must have some understanding of the way in which people view themselves and their society—some understanding of the current tenets of the American Dream." In the 2000 election, most people in America viewed themselves as prosperous and were satisfied with the policies of the current administration. But Gore characterized them as a people suffering because of high drug prices, overcrowded classrooms, fear of crime, and big special interests. To combat these problems, Gore announced that he would "fight for the people." But if most Americans were satisfied with the current state of the nation, there were few crying out for someone to fight for them. Thus, Gore's "fighter" message was inconsistent with the mood of the country. Gore should have capitalized on the positive mood in the country by arguing that he had contributed to the current prosperity and had helped improve upon the situation left by the earlier Bush administration.

Gore also mishandled the challenger strategy of "emphasizing optimism for the future" (Trent and Friedenberg, 1995). Although he discussed his vision for a better America, his rhetoric had more despair than optimism. He talked about the "powerful drug companies" and the "wealthiest one percent" and how he would "take them on." But there was no indication of how doing so would create a better America. Indeed, if he were truly optimistic about the future there would be little need to fight. Ironically, Gore's lack of optimism undermined his potential to run successfully as either challenger or incumbent.

The Bush Challenge

George W. Bush used the challenger campaign style and attacked the Clinton-Gore record. "For eight years," he said in his acceptance address, "the Clinton/Gore administration has coasted through prosperity." Rather than making the most of the end of the Cold War, he said, "the Clinton/Gore administration has squandered it. We have seen a steady erosion of American power and an unsteady exercise of American influence" (Bush, 2000a). Bush took the "offensive position on the issues" by attacking Gore's proposals, as in this late September speech:

> My opponent has a plan for the surplus as well. He is proposing the largest increase in federal spending in 35 years—since the presidency of Lyndon Johnson. Over two hundred new or expanded federal programs. An estimated 20 to 30 thousand new Washington bureaucrats. Four hundred and twelve new regulations on Medicare—a plan that could double the size of the current bureauc-

racy. More IRS agents—because targeted tax cuts mean targeted audits. All this could amount to over $2 trillion in bigger government over 10 years—costing about $20,000, on average, for every household. (Bush, 2000b)

He took a similar tack in the first debate, observing:

[Gore's] plan is three times larger than President Clinton's proposed plan eight years ago. It is a plan that will have 200 new programs—expanded programs and creates 20,000 new bureaucrats. It empowers Washington. My vision is to empower Americans to be able to make decisions for themselves in their own lives. (Commission on Presidential Debates, 2000a)

Clearly, Bush was willing to challenge both the administration's record and Gore's proposals.

But Bush attacked by taking peace and prosperity for granted and calling mostly for incremental change. This was important because attacks based on the Clinton-Gore record could have resurrected the concerns that had led to Clinton's defeat of Bush's father. Instead, Bush generally embraced the Clinton-Gore agenda, minimized their accomplishments, and characterized their leadership as ineffective. "This administration had its chance," Bush said four times during his acceptance speech. "They have not led. We will" (Bush, 2000a).

He was therefore able to use the recovery as a rationale for tax cuts even as he denied credit to the administration. His most prominent such statement occurred in his acceptance address:

Prosperity can be a tool in our hands—used to build and better our country. Or it can be a drug in our system—dulling our sense of urgency, of empathy, of duty. Our opportunities are too great, our lives too short, to waste this moment. So tonight we vow to our nation. We will seize this moment of American promise. We will use these good times for great goals. (Bush, 2000a)

He detailed his approach in a September 28 speech on "Maintaining Prosperity." "Our government has a surplus, and our nation has a choice," said Bush. "Will we use that money wisely, or will we spend it on permanently larger government?" (Bush, 2000b). He described the $4.6 trillion surplus "as an opportunity to protect and extend our present prosperity."

The Texas governor called for change in two key areas: improved working relationships between the parties and effective leadership and moral character in the White House. He called for change in working relationships by saying that "it's time to get somebody in Washington who is going to work with both Republicans and Democrats to get some positive things done when it comes to our seniors." Bush also characterized the administration as rudderless and inactive by charging that "this administration has failed to [reform Medicare]," that it was time for a "new administration to deal with the energy problem [source]," and that "this administration continues on the same old path with the same old programs—while millions are trapped in schools where violence is common and learning is rare" (Bush, 2000a). Bush also suggested that the administration lacked honor and integrity. In his acceptance address he reflected: "Our current president embodied the potential of a generation. So many talents. So much charm. Such great skill. But, in the end, to what end? So much promise, to no great purpose" (Bush, 2000a). In the third debate, Bush argued that the country needs "someone in the White House who will tell the truth" (Commission on Presidential Debates, 2000c).

Bush represented the philosophical center of the political party because he took the centrist positions on issues such as education, abortion, and health care. Importantly, he often blended values and themes that are often seen as disparate, as he did in a December 1999 speech: "We believe in the profit motive—and in the Golden Rule. We are a land of rugged individualists—who are committed to a common good. We want a prosperity as broad and diverse as America itself" (Bush, 1999).

This is the blending of contradictions that Clinton had accomplished with his jeremiad. Also like Clinton in 1992, Bush talked about making abortion more rare rather than trying to ban it altogether. His moderate position on abortion was significant because it invited pro-choice Republican women—an issue audience overlooked for many years—to vote for Bush. In addition, he departed from previous presidential campaigns with a Republican platform that did not advocate the elimination of the federal departments of Commerce, Health and Human Services, Energy, and Education. Appearing to represent the philosophical center was important for Bush because many voters were disturbed by the harshness of the conservative tone of the Republican Party in recent years. Because many voters had developed unfavorable impressions of Newt Gingrich, Pat Buchanan, and those associated with Clinton's impeachment, Bush had to align himself with the more moderate voices in the party.

Bush emphasized optimism for the future through one of the central themes of his campaign: restoring "honor and integrity to the White House." He also conveyed optimism by promising a new tone of civility in Washington, D.C. when he took the White House. This provided a message of hope for those who had tired of the partisan bickering in Washington, even if his party deserved much of the blame for that bickering.

BUSH SEIZES INCUMBENCY

Although Bush employed key challenger strategies well, his task in defeating Gore was still formidable. Trent and Friedenberg point out that incumbents nearly always win and, as mentioned earlier, incumbents are significantly advantaged when citizens are generally satisfied with the country's direction. Significantly, the Bush campaign began to prevail upon the American people's general satisfaction with the administration's policies by developing plans and themes that embodied continuity. Unlike previous Republican presidential campaigns, Bush co-opted traditionally Democratic issues such as education, health care, Medicare, and Social Security. Bush also took a position similar to Clinton's and in contrast to Gore's by supporting the "don't ask, don't tell" policy on gays in the military (Stone and Moniz, 2000). Furthermore, the Republican platform dropped the controversial 1996 plank calling for the abolition of the Departments of Education, Energy, Commerce, and Housing and Urban Development, and Bush called for enforcement of existing gun laws (Toner, 2000). Furthermore, Bush praised the Clinton administration for downsizing government and for its general conduct of foreign policy. For instance, in the second presidential debate, he supported five separate Clinton foreign policy initiatives. Bush's "compassionate conservatism" discourse stood in stark contrast to the harsh tone of recent Republican presidential campaigns. While Bush tried to capitalize on the current policies, he also had to employ other incumbent strategies as well, such as consulting with world leaders, receiving endorsements by other leaders, emphasizing accomplishments, and taking an "above the politics" posture.

George Bush had to overcome the perception that he was underinformed and unprepared to conduct foreign policy. He did so by using the incumbent strategy of consulting with world leaders. Bush met with newly elected Mexican President Vicente Fox and used it to convey a sense of legitimacy. In addition, he discussed his conversation with Fox in the first presidential debate:

> We also need to have a hemispheric energy policy where Canada, Mexico, and the United States come together. I brought this up recently with the newly elected president in Mexico, he's a man I know from Mexico. I talked to him about how best to expedite the exploration of natural gas in Mexico and transport it up to the United States so we become less dependent on foreign sources of crude oil. (Commission on Presidential Debates, 2000a)

Although Bush and Gore both met with President Fox, Bush got more mileage out of the meeting by using it discursively to enact his preparedness for foreign policy leadership.

Bush also used endorsements by other leaders to establish his legitimacy. He had a photo opportunity by holding hands with retired General Norman Schwarzkopf and former Joint Chiefs of Staff chairman Colin Powell, two highly respected military heroes. Such events demonstrated their trust and support for him and their regard for him as a competent leader in foreign policy and military affairs. Bush also mentioned his endorsement by Powell and Schwarzkopf in the first presidential debate, saying "I was honored to be flanked by Colin Powell and General Norman Schwarzkopf [who] recently stood by my side and agreed with me" (Commission on Presidential Debates, 2000a).

Additionally, all Republican governors publicly endorsed Bush during the last two weeks of the campaign. They stood behind him as part of their "Barnstorm for Reform" campaign. Former President Bush also went out on the stump for his son. Even John McCain, Bush's chief rival in the primaries, appeared publicly and enthusiastically with Bush. McCain's endorsement was significant because of his appeal to many independent and Democratic voters. Bush even picked up a late endorsement from Ross Perot—an endorsement that did little to help Reform Party candidate Pat Buchanan, whose campaign had the potential to cost the Republicans important electoral votes in close states.

Bush spoke frequently about his accomplishments in Texas. In his acceptance speech, for example, Bush said:

> So we improved our schools, dramatically, for children of every accent, of every background. We moved people from welfare to work. We strengthened our juvenile justice laws. Our budgets have been balanced, with surpluses, and we cut taxes not only once, but twice. We accomplished a lot. I don't deserve all the credit, and don't attempt to take it. I worked with Republicans and Democrats to get things done.... As governor, I've made difficult decisions, and stood by them under pressure. I've been where the buck stops—in business and in government. I've been a chief executive who sets an agenda, sets big goals, and rallies people to believe and achieve them. I am proud of this record, and I'm prepared for the work ahead. (Bush, 2000a)

Here, Bush attempts several incumbent moves. First, he emphasizes not only his policy accomplishments but also his ability to rise above partisan politics. He refers to himself as "Governor" and as a chief executive to convey the sense that he is a legitimate executive leader. This stood in stark contrast to Gore, who shed the vice president image to speak as "himself." This was important because, unlike Gore, he spoke with pride of his record and was willing to defend it. Some thought that Bush seemed to be running for reelection as governor of Texas, but doing so enacted confidence and executive character.

The final strategy of incumbency that Bush used was to appear to be "above the political trenches." Trent and Friedenberg (1995) argue that for a candidate to present himself as a "statesman" he or she has to appear "above the hurly-burly of politics." They have to present the image that the office has sought them rather than the other way around. Bush attempted to accomplish this image by arguing that the people called on him to run. He stated in his acceptance speech that "gaining this office is not the ambition of a lifetime, but is the opportunity of a lifetime." Bush also assumed an "above politics" posture by rejecting easy opportunities to attack Gore's character. When debate moderator Jim Lehrer asked him if he were satisfied with Gore's statement that he had never questioned Bush's experience, Bush replied:

> Yes. I take him for his word. Look, I fully recognize I'm not of Washington. I'm from Texas. And he's got a lot of experience, but so do I. And I've been the chief executive officer of the second biggest state in the union. I have a proud record of working with both Republicans and Democrats, which is what our nation needs. Somebody that can come to Washington and say let's forget all the finger pointing and get positive things done on Medicare, prescription drugs, Social Security, and so I take him for his word. (Commission on Presidential Debates, 2000a)

Of course Bush could have said something like, "Who is he trying to kid? His campaign has repeatedly impugned my experience and he must take responsibility for those attacks." But this approach enabled him to rise above the "finger pointing" and to discuss his executive experience while distancing himself from the proverbial mess in Washington.

CONCLUSIONS

This chapter has argued that the presidential election of 2000 came down to the postelection campaign in Florida despite a scenario that favored continuity over change. A number of challenger-incumbent dynamics served to tighten the race to the point where it fell to the courts to decide. This argument resonates with that of German (2001), whose content analysis of 197 photographs of Bush and Gore in the *New York Times* led her to conclude that Gore was portrayed as the challenger to Bush's incumbent. Our analysis leads us to three observations about the campaign.

The first observation is that Al Gore either relinquished or executed poorly most of the strategies available to incumbents. Gore seemed unable to differentiate between popular policies and a personally unpopular president. So rather than associating himself with the eight-year policy record of the Clinton-Gore administration, he distanced himself from it. Rather than bolstering the administration's accomplishments he minimized them and called for new changes. Rather than emphasizing progress since the last Bush administration he critiqued the status quo and promised to fight for change. By relinquishing the role of incumbent, Gore did something that Bush could not do for himself—he created a contest between two challengers for the post-Clinton presidency.

The second observation is that Bush executed challenger strategies at least as well as Gore. Bush read the mood of the country as satisfied with the direction of policies and charged that Clinton and Gore had been ineffective, while Gore described a nation fraught with problems and promised to fight for the people against the system. Gore proposed costly plans and pledged specifics, while Bush stressed civility, cooperation, implementation of existing policies, and tax cuts premised on the sound economy.

The third observation is that the Bush people took advantage of Gore's abandoning of incumbency. It was Bush who ran on his record. It was Bush who sought the endorsement of government and military officials. It was Bush, rather than Gore, for example, who backed the "don't ask, don't tell" policy on gays in the military. When Gore tried to soften his image with casual clothing, Bush looked all the more presidential. When in the second debate attention turned to foreign policy Bush endorsed most of the administration's decisions, while Gore suggested alterations.

Our three observations attest to the utility of Trent and Friedenberg's typology as an analytical tool as well as a prescriptive one. But it fails to fully address several features of the challenger and incumbent styles. For example, Trent and Friedenberg's incumbent-challenger distinction is based on the link between one's political role and the discursive constraints and opportunities each affords. We believe that it is now important to identify three dimensions of the challenger and incumbent roles that provide important rhetorical topoi for campaigns. Those dimensions are insider-outsider, continuity-change, and persona (see Table 4.2).

The insider-outsider dimension of the challenger/incumbent typology concerns the candidate's location in the political universe. In its simplest form the incumbent works in the White House and the challenger works elsewhere. But of course "Give 'em Hell" President Harry S Truman won in 1948 by running as the challenger to the Republican Congress's Washington establishment, a script that would later guide the 1984 Reagan campaign.

The insider-outsider dimension, in turn, has positional and geographic components. One can be a positional leader or not—as when Ross Perot mounted his first presidential campaign without a party or legitimate political office. The "positional insider" stance—identifiable in the campaigns of Michael Dukakis and Bob Dole—is "I can do this job because I have credentials, experience, and access that will benefit those who

Table 4.2
The Dimensions of Incumbent and Challenger Styles

Dimension	Component	Incumbent	Challenger
Insider-outsider	Positional	• Use the symbolic trappings of the office • Borrow the legitimacy of the office • Bestow rewards and benefits • Meet with symbolic leaders	• Sympathizers who are positional insiders attack incumbent • Attack "old politics" of quid pro quo • Suggest incumbent has misused the position
Insider-outsider	Geographic	• Affirm relationships at the center of power • Preempt "out-of-touch" characterizations	• Turn distance from power center into populist appeal • Change beltway isolation
Continuity-change	Policy proposals	• Run on policy record • Offer incremental proposals • Connect proposals to record	• Call for change • Offer new policies • Differentiate proposals from incumbent's
Continuity-change	Policy discourse	• Portray the challenge as a threat to undo major accomplishments • Counterattack over legislative balance and states	• Attack the record as misdirected, inadequate, and counterproductive • Depict fellow partisans as having been the last line of defense against the incumbent
Personae	Managerial style	• Affirm one's competency in the office • Nurture doubts about challengers' competence • Use surrogates to advantage	• Redefine the expertise needed for the job • Establish superiority in the new expertise • Attack incumbent's competence
Personae	Personal conduct	• "Act presidential" • Use personal charisma • Elevate self relative to challengers • Nurture personal legitimacy	• Establish trustworthiness • Affirm traditional values • "Act presidential" • Establish level playing field with the incumbent

support me." The positional outsider—Jesse Ventura, Ross Perot, and Jimmy Carter—says, "I can do this job because I have no political/governmental credentials, I am not part of the problems that face us, and I have spent my working life understanding the real world and ordinary Americans." The geographic insider is a creature of Washington (or city hall or the state capital, as the case may be).

The geographic component of the insider-outsider dimension relates to the campaign's decision to situate itself. At one end of the continuum is Richard Neustadt's (1990) emphasis of the importance of Washingtonians to presidential success—a position that is today reflected in the equation of being "inside the Beltway" with being in the loop. The beltway stance implies that the barbarians are at the gates, anxious to destroy all that they are accomplishing. At the other end of that continuum is what Charles U. Larson (2001) terms the wisdom of the rustic—the claim to wisdom by those like Will Rogers, Harry Truman, and Lamar Alexander because of their distance from decision making. This rusticity often carries the presumption of purity as well as wisdom and has been offered often as an antidote to the quadrennial "mess in Washington."

In short, an insider would claim positional experience and familiarity with the geographic power center (whether accurate or not), whereas an outsider would identify a source of expertise apparently unrelated to the office sought and a geographic identity outside the beltway. Bush continually emphasized Texas to distance himself from Washington and his executive experience. For his part, Gore minimized his positional importance and aligned himself with neither Washington nor the hinterland but engaged in a populist fighting record that served neither purpose well.

The *continuity-change dimension* of the challenger/incumbent typology concerns the candidate's policy rhetoric. The first dimension is the actual set of policy proposals embedded in the candidate's rhetoric and the party's platform. Pundits and opposition candidates often characterize these "micropolicies" as "promises"—putting more teachers in the schools and more police on the street, restoring pride in the military, cutting taxes, and so forth.

The second component of the continuity-change dimension is the candidate's overarching discourse as a candidate of continuity or change—a persona that may or may not match the policy proposals. A discourse of change can urge us forward toward a utopian age or back toward a golden age, but it is unwilling to settle for things as they are. A discourse of continuity urges patience, incrementalism, and the risks of change. These personae are a mix of liberal/conservative ideology and power—liberals may like change, but not if it puts their policies at risk, and conservatives may oppose change but not their own initiatives. Ronald

Reagan personified the activist conservative, whereas Democrats' defense of Great Society programs illustrates retentive liberalism.

In short, a candidate of continuity would reiterate its goals and urge incremental pursuit of its agenda, whereas a candidate of change would articulate new goals and set forth a new agenda. In between the two archetypes we can identify candidates who cloak a lengthy list of policy initiatives in a rhetoric of continuity and those who urge major change without articulating the policies that would produce that change. Gore urged change rather than continuity despite widespread support for the administration's policies. Bush aligned himself with the administration's general conduct of foreign policy, supported (perhaps reluctantly) existing gun control and abortion laws, and pursued a course of incremental change. The differences between Gore and Bush in terms of continuity-change were minimal, with Gore seeming to be the candidate with grander goals and aspirations.

The *same persona–new persona dimension* draws our attention to the face and character of the administration. A positional incumbent can suggest that the next term will be similar to or different from the first term, and a challenger can suggest a new style or more of the same style. In 1988 George Bush was able to cultivate the impression that he would be the extension of the Reagan-Bush administration, partly with the help of Reagan speechwriter Peggy Noonan. Similarly, Lyndon Johnson's 1964 landslide election was attributable in part to the Kennedy holdovers and his "Let Us Continue" theme.

Normally, we would expect a challenger to critique the incumbent's persona and to call for a new style of leadership. For example, the Carter campaign described the Nixon-Ford administration as dishonest and pledged never to lie, the Reagan campaign characterized President Carter as overwhelmed by the demands of the office and pledged to take charge, and the Clinton campaign depicted Reagan's heir, Bush, as being afraid to change in a changing world. Embedded in these depictions is the incumbent's willingness and ability to use wisely the resources of the office for the good of the country. In 2000 Bush pressed for a persona change—from incivility to cooperation and from "making change our friend" to "compassionate conservatism." Gore's persona was unpredictable—would he be another Clinton, a casual everyman, a tax-and-spend liberal, a rude know-it-all, or some combination of them all? Bush presented a steady persona that contrasted with Clinton; in his effort to avoid Clinton's and his own plasticity, Gore presented too many personae.

The election of 2000 was not decided by the courts or the chads or even by Ralph Nader. It was an election that, situationally, was Gore's to lose—and lose it he did. He lost it by relinquishing the positional insider, continuity, and consistent persona advantages of the incumbent.

By doing so Gore made it a race between two challengers, and Bush was better able than Gore to present a case for change. More than that, Gore allowed Bush to claim elements of incumbency—a sound economy that permitted tax cuts, enforcement of existing laws and implementation of existing policies, and a consistent persona. By election day, many voters were able to prefer Bush to preside over an era of presumed peace, prosperity, and incremental change. Only then were ballots counted.

REFERENCES

"ABC, CBS Won't Carry Rival's Debates." 2000. *USA Today*, September 5. http://www.usatoday.com/news/e98/e2574.htm

Baker, G. 2000. "Can't Buy Me Love: Americans Have Refused to Give Al Gore the Credit for a Prolonged Economic Expansion." *Financial Times* (London), June 17, 12.

Berke, R.L. 2000. "Personality, Not Policy, Sways Voters in a Primary. *New York Times on the Web*, January 13, 1–4.

Berke, R.L. and J. Elder. 2000. The Electorate; Bush Loses Luster in a Poll as Gore Sheds Poor Image." *New York Times*, February 17, A1.

Broder, J.M. and M. Hennenberger. 2000. "Few in No. 2 Spot Have Been as Involved as Gore." *New York Times on the Web*, October 30. http://nytimes.com/2000/10/31/politics/31RECO.html

Brownstein, R. 2000a. "Washington Outlook, National Perspective: Gore Curiously Fails to Take Credit for Policy Achievements." *Los Angeles Times*, October 16, A1.

Brownstein, R. 2000b. "Gore Turns Down Offer by Clinton to Visit Critical States." *Los Angeles Times*, November 2, A1.

Bush, G.W. 1999. "A Tax Cut with a Purpose." Des Moines, IA, December 1. http://www.georgewbush.com/News/speeches/120100_purpose.html

Bush, G.W. 2000a. "Nomination Acceptance Speech, Republican National Convention." *New York Times on the Web*, August 3. http://www.nytimes.com/library/politics/camp/080400wh-bush-speech.html

Bush, G.W. 2000b. "Maintaining Prosperity." Green Bay, WI, September 28. http://www.georgewbush.com/News/speeches/092800_prosperity.html

Clinton, B. and A. Gore. 1992. *Putting People First: How We Can All Change America*. New York: Times Books.

Commission on Presidential Debates. 2000a. *First 2000 General Election Presidential Debate*. Boston: University of Massachusetts, October 3.

Commission on Presidential Debates. 2000b. *Second 2000 General Election Presidential Debate*. Winston-Salem, NC: Wake Forest University, October 11.

Commission on Presidential Debates. 2000c. *Third 2000 General Election Presidential Debate*. St. Louis: Washington University, October 17.

Fineman, H. 2000. "A Time for Prayer." *Newsweek*, October 23. http://www.msnbc.com/news/479668.asp

Frolik, J. 2000. "Ohioans Like Clinton Policies More Than Him." *Plain Dealer* (Cleveland), March 6, 1A.

Gallup Organization. 2001a. "Satisfaction with U.S. trend." April 1. http://www.gallup.com/poll/trends/ptsatus.asp

Gallup Organization. 2001b. "Presidential Ratings: Issue Approval for Bill Clinton." April 12. http://www.gallup.com/poll/trends/Ptissues_BC.asp

German, K. 2001. "*New York Times* Photographic Coverage of the 2000 Presidential Campaign: Assessing Factors of Attention, Credibility and Emotion." Paper presented at the Central States Communication Association Convention, Cincinnati, April 6.

Gore, A. 2000a. "Remarks to the New York Historical Society. June 13." *In Their Own Words*. Palo Alto, CA: Stanford Mediaworks Ebook.

Gore, A. 2000b. "Remarks. Green Bay, WI. July 13." *In Their Own Words*. Palo Alto, CA: Stanford Mediaworks Ebook.

Gore, A. 2000c. "Nomination Acceptance Address. Democratic National Convention. Los Angeles, CA." August 20. http://algore.com/speeches/sp_08172000_dnc.html

Jordan, R.A. 2000. "Gore's Got Something to Learn from His More Centered Rival." *Boston Globe*, June 4, E4.

Larson, C.U. 2001. *Persuasion: Reception and Responsibility* (9th ed.). Belmont, CA: Wadsworth/Thomson Learning.

Neustadt, R. 1990. *Presidential Power and the Modern Presidents: The Politics of Leadership from Roosevelt to Reagan*. New York: Free Press.

Quinn, J.B. 2000. "In the Voters' Pocketbooks: We're Better Off Now Than We Were Eight Years Ago. But for Al, Is It Better Enough?" *Newsweek*, November 6. http://www.msnnbc.com/news/482541.asp

Smith, C.A. 1994. "The Jeremiadic Logic of Clinton's Policy Speeches." in S.A. Smith, ed., *Bill Clinton on Stump, State, and Stage: The Rhetorical Road to the White House*. Fayetteville: University of Arkansas Press, 73–100.

Smith, C.A. 1998. "The Rhetorical Transformation of Political Coalitions: Bill Clinton, 1992–1996." In R.E. Denton, Jr., ed., *The 1996 Presidential Campaign: A Communication Perspective*. Westport, CT: Praeger, 229–264.

Stephanopoulos, G. 1999. *All Too Human: A Political Education*. Boston: Little, Brown.

Stone, A. and D. Moniz. 2000. "Next President Must Transform USA's Forces. Nation's Military Faces a Dual Challenge: It Must Be Able to Wage War and Keep Peace." *USA Today*, October 3, 17A.

Toner, R. 2000. "The Platform; Draft Platform for G.O.P. Softens Hard-Line Stances." *New York Times*, July 28, A1.

Trent, J.S. and R.V. Friedenberg. 1995. *Political Campaign Communication* (3rd ed.) Westport, CT: Praeger.

Chapter 5

One Nation, After All: Convention Frames and Political Culture

Rachel L. Holloway

Presidential nominating conventions in the United States are made-for-television campaign rallies designed to frame the coming election and position the candidate for the November election. Each party works to solidify its political base, reach out to undecided voters, and set the agenda for news coverage of its candidate. If all goes as planned, the conventions produce a bounce in the public opinion polls to launch the candidates into the fall campaign.

Reaching the public through the convention is increasingly difficult, however, because most citizens simply do not watch. According to a Pew Research Center survey, just 1 in 10 Americans, or approximately 13 percent, said they planned to watch all or most of the television coverage of the 2000 Republican convention; another 28 percent said they would watch some of the convention coverage ("Much Less Convention Interest," 2000). Reluctant to lose prime-time ratings and advertising dollars, the major broadcast networks offered less convention coverage in 2000 than ever before, although the range of cable coverage increased (Hodges, 2000). Nielson Media Research reported the lowest number of homes watching the Democratic convention since 1972 (Marks, 2000). Even fewer homes tuned in to the Republican convention each night than watched the Democrats (McDaniel, 2000).

Despite limited attention from television viewers, the Republican and Democratic conventions both produced the desired response in public opinion polls. Bush jumped from an 11-point lead to a 17-point lead immediately after the Republican convention (Newport, 2000). Gore rebounded strongly after the Democratic convention, moving into a 1-point lead over Bush (Morin and Deane, 2000). Bush established "gravitas," and Gore became "his own man," one with passion, as demonstrated by a notable onstage kiss. The Republican convention created images of inclusion and party unity. The Democrats effectively reshaped the media agenda, reorienting news coverage to focus on Gore's leadership ability and issues central to his campaign (Hershey, 2001, 57–58).

Thus, the political nominating conventions did produce results in the 2000 election. Yet determining exactly *what* produced the results is problematic. Wildavsky (1989) contends that an answer may rest in an understanding of political culture. Voters listen for the cultural assumptions that guide their worldviews. Even with fragmented attention and sound bite news coverage, they can identify fundamental ideas about the world consistent with the structure of social relationships they prefer. Inasmuch as nomination acceptance speeches are carefully constructed frames for the general election, rhetorical analysis of the speeches provides insight into the values, beliefs, and policies presented by each campaign. To the degree that candidates stay "on message," the general philosophy and appeals evident at the convention characterize their campaign discourse and may offer explanations of voter response and the outcome of the campaign.

In 2000, the close outcome and contentious resolution of the presidential campaign promoted perceptions of national division. Crotty (2001) reported that "minorities, women, liberals, Democratic party identifiers and the less educated favored Gore consistently. Males, whites, republican party identifiers, southerners, conservatives, and those with some college favored Bush" (14). Geographically, clear distinctions emerged. Gore voters lived in the Northeast, Mid-Atlantic, and Pacific Coasts. Bush voters lived in rural and suburban areas, primarily in the Midwest and South. On multiple measures, the nation split into what became a statistical tie.

Rhetorical analysis of the convention addresses suggests a different reading of the split. Much as Bill Clinton successfully captured Republican rhetorical territory in 1992 and 1996, George W. Bush's compassionate conservatism moved sharply into the rhetorical frame consistently held by the Democratic Party, pushing Gore to a more liberal position. With Bush's move to capture the middle ground, Bush and Gore actually asked voters without a strong party affiliation to choose between two forms of egalitarianism, progressivism, and populism. Thus, the closeness of the election outcome is as much a product of similarity as of difference.

This alternative reading of the campaign requires an explanation of American political culture as described in the works of Ellis, Wildavsky, and Thompson, among others. The cultural topoi then are used to analyze Bush's and Gore's acceptance addresses. The final section identifies the significant similarities in the candidates' positions as well as the key differences.

FRAMING AND POLITICAL CULTURE

Because neither the Republican nor the Democratic campaign can win an election with only the political base of its party, presidential candidates must secure the support of moderate, generally nonpartisan, and undecided voters. At the opening of the general election campaign, nomination acceptance addresses must convey a vision or worldview that will resonate with a broad constituency without repelling those loyal to the party. The primary objective of the convention is to frame the themes and issues of the coming election. Entman (1993) defines framing as a combination of selection and salience:

> To frame is to select some aspects of perceived reality and make them more salient in the communicating text, in such a way as to promote a particular problem definition, causal interpretation, moral evaluation and/or treatment recommendation for the item described. Frames, then, define problems—determine what a causal agent is doing and costs and benefits, usually measured in terms of cultural values; diagnose causes—identify the forces creating the problem; make moral judgements—evaluate causal agents and their effects; and suggest remedies—offer and justify treatments for the problem and predict their likely effects. (55)

The public's acceptance or rejection of a particular framing of a problem or situation depends on their prior experiences and beliefs. Through experience, individuals develop a preferred pattern of social relations—"how we wish to live with others and how we wish others to live with us" (Boyle and Coughlin, 1994, 192). These patterns, called a way of life in cultural theory, interact with a cultural bias or a set of shared values and beliefs about human society and the natural world. As people participate in the world, they express their perceptions and analysis of situations or pattern of experience; they give voice to their cultural bias. As interaction spreads among individuals, they come to represent common events, experiences, and judgments through a shared set of "cultural topoi" or "systematic line[s] of assumptions and arguments that reinforces a preferred pattern of relationships" (Leichty and Warner, 2000, 62). Each person builds what Kenneth Burke calls an "orientation" or "a bundle of judgments as to how things were, how things are, and how they may be" (Burke, 1984, 140). The orientation guides an individual's analysis of what is important in a situation and what can be ignored. It justifies and evaluates a concern, distributes responsibility and assigns blame, and thereby advocates a response. A cultural bias leads individuals toward patterns of social relations that in turn reinforce the cultural bias, including patterns of political choice. Previous studies have linked political cultures to public responses to risk, responses to environmental issues, and political ideology (Chai and Swedlow, 1998; Coyle and Ellis, 1994; Ellis and Thompson, 1997).

Cultural theory posits that the basic preferred patterns of experience and cultural bias are limited and can be described along two continua of social relations described first by Mary Douglas (1982). The "grid" continuum represents "the degree to which an individual's life is circumscribed by externally imposed prescriptions" (Thompson, Ellis, and Wildavsky, 1990, 5). In a high-grid social context, individual action is directed through institutionalized role classification. The rules governing interaction between boss and employee, husband and wife, governor and governed are explicit and nonnegotiable. People know their place and act accordingly. In a low-grid social context, relationships are negotiated between and among individuals.

The group dimension of social relations is "the extent to which an individual's life is absorbed in and sustained by group membership" (Thompson, Ellis, and Wildavsky, 1990, 5). The greater the group dimension, the more stringent the group boundaries become and the more an individual will be controlled by group expectations and norms. A low-group way of life emphasizes individual choice and self-interest.

The combined grid-group continua produce five dominant ways of life. Individualists form the low-grid–low-group quadrant in cultural theory and adhere to two ways of life. The first, competitive individualists, are guided by the key values of freedom, equality of opportunity, and reward for achievement. Individualists believe in the basic goodness of humans and are committed to the full development of each individual's unlimited potential. That is possible, they believe, only when individual liberty is maximized. They trust individuals to self-regulate and believe cooperation is best achieved through networks of voluntary, contractual relations among persons they perceive as equal in broad capacities such as rationality (Wildavsky, 1998, 118). As true optimists, individualists take risks to seek out opportunity. Often characterized by others as unconcerned for the common good, individualists would counter that personal success translates into societal success. The maxims "a rising tide lifts all boats" or "a poor man never gave someone else a job" express the idealized individualist perspective.

The second form of individualism, the autonomous individualist, is low group and low grid but rejects the relationships sought out by the competitive individualist. The autonomous individualist withdraws from social life, ideally to pursue an inner, spiritual life and to be one with Nature, thinking neither of the past nor of the future. The autonomous individualist, whether a hermit, a monk, an artist, or a writer, will live simply, reducing needs and working toward self-sufficiency (Leichty and Werner, 2000; Ellis, 1993, 140–148).

A high grid–high-group way of life produces a commitment to hierarchy. Those who accept a hierarchical way of life seek stability and security through the creation of order in the world. Hierarchists believe that human nature is flawed and must be directed through rules and structure in order to maximize the common good. Hierarchy creates and privileges authority and promotes values of deference, obedience, and sacrifice of individual interests for those of the group (Ellis, 1993, 95).

Relative to other nations, American political culture is not committed to hierarchy, although its proponents may be found in the nation's military tradition, organized religion, the patriarchal family, and the nation's organization of commerce, either historically on the large plantation or today in many modern corporations (Ellis, 1993, 95). For a hierarchist, bureaucracy serves to dampen and restrain self-interested, ambitious individuals. The term *civil servant* captures the hierarchical ideal of sacrifice for the common good. For all their emphasis on sacrifice, hierarchists accept capitalism as consistent with many of their goals. Social stratification, private property, and a merit-based reward structure create the order, stability, and incentives for discipline and hard work favored by adherents of a hierarchical worldview (Ellis, 1993).

One of the distinguishing characteristics in American hierarchical political culture is the development of noblesse oblige. The American hierarchical worldview instills in its privileged classes a sense of intellectual and moral superiority and a concomitant responsibility, obligation and duty to the public good (Ellis, 1993). Hierarchists turn to experts and heroic leaders who will use knowledge and government power to order the world in such a way as to advance the interests of all the people, especially those less fortunate.

A low-grid–high-group worldview is egalitarian. Egalitarians share the hierarchists' commitment to the collective (high group), but unlike the hierarchists, egalitarians believe humans are by nature good. They emphasize equality and community, make decisions by consensus, prize solidarity and loyalty, and favor participation as a guiding precept. Hierarchists create a beneficial social order through external proscriptions; egalitarians win assent through individual commitments.

In an egalitarian worldview, problems arise only when social and political institutions create inequality and individuals are corrupted through material status and power (Leichty and Warner, 2000, 65). Egalitarians work to secure justice and equality for those disenfranchised and oppressed by capitalism and hierarchy. For many egalitarians, government is a tool to promote equality, especially through regulating the negative effects of competitive individualism (Leichty and Warner, 2000, 66). They focus on the process of "harmonizing personal concerns with group welfare through discussion leading to consensus" (Wildavsky, 1998, 121). More than other ways of life, egalitarians express concern for the internal life of individuals, focusing on the quality of personal relationships and others' feelings. Egalitarians see no need for sacrifice per se because if uncorrupted by hierarchy or market stratification, humans will act supportively toward other group members.

Egalitarians traditionally are the champions of fatalists, who inhabit a high-grid–low-group way of life. Fatalists perceive life as directed by external forces that they can neither predict nor control. Their strategy is to cope with whatever comes, living day to day. They lack any sense of efficacy gained through social relationships. Fatalists believe cooperation fails because individuals sabotage collaborative efforts in order to gain advantage. Competition fails because victory is not won by hard work, honesty, or skill but by luck or more often deceit. Those who make the rules always win. Since fatalists have no influence in making the rules, they attempt to cope with whatever comes (Ellis, 1993, 132–133).

Political success rests in creating a set of themes and appeals that includes the cultural assumptions of each party's political base and stretches across cultural lines to form a constituency large enough to win the election. In recent elections, Republicans created a coalition of fiscal conservatives, who adopt a competitive individualist way of life, and social conservatives, who follow the hierarchical philosophy. Despite their somewhat opposed worldviews, both groups favor small federal government. The fiscal conservatives want limited regulation and intervention in the market economy, believing ultimately that government limits the ability of individuals to excel. Social conservatives are suspicious of government intervention in their private lives. Ellis notes that "contemporary fundamentalists express respect for authority in the family, school, church, and country, yet often evidence little trust in government and openly attack institutions such as the Supreme Court" (Ellis, 1993, 119).

The Democrats traditionally formed a cultural alliance between liberal egalitarians and the disenfranchised fatalists, turning to government to counter the growth of economic disparity and the oppression of hierarchy (Wildavsky, 1998; Ellis, 1998) Clinton, as a "New" Democrat, secured his base in liberal egalitarianism but adopted fiscal policy and a set of social values acceptable to moderates who, while not liberal, were increasingly suspicious of the rise of social conservatives within the Republican Party.

The 2000 presidential election produced a similar rhetorical shift, this time from the Right. By leaving the traditional home of both the fiscal and social conservatives, but adopting an egalitarian position that shared values of each, Bush's compassionate conservatism moved him into new rhetorical territory. At the same time, Gore moved away from Clinton's middle-ground strategy, invoking a populist rhetoric to unite the liberal elite and the partisan poor. The fundamental similarities outweighed the differences and produced a nearly perfect tie among voters.

BUSH'S COMPASSIONATE CONSERVATISM

Bush faced several challenges as he set the frame for the general election. He needed to establish his mastery of the issues and to appear "presidential." He needed to secure the support of key constituencies—fiscal conservatives who favored a small central government, privatization, and tax cuts; and social conservatives, especially the Christian Right, who viewed government as increasingly hostile to their values.

Bush's discourse appealed to both groups. Individualism, a value shared by egalitarians and competitive individualists, appeared as a central theme and was evident in Bush's references to people: "Every man and woman . . . every child . . . every family." When Bush spoke about the costs of prescription drugs, he promised to extend affordability to "every" senior. Although referring to groups, Bush's use of "every" and "each" throughout his speech elevated the individual's needs as primary ("George W. Bush Accepts," 2000. All subsequent references to Bush's speech come from this source.)

Bush also privileged individual ownership and choice. When he discussed Social Security, he spoke to seniors as individual workers: "[Y]ou earned your benefits, you made your plans." He offered younger workers a choice to invest payroll taxes privately, saying, "When this money is in *your* name, in *your* account, it's not just a program, it's *your* property" (emphasis added). He argued that "those who spend *your* tax dollars must be held accountable" (emphasis added). He said he would abolish the "death tax" so that "every family, every farmer and small business person, should be *free* to pass on their life's work to those they love" (emphasis added).

Bush advocated a reduction in taxes because the surplus is not "the government's money. The surplus is the people's money." Bush hit the key themes of the competitive individualist: choice, freedom, and independence to direct one's personal affairs without government interference.

Bush also voiced the concerns of those who embrace hierarchy. He emphasized a generational commitment, asking Americans to meet their obligations to their parents and grandparents and to future generations. He emphasized security, a key value of hierarchy, through his calls for a strong military and a missile defense. He argued from "principle," he said, noting that he would not need to take a poll to know his own mind. The externally imposed order of rules is an expression of hierarchy; being directed by inner convictions is egalitarian. He honored the role of parents and the family, called on schools to "support the ideals of parents," promised to provide safety to children through enforcement of gun laws, and promised to lead the nation "toward a culture that values life." He identified a range of issues and beliefs that would resonate with those who are socially conservative specifically and who embrace hierarchy generally.

Had George W. Bush said no more, his position would have created the coalition of conservatives across the competitive individualist and hierarchical cultures. Bush, however, was a "new" kind of Republican, an egalitarian one.

Bush's egalitarianism is revealed most clearly in his characterization of the nation's problems involving the most needy in society. For instance, he called poor educational performance a form of discrimination: "Too many American children are segregated into schools without standards, shuffled from grade to grade because of their age, regardless of their knowledge. This is discrimination pure and simple, the soft bigotry of low expectations. And our nation—and our nation should treat it like other forms of discrimination, we should end it." Such discrimination and lack of hope lead to fatalism, in Bush's view. Fatalism, in turn, is a sign of failed society and government. He conveyed his understanding of a growing fatalism through an interaction with a boy in jail:

> Toward the end of conversation, one young man, about 15, raised his hand and asked a haunting question, "What do you think of me?" He seemed to be asking, like many Americans who struggle . . . "Is there hope for me? Do I have a chance?" and, frankly, "Do you, a white man in a suit, really care what happens to me?" A small voice, but it speaks for so many. Single moms struggling to feed the kids and pay the rent. Immigrants starting a hard life in a new world. Children without fathers, and neighborhoods where gangs seem like friendship, where drugs promise peace and where sex sadly seems the closest thing to belonging. We are their country, too. And each of us must share in this promise, or the promise is diminished for all.

He says the largest lesson he learned growing up was that "everyone, from immigrant to entrepreneur, has an equal claim on this country's promise." Bush gives voice to an egalitarian commitment to equality and inclusion.

In Bush's philosophy, just as each person must be included in the promise of the nation, each person must participate in the response. He turned to two additional key principles of egalitarianism, participation and community. He says, "Big government is not the answer, but the alternative to bureaucracy is not indifference. It is to put conservative values and conservative ideals into the thick of the fight for justice and opportunity." He supported local control of local schools combined with accountability for federal tax support; he called for Head Start in all public schools and for tax relief for all Americans. But for the problems of entrenched poverty, Bush proposed federal funding for faith-based organizations to provide social services. He said, "[W]e will support the heroic work of homeless shelters and hospices, food pantry and crisis pregnancy centers, people reclaiming their communities block by block and heart by heart." In a true egalitarian spirit, Bush focuses on the internal life of the individual. The key to the future is giving children "moral courage." Government, Bush said, cannot enact the values of egalitarianism in this regard. He said government "can feed the body, but it cannot reach the soul. Yet government can take the side of these groups, helping the helper, encouraging the inspired." In what he calls the era of responsibility, individuals have a responsibility to community: "[E]ach of us has important tasks—work that only we can do." The market, hierarchical proscriptions, and government programs cannot meet society's need.

Bush's emphasis on the role of faith-based organizations in the nation and his calls for "each of us" to "love and guide our children, and help a neighbor in need" were welcomed by social conservatives, but the inclusiveness of his message was far broader, including "synagogues, churches, and mosques." In speaking of his own faith, Bush expressed a social gospel broadly practiced by members of the political Left as well as the Right: "I believe in tolerance, not in spite of my faith, but because of it. I believe in a God who calls us, not to judge our neighbors, but to love them. I believe in grace, because I have seen it. . . . In peace, because I have felt it. . . . In forgiveness, because I have needed it." Bush's interest in the internal life of individuals and the belief that change comes only from changing the "hearts and minds" of individuals are egalitarian beliefs. The action principle of egalitarians is "do it for love" (Leichty and Werner, 2000).

Another element that distinguishes Bush's worldview from competitive individualism is a distrust of prosperity. In Bush's philosophy, "prosperity with a purpose" elevates society; prosperity without purpose degrades society. Bush argued that prosperity without a purpose could be "a drug in our system—dulling our sense of urgency, of empathy, of duty." He accused the Clinton/Gore administration of coasting through prosperity and leading "downhill" toward moral bankruptcy. Not surprisingly, Bush used President Clinton as his symbol of squandered prosperity: "Our current president embodied the potential of a generation. So many talents. So much charm. Such great skill. But, in the end, to what end? So much promise, to no great purpose."

He argued that the "rising generations of this country have our own appointment with greatness" that does not "rise or fall with the stock market. It cannot be bought with our wealth." The generation that tested limits and improved the country in many ways, Bush said, also "lost its way" but began to come home when its members "held our first child, and saw a better self reflected in her eyes." To have goals, purposes, and duties and to live up to those values, Bush says, gives his generation the chance "to show we have grown up before we grow old." Through family and faith, Bush's generation had discovered "that who we are is more important than what we have. And we know we must renew our values to restore our country." The vision of the founders was centered on character: "They never saw our nation's greatness in rising wealth or advancing armies, but in small, unnumbered acts of caring and courage and self-denial." Read Bush's statement "[W]e cannot embrace the values of competitive individualism or of hierarchy alone." The foundation must be in subordination of self to community, motivated by caring and concern. In other words, egalitarian values provide the foundation of his new Republican vision.

Bush's rhetoric is in fact not new but draws on an egalitarian critique of competitive individualism found in progressivism. The progressive movement of the early twentieth century, led by social scientists such as Charles Horton Cooley, Jane Addams, and Mary Parker Follett, turned away from formal institutions and from the division of labor and specialization of the marketplace in favor of small, face-to-face communities as remedies both to isolation of the workplace and to the oppression of hierarchy. The Social Gospel movement of the same time believed public life should be guided by "brotherhood and love," fundamental principles of egalitarians and the exact words Bush used to describe the "compassion" of his conservatism (Ellis, 1993). Contemporary faith-based organizations are modern equivalents to the settlement houses and community centers in turn-of-the-century Chicago. Richard Hofstadter described progressivism as more than an effort to "recreate the old nation of limited and decentralized power, genuine competition, democratic opportunity and enterprise." It also idealized small town virtues of fraternity, equality, and civic participation" (cited in Ellis, 1993, 23).

Bush's focus on values, families, children, character, moral courage, sacrifice, security on our streets, and protection from threats abroad appealed to the spirit of hierarchy. His emphasis on individual freedom and choice, opportunity, and the optimistic promise of the future expressed the spirit of competitive individualism. Yet his position was neither. Ellis (1998) notes that multiple voices can be heard in progressivism: "If one focuses on its commitment to individual conscience and autonomy, its adherents seem to be forerunners of a modern individualistic age. But if attention is turned to its vision of the individual subordinated to the collective will, progressivism seems to point backward to a bygone age of hierarchy" (2). What makes the progressive strain of egalitarianism so politically appealing is its connections to competitive individualism and hierarchy and its rejections of the extremes embedded in each. Both competitive individualism and egalitarianism focus on human nature as good, on individual self-determination, and on free will. Yet egalitarianism rejects competition and the fluid, short-term associations of the market.

At the same time, egalitarianism shares a commitment to group affiliation with hierarchy. The individual is subordinated to the needs of the group, rejecting selfish and undirected ambition of competitive individualism. Yet, as an egalitarian, Bush rejects distinctions of class, race, and religion embedded in hierarchy and embraces values of equality and justice, calling for and representing inclusion in his own message and in the symbolism of the convention. Change comes not from external proscriptions but from internal convictions. Bush's vision integrates individual autonomy with a commitment to community, responding to society's problems without increasing the role of federal government.

GORE'S POPULISM

Gore launched his general election campaign with populist rhetoric, a second dominant strain of egalitarian rhetoric. Captured in the phrase "I'm for the people, not the powerful" Gore adopted a position favored by Democrats, in varying degrees, throughout the twentieth century. Populism emerged first in the late 1800s as egalitarians abandoned hopes that a self-regulating market would create and support equality among all people. Taking a different egalitarian path from the progressives, populists turned to government to counter the marketplace, stating that "the powers of government—in other words, of the people—should be expanded . . . as rapidly and as far as the good sense of an intelligent people and the teachings of experience shall justify, to the end that oppression, justice, and poverty shall eventually cease in the land" (Ellis, 1993, 54).

The populists' use of government was primarily targeted at those in greatest need, the fatalists trapped in poverty and discrimination. Gore's nomination address adopts this perspective explicitly. The hand of the market, competitive individualism, has trapped the less fortunate in society: "[P]owerful forces and powerful interests stand in your way, and the odds seem stacked against you, even as you do what's right for you and your family." Gore says that the election is not "just between my opponent and me. It's about our people, our families and our future and whether forces standing in your way will keep you from living a better life." Gore focuses on families that "work" and "struggle," using the phrase "working families" eight times in his speech ("Vice President Al

Gore's Walk," 2000. All subsequent references to Gore's speech are available in this document.)

Using a now-common strategy, Gore invited people he met on the campaign trail to the convention and then featured their stories in his speech. He recounted Mildred Nystel's dream of sending her daughter to college and finished her story by promising to fight for targeted tax cuts "to help working families save and pay for college." He then says that "*they* need *our* help" (emphasis added).

In a second story, Gore told the story of Jacqueline Johnson, who after years working as a medical assistant could not afford prescription medicines. Gore promised, "I will fight for a prescription drug benefit for all seniors under Medicare. It's just wrong for seniors to have to choose between food and medicine, while the big drug companies run up record profits. That is wrong."

The powerful forces and interests against which working families struggle include "big tobacco, big oil, the big polluters, the pharmaceutical companies, the HMOs." The president, says Gore, is "charged with the responsibility of fighting for all the people, not just the people of one state or one district, not just the wealthy or the powerful. All the people, especially those who need a voice, those who need a champion, those who need to be lifted up so they are never left behind." And Gore then promised to fight, using the word or some variation twenty times.

Gore's fight would be for federal government action to respond to the problems of the powerless. He promised to fight for affordable health care, to double the federal investment in medical research, to save and strengthen Social Security and Medicare, to make the greatest single investment in education since the GI bill, to provide universal preschool, to offer a range of tax reforms targeted at working families, to expand child care, after-school care, and family and medical leave, to increase the minimum wage, to increase community policing, to support a meaningful Patient's Bill of Rights, to offer a new prescription drug benefit under Medicare, to pass hate crimes legislation and crime victims' bill of rights, to preserve affirmative action and a woman's right to choose, and to secure drug-free and gun-free schools. In the voice of modern egalitarianism, Gore offered government programs to respond to the oppression, injustice, and suffering caused by the ambition of the powerful. He promised to use government to defend and extend the rights of citizens. In fact, Gore used the word "rights" six times. Perhaps just as significantly, he distinguished between the "right kind of education," the "right" kind of tax relief for the "right people" and identified the actions of the powerful, and his opponent, by implication as "wrong."

In advocating government programs and planning, Gore turned to the external proscriptions and order of hierarchy. At several points in the speech, Gore reaches across the cultural line to those who embrace hierarchy more explicitly, most notably in acknowledging concerns about American popular culture:

> To all the families—to all the families who are struggling with things that money can't measure, like trying to find a little more time to spend with your children or protecting your children from entertainment that you think glorifies violence and indecency, I want you to know I believe we must challenge a culture with too much meanness and not enough meaning. And as president, I will stand with you for a goal we share: to give more power back to parents; to choose what your own children are exposed to, so you can pass on your family's basic lessons of responsibility and decency. The power should be in your hands.

In addition, Gore's appeals to security and stability may appeal to those who favor central and bureaucratic authority, supported by expertise and planning. Gore's characterization of Bush's proposals as "risky schemes" matches a hierarchical worldview. Hierarchists distrust the fluid negotiations of competitive individualists; the hierarchical worldview favors stability and security created through order and bureaucracy as a corrective to the ambition and risk embedded in fluid and voluntary negotiation of competitive individualism. His appeals to physical security (community policing, gun control) and to financial security (Social Security, tax relief) appeal to hierarchy's emphasis on stability. Only in highlighting his role in reforming welfare did Gore ever signal that government programs might sometimes become the problem. Taken in total, Gore's convention address frames his campaign in populism.

While still egalitarian, populism turned to government to counter the power of corporate interests. The affiliation between egalitarians and hierarchists (external, group-based programs) in opposition to competitive individualists emerged in Roosevelt's New Deal (Ellis, 1993; Wildavski, 1998) and remained a primary coalition for Democrats through the 1960s. As government became hostile to their social values, hierarchists moved away from egalitarians and made an uneasy alliance with the fiscal conservative individualists. Gore's discourse, therefore, captured the remaining coalition—the liberal elite and the fatalists.

SHARED VALUES, DIFFERENT VISION

Both Bush and Gore stayed generally "on message" throughout the remainder of the campaign, although Gore softened his populism, to some degree. After Labor Day, Gore's stump speech mentioned "middle-class families" 12 times and working families only once ("Gore's Summer Surprise," 78). And although he criticized Bush's tax cut plan for favoring the wealthy, his own proposals were careful not to target the rich. In the end, Gore attracted the traditional Democratic voter committed to the use of federal government to secure rights and to provide help to those most often identified with the struggles of fatalism. The combination of liberal elite voters, those committed to the liberal stance on issues available to egalitarians, and the working-class and lower-middle-class voters attracted to government assistance to the economically disadvantaged came together as the Gore constituency.

Bush's speech also secured his Republican base. Fiscal conservatives who embraced self-regulation and limited government indicative responded to Bush's call for limited government and tax cuts. An emphasis on character and responsibility, local control, and national security appealed to traditional conservatives and social conservatives.

What is most interesting in the issue frames is the relationship to the broad middle class in America, those not tied specifically to either political party, what Ceaser and Busch (2001) call the "floater voter." The floater voter includes most of the nonpartisans as well as a portion of weaker partisans that reject both the strong government and permissive cultural politics of the Left and the antigovernment, divisive cultural rhetoric of the Right. These "middle-ground" voters follow a middle-class morality (Wolfe, 1998) and represent a resurgence of a more moderate egalitarianism as predicted by Wildavsky (1998). Middle-class Americans, whether they identify themselves as Republicans or Democrats or offer no political affiliation, embrace a range of beliefs often misinterpreted by both academics and pundits, occupying a middle ground that resonates both with the New Democratic vision of Clinton and the compassionate conservatism of George W. Bush.

Middle-class Americans, as described by Wolfe (1998), follow a morality captured in Bush's term "compassion." The majority call themselves "people of faith," but they are suspicious of overly public or judgmental religious practice. They embrace what Wolfe (1998) calls a quiet faith. They balance religious belief with tolerance, favor private practice of religion over public declarations, reject lectures about right and wrong in favor of personal example, and balance what is right with what is practical.

Moreover, like Bush, many of those who support public expression of religious faith root their argument in a commitment to free exercise of religion and to diversity, favoring the broadest and most inclusive expression of faith possible. If a cultural war exists for these people, it is not between and among religious sects but between believers and nonbelievers. Wolfe concluded, "The conflict between believers and nonbelievers is as deep as it ever has been in America, but it is no longer a conflict between know-nothings and an enlightened elite. Those who want prayer in schools or crosses on mountains are anything but know-nothings: They have arguments on their side and, even more important, those arguments are lodged not in blind acceptance, but in a liberal language of inclusion and accommodation" (Wolfe, 1998, 71).

Understanding American middle-class morality helps to explain the public response to Bush's call for federal support of faith-based organizations. A Pew Research Center survey found that Democratic support was greater than Republican support for proposals to give government funding to religious organizations (61 percent among Democrats, 46 percent among Republicans). Support increased among both groups when asked if they approved of proposals to allow religious organizations to *apply* for funding (74 percent Democrats, 63 percent Republicans). The voter group indicating the highest support (74 percent) was the Democrat-oriented Partisan Poor—a group with significant representation of low-income and minority voters. The groups who provided the weakest support were liberals (41 percent) and staunch conservatives (41 percent) ("Religion and Politics," 2000). Both groups feared government intrusion, either government support for religion or government intrusion in religion. Bush's extension of federal support to faith-based organizations cannot be explained by a simple liberal-conservative or a Democrat-Republican dichotomy. When understood as an expression of a moderate egalitarian view, the responses not only make sense but also demonstrate the appeal across party lines.

Values of tolerance and responsibility direct this group's evaluation of social programs, such as welfare. The middle-class supports welfare—society should provide assistance for all people who need help—but those in need have a responsibility to help themselves whenever possible (Wolfe, 1998). Gore adopted this view explicitly in a brief reference to welfare reform:

> Over and over again, I talked to folks who told me how they were trapped in the old welfare system. I saw what it did to families. So I fought to end welfare as we—we then knew it, to help those in trouble, but to insist on work and responsibility. Others talked about welfare reform. We actually reformed welfare and set time limits. Instead of handouts, we gave people training to go from welfare to work, and we have cut the welfare rolls in half and moved millions into good jobs. And it's helped lift them up.

Bush's call for a responsibility era hit these same values directly and without offering additional government programs in response.

Interestingly, both Gore and Bush described wealth as a potential threat to society. Gore focused on the impact of big business on the poor; Bush tied social decay to wealth. In this regard, Bush better matches the concerns of the middle class. They strive to provide financial security for their families and at the same time worry that their ability to give their children material security is diminishing their ability to guide their children morally. Wolfe's interviews revealed a persistent belief that hard times strengthen character, especially among older Americans. Inasmuch as the children of the affluent have unlimited choices and few hard times, their parents worry that they will not develop strong moral character. Middle-class Americans also recognize the role of poverty in social problems and identify strongly with the struggles of poor parents against drugs, violence, and sex in inner-city communities (Wolfe, 1998). Both Bush and Gore spoke to the concerns of parents. Again, the difference between the candidates in the role they assigned to government in responding to the problem.

In the end, the suburban middle class studied by Wolfe voted for Bush. And not surprisingly, because Bush fits their worldview. In describing where he developed his way of life, Bush talked of a "different place" far from Washington, D.C.:

> In Midland, Texas, where I grew up, the town motto was "the sky is the limit" . . . and we believed it. There was a restless energy, a basic conviction that, with hard work, anybody could succeed, and everybody deserved a chance. Our sense of community was just as strong as that sense of promise. Neighbors helped each other. There were drywells and sandstorms to keep you humble, and lifelong friends to take your side, and churches to remind us that every soul is equal in value and equal in need. This background leaves an accent, it leaves an outlook.

Bush's outlook, compassionate conservatism, a product of middle America in many ways, resonated with the attempts of voters to find a new way to reconcile their commitment to the individual with their belief in community. Egalitarianism has always been that place in American political culture. In attempting to appeal to partisan Democrats and to distance himself from Clinton, Gore also distanced himself from Clinton's well-established middle ground, opening the door for Bush's message. What is intriguing rhetorically is that Bush and Gore made their stand within the same political culture, tapping into related, although distinct, currents of American political thought and expression. At the level of values, Bush and Gore are more similar than different. A close reading of the rhetoric of the two candidates and of the responses of the American people reveals a consensus around a set of American values—freedom, equality, community, individualism, and tolerance. Their disagreements among those in the middle ground centered around the role of government in reaching the nation's goals. The goals themselves were not in dispute. That an election turned, in the end, on choices about the role of government to meet society's needs is actually not a sign of a cultural war but an indication that America is, as Wolfe contends, one nation, after all.

REFERENCES

Barnes, James A. 1000. "Now for the Post-Mortems." *National Journal*, 32(52) (December 23), 3980–3981.

Boyle, Richard P. and Richard M. Coughlin. 1994. "Conceptualizing and Operationalizing Cultural Theory." In Dennis J. Coyle and Richard J. Ellis, eds., *Politics, Policy, and Culture*. Boulder, CO: Westview Press, 191–218.

Burke, Kenneth. 1984. *Permanence and Change: The Anatomy of Purpose* (3rd ed.). Berkeley: University of California Press.

Ceaser, James and Andrew Busch. 2001. *The Perfect Tie: The True Story of the 2000 Presidential Election*. Lanham, MD: Rowman & Littlefield.

Coyle, Dennis J. and Richard Ellis, eds. 1994. *Politics, Policy, and Culture*. Boulder, CO: Westview Press.

Crotty, William, ed. 2001. *America's Choice 2000*. Boulder, CO: Westview Press.

Douglas, Mary. 1982. *In the Active Voice*. London: Routledge and Kegan Paul.

Ellis, Richard J. 1998. *The Dark Side of the Left: Illiberal Egalitarianism in America*. Lawrence: University Press of Kansas.

Ellis, Richard. J. 1993. *American Political Cultures*. New York: Oxford University Press.

Ellis, Richard J. and Fred Thompson. 1997. "Seeing Green: Cultural Biases and Environmental Preferences." In Richard J. Ellis and Michael Thompson, eds., *Culture Matters*. Boulder, CO: Westview Press, 169–190.

Entman, Robert. M. 1993. "Framing: Toward Clarification of a Fractured Paradigm." *Journal of Communication*, 43(4), 51–58.

"George W. Bush Accepts the Republican Presidential Nomination." 2000. CBS News Transcripts, Burrelle's Information Services, August 3. Lexis-Nexis Academic Universe. http://web.lexis-nexis.com/universe/

"Gore's Summer Surprise." 2000. *Newsweek*, November 20, 78.

Hershey, Marjorie Randon. 2001. "The Campaign and the Media." In Gerald M. Pomper, ed., *The Election of 2000: Reports and Interpretations*. New York: Seven Bridges Press, 46–72.

Hodges, Ann. 2000. "Campaign 2000: Public Service Loses to Profits." *Houston Chronicle*, August 19, A19.

Leichty, Greg and Ede Warner. 2000. "Cultural Topoi: Implications for Public Relations." In Robert L. Heath, ed., *Handbook of Public Relations*. Thousand Oaks, CA: Sage Publications, 61–74.

Marks, Peter. 2000. "The 2000 Campaign: The Media; At Their National Convention, Democrats Shined Spotlight on Local Races." *New York Times*, August 20, A26.

McDaniel, Mike. 2000. "Democratic Convention in Los Angeles: Cable Networks Dominate in Coverage of Political Conventions." *Houston Chronicle*, August 18, A21.

Morin, Richard and Claudia Deane. 2000. "Bounce Gives Bush Biggest Lead; Poll Shows Gain in Voter Perception of GOP Tolerance." *Washington Post*, August 8, A11.

"Much Less Convention Interest." 2000. Pew Research Center for the People and the Press. http://www.people-press.org/july00rpt.htm

Newport, Frank. 2000. "Bush Up 54% to 37% over Gore After GOP Convention." Gallup Organization, August 7. http://www.gallup.com/poll/releases/pr000807.asp

"Religion and Politics: The Ambivalent Majority." 2000. Pew Research Center for the People and the Press. http://www.people-press.org/reli00rpt.htm

Rutenberg, Jim. 2000. "The 2000 Campaign: The Television Audience; Democrats' Party Outdrew the G.O.P.'s." *New York Times*, August 19, A12.

Thompson, Michael, Richard Ellis, and Aaron Wildavsky. 1990. *Cultural Theory*. Boulder, CO: Westview Press.

"Vice President Al Gore's Walk to the Podium to Make his Acceptance Speech." 2000. CBS News Transcripts, Burrelle's Information Services, August 17. Lexis-Nexis Academic Universe. http://web.lexis-nexis.com/universe/

Wildavsky, Aaron. 1998. *Culture and Social Theory*. New Brunswick, NJ: Transaction Publishers.

Wildavsky, Aaron. 1989. "Choosing Preferences by Constructing Institutions: A Cultural Theory of Preference Formation." In Arthur Asa Berger, ed., *Political Culture and Public Opinion*. New Brunswick, NJ: Transaction Publishers, 21–48.

Wolfe, Alan. 1998. *One Nation, After All*. New York: Penguin Books.

Chapter 6

The 2000 Presidential Debates

Robert V. Friedenberg

At the dawn of the new millennium, for the seventh consecutive presidential election, the major party candidates engaged in a series of nationally broadcast debates. As in each of the preceding six presidential elections, the debates were the end product of considerable arguing and compromise between the candidates and the sponsoring organization. Overwhelming public opinion in favor of holding presidential debates has institutionalized presidential debates. Nevertheless, as in the past, the debates themselves were preceded by controversy.

DECISION TO DEBATE

In 1987, the Commission on Presidential Debates (CPD) was established "to ensure that debates, as a permanent part of every general election, provide the best possible information to viewers and listeners." The commission's primary purpose "is to sponsor and produce debates for the United States leading presidential and vice presidential candidates" (Commission on Presidential Debates, 2000a). The Commission on Presidential Debates has been in charge of all of the general election presidential debates since 1988. In prior years, the commission and the candidates had argued over who would participate in the debates as well as the format of the debates. Hence, in 2000, well in advance of the general election period, the commission attempted to remove the controversy over participation by developing criteria that could be utilized to determine who would be allowed to participate.

The key test that the commission determined would be used to limit the field of potential presidential debaters was found in part three of the selection criteria. It reads as follows.

> The CPD's third criterion requires that the candidate have a level of support of at least 15% (fifteen percent) of the national electorate as determined by five selected national public opinion polling organizations, using the average of those organizations' most recent publicly reported results at the time of the determination.
>
> The Commission on Presidential Debates will use an average of the following five polls to determine whether a candidate has 15% support.
>
> - ABC News/*Washington Post*
> - CBS News/*New York Times*
> - NBC News/*Wall Street Journal*
> - CNN/*USA Today*/Gallup
> - Fox News/Opinion Dynamics

The commission added that it would consult these polls after labor day "but sufficiently in advance of the first scheduled debate to allow for orderly planning" (Commission on Presidential Debates, 2000b).

Predictably, minor party candidates, most notably Green Party candidate Ralph Nader and Reform Party candidate Patrick Buchanan, were immediately upset, recognizing that it was highly unlikely that they or any other minor party candidates would reach the 15 percent threshold established by the commission. Buchanan accused the presidential debate commission of attempting to "shut off real debate, to squelch new dissent, to segregate third parties and to control the White House in perpetuity for the two beltway parties" (Burns, 2000a). Nader argued that the commission was in effect stifling debate by excluding candidates. Moreover, the famed consumer advocate filed suit with the Federal Elections Commission, claiming that corporate contributions to the Commission on Presidential Debates, used primarily to help defray the $550,000 cost of staging each debate, were "unlawful" and "corrupts the political process, tilts the electoral playing field sharply toward the Democratic and Republican parties, undermining third parties and limiting the choices of voters" ("Companies Sponsor Presidential Debates," 2000).

The commission defended their decision. Paul G. Kirk, cochairman of the commission, claimed that "it's not a perfect analogy, but in sports, people understand you don't make the playoffs unless you start to accumulate enough wins to show you're competitive" (Meckler, 2000a, A9). Commission Executive Director Janet Brown defended the corporate sponsors such as AT&T, Sun Microsystems, and Anheuser-Busch. Brown pointed out that the Federal Elections Commission had approved of these contributions and that though many presidential commission sponsors did spend money lobbying Congress, their donations to the Commission on Presidential Debates was nothing more than an act of good citizenship (Meckler, 2000a). The protests and legal actions of minor party candidates not withstanding, the Commission on Presidential Debates developed a calendar and formats for the 2000 presidential debates.

The calendar developed by the commission prevented a conflict between the debates and several heavily watched athletic events. Thus, all three presidential debates, as well as the vice presidential debate, were scheduled to be held within a 14-day period between October 3 and October 17. This schedule allowed them to be held after the Olympics were over and before the World Series would start. However, it did result in scheduling the first debate on the same evening as a baseball divisional playoff game. The National Broadcasting Company, which had the contract to broadcast the game, made plans to make both the game and the debate available to its local affiliate stations, allowing each affiliate station to determine what it wished to carry. NBC's affiliated cable outlet, MSNBC, would carry the debate. Similarly, the Fox Network decided to carry its regular programming, rather than the debate. Fox Executive Vice President Preston Beckman pointed out that the Fox News Channel would carry the debate (Bauder, 2000).

The final format that the debate commission offered to the two major party candidates called for three presidential debates. Each was to be 90 minutes long. During the first, the candidates would stand behind podiums and answer questions directed to them by a moderator. During the second, the candidates would both be seated at a table and answer questions directed to them by a moderator who would share the table with them. During the third, the candidates would utilize a "town meeting" format. They would both be seated on stools but were free to move about the stage as they answered questions directed to them by a moderator. The moderator would screen previously submitted questions from members of the audience. The moderator would identify the individuals who submitted the questions so that the candidates could answer these audience members directly. The Gallup polling firm would identify undecided voters who would comprise the audience.

Predictably, the commission recommendation on format was not immediately acceptable to both candidates. Al Gore's staff considered Gore to be an outstanding political debater. Hence, from the primary period forward, the Gore campaign indicated that it would accept the recommendation of the Commission on Presidential Debates and attempted to score political points with their rapid agreement. Throughout the spring, the Gore campaign posted a section on its homepage "Bush Debate Duck" indicating how long Bush had avoided accepting Gore's offer to debate him (Gore 2000, 2000). Gore repeatedly indicated his willingness to debate, attempting to contrast it with Bush's reluctance. Indeed, during a television interview he claimed that he would "debate Bush anywhere, anytime" (Thomas, 2000, 90).

Upon securing the nomination, Texas Governor George Bush made it clear that he would debate Gore. However, his campaign indicated it was not entirely pleased with the format and schedule recommended by the commission. Bush had never cared for debates. He believed that the formal format, in which candidates stood behind a lectern while answering reporters' questions, was contrived and fake. In Bush's view such a format was nothing more than reporters playing "gotcha" with candidates who were carefully rehearsed with poll-tested one-liners. He preferred the more casual sit-down talk show format. Off the record, Bush told reporters that "my best moments come when I'm more relaxed and I can get a couple of quips in. I don't want it to be too planned and structured" (Thomas, 2000, 89).

Consequently, in a September 3 press conference, Bush challenged Gore to three debates. Bush played tapes of Gore appearances on NBC's *Meet the Press* and CNN's *Larry King Live*. During those appearances Gore had challenged Bush to debate him "anywhere, anytime," including on those two talk shows. Bush offered to accept Gore's challenges and debate him on those two shows. Additionally, he accepted the recommendation of the Commission on Presidential Debates for a final town hall–style debate on October 17 at Washington University of St. Louis and suggested that the vice presidential candidates debate twice, instead of the single debate recommended by the commission. Bush concluded by observing that "my opponent has said he will debate any time, any place and he has already accepted the debates that I am accepting today. I take Al Gore at his word that he will be there" (Sammon, 2000).

With his September 3 press conference, Bush no doubt hoped to go on the offensive with the debate issue and portray Gore as the one who was ducking the debates. But the Gore campaign accepted the Bush challenge—with one proviso. The vice president would be glad to debate the governor on the two talk shows, but only after the series of debates recommended by the Commission on Presidential Debates had concluded. "George Bush is trying to do everything he can to avoid prime-time presidential debates that will be seen on all three networks," claimed Gore spokesman Mark Fabiani (Boyer, 2000). By accepting Bush's proposal, with the proviso that the talk show debates come after those the commission was recommending, Gore and his staff had once more placed Bush on the defensive.

As this public argument continued, the candidates and the commission were widely reported to be privately meeting to work out a debate schedule. The Gore campaign refused to budge from the proposal of the Commission on Presidential Debates. William M. Daley, chairman of the Gore-Lieberman campaign, claimed that the commission proposal accepted by Gore "would give the greatest number of voters the chance to hear the candidates directly" ("Gore Pressures Bush," 2000). By the first week of September, the Bush campaign was reported to be on the verge of agreeing to the entire proposal of the Commission on Presidential Debates, as Gore had been urging (Harwood and Calmes, 2000).

Finally, on Sunday morning, September 17, after what was reported to be almost eight hours of meetings throughout the weekend ("Bush, Gore Set Debate Format," 2000), the two campaigns accepted the original recommendations of the Commission on Presidential Debates. There would be three presidential debates with three different formats. Between the first and second presidential debates, there would be a vice presidential debate. Moreover, the campaigns agreed that Jim Lehrer, host of the Public Broadcast System's nightly news show, would serve as the moderator for all three of the debates (Balz, 2000).

The press portrayed the final debate settlement as a Gore victory. Such an interpretation was not entirely unwarranted. The Gore campaign had steadfastly refused to budge from the commission proposal. They had utilized their early acceptance of the nonpartisan commission proposal to portray Gore as willing to debate and Bush as reluctant and afraid to debate. They had portrayed Gore as anxious to debate in front of a massive national audience, implying that Bush was attempting to avoid a large audience. The *Los Angeles Times* reported that Bush had "balked" at the formats and schedule of the commission, but his aids "gave in" when they accepted the commission proposal (Kiker, 2000). The *Washington Post* found that "Bush campaign officials had pushed hard for less rigid rules of engagement and earlier had complained about past commission sponsored debates, calling them 'canned' and 'phony.' " But Bush "eventually reversed course and agreed to debate under the Commission's auspices" (Balz, 2000, A6). Even months after the debates, *Newsweek* characterized Bush's performance during the debate over debates as one in which "in the end he caved in and achieved almost nothing" (Thomas, 2000, 89).

The conventional analysis exemplified by the *Los Angeles Times*, the *Washington Post*, and *Newsweek* was correct in suggesting that Bush had accepted formats that he did not like for two of the three debates. Moreover, it is reasonable to conclude that as a consequence Gore seemed to have won the "debate over debates." However, in stopping there, the conventional press analysis was shallow. It ignores two key points that would prove exceedingly helpful to George W. Bush's quest for the presidency.

First, the "debate over debates" established Bush as a clear underdog. It dramatically lowered expectations for him. By portraying Gore as a formidable debater who wanted a massive audience to witness the debates, presumably because he would decisively best Bush in them, the

Gore campaign was setting high expectations for their candidate and helping lower the expectations that would be placed on Bush. The Bush campaign's approach, making clear their aversion to two of the three formats ultimately used, reinforced the public perception that Gore was clearly the better debater. Gore got the formats that he wanted, and he secured a prime-time audience. But in doing so, expectations on him were increased and those on Bush were lowered. On balance, Bush entered the debates as a distinct underdog and had a clear excuse if he did poorly in at least two of them.

Curiously enough, the one person in Gore's camp who seemed to recognize the potential negative consequence the debate over debates might have on their campaign was Gore himself. As the two sides quibbled over the debates, and account after account portrayed the Bush team as hesitating to debate and concerned about formats because of Gore's overwhelming ability, Gore told his staff that he would never be able to win the debates. The expectations for Bush, he claimed, were just too low (Kurtz, 2000, C1).

The second advantage Bush gained from the debate over debates was largely dismissed at the time, and its ultimate effect cannot be measured. But millions of Americans saw that Gore had unquestionably exaggerated about his willingness to debate Bush. In his press conference of September 3, Bush pressed Gore on those exaggerations, showing clips of Gore's unqualified statement that he would debate Bush anywhere and anytime. Gore's statement was replayed on a wide variety of news and talk shows in the days after Bush's press conference as the negotiations over the debates continued between September 3 and 14.

In isolation, Gore's exaggerations might not have been serious. However, Gore's honesty and credibility were ultimately questioned repeatedly during the campaign. After the first debate, Gore's veracity, always somewhat questionable at best, became a major issue that was exploited by Bush throughout the rest of the campaign. Gore's demonstrable exaggerations about his unqualified willingness to debate may have served many Americans as yet another example of his exaggerating.

The "debate over debates" seemed, at first glance, to have been won by Al Gore. He secured the format and the exposure he wanted by accepting the format and schedule of the Commission on Presidential Debates. In the short run, he was able to effectively position himself as serving the public interest, advancing the cause of debates that could be viewed by millions of Americans. However, though Gore clearly won the battle for formats and schedule, it is not so clear that he won the war. Gore's very self-righteousness about the debates, combined with Bush's reluctance to immediately accept the commission proposals and his obvious desire to utilize other formats and schedules, ultimately contributed to the public perception that Gore was a formidable political debater and that Bush lacked debate and verbal skills. Arguably, more than any contemporary presidential debater, Bush had successfully lowered the expectations on himself and dramatically increased those on his opponent. Moreover, the debate on debates facilitated Bush's exposing, in a well-publicized fashion, which could not be denied, Gore's propensity to exaggerate. Though largely unremarked upon at the time, it was yet another example of a problem that would grow to haunt Gore as the campaign progressed.

DEBATE ONE

Characteristically, successful presidential and vice presidential debaters have utilized a variety of rhetorical and image strategies in presenting themselves to the public. The most successful debaters typically are those best able to

1. Direct their remarks at highly targeted audiences;
2. Develop an overall theme throughout the debate;
3. Debate not to lose by avoiding specifics and making use of proven safe responses;
4. Present themselves as vigorous active leaders;
5. Foster identification of themselves with national aspirations;
6. Foster identification of themselves with the dominant political party/philosophy;
7. Personify themselves as exemplifying a desirable characteristic (Friedenberg, 1997).

These practices of successful national political debaters provide us criteria to utilize in evaluating the 2000 debates.

In past elections, the first debate between the candidates tended to be the defining debate. It was more eagerly anticipated, viewed by more people, and set the tone for those that followed. The traditional importance of the first debate was reaffirmed in 2000. Hence, though this study will touch on all the debates, it will focus more extensively on the first.

The first debate was held on October 3, on the campus of the University of Massachusetts in Boston. The format called for the single moderator, Jim Lehrer of the Public Broadcasting System, to ask questions of each candidate alternately. A coin flip gave the first question to Vice President Gore. Each candidate had two minutes to answer questions directed to him by Lehrer. The opponent was given one minute for a rebuttal. Lehrer was given the option to follow up the initial exchange between candidates on a topic for a total of three and a half minutes, but within that time no single answer could exceed two minutes. Though the format eliminated opening statements, it did provide for a two-minute closing statement by each candidate.

The first exchanges exemplified much of what would follow. Lehrer opened with a pair of questions that were meant to force each candidate to confront one of their harsh past statements about their opponent. But, in effect, the candidates used the first two minutes of their speaking time to present an opening statement. Lehrer's first question went to Gore. "Vice President Gore, you have questioned whether Governor Bush has the experience to be president of the United States. What exactly do you mean?" Gore responded:

> I have actually not questioned Governor Bush's experience; I have questioned his proposals. And here's why: I think this is a very important moment for our country. We have achieved extraordinary prosperity. And in this election America has to make an important choice. Will we use our prosperity to enrich not just the few but all of our families? I believe we have to make the right and responsible choices. If I am entrusted with the presidency, here are the choices that I will make. I'll balance the budget every year. I will pay down the national debt. I will put Medicare and Social Security in a lockbox and protect it. And I will cut taxes for middle class families.
>
> I believe it's important to resist the temptation to squander our surplus. If we make the right choices we can have a prosperity that endures and enriches all of our people. If I'm entrusted with the presidency, I will help parents and strengthen families, because you know, if we have prosperity that grows and grows, we still won't be successful unless we strengthen families by, for example, ensuring that children can always go to schools that are safe, by giving parents the tools to protect their children against cultural pollution.
>
> I will make sure that we invest in our country and our families. And I mean investing in education, health care, the environment, and middle class tax cuts and retirement security. That's my agenda, and that's why I think that it's not just a question of experience.

In this answer Gore attempted to answer Lehrer's question briefly, essentially with the one-sentence claim that "I have actually not questioned Governor Bush's experience; I have questioned his proposals," and then launched into an opening statement. His dismissal of Lehrer's question was the weakest point of a response that served as an effective opening statement.

In these two minutes Gore made five references to families. He made two additional references to parents. Gore was targeting his remarks to America's families. In addition to the references to families and parents, Gore drew a distinction between "the few" and "all our families." Twice he spoke of cutting taxes "for middle class families" and claimed his policies would "enrich all of our people." Clearly, Gore was attempting to portray himself as the defender of middle-class American families and, at least by implication in this opening statement, suggest that Bush was more interested in the "few" wealthy.

By targeting the middle class, Gore also began to develop his overarching theme. In this quasi-opening statement, Gore was clearly suggesting that as president he would fight for middle-class America. He spoke of protecting children from "cultural pollution," investing in education, health care, and retirement security, issues that resonate exceptionally well with the middle class. Gore was constrained by having to adapt to Lehrer's question. But he successfully introduced his overarching theme, that he would fight for middle-class America, in his first answer.

Gore's answer drew on general themes he had developed throughout the campaign and avoided specifics. He was debating not to lose. He spoke in generalities, three times telling his audience that he would make the right choices without getting into the specifics of those choices beyond indicating that he would balance the budget, pay down the national debt, protect Medicare and Social Security, and cut taxes. Indeed, Bush could have agreed with each of the choices that Gore endorsed, they were so vague in this answer.

As Gore presented himself to the public there could be no doubt that he would be a vigorous and active leader. In two minutes he used the word *I* or variants of it (*I'll, I'm*) 20 times, on average once every six seconds. In this opening statement Gore made reference to no less than 13 programs he would implement as president. He was clearly presenting himself as an activist president.

That activity was largely dedicated to attaining and preserving the economic aspirations of middle-class America. The overall effect of Gore's initial answer was to portray himself as a fighter for the aspirations of his targeted audience, the middle class. Curiously, Gore made no reference in this statement, and virtually none throughout the debate, to either the Democratic Party or the president with whom he had served for eight years, Bill Clinton.

In sum, Gore had turned the opening question into an opportunity to make an opening statement. In doing so, he clearly indicated his target audience, began to develop an overarching theme aimed at that audience, did so while debating not to lose by avoiding specifics and making use of proven safe responses, and presented himself as a vigorous active leader. It was a strong start for the vice president.

The format provided that Governor Bush could respond after the vice president answered. He did not explicitly address the question of his experience but did so implicitly. "We do come from different places. And I come from West Texas. I've been a governor. Governor is the chief executive officer and learns how to set agendas and I think you're going to find the difference reflected in our budgets." In addition to the difference in their experience, Bush then pointed to two additional distinctions between himself and Gore. First, while he too wished to preserve Social Security, he would provide a tax cut to everyone who paid taxes, not just the middle class. Second, he would not dramatically increase the activity and size of government. Rather, he wanted to free Americans from big government so that they might make decisions for themselves.

While Bush did not explicitly respond to Gore's evasion of Lehrer's original question, Lehrer did. "I take it by your answer then, Mr. Vice President, that in your—an interview recently with the *New York Times*, when you said that you question whether Vice President—or Governor Bush was experienced enough to be president, you were talking about strictly policy differences?" Lehrer's reference to the *New York Times* the second time he asked the question, and his own credibility, drew attention to Gore's original statement. Gore reiterated his claim that he simply meant that the men had policy differences, then went on to use his time to assert that his policies would help education, health care, prescription drugs, and national defense, while Bush's tax cut would make it impossible to aid these programs and would favor the wealthiest 1 percent of the country. Gore was developing his overarching theme, but he was doing so at the cost of appearing evasive. When Lehrer asked Bush to comment on Gore's remarks, Bush again drew the distinction between the two men clearly. He observed, "There's a difference of opinion. My opponent thinks the government—the surplus is the government's money. That's not what I think. I think it's the hard-working people of America's money, and I want to share some of that money with you, so you've got more money to build and save and dream for your families." As he attacked Gore's desire to spend on government programs and his own desire to provide tax relief, Bush attempted to identify with the middle class.

Lehrer was persistent. Having twice elicited from Gore the statement that his criticism of Bush's experience was really criticism of his policies, Lehrer concluded this exchange by turning to Bush. "When you hear Vice President Gore question your experience, do you read it the same way, that he's talking about policy differences only?" Bush used the opportunity presented him to attack Gore's evasiveness, exaggeration, or lying to instead bolster his own experience and reaffirm a major distinction between himself and Gore.

> Yes, I take him for his word. I mean, look, I fully recognize I'm not of Washington. I'm from Texas. And he's got a lot of experience, but so do I. And I've been the chief executive officer of the second-biggest state in the Union. And I've had a proud record of working with both Republicans and Democrats, which is what our nation needs. We need somebody who can come up to Washington and say, "Look let's forget all the politics and finger-pointing and get some positive things

done on Medicare and prescription drugs and Social Security." And so, I take him for his word.

Even in this opening exchange both men were directing their remarks to their targeted audiences, developing an overall theme, debating not to lose, and presenting themselves as vigorous leaders. Gore, with more time, was able to develop and implement these strategies more fully initially. However, the second question and the exchange it provoked would provide Bush with the time edge.

Lehrer asked Bush, "You have questioned whether Vice President Gore has demonstrated the leadership qualities necessary to be president of the United States. What do you mean by that?" Like Gore, Bush used the first opportunity that he had to speak uninterrupted for two minutes not to simply answer the question but to deliver what was in effect his opening statement.

Well, here's what I've said: I've said, Jim, I've said that eight years ago they campaigned on prescription drugs for seniors, and four years ago they campaigned on getting prescription drugs for seniors. It seems like they can't get it done. Now they may blame other folks, but it's time to get somebody in Washington who is going to work with both Republicans and Democrats to get some positive things done when it comes to our seniors.

And so what I've said is, is there's been some missed opportunities. They've had a chance. They've had a chance to form consensus. I've got a plan on Medicare, for example, that's a two-stage plan that says we're going to have immediate help for seniors in what I call "Immediate Helping Hand," a $48 billion program.

But I also want to say to seniors, if you're happy with Medicare the way it is, fine, you can stay in the program. But we're going to give you additional choices just like they give federal employees in the federal employee health plan. Federal employees have got a variety of choices from which to choose, so should seniors.

And my point has been, as opposed to politicizing an issue like Medicare—in other words, holding it up as an issue, hoping somebody bites and then try to clobber them over the head with it for political purposes—this year, in the year 2000, it's time to say let's get it done once and for all. And that's what I have been critical about the administration for. Same with Social Security. I think there was a good opportunity to bring Republicans and Democrats together to reform the Social Security system so the seniors will never go without. Those on Social Security today will have their promise made.

But also to give younger workers the option at their choice of being able to manage some of their own money in the private sectors to make sure there's a Social Security system around tomorrow. There's a lot of young workers at our rallies we go to, that when they hear that I'm going to trust them at their option to be able to manage, under certain guidelines, some of their own money to get a better rate of return so that they'll have a retirement plan in the future, they begin to nod their heads. And they want a different attitude in Washington.

This, Bush's first opportunity to speak for two minutes without interruption, came approximately six minutes into the debate. Unlike Gore, Bush utilized most of his two minutes to answer Lehrer's question. In doing so he aimed his remarks at seniors and younger workers. Bush did not explicitly express a clear overall theme. He gave two examples of how he would empower people, at the expense of government programs. He presented himself as a vigorous leader who would resolve issues for the public good, rather than play politics with them. He personified himself as exemplifying action. He would be a man who got things done.

Lehrer gave Gore his one-minute rebuttal time. Gore offered a defense of Medicare and concluded his minute by getting back to Bush's tax plan, pointing out that it provides immediate tax relief to the wealthiest 1 percent. Clearly, Gore was taking every opportunity to portray Bush as the tool of the wealthy and himself as a champion of "the people." As this extension of only the second question that Lehrer had asked progressed, Gore began to engage in activities that subsequent focus groups and research indicated the public found annoying. As Lehrer tried to maintain time limits, Gore interrupted, "Jim can I . . ." And again Gore interrupted, "Can I make one other point?"

Lehrer was being placed in an unprecedented position. As the only other individual involved in the dialogue between the candidates, it was his responsibility to enforce the rules and ask questions. The format gave him latitude to allow the candidates a combined three minutes and thirty seconds to expand on the initial two-minute answer and one-minute rebuttal they gave to a question. Presumably both Gore and Bush would get an approximately equal amount of that extra time. But clearly Lehrer was having trouble both in limiting the additional time to three minutes and thirty seconds and in ensuring that it was divided approximately equally.

Illustrative of the problem Lehrer faced was the end of the exchange Lehrer had initiated by asking Bush about Gore's leadership ability. Lehrer addressed the candidates. "One quick thing, gentlemen. These are your rules. I'm doing my best. We're way over the three-and-a-half. I have no problems with it, but we wanted—do you want to have a quick response, and we'll move on. We're already almost five minutes on this, alright?" As Lehrer finished, Gore immediately jumped in to extend his prior remarks. Lehrer then tried to conclude the exchange with what seemed like a simple yes or no question. "Let me ask you both this, and we'll move on," observed Lehrer. "As a practical matter, both of you want to bring prescription drugs to seniors. Correct?" Bush responded, "Correct." Gore responded. "Correct, but the difference is—the difference is I want to bring it to 100 percent and he brings it to only five percent." Again Lehrer attempted to terminate this exchange. "All right. All right. All right," he said, attempting to move on.

But Gore's late dig at Bush caused the Texas governor to respond, and in all fairness Lehrer could hardly cut him off after Gore had used extra time to essentially claim Bush was a liar. Bush then explained his prescription drug plan for seniors. Gore began to question him about it, and Bush then responded by claiming that Gore's plan would take eight years to fully implement. Lehrer had evidently had enough, telling both men, "You have any more to say about this you can say it in your closing statement, so we'll move on, OK?" Without waiting for an answer, Lehrer moved on to the next question.

The exchange illustrates several characteristics that contributed to the subsequent public reaction to both men. First, Gore could not seem to take no for an answer. When his time was up, he frequently attempted to extend it, to add yet another comment, to get in the last word. Second, he could not even answer a simple yes or no question briefly. Gore was debating well. But as events would prove, he was irritating his audience. Moreover, Bush was holding his own. He was responding to every charge that Gore made, to every question that Lehrer asked. Both men were reaffirming the confidence placed in them by their supporters. But the very fact that Gore was so heavily favored, that so little was expected out of Bush, magnified the significance of Bush's ability to appear on roughly equal terms with Gore.

Moreover, throughout these early exchanges Bush raised another issue that would subsequently cause trouble for Gore. The second time he spoke, Bush started his response to Gore's preceding remarks about taxes by observing, "Well, let me just say that obviously tonight we're going to hear some phony numbers about what I think and what we ought to do." As the evening progressed, Bush raised questions about Gore's accuracy, particularly when Gore attacked his proposals. At one point Gore referred to an audience member by name and claimed that this person would not receive federal help paying for prescription drugs under Bush's plan because his earnings were too high. Bush responded, "Look, this is the man who's got great numbers. He talks about numbers. I'm beginning to think not only did he invent the Internet, but he invented the calculator." Bush's remark cleverly linked Gore's debate comment to one of his most famous exaggerations and in doing so implied that they were both about equally accurate. Moreover, Bush repeatedly characterized Gore's figures as "fuzzy math." He used it first to describe a Gore characterization of a Bush proposal. After his first early use of the phrase, subsequently in response to yet another Gore answer, Bush claimed, "The man's practicing fuzzy math again." Later, Bush observed, "This man's disparaging my plan with all this Washington-fuzzy math." Toward the end of the debate, after Gore attacked Bush's tax proposals, claiming they would amount to cutting taxes by $1.9 trillion, "almost half of which goes to the wealthy," Bush responded, "I can't let the man continue with fuzzy math. It's $1.3 trillion, Mr. Vice President. It's going to go to everybody who pays taxes. I'm not going to be one of these kinds of presidents that says 'you get tax relief and you don't.' I'm not going to be a pick and chooser."

Most members of the audience were not in a position to judge the disputed numbers: But many of them may well have noticed that when Bush referred to Gore's "fuzzy math" it was in the context of responding to a Gore attack on a Bush proposal. It is not unreasonable for many in the audience to believe that Bush knew what he was proposing and that perhaps Gore was indeed "fuzzying" the numbers to discredit his opponent.

Moreover, as Bush raised questions about Gore's numbers, the average viewer might well have perceived him as Gore's equal. But Gore was touted before the debate as the policy wonk, the experienced debater, who would easily dispense with Bush. Bush's ability to question Gore's use of numbers as well as three other exchanges in the debate all combined to undermine the predebate claims of Gore's superior fitness for the office.

Approximately one-third of the way through the debate Lehrer asked Gore, "If President Milosevic of Yugoslavia refuses to accept the election results and leave office, what action, if any, should the United States take to get him out of there?" It was the first question that Lehrer had asked that could direct the debate into the conduct of American foreign policy, widely perceived to be Bush's weakness. Questions, such as this one, according to the conventional wisdom, were ones where Gore would excel. Gore responded.

> Well, Milosevic has lost the election. His opponent, Kostunica, has won the election. It's overwhelming. Milosevic's government refuses to release the vote count. There's now a general strike going on. They're demonstrating. I think we should support the people of Serbia and Yugoslavia as they call Serbia plus Montenegro and put pressure in every way to recognize the outcome of the election. . . . Now, we've made it clear, along with our allies, that when Milosevic leaves, then Serbia will be able to have a more normal relationship with the rest of the world. That is a very strong incentive that we have given them to do the right thing. Bear in mind, also, Milosevic has been indicted as a war criminal, and he should be held accountable for his actions. Now we have to take measured steps, because the sentiment within Serbia is, for understandable reasons, still against the United States, because their nationalism has led—even if they don't like Milosevic, they still have some feelings lingering from the NATO action there. So we have to be intelligent in the way we go about it.

Rather than an answer in which he enunciated specific policies we could implement, as the question called for, Gore played it safe. He relied on generalities and safe statements such as "We should support the people of Yugoslavia," "We have to take measured steps," and "We have to be intelligent in how we go about it." While Gore illustrated that he was clearly conversant with the situation in that part of the world, he provided no real answer to Lehrer's question.

When Bush was given his one minute to respond to the same question, he quickly agreed with Gore that it was time for Milosevic to go. Then Bush continued.

> But this'll be an interesting moment for the Russians to step up and lead as well, be a wonderful time for the—for the Russians to step into the Balkans and convince Mr. Milosevic it's in his best interest and his country's best interest to leave office. The Russians have got a lot of sway in that part of the world, and we'd like to see them use that sway to encourage democracy to take hold.

Bush had not played it safe. He had answered the question more directly than Gore by suggesting action the United States might take, namely, encouraging Russia to handle Milosevic. Gore perceived Bush's suggestion that we might wish to see Russia exert influence in dealing with Milosevic as an error and pounced.

> Now, I understand what the governor has said about asking the Russians to be involved. And under some circumstances, that might be a good idea. But being as they have not yet been willing to recognize Kostunica as the lawful winner of the election, I'm not sure that it's right for us to invite the president of Russia to mediate this dispute there, because we might not like the result that comes out of that. They currently favor going forward with a runoff election. I think that's the wrong thing. I think the governor's instinct is not necessarily bad, because we have worked with the Russians in a constructive way, in Kosovo, for example, to end the conflict there. But I think we need to be very careful in the present situation before we invite the Russians to play the leading role in mediating.

At first glance this exchange seems to have been predictable. Gore displayed his knowledge of foreign affairs and debated not to lose by offering bland, safe, stock responses. Bush agreed with Gore but offered one specific change, encouraging greater Russian diplomatic involvement. Gore predictably attempted to refute the merit of that idea, again displaying his knowledge of the situation.

However, within days of the debate it was being widely reported that, as, the *Washington Post* wrote, "the Clinton administration has been trying for weeks to do precisely what the Republican candidate proposed." The paper went on to provide the details, observing that "President Clinton spoke to Russian President Vladimir Putin for 35 minutes in an effort to solicit his support for promoting democratic change in Belgrade. Secretary of State Madeleine Albright and national security adviser Samuel R. "Sandy" Berger have been trying to do the same thing in regular conversations with their counterparts" (Lancaster, 2000, A14). Moreover, the Clinton administration policies were widely publicized when Bush's vice presidential candidate Richard Cheney made reference to them in his debate a few nights later with his Democratic counterpart, Joseph Lieberman.

Hence, Gore's remarks were quickly perceived to be indicative of one of two problems. Either the vice president was simply unaware of what his own administration was doing, or he was deliberately ignoring the efforts of his own administration in order to suggest that he had a greater understanding of how to handle American foreign policy in this part of the world. Neither option reflected well on Gore. Moreover, the second played right into the hands of those who had claimed that he repeatedly tended to exaggerate his own abilities.

Second, approximately two-thirds of the way through the debate, in the midst of an exchange about the candidate's respective educational policies, Gore tried to illustrate that Bush's voucher proposal would hurt public schools by taking money from them.

> I'd like to tell you a quick story. I got a letter today, as I left Sarasota, Florida. I'm here with a group of 13 people from around the country who helped me prepare and we had a great time. But two days ago we ate lunch at a restaurant and the guy who served us lunch gave me a letter today. His name is Randy Ellis. He has a 15-year-old daughter named Kaylee who's in Sarasota High School. Her science class was supposed to be for 24 students. She is the 36th student in that classroom, sent me a picture of her in the classroom. They can't squeeze another desk in for her, so she has to stand during class. I want the federal government, consistent with local control and new accountability, to make improvements of our schools the number one priority so Kaylee will have a desk and can sit down in a classroom where she can learn.

Gore also made a subsequent reference to the plight of Kaylee Ellis in a later question about education.

However, in press interviews after the debate, Sarasota High School principal Daniel Kennedy said that Gore was incorrect. He claimed that Kaylee did not have to stand in her science class. He suggested that might have been true on the first day due to the fact that $150,000 worth of new science equipment for her lab was stacked up and waiting installation in the opening days of the school year. Principal Kennedy suggested that "it would have been good if the facts had been checked before he was encouraged to use that information on a national debate." Kennedy went on to badly damage the Gore contention that the school needed federal money by observing that his school has a "practically brand-new campus," and "it's one of the top high schools in the nation right now," adding that "all of our students are in regular classes and we have 900 computers, 600 Internet sites." Kennedy concluded that "we'd never allow a student to have to stand up during class" (Burns, 2000b; Hogenson, 2000). Thus, yet another of Gore's statements during the debate was found to be a questionable exaggeration.

Late in the debate moderator Lehrer asked the candidates to "point to a decision, an action, you have taken, that illustrates your ability to handle the unexpected, the crisis under fire." Bush responded by citing the emergency responses he had been involved with when fires and floods swept parts of Texas during his administration. After discussing his own activities, Bush added, "And I've got to pay the administration a compliment. James Lee Witt of FEMA has done a really good job of working with governors during times of crisis." Gore immediately attempted to take some of the credit, claiming, "I want to compliment the governor on his response to those fires and floods in Texas. I accompanied James Lee Witt down to Texas when those fires broke out. And FEMA has been a major flagship project of our reinventing government efforts. And I agree, it works extremely well now."

Once again, Gore had misstated himself. Gore had not accompanied the FEMA head to Texas on the occasion of the fires about which Bush spoke. Rather, his staff claimed that two years after the disastrous fires of 1996, in June 1998, Gore visited Texas during a spate of smaller fires. He never visited the scene of the lesser fires, nor did he involve himself in the relief efforts. Rather, he held an airport briefing in Houston, visited a local school, and attended a fund-raising dinner for Democratic Congressman Jim Turner (Meckler, 2000b; Hogenson, 2000). Though the issue itself was trivial, it soon became known as yet another example of Gore's propensity to exaggerate his own role in events.

Bush delivered the first closing statement. He used it as an opportunity to clearly reiterate the overarching theme he had been attempting to develop all evening. "I want to empower people in their own lives. I also want to go to Washington to get some positive things done." Bush then went on to reiterate his stock positions on Medicare, prescription drugs, Social Security, rebuilding the military and improving education. Given the campaign and the preceding 90 minutes, Bush's conclusion was entirely predictable. Nevertheless, it accomplished what Bush no doubt wanted to do. He was able to enunciate his overall theme and portray himself as an active leader. He attempted to reinforce what was likely his principal target audience, conservative Republican voters, and attempted to reach out to others by stressing how though his proposals for prescription drugs, Social Security, and education would give people choices, he nevertheless recognized the need for using the federal government. He largely avoided specifics, debating not to lose, and personified himself as a less divisive figure than his opponent, exemplifying a trait he no doubt felt the American public wanted. In sum, it was a solid, if not spectacular, closing statement that highlighted the differences in both policy and tone that Bush saw between himself and his opponent.

Gore used virtually identical language in his concluding statement as he had used almost 90 minutes earlier in responding to the first question that facilitated his developing an opening statement. In both cases he enunciated his overarching theme, that he would see to it that America used "its prosperity to enrich all of our families, not just the few." Moreover, Gore presented himself as a vigorous active leader. Like Bush, he identified with national aspirations for sound health care and education, using proven safe statements to express his views. Unlike Bush who stressed the need for rebuilding the military and being a peacemaker, Gore made no mention whatsoever of the military or of foreign policy in his concluding remarks.

Perhaps the main difference between Gore's first answer/opening statement and his closing statement was one of tone. In his opening statement, Gore claimed that "America has to make an important choice" about how to use its prosperity. "I believe," he claimed, "we have to make the right and responsible choices." On four occasions in the answer that served as his opening statement, he spoke about making choices.

But by his concluding statement Gore was no longer satisfied to "make choices." Rather, he had to fight. In his two-minute conclusion he used the words "fight" or "fought" seven times. The tone of his opening remarks was that of the rational decision maker. The tone of his closing remarks was that of the passionate advocate. Gore had targeted the middle class and utilized his concluding remarks to portray himself as their champion.

Both Gore and Bush had done a credible job in the first debate. Both had directed their remarks at targeted audiences. Bush had made numerous appeals to his conservative Republican base and often reached out, attempting to appeal to others. Gore had portrayed himself as the champion of middle-class working men and women, the traditional Democratic voter. Both had developed an overall theme. Bush would empower people by reducing government, yet he would maintain key government programs as a safety net for those who needed them. Gore would fight for middle-class America by protecting key government programs such as Medicare and Social Security while expanding government in such areas as education. Both men had relied heavily on remarks they had been repeating throughout the campaign. They both presented themselves as men who would be vigorous and active presidents.

At first glance, this was a close debate, with perhaps a slight edge going to Vice President Gore, who was more fluent. Both candidates repeatedly stressed their differences with the other and clearly satisfied their supporters in doing so. Gore bested Bush in three of the four "instant polls" taken moments after the debate concluded and on that basis claimed victory (Ferrano, 2000; Lester, 2000a). Press accounts written minutes after the debate stressed the clash between the two men on issues such as taxes and the role of government but also noted that both candidates were attempting to move their parties to the center of the political spectrum (Brownstein, 2000; Balz and Neal, 2000).

However, though the immediate results suggested a close debate with a slight edge to Gore, by the next day three story lines were developing out of the debate that all favored Bush and contributed to the judgment that ultimately he won this debate.

First, Gore had gone into the debate heavily favored. Yet he had not scored a decisive victory. Bush had raised questions about Gore's use of statistics; he had challenged Gore sharply on such issues as tax policy, Social Security, prescription drugs for the elderly, education, and rebuilding the military. Both candidates reaffirmed the confidence of their partisans by effectively voicing their positions. For the most part, Bush had given as good as he got. Hence, Gore failed to live up to expectations and Bush exceeded expectations. The perception of Gore as the vastly more experienced and more intelligent candidate was largely nullified in the first debate. Much as in the 1960 debates between Kennedy and Nixon, and the 1980 debate between Reagan and Carter, the heavily favored candidate with experience in the federal executive branch of government was unable to distinctly illustrate that he would be a clearly better president than his opponent. Gore had won the debate over debates, but in doing so, he had created expectations that were difficult to meet and had helped lower expectations for Bush. Bush met the expectations placed on him; Gore had difficulty meeting the expectations that had been created for him during the predebate period.

Second, throughout the campaign Gore, as we have noted, had been criticized for exaggerating his accomplishments. In the wake of the first debate Gore's exaggerations, which for many observers was little more than a euphemism for lies, became a major issue. Gore's statements in the debate were examined, and as we have seen, on at least three occasions during the debate he appeared to again exaggerate. Moreover, Gore's constant assertions about the cost of his programs and those of Bush were also sharply questioned and disputed by Bush, suggesting yet other possible errors.

Moreover, within three days of the debate, as the controversy over Gore's exaggerations mounted, Internet muckraker Matt Drudge published the full text of memos that had been frequently mentioned as early as the Democratic primaries. Drudge published two memos sent to Gore during his first run for the Democratic Party presidential nomination in 1987 and 1988 by his then–deputy campaign press secretary Mike Kopp and his then–campaign press secretary Arlie Schardt. Kopp observed that "this impression that you stretch the truth (or say something one place and something different elsewhere) had already reared its ugly head" (Drudge, 2000). In his memo, Kopp mentioned four different occasions in the early months of the 1988 primaries where Gore had stretched the truth and observed that other campaigns, particularly that of Richard Gephardt, were using this tendency against him. Kopp cited reporters he had tried to do damage control with but concluded that "the point of all this is to caution you about your press image, and how it may continue to suffer if you continue to go out on a limb with remarks that may be impossible to back up."

Schardt, Gore's press secretary at the time, started his memo with the statement, "This is very important." He then went on to detail how reporter Nolan Walters of Knight-Ridder newspapers was investigating Gore and seemed to have found discrepancies in Gore's claims (1) to be a farmer, (2) to be a homebuilder, (3) about the sources of funding for his first congressional campaign. Walters treated each issue, laying out how Gore ought to handle reporters questioning him about them. He constantly urged Gore not to overstate his accomplishments.

- Do not overstate your degree of involvement as a farmer or former homebuilder.
- The main point is to be careful not to overstate your role.
- As I see these 2 subjects, your main pitfall is exaggeration. Be careful not to overstate your accomplishments in these 2 fields. (Woodward, 2000, A14)

The timing of Drudge's release of these memos, which were subsequently quoted and mentioned by the mainstream press, seemed to clearly illustrate that the errors Gore might have made in the debate were not isolated examples but rather seemed to be simply the most recent manifestations of a habitual tendency to exaggerate that extended back a decade or more. Within three days of the debate Calvin Woodward of the Associated Press was observing "the [Gore] campaign knows no claim by the Democratic candidate about his family or professional resume will be taken at face value. His occasional tendency to embellish has not stopped, even in the campaign spotlight" (Woodward, 2000, A14).

Bush's running mate, Dick Cheney, used his own expertise and credibility as a former secretary of defense to extend the argument and reinforce a key position of the Republican ticket. Four days after the debate, Cheney focused on Gore's statement in the debate that the American military was stronger than ever before. Cheney claimed that the military

> is clearly worse off today than it was eight years ago. There are only two ways to interpret Al Gore's refusal to admit what's going on here. Either he doesn't

know what the state of the U.S. military is. Or there's an alternative—he's decided not to tell the truth about it. Either alternative is a terrible indictment of a man who would be commander in chief. (Walsh, 2000, A14)

The end result of the focus on Gore's "exaggerations" and the questions about Gore's credibility created by the debate was evident in a poll taken three days after the debate. According to the CNN-*Time* poll, barely over half the public, only 54 percent, felt that Gore was trustworthy enough to be president, and 60 percent felt that he would say anything to get elected president. In contrast, over two-thirds of the voters found Bush trustworthy, and only 40 percent found that Bush would say anything to get elected. The poll concluded that concerns about Gore's exaggerations and credibility had largely receded after the Democratic National Convention, but they had been resurfaced by the first debate (Lester, 2000b).

The third major story to come out of the first debate involved Gore's attitude and mannerisms throughout the debate. Viewers found him condescending toward Bush, arrogant, and even a bit petulant. Throughout the debate Gore could be heard sighing into the microphone when Bush spoke. His facial expressions when Bush spoke also suggested to many viewers that Gore had little respect for Bush. Moreover, viewers found Gore's attempts to interrupt both Bush and Lehrer and to have the last word and to extend his time limits irritating, annoying, and somewhat childish. Within 48 hours of the debate Bush's pollster, Matthew Dowd, briefed the Bush team. Dowd told the Bush staff that the debate itself was judged a draw but that the voters "had focused on Gore's grimace, his sighs, his mannerisms." Dowd observed that one of those in his focus group likened Gore to "Eddie Haskell, the unctuous character in 'Leave It to Beaver.' " The message, Dowd told the Bush camp, was clear: Gore was hurting himself (Thomas, 2000). Stan Greenberg, Gore's pollster, had drawn similar conclusions and was unhappy with Gore's performance. Greenberg urged Gore to show a little more grace and to exhibit more passion for his own programs and less eagerness to rip his opponent. Greenberg urged that Gore defend his ideas more and attack Bush less (Thomas, 2000).

Although the instant polls taken on the same evening as the debate showed Gore winning, it soon became apparent that the debate had benefited Bush in at least three ways. First, he had met the expectations placed on him, and Gore did not. The Bush team and the press had placed high expectations on Gore due to his 24 years of government experience and his 44 prior debates. Expectations on Bush were low. Bush met or exceeded them. He came across as more than able to contest Gore on a host of issues and perhaps more knowledgeable than many had thought. He had met what the press called the "gravitas" threshold. Side by side with Gore, he seemed to have the stature of a president.

Second, the debate resurfaced the issue of Gore's credibility, which had seemingly been put behind him during the Democratic convention. Bush's attack on Gore's use of statistics as well as a variety of other Gore "exaggerations" once more focused public attention on Gore's credibility. News of Gore's long-standing propensity to exaggerate and the Bush team's linking of those exaggerations to major issues such as military preparedness and major personality characteristics that Americans wanted in their leaders, such as trustworthiness, made this a damaging consequence of the debate for Gore.

Finally, Gore's personal mannerisms and aggressiveness during the debate resonated poorly with the public. Even within the Gore camp, by the end of the week, there was dismay at the image Gore had created of a somewhat arrogant, bullying figure who was reluctant to play by the rules and kept trying to get his own way. The Bush camp, aware of the negative public reaction to Gore's personal style, chose not to comment whatsoever, believing that Gore was hurting himself without their help.

DEBATE TWO

The second presidential debate of 2000 was held on October 11. The two candidates and moderator Jim Lehrer sat at a conference table. Lehrer observed in the opening seconds, "The format tonight is that of a conversation. The only prevailing rule is that no single response can ever, ever, exceed two minutes." This was the format most favored by Bush. Lehrer's opening questions to the candidates focused on the use of American power as a tool of foreign policy. Foreign policy was the subject area in which Bush was widely perceived to be the weakest.

Nevertheless, from the outset, as he had eight days earlier, Bush appeared to be on equal footing with Gore. Indeed, no doubt in response to the criticism he had taken for his arrogance in the first debate, throughout the opening third of the debate and its focus on foreign policy, Gore constantly expressed his agreement with Bush. After a five-minute discussion of how to project American power throughout the rest of the world, in which Gore had the last word, he followed Bush's final comments by saying, "I agree with that. I agree with that."

Five minutes later, after giving the two men an opportunity to discuss their Middle East policies, Lehrer observed that "people watching here tonight are very interested in Middle East policy. They want to base their vote on differences between the two of you as president, how you would handle Middle East policy. Is there any difference?" Gore immediately responded, "I haven't heard a big difference right in the last few exchanges." Moments later Lehrer listed the eight occasions within the last 20 years in which both Democratic and Republican presidents had sent U.S. ground troops overseas. Both men agreed that six of those actions were warranted, including the massive use of American force in Kosovo and Iraq. Bush questioned the Clinton-Gore administration's use of troops in both Somalia and Haiti. Bush claimed that in both instances the missions were changed during the course of the incident. He offered an overall policy. "I don't think our troops ought to be used for what is called nation building. Our troops ought to be used to fight and win war." Gore defended the actions in Somalia and Haiti but acknowledged that both situations might have been handled better by the United States if we had reacted sooner.

In response to additional questions about the use of military force Bush suggested that we should remove our remaining forces from Haiti but that our forces might play a limited role in training in Colombia. He reiterated his desire to use the military only for fighting and winning wars. He claimed that the use of the military should not be undertaken without a clear exit strategy. "I don't disagree with that," responded Gore. In sum, throughout the first third of the debate Gore was largely agreeing with Bush. Moreover, he was doing so on questions of foreign policy, where Bush was believed to be weak. Once more, Bush was holding his own against Gore.

Moreover, in contrast to the first debate, Gore had toned down his annoying mannerisms. Indeed, he was deferential to Lehrer, on occasion making comments like, "I don't want to jump in. May I reply?" Additionally, on several other issues, most notably violence in our culture, Gore expressed his agreement with Bush. Gore was clearly attempting to be less contentious than in the first debate. However, by doing so, he found himself frequently expressing agreement with Bush on the very issues that Bush was often accused of having little knowledge or experience. Gore's personality might be perceived more favorably, but Bush's stature vis-à-vis Gore was growing.

During the last third of the debate Gore and Bush began to clash more seriously. Lehrer was questioning the candidates about tax cuts and their policies toward the environment. Bush strongly defended his across-the-board tax cuts, claiming that Gore's proposal would not provide tax relief to 50 million Americans. "We have a different point of view," observed Bush. "He believes only the right people ought to get tax relief. I think everybody who pays taxes ought to get tax relief."

Bush and Gore agreed on the importance of a clean environment but differed on how to attain it. Bush defended his programs to protect the Texas environment and claimed that "command and control" of the environment out of Washington was not the way to attain a clean environment. He provided examples of unilateral actions by the federal government, taken without consulting the state and local authorities, suggesting that at the least those who were affected by these environmental decisions, or their elected officials, should have been consulted.

Moreover, he attacked the Gore-supported treaty on the environment for exempting China and India from the standards imposed on the United States and observed that it was defeated by a vote of 99–0 in the Senate. Gore agreed that "command and control" from Washington was not good but defended the treaty.

Lehrer closed the questioning by asking each man about the harsh statements coming from their campaigns about the other. Both claimed not to have made harsh statements themselves, but Bush did not deny that his campaign officials had taken to calling Gore a serial exaggerator, nor did Gore deny that his campaign officials had taken to calling Bush a bumbler. Both men used their one-minute closing statements to reiterate their positions on key issues. Both spoke of education, taxes, Social Security, and health care. Gore added the environment. Bush added the military.

The first debate placed Gore in a difficult position for the second debate. He could continue his aggressiveness—and risk reinforcing the overbearing persona he created in the first debate that had resonated against him—or he could be more agreeable and risk not drawing major distinctions between himself and Bush. He chose the latter. He was more likable. Gore's failure to draw major distinctions between himself and Bush, most notably in what had heretofore been perceived as his strength and Bush's weakness, foreign policy, meant that in the second debate Gore was unable to decisively illustrate that he was better prepared to direct American foreign policy. In the second debate Gore's personality was less abrasive than in the first, though Bush was still perceived to be more likable than Gore. Moreover, Bush's suitability for the presidency vis-à-vis Gore was enhanced. Gore's own focus groups immediately made his shortcomings obvious to the campaign (Kurtz, 2000). Moreover, virtually all of the instant polls, including those done by CNN/*USA Today*/Gallup, CBS News, and Reuters/MSNBC, found that Bush won the debate (Holland, 2000; CBS, 2000; Eisner, 2000).

DEBATE THREE

The final debate was held on October 17. It utilized the "town hall" format, Bush's least favorite. The candidates sat on stools but were free to move about on the stage. Each audience member, all undecided voters, had written out a potential question. Moderator Lehrer then selected the questions. As the debate progressed Lehrer called on audience members to read their questions. The audience member called upon would stand and do so. Typically the candidate would move toward the questioner during the initial portion of the answer and address that person. As in the prior debates, there were no opening statements, though there were closing statements.

Gore was more aggressive in this debate than in the second debate. But he toned down much of the sighing, facial expressions, and other nonverbal communication that had caused him trouble in the first debate. Nevertheless, on one occasion, as Bush was talking, he attempted to rattle Bush by moving right behind him, essentially invading his personal space. Bush turned partway toward Gore and did a double take with a quizzical expression on his face. As the audience laughed, Gore backed off. The exchange made Gore appear overbearing and perhaps a bit foolish. On several occasions, Gore tried to stretch the time limit and get in the last word by speaking out of order. Lehrer repeatedly refused to allow him to do so.

Additionally, although the rules expressly prohibited one candidate from asking a question of the other, on several occasions Gore directed questions at Bush. Each time, Lehrer interceded, reminding the candidates of the rules. But late in the debate, in an exchange over affirmative action, Gore tried again.

Gore: He said if affirmative action means quotas, he's against it. Affirmative action doesn't mean quotas.

Bush: Good.

Gore: Are you for it without quotas?

Bush: I may not be for your version, Mr. Vice President. But I'm for what I just described to the lady [affirmative action and equal opportunity]. She heard my answer.

Gore: Are you for what the Supreme Court says is a constitutional way of having affirmative action?

Bush: Jim, is this . . .

Lehrer: Let's go on to another . . .

Gore: I think that speaks for itself.

Bush: No. Doesn't speak for itself, Mr. Vice President. It speaks for the fact that there are certain rules in this that we all agreed to, but evidently rules don't mean anything.

Coming late in the debate, Bush's sharp reminder that Gore was breaking the rules seemed to encapsulate much of the reaction to Gore's behavior. Perhaps not to the degree he had nonverbally in the first debate but certainly verbally, Gore continued to appear unjustifiably aggressive. He forced moderator Lehrer to restrain him on several occasions, and on other occasions he broke the rules.

The distinctions between the two men were drawn more sharply in this debate than in the second. Bush defended himself aggressively against Gore's attacks, contributing appreciably to drawing the distinctions between the two men. There were few actual agreements between the two, other than when Gore agreed with Bush that the death penalty was a deterrent to crime. Otherwise, the debate was marked by serious clash.

- Gore claimed vouchers were "a mistake." Bush believed vouchers "are up to the states . . . I don't like it when the federal government tells us what to do. I believe in local control of the schools."
- Bush claimed that "when you total up all the federal spending he [Gore] wants to do, it's the largest increase in federal spending in years. And there's just not going to be enough money." Gore claimed his plan "would balance the budget every year."
- Bush claimed "50 million Americans get no tax relief under his [Gore's] plan." Gore claimed, "I would fight to have middle class tax cuts."
- Gore would eliminate the estate tax or "death tax" on 80 percent of all family farms and family businesses, still keeping it "on the very wealthiest," to provide government income that otherwise would be "an extra heavy burden on middle class families." Bush would eliminate it entirely, "because people shouldn't be taxed twice on their assets. It's either unfair for some or unfair for all. Again, this is just a difference of opinion. If you're from Washington, you want to pick and choose winners."
- Gore favored "moving step by step towards universal health coverage." Bush was "absolutely opposed to a national health care plan."

In their closing statements, both men attempted to draw the distinctions between themselves once again. Gore claimed that we needed campaign finance reform, implying that Bush did not agree. Gore claimed that he would fight for middle-class working men and women, implying that Bush would not. Gore claimed that during the past eight years the economy had grown remarkably and crime rates were down, implying that such would be unlikely under a Bush administration.

Bush concluded by suggesting that the difference between himself and Gore was "the difference between big federal government and somebody who's coming from outside of Washington who will trust individuals." He highlighted his tax program, his education program, his programs for seniors, and his desire to rebuild the military, implying that in each instance he differed sharply from Gore.

The third debate was Gore's best debate. His persona seemed more acceptable to the public than either the overbearing persona of the first debate or the artificial persona of the second debate. By the same token, Bush also did well in the third debate. Bush seemed more articulate and confident as the series of debates progressed. On balance the instant polls that followed the third debate gave a slight edge to Gore, but that edge was so slight that the *Washington Post*'s director of polling, Richard Morin, summarized the findings of the overnight snap polls by observing that "overall, the instant polls found that few voters changed their minds about which candidate to support" (Morin and Deane, 2000).

CONCLUSION

Bush and Gore both debated well throughout these three debates. Both men appeared presidential enough and provided sufficient rational for their programs to reinforce those leaning toward them at the outset of the debates. They had largely targeted their respective base voters and had done nothing to diminish those respective bases.

Bush stuck to his basic issues, using them to support his overall thesis that he would empower people at the expense of the federal government. Bush used responses that he had been using throughout the campaign. He was able to enunciate specific policies and policy differences, particularly concerning foreign policy, to appear credible. Yet he did so while making use of proven, largely safe responses. He suggested that he would be an activist, getting things done in a Washington where his opponent had largely failed to get things done for eight years. He identified himself with a host of national aspirations involving education, help for the elderly, and medical care. He consistently identified himself as a conservative and attempted to personify himself as one who got things done, who could work across partisan lines to accomplish the public's business. It was a highly credible series of debates for a candidate who himself was considered a poor debater and whose opponent was considered a formidable debater.

Gore too debated well. Like Bush he directed most of his remarks at his targeted base voter audience. He used the issues he developed, his selective tax cuts, educational policies, health policies, and Social Security policies, to reinforce his overall theme that he would fight for the middle class. He too debated not to lose, displaying a command of the issues but a reluctance to offer new arguments or examples. More than Bush, Gore came across as an activist. He offered a program or policy in answer to almost every question and made frequent references to his 24 years of government service and his accomplishments during that service. Like Bush, he identified with a host of national aspirations. Gore made little reference to his Democratic Party, rather remarkably totally avoided ever mentioning incumbent president Bill Clinton, under whom he had served for 8 years, and made no references to a political philosophy, though Bush repeatedly suggested that Gore was a liberal. As the debates ended, he personified himself as a fighter.

In sum, both men debated well. Nevertheless, there was a winner. Al Gore had been right to worry back in August that the debate expectations on himself and Bush were vastly different. Bush had met the expectations placed on him. He appeared up to the job of being president.

He appeared roughly equal in knowledge and ability to Gore. While the two men differed sharply on a host of positions, Gore did not, as his supporters had anticipated, come across as having more gravitas, as being more presidential, than Bush. Indeed, a CBS poll taken after the last debate suggested that 36 percent of the country felt more comfortable with the idea of Bush as president than had felt that way before the debates, and only 25 percent felt less comfortable, a net gain of 11 percent more people feeling more comfortable with Bush. In contrast, that same poll found that 34 percent felt more comfortable with Gore, but almost the same number, 31 percent, felt less comfortable, a net gain of only 3 percent (Morin and Deane, 2000). Moreover, according to Democratic pollster Celinda Lake, Gore lost among voters who made up their minds during the debates (Lake, 2000).

Second, the debates had once again surfaced the issue of Gore's penchant for exaggeration. It is bad enough for any political figure when his truthfulness is questioned. Given the ethical clouds that hung over the administration in which he served, it may be a tribute to Gore that even though questions about his own veracity were raised during this campaign, only 44 percent of all voters told exit pollsters that the Clinton scandals were important to them during this election. Nevertheless, as David Broder (2000) has observed, those voters "voted overwhelmingly for Bush" (A45). Had Gore been able to put concerns over his exaggerations behind him early in the campaign, and had they not resurfaced during these debates, perhaps that 44 percent might not have voted so overwhelmingly for Bush.

Finally, the image that Gore projected of himself, the Gore persona to which many Americans were exposed during the debates, detracted from the vice president's candidacy, particularly when contrasted to the persona of Governor Bush. Gore was perceived as a rather dislikable fellow. He was perceived as impolite almost to the point of being rude, a whiner who seemed unable to abide by the rules, and overly aggressive. Whether or not these perceptions are accurate, they became widespread as a consequence of the debate. Even Gore's own staff admitted that he had a "likeability" problem when contrasted to Bush (Thomas, 2000). Additionally, while Bush had been himself throughout the debates, Gore came across as a somewhat different person in each of the debates. This too was not reassuring to a public that traditionally perceives the debates as one of their few means of really getting to know the candidates. For all of these reasons, the presidential debates of 2000 ultimately helped Governor George W. Bush more than they helped Vice President Albert Gore.

REFERENCES

All direct quotations from the debates are taken from the transcripts of the debates provided by the Commission on Presidential Debates through their Internet site, which can be found at www.debates.org/index.html.

Balz, Dan. 2000. "Presidential Debates Take Several Forms." *Washington Post*, September 17, A6.

Balz, Dan and Terry Neal. 2000. "Gore and Bush Clash Sharply on Policy Issues." *Washington Post*, October 4, A1.

Bauder, David. 2000. "NBC, Fox Choose Sports Over Debates," September 23. (Originally found on the Internet site of the *Washington Post*. This AP story is not archived by the *Washington Post*. Hard copy is available from the author.)

Boyer, Dave. 2000. "Bush Team Prepares for Debates." *Washington Times*, August 31. (Originally found on the Internet site of the *Washington Times*, where it is archived as article i.d. # 2000244083. Hard copy is available from the author.)

Broder, David. 2000. "Burying the Hatchet." *Washington Post*, November 10, A45.

Brownstein, Ronald. 2000. "Miles Apart, But Both Play to the Center." *Los Angeles Times*, October 4. (Originally found on the Internet site of the *Los Angeles Times*, which does not archive back stories. Hard copy is available from the author.)

Burns, Jim, 2000a. "Buchanan Fumes Over Exclusion from Debates." CNSNews, July 20. (Originally found on the Internet site of CNSNews. CNSNews does not archive old stories. Hard copy is available from the author.)

Burns, Jim. 2000b. "Florida High School Principle Says Gore Has Facts Wrong." CNSNews, October 4. (Originally found on the Internet site of CNSNews. CNSNews does not archive old stories. Hard copy is available from the author.)

"Bush, Gore Set Debate Format." 2000. *Birmingham News*, September 17, 3A.

CBS News. 2000. "CBS Poll; Slender Edge to Bush." CBS News, October 11. (Originally found at the Internet site of CBS News. CBS News does not archive old stories. Hard copy is available from the author.)

Commission on Presidential Debates. 2000a. "Homepage-Debate." http://www.debates.org/indes.html

Commission on Presidential Debates. 2000b. "Candidate Selection Process." http://www.debates.org/pages/Candsel.html

"Companies Sponsor Presidential Debates." 2000. Capitol Hill Blue, July 19. (Originally found at the Internet site Capitol Hill Blue. This Associated Press story is not currently available in the CHB archives. Hard copy is available from the author.)

Drudge, Matt. 2000. "Released: Memos to Gore Warned of 'Stretching Truth' Full Text Made Public." October 6. (Originally found at Drudge Report.Com. Drudge does not archive his articles. Hard copy is available from the author.)

Eisner, Alan. 2000. "Bush Gore Hit Trail Again after Second Debate." Reuters: Breaking News, October 12. (Originally found at the Internet site of Reuters. Reuters does not archive old stories. Hard copy is available from the author.)

Ferrano, Thomas. 2000. "Gore Buoyed by Polls, Raises Fists in Victory." October 4. (Originally found at Excite News.com. This Reuters news service story is not archived by Excite News or Reuters. Hard copy is available from the author.)

Friedenberg, Robert V. 1997. "Patterns and Trends in National Political Debates 1960–1996." In Robert V. Friedenberg, ed., *Rhetorical Studies of National Political Debates—1996*. Westport, CT: Praeger, 61–90.

"Gore Pressures Bush for Televised Debates." 2000. *Cincinnati Enquirer*, August 30, A5.

Gore 2000. 2000. "Bush Debate Duck." Found daily throughout the spring of 2000 at http://www.algore2000.com

Harwood, John and Jackie Calmes. 2000. "Bush Moves toward Accepting 2 Debates of 3 Proposed by Bipartisan Commission." *Wall Street Journal*, September 8, A20.

Hillman, Robert. 2000. "Gore Says Bush Afraid of Debates." *Dallas Morning News*, August 22. (Originally found at the Internet site of the *Dallas Morning News*. The *Dallas Morning News* does not archive old stories. Hard copy is available from the author.)

Hogenson, Scott. 2000. "String of Misstatements Haunts Gore." CNSNews, October 4. (Originally found at the Internet site of CNSNews. CNSNews does not archive back articles. Hard copy is available from the author.)

Holland, Keating. 2000. "Bush Gets the Edge in Debate Performance Poll." October 12. (Originally found at the Internet site of CNN. CNN does not archive old stories. Hard copy is available from the author.)

Kiker, Douglas. 2000. "Bush, Gore Camps Agree on Debates." *Los Angeles Times*, September 17. (Originally found on the Internet site of the *Los Angeles Times*, which does not archive back stories. Hard copy is available from the author.)

Kurtz, Howard. 2000. "Feeding the Media Beast: Leaks, Rats and Blackberries." *Washington Post*, December 17, C1.

Lake, Celinda. 2000. "Issue Kleptomania." *Campaigns and Elections*, December–January 2001, 81.

Lancaster, John. 2000. "Bush Team Hits Gore on Role of Russia." *Washington Post*, October 7, A14.

Lester, Will. 2000a. "Gore Fares Better in 3 of 4 Polls." Associated Press Wire, October 4. (Originally found at the Associated Press Election 2000 site on the Internet. The Associated Press does not archive old stories. Hard copy is available from the author.)

Lester, Will. 2000b. "Poll: Bush More Trusted Than Gore." *Washington Post*, October 6. (Originally found at the Internet site of the *Washington Post*. This Associated Press article is not archived by the *Washington Post*. Hard copy is available from the author.)

Meckler, Laura. 2000a. "Debate Threshold Defended." *Cinicinnati Enquirer*, June 22, A9.

Meckler, Laura. 2000b. "Truthfulness First Issue in Debate." Associated Press Wire, October 4. (Originally found at the Associated Press Election 2000

Internet site. AP does not archive stories. Hard copy is available from the author.)

Morin, Richard and Claudia Deane. 2000. "Instant Polls: Debates Leave Race at a Draw." *Washington Post*, October 18. (Originally taken from the Internet site of the *Washington Post*. This story is not archived by that paper. Hard copy is available from the author.)

Sammon, Bill. 2000. "Bush Proposes Network Debates." *Washington Times*, November 4. (Originally found at the Internet site of the *Washington Times*, where it is archived as article i.d. # 2000248045. Hard copy is also available from the author.)

Thomas, Evan (and *Newsweek's* Special-Projects Team). 2000. "The Inside Story: What a Long Strange Trip." *Newsweek*, November 20, 89.

Walsh, Edward. 2000. "Cheney Rips Gore's 'Problem' with Credibility." *Washington Post*, October 7, A14.

Woodward, Calvin. 2000. "Gore's Embellishments Persist, Even in the Spotlight." *Cincinnati Enquirer*, October 6, A14.

Chapter 7

Digital Democracy 2000

Rita Kirk Whillock and David E. Whillock

This year's James K. Batten Award for Excellence in Civic Journalism awarded by the Pew Center for Civic Journalism lauds the advent of a new vein of political information: the Internet. America Online received the award for its "one-stop election shopping" site (Pew Center, 2001). This award underscores how the Internet has begun to take its position alongside the traditional media of newspapers, television, and radio. At a minimum, the award suggests that scholars have not been wrong in the past when they suggested the medium might have its place in the political discourse of the nation. Writing in 1998, John Pavlik discussed the Internet's future role, suggesting that "[m]ost fundamental is perhaps the use of the new technologies to facilitate an informed public citizenry and to increase and improve public participation in the political process" (293).

Having traced the development of the Internet in presidential elections over the last three election cycles, our contention has been—and continues to be—that the Internet will discover its unique capabilities and in doing so will find itself important in the company of traditional forms of information dissemination.

That said, the Internet is still in the process of discovery. The 2000 election cycle did not develop as rapidly as a tool of American politics as some people expected. However, the areas where the Internet was successful gave credence to the argument that eventually this new technology will indeed be a cornerstone for election strategists, especially in those elections that demand information dissemination over a large and varied election demographic group.

Internet use in the 2000 presidential election was notable for several reasons that will be explained in this chapter. First, election regulations regarding citizen and campaign use of the Internet changed in significant ways, allowing for its legal use while attempting to tame its revolutionary character. Second, campaigns learned to raise an inordinate amount of money using the Internet for fund-raising. Third, campaigns developed ways of better utilizing the Internet as a method of organization and information dissemination. Concurrently, the political parties began using the Internet as a means of party building. And in the midst of the fevered discussion, the public began talking back and talking to each other.

Each of these developments in the use of Internet communication is significant through the eyes of those who are watching the Internet revolution take hold. But, as we will discuss, whether these developments necessarily are important for the *outcomes* of future elections, or when that might take place, remains in question.

CHANGES IN THE DEMOGRAPHIC PROFILES OF INTERNET USERS

By election day, the Internet had proven its utility as an information medium. Some 104 million American adults accessed the Internet specifically for election information (see Rainie and Packel, 2001). Confirming the anecdotal suspicion that the Internet is primarily an information source, a Pew Center study found that "48% of Internet users, or about 50 million Americans, got news about the campaign from the Web" ("Internet Election News," 2000). In comparison, that figure dwarfs the 4 percent use of the Internet recorded in the 1996 election (Schafer, 2001, 1).

Evidence supports the assertion that the immediacy of news events such as contested elections or hurricane watches delivers information consumers to the Internet. The Pew Center reports that "on a typical day in later 2000, 17% of Internet users were getting political news [from the Internet], a doubling of the number who were getting it on a typical day in October and a tripling of the number getting political news at midyear" (Rainie and Packel, 2001). Notably, during the same period of time, while the political information use increased, general news events did not. "The overall increase in those getting general news online (as distinct from political and campaign news) was modest at the end of 2000" (Rainie and Packel, 2001).

The rapidly unfolding news events resulting from the disputed election results were one of the driving factors for the high Internet traffic in November. In fact, the Web site for a West Palm Beach television station, WPBFChannel.com, was the first to break the story about the ballot controversy. Up-to-the-minute news coverage unfolded online in ways that local print news media could not and standard television news chose, for programming reasons, not to deliver.

Concurrently, the party machines and their Web site assistants sought to drum up public sympathy in support of their candidate's positions. Thus, online spin control became an important partisan task.

The election controversy showcased how the Internet has begun to assume the role talk radio held in previous elections—it permitted the public to vent their frustrations and election angst. Grassroots activists permitted public venting over the controversy through sites such as www.whoshouldwin.com. The basic anonymity of the Internet allowed those who might not otherwise voice their opinions a platform. Those who might not be so shy were also given a platform from which to speak. They no longer had to wait for the local news media to ask questions. They could, without recourse or identification, state their feelings for the candidates and issues in what they considered a free speech forum. And there was room for party hacks that used multiple identities to stack perceptions of online opinion.

While presidential contenders moved to the Internet in force, other regional and local political hopefuls did not. In election 2000, the lower on the ballot the election contest appeared, the lower the chances of having an online presence. For example, the 2000 election cycle produced Web sites from only 56 percent of congressional campaigns (Derfner, 2001), leaving a significant margin with no presence on the Internet.

Even with this margin, this election did not produce evidence of the significant impact of the Internet on an election's outcome. Thus, by using the Internet, a candidate did not necessarily have a proven advantage over a candidate who chose not to use it. In national campaigns the use of the Internet remained a tool that was considered imperative to use. To have an Internet presence seemed important if for no other reason than those who used it sent the symbolic message that they were current in new technologies and would be active in the future.

Clearly, the Internet can no longer be dismissed as irrelevant. One poll conducted of over 9,000 people in January 2001 found that television remained the primary sources for news information on world events (56 percent). Yet the Internet ranked second (19.5 percent) for obtaining news information, narrowly ahead of newspapers (17.3 percent), but overwhelmingly favored over other traditional media such as radio (9.1 percent) or magazines (1.4 percent) (BIGResearch, 2001, 2). As consumers grow more comfortable with the Internet, the number using the technology will increase. Its use as an information source is no longer in dispute. The question is how it will become a tool of politics.

TAMING THE BEAST: LAWSUITS AND FEDERAL REGULATORY OVERSIGHT

When scholars look back at the election of 2000, one of the benchmarks will be when the Supreme Court made the unprecedented step of providing a complete online transcript of the Florida election case immediately after the justices heard the oral arguments. The Court's action elevated the Internet to a new role, replacing television's spot reporting for analysis of breaking stories. Readers were able to assess the transcript themselves in real time with reporters covering the story. No other medium was able to provide the immediate text of the Court's hearing in such detail.

The Court's battle with information distribution has been notable. Historically, cameras have been denied in the Supreme Court, and Chief Justice William Rehnquist upheld that policy in this precedent setting case. The posting of the transcript on the Supreme Court Web site, www.supremecourt.gov, brought immediate positive reaction from groups who customarily receive such transcripts only through the National Archives and then only after the Court's term is completed for the year. Even before the Court rendered its verdict, the outcome of the Florida case was debated on news shows and chat groups around the country and followed around the world.

This event was called by some "the most famous week in Web news history" (Weiner, 2000). Outgunned by Internet news sites, traditional news outlets began changing their mind-set on dissemination of information to an interested public. "There is . . . evidence that newspapers are putting more resources behind their online products. The news following this past Election Day was anything by static, which forced online newsrooms to think less like print products and more like news radio stations. The result was a plus for consumers who received timely and insightful coverage of a historic event" (Weiner, 2000). Consumers were not the only group that understood the developing importance of the Internet on political campaigns.

The 2000 election season produced three regulatory advisory opinions on the Internet that have consequences for future elections. The first opinion—later challenged for clarification—regards Internet uses by third parties. The second seeks clarification on a host of campaign reporting issues and brings into light future applications and regulation of shadow campaigns. The third is significant for opening the Internet as a campaign revenue stream.

Internet Use by Third Parties

On three separate occasions (September 18, September 23, and October 2, 1998), a private citizen named Leo Smith contacted the Federal Election Commission requesting an advisory opinion. Smith, a Web site designer by profession, created a site to protest House Republican efforts he felt were directed against President Clinton. Also, the site openly advocated the defeat of Republican incumbent Nancy Johnson and advocated the election of Democrat Charlotte Koskoff in the race for the Sixth Congressional District of Connecticut. The Smith site had been accessible online since September 17, 1998. Important to the ruling on this case, the site used specific advocacy terms: "defeat Nancy Johnson" and "work to elect Koskoff for Congress" (see "Federal Election Commission Advisory Opinion Number 1998–2," 1998). Additionally, the site offered browsers the opportunity to contribute money and to volunteer for the Koskoff campaign. Smith would send the information collected from the Web site to the campaign but claimed that he had no connection with the campaign and was working as an independent third party.

The question Smith posed to the commission was whether regulation required him to identify himself as the payer of costs related to the Web site or sponsor of the Web site, rather than the "independent voter" identification that Smith preferred.

Taken in total, the commission ruled that Smith must identify himself. The committee reiterated that a statement is required if the site is sponsored or approved by the Koskoff Committee, which this one was not. Yet it is also required if the message expressly advocates "the election or defeat" of a clearly identified candidate *or* if it solicits money *or* if it does so through various types of mass media (see "Federal Election Commission Advisory Opinion Number 1998–2," 1998).

Significantly, this is the first ruling where Internet Web sites are identified as a form of mass media to the general public. This is also the first ruling to declare that Web sites have value because of expressions of advocacy or defeat regarding federal election candidates.

As such, the commission ruled that the Web site must meet the requirements set in 2 U.S.C. 441d and 11 CFR 110.11. It must include the full name of the Web advocate and not merely an "independent voter." It must also include a truthful statement as to whether or not your communication via the Web site is authorized by any candidate.

The commission's statement that "any value of services over $250 would require the individual to report" is what stirred a later controversy with the Bush campaign. In the Smith case, the commission ruled that there are minimal costs associated with the Web site: fee to secure domain name, amount invested in hardware, utility cost to create such a site. Should the cost figure meet the threshold of campaign contribution, reporting would be required.

Regulation of Shadow Campaigns

A second case is a rather lengthy request from the Bush campaign for clarification on the reporting obligations for campaigns, the value of links, and the ability of a campaign to reproduce (or link to) data such as opinion polls or opinion sites. The commission responded to three Bush letters dated June 7, July 8, and September 23, 1999 (see "Federal Election Commission Advisory Opinion Number 1999–17," 1999).

The Bush campaign sought to determine the value of Web links to the campaign site from both sites they know and approve of and those that do so freely but without approval of the campaign. As anticipated, such activities constitute third-party activity over which the commission has no control or comment. The commission responded that "anything of value" as found in 2 U.S.C. 441b(a); 11 CFR 114.2(b) "includes goods or services provided without charge or at less than the usual and normal charge." *But* that does *not* include "the value of services provided without compensation by any individual who volunteers on behalf of a candidate or political committee," as expressed in (2 U.S.C. 431 (8)(b)(i). As long as the Bush campaign does *not* offer such Internet providers with items of value or coordinate the activities, there is no obligation to report the financial value. Several of the specific issues asked by the Bush campaign resulted in this ruling including the value related if vendors, volunteers, media outlets, or commercial enterprises listed campaign links.

The second issue raised by the commission was the value of Internet polls: Do these fall under news media exceptions, regardless of the sponsor or source of the polls? Does the dissemination of these results become reportable? Examples include straw polls by the Indiana Republican Party, shopping site Shabang, and news sites. The commission did not rule on the news media exemption except to say that it must meet the guidelines of "press exemption" under 2 U.S.C. 431(9)(b)(i). This is significant since more sites self-identify the work they do as that of the press.

From a campaign vantage, the value of this ruling is that as long as such links are covered as operating expenditures, campaigns can selectively link to whatever sites provide them the most persuasive power. The illusion of momentum, the use of credibility from third-party (and supposedly unbiased) sources, or the value of those links when the campaign itself is referenced by most every reputable news agency is each a viable campaign strategy.

The Internet as a Campaign Revenue Stream

A third case proved to be the most lucrative ruling for campaigns. Bill Bradley requested an opinion regarding 26 U.S.C. 9031–9042 and commission regulations regarding the matching of credit card contributions made through the Internet. The request also referenced the Federal Election Campaign Act of 1972, as amended.

Specifically, Bradley requested that the campaign be allowed to solicit contributions through its Web site; be able to process credit card, debit card, or other electronic transfer payments; confirm contributions via electronic mail; pay processing fees to avoid recording a "corporate contribution"; have these funds qualify for federal matching funds; and allow the committee to use an Internet credit card processing vendor in order to obtain contributor information such as name, address, "and other billing information" on file with the issuer of the credit/debit card (see "Federal Election Commission Advisory Opinion Number 1999–9," 1999).

The commission noted within their report the "rising popularity" of the internet "*both as a form of information gathering* and as a vehicle for financial transactions" (5; emphasis added). The significance of information gathering permitted by campaign access to "other billing information" on file with the issuer of the credit/debit card has yet to be fully explored but may grant access to a great deal of demographic information campaigns would have had paid for through other sources. The commission itself granted permission for information gathering by requiring campaigns to solicit the name of the employer and the person's occupation if the contribution is above $200.

The more obvious effect of the ruling is that the commission, noting the contradiction with the Bradley proposal, revised its regulations to permit credit card contributions to be eligible for federal matching funds. After the 30-day legislative review period, the regulations took retroactive effect to January 1, 1999.

UNIQUE DOMAINS: FUND-RAISING ON THE NET

The ability of campaigns to use the Internet as a fund-raising vehicle eligible for federal matching funds is the most significant development for the Internet in campaign 2000. Politics is often seen as a game of beating expectations. The Internet certainly did that. Three features of the medium made it particularly promising as the election year opened: its dramatic speed, relatively low cost, and ability to attract voter-initiated contact. Phil Noble, president of Politics Online, comments, "We all expected online fundraising to take off in the presidential campaign, but no one expected it to continue to skyrocket to such levels" ("Follow the Money," 2000).

As mentioned earlier, Bill Bradley opened the door by getting approval for federal matching funds of Internet dollars. Bradley was also the first candidate in U.S. history to break the $1 million level in Internet donations. Like many things in politics, records are made to be broken.

Initially, John McCain's campaign turned to the Internet to establish a grassroots movement. Max Fose, the then-28-year-old Internet director, noted that the Internet is the "ultimate grassroots-organizing tool" (Moore, 2000). That organization got people involved, and involvement—even through the limited connections the Internet provides—turned into contributions. "In the hours of darkness between John McCain's victory in New Hampshire and the start of the next business day, he raised $300,000 . . . through his website. By week's end the total was $2 million—numbers that would have been higher had the site not become temporarily dysfunctional because of heavy traffic" (Birnbaum, 2000).

The Internet made cash readily available to campaigns at critical junctures. Campaigns are not able to spend on the promise of money pledged, nor can they draw upon money until the checks are deposited (during regular business hours) and are credited to the campaign's account. Even though McCain lost to Bush in the South Carolina primary, the immediate transference of Web donations provided him the momentum to engage throughout the southern campaign. Without such an infusion of cash, the McCain campaign likely would have folded.

Momentum cannot be underestimated. The old saying that nothing breeds success like success proved true in the McCain campaign. As the campaign developed new modes of Internet interaction from online chats with donors to increased information about how money would be spent, the McCain campaign's fund-raising prowess became even more evident. While Bradley was the first to break the $1 million benchmark, McCain was the first candidate to raise the $1 million on the Internet within 48 hours ("Who's First?" 2001).

The McCain campaign demonstrated the power of the Internet as a fund-raising tool: "roughly 22% of his total campaign contributions on line" ("Who's First?" 2001), which was more than any other candidate in the primaries. Other than the fact that the contributions were online, McCain opened the political process to two much-sought-after groups of voters: first-time donors and those with younger demographics. Becky Donatelli, an Internet strategist for McCain, claimed that almost half of the online donors were first-time donors and that nearly 60 percent were under the age of 45 ("McCain Fundraising," 2000).

Generally, political fund-raisers go after the big donors. The reasons are simple. Those who are willing and able to give the maximum legal contribution require less time than going after multiple donors for the same total amount. Those donors often require face time with the candidate at some major function. Such functions also serve as good press events, assisting the campaign in reaching a wider audience.

The Internet upset the traditional fund-raising strategies. In part, the Internet served as a vehicle to enable donors to contribute at any level. The average credit card donation to McCain was $110 ("Digital Democracy," 2000). That does not seem impressive until we realize that McCain raised over $6 million in his online campaign ("McCain Fundraising," 2000). Further, the 2000 election demonstrated that "online fundraising beats offline in terms of speed, ease, and cost" (Derfner, 2001). Finally, donors were also visitors to the Web site, exposing them to the McCain message of the day.

The Bradley and McCain campaigns were so successful that in the 2000 presidential election all candidates had "Internet departments that raise money, recruit, and direct volunteers, and produce so-called banner ads that run on the bottom of widely read Web pages" (Birnbaum, 2000).

The Internet in other federal races did not enjoy such widespread use. Nearly 40 percent of federal election campaigns existed "without a mechanism to accept contributions" (Derfner, 2001).

As successful as the Internet proved to be in election 2000, the breakthrough came in the form of potential unrealized opportunity. Less than 14 million Americans have used credit cards for online transactions ("Digital Democracy," 2000). There is still widespread distrust of how credit numbers can be abused by hackers, and users are skeptical of unseen processors who are accessing information on the other end of the line. Further, the Internet still accounts for a small percentage of a campaign's overall budget. In relation to all federal candidates, one study found that candidates "raised 95% of their money offline" (Derfner, 2001).

The 2000 elections proved how the Internet might be a potential for functional and significant campaign resources. We may anticipate that a great percentage of campaigns will be ready to tap its capabilities in elections to follow.

DISPERSING INFORMATION, ORGANIZING PEOPLE

The use of the Internet by the everyday consumer is becoming more distinct. Seventy-four percent of people who use the Internet claim that their primary use is to send or receive email (Harris Polling, 2001). The next major use categories are "to check on news updates, weather, etc." and "to get information about a hobby or special interest" (Harris Polling, 2001). With the target audience clear, political parties began to find ways to incorporate potential voter use with political purposes.

The Democratic Party did less with the medium at the convention than the Republicans. However, the Democrats took on an enormous amount of grassroots feedback in developing the party platform, a document that is usually rather meaningless to the campaign agenda. Joe Andres, chairman of the Democratic National Convention, noted that this was "the first interactive platform in the history of the United States of America. We had more than 45,000 Americans who wrote in their ideas for what should be in the platform [and] how our platform should reflect their values as they go through this process. . . . That clearly changed the way in which we saw the very process. . . . We think the platform has much more moral authority than it would otherwise because of that" (Hoefer, 2000a). Andres reported that 60 million people looked at the platform that year, making it appear that the platform is not an irrelevant party identifier.

Republicans made their own inroads to the Internet. As a category of user, Republicans "were more likely to be checking the daily story than Democrats or Independents" (Rainie and Packel, 2001). Also, Republicans were the first to find that the Internet proved to be a needed outlet for those who did not find coverage through traditional media outlets. For example, when ABC elected to run *Monday Night Football* instead of the opening night of the Republican National Convention, those preferring Peter Jennings's coverage were reduced to the half-time report on politics. Meanwhile, ABCNews.com produced five programs a day for its Internet audience. The Republican Party assisted the effort by establishing the first press tent dedicated to Internet coverage. The "Internet Ally" became a nonstop parade of political leaders who dropped by for interviews and for the curious who gathered to judge the public relations spin that the convention was receiving.

Online news organizations began to find their stride this election. America Online (AOL), for example, argued that there were four distinctions in online news coverage (deLaski in Hoefer, 2000b). One is the interactivity of the event. The audience felt a real-time connection to the campaigns and the issues. Second is the sense of community you can get online from other people around the country and commune with them while you're watching an event. The third is the research nature—the fact that it's a better research tool than any other medium. And fourth is "on demand"—the fact that if you don't want to watch it while the networks put it on, you can come back anytime.

The interactive nature of what has been traditional news sites has fueled the ethical debate about the proper role of the journalist. For example, many news organizations provided links to nonpartisan groups like www.BeAVoter.org, which invites people to register to vote. Similarly, online polls and instantaneous ratings of the convention speeches blend reporting with entertainment. Such public journalism has produced widespread debate in traditional journalistic circles but does not seem to weigh in with the new dot.com world of journalism. While dispersing information was important for the party at the national and local level, the candidates began using the Internet to develop stronger organizational ties to their constituents and campaigns.

Candidates led the way in developing organizing structures for involvement. Notably, Bill Bradley was able to use a cyber-precinct system that proved interesting. The system is built around the organizing personality of the volunteer. A volunteer who can get 25 people to join his or her group obtains a campaign title. Various levels of membership permit greater levels of access to campaign information and even privileges at political events in the area. The organizing principle is interpersonal communication.

This model stands in contrast to what Robert Putnam (1995) has labeled "tertiary associations." These are groups where for the "vast majority of their members, the only act of membership consists in writing a check for dues, or perhaps occasionally reading a newsletter. Few ever attend any meetings of such organizations, and most are unlikely ever (knowingly) to encounter any other member" (70). Online chat rooms provided encounters that established a sense of connectivity for the participants.

Notably, one of the clear developments of this election cycle was the recruitment and use of online volunteers. Volunteers could sign up online to work with action groups or campaigns, saving hours of needless waiting and more efficiently putting volunteers to work. President Clinton's Summit for America's Future, highlighting the role of volunteerism by Americans, is a model for how organizations learned about organizing groups for specific action (see Volunteer America, 2001).

In elections, unlike the periods of governing in off-election years, Internet user groups consisted of more like-minded individuals. This is a notable shift. Traditionally, campaigns rally people around the candidates and not necessarily those with overall common interests. Virtual organizers this election cycle began organizing people who had common interests and moving those groups toward candidate identification. For this election cycle, this permitted virtual activists to enter the mainstream in force. The magnitude of effort compelled at least one company to form for the express purpose of training people how to organize and network (see, e.g., Net Action, 2000).

Some activists are mainstream politicians, like House Majority Leader Dick Armey, whose, Web site serves his district as well as the broader conservative activists across the nation (www.armey.com). Others are aggregations of citizens forging relationships around a common cause. Notable groups include Citizens for Balanced Growth (www.carycbh.org), which was started in Cary, North Carolina, and soon became the local public's venting station, or the Conservation Action Network (http://takeaction.worldwildlife.org), which permits users to contact government officials, media outlets, and regulatory agencies about environmental advocacy issues. Typically, traditional lobbying groups do not encourage participant involvement less the discussions dilute the power of the lobbying efforts. Regardless of position or title, those involved in the political process are beginning to recognize that the Internet as a medium makes it easier for voters to debate topics and find information.

Finally, Internet users this election cycle used humor as a means of developing cohesion. The daily outpouring of Internet jokes kept email boxes full. One study noted that "54% of Net users trafficked in e-mail jokes about the election" (Derfner, 2001). Such messages with attitudinal intent have yet to be fully studied but are bound to be the substance of future election studies.

FUTURE CHANGES

One of the directions scholars will watch is the customization of the Internet. The technology already exists for such customization, but as with many other phases of technology, the public must be ready to accept it and the providers must find ways of making it profitable. Currently, the Internet serves as a one-size-fits-all source of information, used like traditional news outlets. A person wanting national news goes to national news sites but must go to other locations to find state news and perhaps still others for local news. Those wanting political information do not have customized access. That will surely change. Lee Rainie with the PEW Center suggests that "probably a lot of sites will figure out it's not that hard to plug in data like a ZIP code and kick out a lot of local information—the databases already exist" (Schafer, 2001, 3). AOL has already introduced such services, with CNN planning to make alliances with local providers to give similar information in the next few years. Commenting on National Public Radio, editor Andy Brack at Netpulse noted, "The Internet currently does not provide huge amounts of targeting. And that's what makes it difficult for candidates, more than likely, to make purchasing decisions for banner ads" (Abramson, 2000).

Another must for the Internet is to provide more than ease of use for information. The medium has yet to discover a unique platform. Just as early television took on the traits of radio before it emerged as a visual medium, the Internet has yet to find what combination of factors will provide it with a unique voice. "Today's Web news is often fairly detailed, but otherwise it looks, reads, and sounds a lot like newspapers, radio and TV (except in terms of video quality, where it doesn't look as good as broadcast" (Schafer, 2001, 1).

The Internet is not currently limited by the self-imposed ethics of traditional journalistic practices. Thus, the medium will result in the development of a new ethic, policed not by the industry itself but by the users. For example, one of the issues that surfaced in the 2000 election was the publication of raw exit poll data. Matt Drudge, known for breaking the Clinton-Lewinsky scandal, also ignored the journalistic embargo of such data until after the polls were closed. His site was so overwhelmed that the system crashed for a while, even though other sites mirrored it. The bottom line is that people want information and will go to whatever source can offer it.

The increased use of the Internet will also pave the way for a new type of political consultant whose job it is to master the Internet spin control. In its infancy, campaigns have demonstrated fear that subversive individuals or groups will spread gossip, rumors, and lies to unduly sway unwary voters. Speed has been more valued in the decision-making processes than deliberative—or even correct—decisions. The new Internet politics uses a different model. It relies on the use of experts who understand that campaigns also have access to email discussion groups and virtual information portals to rebut information. Essentially, campaigns are beginning to recognize that simply posting material on the Web does not easily manipulate decisions. Not only has the credibility for online sources failed to emerge, but the manipulation of decision-making criteria is not easily achieved. The process is simple: to allow corrections to erroneous information through more expression rather than to insert controls to prevent errors in the first place. Finding Internet specialists with the tools to monitor the Internet and the knowledge to intervene appropriately on behalf of a campaign will be critical to future electoral success. Noting the fact that news cycles on the Internet have virtually disappeared, "candidates responded to criticisms before the criticisms were actually uttered; the dialogue was essentially constant" (Derfner, 2001).

The area for strategists to watch is voter insurgencies—not campaign-driven events. This year, for example, the idea of vote trading emerged as a grassroots effort. The idea was that Gore supporters in states leaning heavily toward Gore would trade votes with Nader voters in key swing states. Thus, the Nader voters stood a better chance of helping Nader achieve the 5 percent threshold required for federal matching funds for the Green Party in 2004 and Gore would be assisted in taking the presidency. The tactic developed online as "Nader Trade," and www.voteswap2000.com was quickly eliminated through legal action. Before it was stopped, nearly 1,400 Nader voters in Florida pledged to vote for Gore (Harris, 2000). The idea that a voter-generated movement could tilt the balance of power among competing groups is significant. As one writer puts it, "[T]he Web can shift the center of political gravity to the voters" (Derfner, 2001).

One such shift is toward the small donor, making more people part of the political structure. If the trend toward online fund-raising continues, what will be its political effects? One conclusion is that there will be greater interaction between the campaigns and their publics. "Online fundraising will challenge the essentially passive relationship that the majority of people will have with government and politics" ("Digital Democracy," 2000). A second trend is toward less reliance on the political parties for fund-raising assistance. Party identification and loyalty may very well give way to a more independent voter who identifies with particular issues or candidates.

Fund-raising issues still need to be resolved. Problems with the regulatory environment may very well emerge. "At this time, even the smallest municipalities . . . can impose regulations on charitable solicitations" (Mercer, 1998, 5). Ethical issues related to donor tracking, Web linkages, and campaign responsibility for supporter actions will undoubtedly arise. Yet these problems will be resolved, creating a new series of questions to be determined.

Finally, the age of the traditional, repetitive stump speech may very well be over. Campaigns will find a need to be timely and have a fresh message. The daily repetition of remarks before various geographical audiences will not sustain the Internet's need for new information. Conversely, Internet messages must develop a consonance with the candidate's stump speeches.

REFERENCES

Abramson, Larry. 2000. "Political Internet Use and Advertising." National Public Radio. Cited in Netpulse. August 17. http:www.politicsonline.com/toolbox.fund.asp

BIGResearch. 2001. "Public Policy & Media Influence Study." February. www.bigresearch.com

Birnbaum, Jeffery H. 2000. "Electronic 2000: Politicking on the Internet, We'll Be Voting There Too." *Fortune*, March 6. http://www.elibrary.com/s/edumark/getdoc.cgi?id=18610472x127y34045w0&OIDS=0Q00

Derfner, Jeremy. 2001. "So, Was It a Net Election?" *Slate*, January 25. http://slated.msn.cx/netelection/entries/01-01-25_97767.asp

"Digital Democracy: Stand Online Voting, and More." 2000. *The Economist*, 355, June 24. http://www.elibrary.com/s/edumark/getdoc.cgi?id=188610472x127y34045w0&OIDS=0Q00

"Federal Election Commission Advisory Opinion Number 1998–2." 1998. November 20. http://herndon3.sdrdc.com/ao/a0/980022.html

"Federal Election Commission Advisory Opinion Number 1999–9." 1999. June 10. http://herndon3.sdrdc.com/ao/a0/990009.html

"Federal Election Commission Advisory Opinion Number 1999–17." 1999. November 10. http://herndon3.sdrdc.com/ao/a0/990017.html

"Follow the Money." 2000. Politics Online: Fundraising & Internet Tools for Politics. http://www.politicsonline.com/pol2000/follow_the_money.asp

Harris, Scott. 2000. " 'Nader Traders' May Have Affected Outcome in Florida." *Industry Standard,* November 17. http://www.cnn.com/2000/TECH/computing/11/17/nader.traders.help.gore.idg/index.html

Harris Polling. 2001. "National Polling on the Internet." February 21. http://nationaljournal.com/scripts/printpage.cgi?/members/polltrack/2001/02/0221har

Hoefer, Andy. 2000a. "DNC's Andrew Sees Internet as 'Future of Political Parties.' " *Politics Online,* August 16. http://www.politicsonline.com/specialreports/democratic_convention/polstory

Hoefer, Andy. (17 August 2000b). "The Internet Turns Political Journalism Around, According to AOL's DeLaski." *Politics Online,* August 17. http://www.politicsonline.com/specialreports/democratic_convention/polstory.asp?id=10

"Internet Election News Audience Seeks Convenience, Familiar Names: Youth Vote Influence Online Information." 2000. http://www.pewinternet.org/reports/toc.asp?Report=27

"McCain Fundraising." 2000. "Politics Online: Fundraising & Internet Tools for Politics." www.politicsonline.com/specialreports/000202.mccain02.asp

Mercer, Eric. 1998. "How Can We Use the Internet for Fundraising?" October 27. http://www.nonprofits.org/misc/981027em.html

Moore, John. 2000. "Point, Click, Donate." *ZDNet,* March 6. www.zdnet.com/sp/stories/news/0,4538,2456315.00.html

Net Action. 2000. www.netaction.org/training

Pavlik, John V. 1998. *New Media Technology: Cultural and Commercial Perspectives* (2nd ed.). New York: Allyn and Bacon.

Pew Center for Civic Journalism. 2001. "James K. Batten Award for Excellence in Civic Journalism." *American Journalism Review,* 23(4), 8–9.

Putnam, Robert. 1995. "Bowling Alone: America's Declining Social Capital." *Journal of Democracy,* 6 (January), 65–78.

Rainie, Lee and Dan Packel. 2001. "More Online, Doing More." The Pew Internet & American Life Project. February 18. http://www.pewinternet.org

Schafer, Alison 2001. "2000 Fizzled as *the* Internet Election." *Online Journalism Review,* February 1. http://ojr.usc.edu/content/print.cfm?print=25

Volunteer America. 2001. http://www.impactonline.com

Weiner, Allen. 2000. "Online Newspapers Bask in Overtime Election." *Forbes.com,* November 29. http://www.forbes.com/2000/11/29/1129netratings.html

"Who's First?" 2001. Politics Online: Fundraising & Internet Tools for Politics. January 29. http://www.politicsonline.com/specialreports/fec/fec.asp

Chapter 8

Videostyle and Political Advertising Effects in the 2000 Presidential Campaign

Lynda Lee Kaid

Political advertising has played a role in every presidential campaign for the past five decades. The 2000 campaign was no exception. An open race, with two visible challengers who brought many incumbent characteristics to the contest, this campaign provided an opportunity to assess the videostyle of George W. Bush and Al Gore individually and in the context of prior presidential elections.

POLITICAL ADVERTISING AND THE VIDEOSTYLE CONCEPT

Although the events of the postelection period have overshadowed and dominated discussion of the 2000 campaign, the political spot advertising in the 2000 air war was of historical importance in several ways. For instance, this campaign saw unprecedented levels of spending on political spots, partly as a result of the massive expenditures of soft money by both national political parties (Devlin, 2001). The candidates produced a large number of different spots, but they also blended and coordinated the expenditures and production of their spots with their respective political parties. Thus, many near-identical spots were aired for which the only distinguishable differences were the tag/disclaimer lines, some giving the candidate campaign committee as sponsor, some crediting the respective national party.

Prior research on political advertising has given candidates and parties reason to be optimistic that such expenditures can have an impact on voter perceptions and electoral outcomes (Kaid, 1999). In experimental studies directed specifically to the ads of the presidential candidates in

1988, 1992, and 1996, researchers have shown that exposure to the television spots used in the campaign has effects, sometimes negative and sometimes positive, on the evaluations of the candidates (Kaid, 1997; Kaid and Chanslor, 1995; Kaid, Leland, and Whitney, 1992; Kaid, McKinney, and Tedesco, 2000; Kaid and Tedesco, 1999).

Research on videostyle has been designed to describe the approaches that candidates take in their political advertising. Originally outlined by Kaid and Davidson (1986) in an analysis of U.S. Senate campaigns, videostyle applies Goffman's (1959) notion of "self-presentation" in interpersonal settings to television advertising, taking the position that a candidate seeks ways of presenting a positive image to voters through the techniques available in the visual medium of television. Kaid and Davidson (1986) and later Kaid and Johnston (2001) describe three elements of videostyle, the verbal, the nonverbal, and production techniques. How a candidate uses these three elements of videostyle can be combined to describe that candidate's videostyle.

The verbal components of videostyle relate to the substantive content communicated in a television spot. For instance, does the content of the message focus on the image qualities of the candidate or on issue positions? Does the content have a negative or positive focus? Verbal content also can relate to the type of proof offered for the claims in an ad. Nonverbal content in a political spot has many similarities to the study of nonverbal characteristics in an interpersonal setting (Burgoon, Buller, and Woodall, 1989), analyzing the candidate's speaking rate and tone, body movements, dress and setting, and other similar concerns. The production element of videostyle, of course, refers to the way in which modern audio and video production techniques are used to convey the candidate's message. This can range from use of camera angles to special effects.

Taken together, these three elements of videostyle provide a way of comparing candidate styles with each other and with candidates in previous campaigns. Kaid and Johnston (2001) recently analyzed the videostyle of all general election presidential candidates from 1952 through 1996. Thus, the results from the analysis of the 2000 ads can be compared to the videostyles of earlier candidates.

DESCRIPTION OF THE AD SAMPLE AND ANALYSIS

The procedure for determining videostyle for the 2000 ads followed the content analysis procedures used by Kaid and Johnston (2001) for prior presidential campaigns, and the specific codesheet and categories are detailed in their work. Briefly, the television spot was the unit of analysis. Verbal content categories involved distinguishing between image and issue ads, those with a positive and negative focus, the type of proof used (emotional, logical, or ethical in accordance with Aristotle's typology), and categories that related to the incumbent and challenger strategies used by the candidates, as originally delineated by Trent and Friedenberg (1983).

Spots were coded for the dominant approach used in the ad. The negative and positive focus categories were related to the candidate sponsoring the ad. Ads were coded as positive if the ad concentrated on the positive characteristics of the candidate sponsoring the ad but were considered negative if the dominant focus was on the opponent, criticizing or attacking the opponent. Comparative ads were not a separate category; an ad that included both positive and negative information was placed in one of the two categories according to how dominant the content was in the ad. The issue and image category was coded similarly. If an ad emphasized policy concerns or specific policy proposals as the dominant content of the ad, it was considered an issue ad. If the spot's dominant approach was to emphasize the personal characteristics or qualities of the sponsor or opponent, even if an issue was mentioned, the spot was coded as an image spot. Coding categories also included a series of categories designed by the researcher to supplement the traditional videostyle coding of production techniques by adding categories that identified the technological distortions present in the ads. These distortions are defined as "audio or video technology in a political spot that creates a false, distorted, deceptive, or misleading impression" (Kaid, 1996, 132).[1] Categories of manipulations have been outlined elsewhere to include (1) editing techniques, (2) special effects, (3) visual imagery/dramatizations, (4) computerized alteration techniques, and (5) subliminal messages (Kaid, 1996, 2000).

The ad sample consisted of ads produced for the general election period for both George W. Bush and Al Gore. This sample included ads that started airing after the primary season in May and June, and because of the blending of candidate and party soft money spending, the sample included ads aired by the Republican and Democratic national parties on behalf of the candidacies of their standard-bearers, Bush and Gore. This resulted in a sample of 161 ads made available by the Political Commercial Archive at the University of Oklahoma. In this sample, there were 115 Gore ads and 46 Bush ads. These ads were coded by three trained graduate students. Using Holsti's formula (North, Holsti, Zaninovich, and Zinnes, 1963),[2] intercoder reliability was calculated for a subsample of the spots and averaged +.85 across the entire sample for all categories.

Additional evaluation of the spots and their potential effects on voters is provided by reporting the results of reactions of potential voters to a selection of the campaign spots just before the election. In sessions conducted on November 1–3, 2000, potential voters, primarily from undergraduate speech communication classes at the University of Oklahoma, were recruited to watch a series of eight Bush and Gore spots[3] and to respond to the spots positively or negatively on computer dials that continuously registered responses in relation to the spot content. Although this group was overbalanced toward females (77 percent), the distribution for party affiliation was more even, with 41 percent Democrats, 36 percent Republicans, and 23 percent Independent/other.

BUSH AND GORE VIDEOSTYLE IN CAMPAIGN 2000

Verbal Components of 2000 Videostyle

Of particular interest in the 2000 campaign is the reduction in negative advertising for the winning candidate. Table 8.1 shows that George W. Bush's ads reflected a predominantly positive tone. In contrast, Al Gore's ads were significantly more negative in tone, X^2 (1) = 8.33, p = 02. Thus, while only 37 percent of Bush's ads were negative, Gore ran almost twice as many negative ads (62 percent). Both Bush and Gore focused their attacks on issues; 49 percent of Gore's and 35 percent of Bush's attacks fell into this category (a difference that was not statistically significant). However, Bush was significantly more likely than Gore to attack his opponent on personal qualities (17 percent versus 5 percent, X^2 (1) = 6.13, p = .01.

A striking feature of the negative attack ads in 2000 was the fact that, for both candidates, over three-quarters of the negative ads were sponsored by their respective political parties (both national and individual state party organizations), rather than being attributable directly to the candidate's own campaign committees. For instance, an early Republican National Committee (RNC) ad called "Really" attracted media attention with its ridicule of Gore for his denials about 1996 fund-raising at a Buddhist temple and for taking credit for inventing the Internet. Another RNC ad titled "Nonsense" accused Gore of bending the truth. Even the Ohio Republican Party got into the game with several ads, including an attack on Gore's personal integrity in an ad called "Cookin' in the Kitchen" that shows Gore stumbling and fumbling to answer a question by reporter Lisa Meyers about whether he or Bill Clinton have ever told a lie.

The Gore-Lieberman campaign and their affiliated party organizations concentrated their attacks more on Bush's issue stances and accomplishments in Texas. A Democratic National Committee (DNC) ad called "Oh, Sure" accused Bush of promoting programs to help the oil industry, big industry, and polluters, ending with the tag line "By favoring the few, George W. Bush would hurt the many." Although Lieberman escaped much individual scrutiny in Republican ads, Dick Cheney received some

Table 8.1
Characteristics of the 2000 General Election Ads

	Bush (n = 46)	**Gore (n = 115)**
Verbal Content of Ad		
Ad Focus*		
Positive	63%	38%
Negative	37	62
Use of Appeals		
Logical	89	93
Emotional*	26	47
Ethical	24	37
Fear Appeal*	9	56
Ad Type*		
Issue	63	84
Image	37	16
Nonverbal Content of Ad		
Candidate Is Speaker in Ad*	26	16
Presence of American Symbols*	22	42
Almost Always Makes Eye Contact*	26	6
Smiling Facial Expression*	48	16
Production Content of Ad		
Camera Shot—Tight*	41	24
Slow Motion*	24	53
Split Screen*	4	39
Technological Distortions in Ads	83	92

*Chi-square test indicates difference is significant at $p \leq .05$.

direct hits from the Democrats with criticisms for being sympathetic to oil and big business interests.

Another indicator of the verbal content of ads is the emphasis on issues and image qualities. Here the 2000 ads are very much in line with prior contests. Both candidates placed most of their emphasis on issues. However, Table 8.1 shows that Gore placed significantly more emphasis on issues than did Bush, since 84 percent of Gore's ads versus 63 percent of Bush's ads were predominantly about issues, X^2 (1) = 7.91, p = .01.

The specific issue and image content emphasized is outlined in Table

Table 8.2
Emphasis on Specific Issues and Candidate Qualities in 2000 General Election Spots

	Bush (n = 46)	Gore (n = 115)
Issue Mentions		
Economy*	13%	32%
Deficit	13	11
Crime	0	4
Taxes*	4	25
Drugs	2	0
Children	13	20
Medicare/SS/Elderly	35	37
Health Care	13	17
Education*	46	27
Environment*	4	28
Candidate Character Mentions		
Honesty	15	10
Strength*	4	37
Compassion*	39	20
Competence	7	7
Aggressiveness*	48	9
Activeness	44	47
Qualifications	4	5

*Chi-square indicates difference is significant at $p \leq .05$.

8.2. The biggest differences between the two candidates appear on a few issues. Gore was over twice as likely as Bush to emphasize the economy, trying in 32 percent of his ads to take credit for the prosperity of the Clinton-Gore years. Gore also spoke of taxes much more often than did Bush, mostly in negative ads criticizing Bush's tax plans. Both candidates concentrated equally on Medicare, Social Security, and issues related to the elderly (35 percent of Bush ads and 37 percent of Gore ads). However, two other differences were important. First, by virtue of his claims about accomplishments in Texas, Bush was able to grab and sustain an advantage on the education issue. Nearly half of his spots (46 percent) concentrated on this issue, compared to only 27 percent of Gore ads, a statistically significant difference. In numerous ads, Bush spoke about the Clinton-Gore "education recession" and touted his own "education agenda." Gore, however, easily outpaced Bush on the environment issue, on which he focused seven times as much attention as did Bush. Most of this environment focus was on critical attention to the Bush record on environmental issues in Texas. In one DNC ad called "Oil & Water" Bush was accused of letting polluters run free, while Gore was credited with cleaning up pollution problems. The spot ended by saying, "America's environment is cleaner now. Do we really want it to look like Texas?"

Although issues were the dominant focus of ads for both candidates, image qualities were not missing. Table 8.2 also shows what qualities the candidates emphasized in their spots. George W. Bush was able to bring out his emphasis on "compassion" frequently. In fact, he co-opted this traditionally Democratic value by conveying it in 39 percent of his spots, compared to similar emphasis in only half as many Gore spots (20 percent). Bush also built a big advantage over Gore in the "aggressiveness" category, while Gore conveyed strength and toughness more frequently.

Another important aspect of the verbal style of the ads is the type of proof used to present a candidate's arguments. Table 8.1 demonstrates that both candidates relied a great deal on logical proof, using statistics and graphs, and there was no major difference in their use of ethical proof. The biggest difference between Gore and Bush in 2000 was in the use of emotional proof. Gore was much more likely to use emotional proof in his ads (47 percent) versus 26 percent for Bush), X^2 (1) = 5.92, p = .01. Gore used emotional appeals in both positive and negative ads and often with children. One of his most poignant ads was called "Ian," in which video is shown of a small boy for whose health care needs Gore had fought. Not surprising, given this emphasis on emotional proof, Gore was also the candidate most likely to use some type of fear appeal in his ads. While Bush used a fear appeal in only 9 percent of his spots, Gore used a fear appeal in over half of his ads, X^2 (1) = 30.71, p = .000. Most of the fear appeals used by Gore centered on the health care/elderly care issues and on children. For instance, in "Siding," he accused Bush of hurting seniors by siding with big drug companies, and in "Judge" Bush was chastised for his record on children's issues in Texas.

Incumbent and Challenger Style in the Verbal Message

Verbal style is also conveyed by how a candidate uses the content of messages in the context of electoral position. An incumbent president has certain advantages and underpinnings of the office within which to position a campaign message, while a challenger must rely on the ability to emphasize the need for change while providing reassurance of continuity. Trent and Friedenberg (1983) have outlined a number of verbal strategies that characterize an incumbent or challenger. These categories

Table 8.3
Challenger and Incumbent Strategies in 2000 Presidential Spots

Percent of Spots	Challenger Bush (n = 46)	Assumed Incumbent Gore (n = 115)
Incumbent Strategies		
Use of Symbolic Trappings	2%	4%
Presidency Stands for Legitimacy	0	4
Competency and the Office	7	10
Consulting with World Leaders	0	1
Charisma and the Office*	11	0
Using Endorsements by Leaders	2	0
Emphasizing Accomplishments	2	10
Above-the-Trenches Posture	24	30
Depending on Surrogates to Speak*	13	1
Challenger Strategies		
Calling for Changes*	48	30
Speaking to Traditional Values	17	11
Taking the Offensive Position	26	25
Emphasizing Optimism	20	11
Representing Center of Party	0	0
Attacking the Record of Opponent*	24	63

*Chi-square is significant at $p \leq .05$ for difference between incumbent/challenger.

have been adapted in videostyle analysis to guide an understanding of presidential candidate messages. Table 8.3 shows the application of these various strategies to the Bush and Gore 2000 campaign ads. In this situation, Gore was considered a "presumed incumbent" in that he was the sitting vice president at the time of the campaign, making Bush the challenger.

The findings on use of incumbent and challenger styles in the verbal messages of Gore and Bush may provide interesting clues to Gore's failure. A striking finding is that there is absolutely no category of incumbent strategies in which Gore shows superiority over Bush. In fact, the only two incumbent strategy categories that show a significant difference between the two candidates favor the challenger, Bush, who was better able to convey "charisma" in regard to the presidency and who was better able to attract "surrogates" to speak on his behalf. This latter category reminds political observers that Gore deliberately chose to limit campaign use of the one surrogate who might have helped his cause, at least among certain groups, then-President Bill Clinton.

Bush also claimed an advantage in many challenger strategies, capitalizing on the ability to "call for change." Gore was ahead on only one category, the challenger stance of "attacking the record of the opponent." While Gore's predecessor Bill Clinton was successful in using the attack strategy as an incumbent in his 1996 campaign, he also took advantage of the incumbent strategies at his disposal, particularly "emphasizing accomplishments" of his own. This balance was missing from Gore's positioning and may have been a factor in his inability to convert the substantial political capital of the Clinton-Gore years into a victory.

Nonverbal Content of the Ads

The second component of videostyle relates to the nonverbal aspects of the candidate's self-presentation in political spots. One of the most interesting of these variables has been the simple physical presence/speaking of the candidate. The 2000 campaign conveyed a promising nonverbal message in this regard. For the first time in several campaign cycles, the presidential candidates appeared and spoke for themselves in several campaign spots. As Table 8.1 shows, George Bush was the dominant speaker in over one-fourth of all his campaign spots (26 percent). While Bush was the dominant speaker significantly more than Gore, even Gore was the main speaker in 16 percent of his ads. This compares favorably with the 1996 campaign in which Dole and Clinton were main speakers in only 5 percent of the campaign ads (Kaid, 1998; Kaid and Johnston, 2001). This advantage for Bush is mainly a result of his more positive spot emphasis. In several spots he spoke directly to the camera and made a direct statement to the American people. For instance, in "Hard Things," Bush expressed his belief that doing the right thing is sometimes hard and tried in his reflections to give the voter an insight into his own character and beliefs, In other spots, he appeared with children and his wife, Laura, and spoke directly about his education program and goals. In several spots, Bush was the main speaker in another language, as he attempted to attract Hispanic voters by speaking Spanish. Gore also spoke directly to the camera in some spots or was presented speaking to groups, as in "Beancounters," a spot in which Gore tried to convey his lack of support for turning medical care over to government bureaucrats. Gore also tried out his Spanish-speaking skills in a few spots.

George W. Bush was able to seize a lead in several other nonverbal components of videostyle. Table 8.1 shows an advantage for Bush in establishing eye contact with viewers, which he did in 26 percent of his spots, compared to only 6 percent for Gore. In addition, Bush was three times as likely to be seen with a smiling facial expression as was Gore; Bush was smiling 48 percent of the time, versus 16 percent for Gore. There were no significant differences in the formality/informality of the settings of the two candidates' ads or in the type of dress they favored.

One other nonverbal component did favor Al Gore, however. Gore was able to take advantage of American symbols in his spots more frequently than Bush. That means that Gore was able to position himself in settings where American symbols provided a backdrop for his positions. This included symbols such as the American flag, positioning with the American Capitol building, and other symbolic representations of American politics and culture. The use of such symbols may have provided Gore with at least some of the trappings of office and incumbency that he failed to take advantage of in his verbal messages.

Production Components of Videostyle

In recent campaigns the absence of the candidate as a major speaker in the commercials has limited the ability to compare some aspects of the production components of videostyle, such as camera angles and shots. However, since both Gore and Bush were present and speaking in a number of the 2000 spots, it was possible to compare these aspects of videostyle. Table 8.1 shows the areas in which there were differences in the two candidates' production styles. First, there were no differences in the camera angles used in the presentation of Bush and Gore; both were shot primarily straight on with few differences in high or low angles. However, the type of camera shot did suggest a major difference. Bush was much more frequently shown in close-up or tight shots (41 percent) than was Gore (24 percent). Close-ups are thought to convey more warmth and intimacy and to give the viewer a greater sense of immediacy and sympathy. This production quality indicates a quality that should have been favorable to Bush.

Table 8.1 also shows that there were a few differences in specialized production techniques between the candidates. Gore took greater advantage of slow-motion video and of split-screen techniques in his ads. Such special effects techniques are often seen in negative ads and may have fit well with the Gore strategy of creating negative messages about George W. Bush.

The final production technique considered here is the use of technological distortions designed to create false or misleading impressions for viewers. The evidence in Table 8.1 shows that in presidential campaigns, at least, the trend toward greater use of such techniques continues. In fact, four of every five Bush ads (83 percent) and nine out of every ten Gore ads (92 percent) used some type of computer or video technique for this purpose. Examples abound, of course, but few observers have forgotten the famous "RATS" ad, a spot in which Bush was accused of using subliminal techniques to malign his opponent. Titled "Priority," this ad used fast-paced movement of letters from the word "bureaucrats" to leave some observers with the view that the Bush campaign was trying to implant the word "R-A-T-S" in association with Gore in the minds of American voters. Although not subjected to the same media scrutiny, the Gore campaign ad "Oh, Sure" created a similar effect with the word "NurSINg" that could arguably have been designed to associate the word "S-I-N" with George W. Bush.

Both campaigns also used distorted techniques to convey sinister and emotional images of children and the elderly by converting color footage to black-and-white images and using slow-motion and freeze-frames to highlight distorted images. In an RNC ad called "Let's See," producers reproduced and distorted Gore's picture in a television screen and imposed over it statistics of those indicted and accused of ethical misconduct in the Clinton-Gore administration, ending with a screen that touted the Web site "gorewillsayanything.com."

For their part, Gore and the DNC were quick to use such techniques to their advantage. A frequently seen piece of video showed a distorted Houston skyline, polluted almost beyond recognition. In a spot called "Needle," the video showed the Seattle skyline and then manipulated it to show a sudden haze while ending with the admonition: "Now take a deep breath and imagine Seattle with Bush's Texas-style environmental regulation . . ."

Effects of Videostyle Characteristics on Voters

The effects of any specific political ad or ad component are difficult to pinpoint. However, the reactions of the group of 22 viewers who viewed a sample of the Bush and Gore ads while reacting moment to moment on hand-held computer dials provide some clues about what specific content and techniques were effective in the 2000 ads. As noted earlier, These student voters watched a sample of eight Gore and Bush spots (four for each candidate) and registered their reactions on a scale of 1 (negative/unfavorable to the candidate sponsoring the ad) to 7 (positive/favorable to the sponsor).

First, in terms of the verbal components of videostyle, the viewers in this study were more impressed by positive messages than by negative ones. The highest mean ratings for the candidates throughout the viewing session came during positive messages, and the ratings tended to decline uniformly during negative or attack messages.

Second, issues also rated highly with viewers, validating the candidates' decisions to focus their messages on issue content. In these spots, the highest ratings for Bush and Gore came in spots that focused on education, particularly on the candidates' plans for improving schools and providing help for college educations. Obviously, student subjects probably have a high regard for such issues, but education was also showing up as a leading issue in polls during the 2000 campaign. What issues did not score well? For Bush, his lowest issue-specific ratings (4.04) came when he mentioned his plan to allow private investment of some of the money from Social Security. For Gore, the lowest issue means came when he attacked George Bush for his stance on the minimum wage in Texas (3.73) and for letting pollution worsen in Texas (3.91). It is difficult to be sure if these low scores related to the issues themselves, however, or to the negativity of the message.

The third major pattern relates to a nonverbal aspect of videostyle, the candidate-as-speaker. There is a clear pattern in the reactions to the spots with the computer dial data in favor of the candidate as main speaker in an ad. In the four Bush ads, for instance, Bush received his highest mean score ratings in the ad called "Trust," in which he is the main speaker throughout the ad. This ad focused mainly on Bush as he talked about trusting people to solve problems by giving the people back part of the budget surplus. He got his highest rating of 4.82 when he proclaimed, "And if schools continue to fail, we will give parents different options. I trust you with some of the budget surplus." This ad was much more popular with Republicans, of course, but it also scored well with Independents, and it was more favorably rated by men than by women. A similar pattern emerged in the Gore positive ad "College." Gore received a very high mean rating of 5.41 at the end of this spot when he spoke himself about his own positive platform on college education. Throughout all of the eight spots, the candidates got very high mean ratings from all groups when they were present and speaking themselves in their own spots. This particular nonverbal component of videostyle was very important in the 2000 campaign.

In the production techniques area of videostyle, the most interesting findings came in a spot where there were clear technological alterations, the Gore "Needle" spot, in which the Gore campaign created a haze over the Seattle skyline to suggest what would happen to Seattle if Bush were elected. Viewers did not react well to this technique, and ratings plummeted below the center point of 4.0 at this particular point in the spot. This is an encouraging finding because it may indicate that viewers clearly saw the "trick" as a gimmick and did not react positively toward the candidate's ploy.

CONCLUSION

Overall, the 2000 campaign provided some interesting new trends for videostyle analysis. While some verbal content categories remained similar to past years, with the emphasis on issue content, the overall positivity of the messages was higher as a result of George W. Bush's more positive message. Because Gore had such a high percentage of negative messages and produced so many more commercials than the Bush campaign, the percentage of negative messages for campaign 2000 remained high (77 percent). Nonetheless, George W. Bush is the first candidate since Ronald Reagan in 1984 to present spot messages that have a 2:1 positive/negative ratio. Emotional proof remained a dominant feature of ads, and the tendency of Democratic candidates to use fear appeals was reinforced (Kaid and Johnston, 2001). Finally, Gore's failure to utilize any of the strategies of incumbency may have affected his chances of victory.

From the standpoint of nonverbal characteristics of the spots, the most important development is the reappearance of the candidate as a main speaker in the ads, and voters appeared to reward the candidate who excelled at this, George W. Bush. Bush also established more eye contact with viewers and smiled more. Production characteristics may also have worked in Bush's favor since he was shown in tighter, more intimate camera shots throughout his spots.

A troubling finding in the production area was the high level of technological distortion present in the 2000 ads of both candidates. This is particularly a concern since earlier work has shown that the presence of such distortions can work to the advantage of the sponsoring candidate (Kaid, Lin, and Noggle, 1999; Kaid and Noggle, 1998). However, a study specifically testing the effects of the Bush "RATS" ("Priority") ad showed that the presence of the supposedly subliminal message did not affect viewer evaluation of the candidates (Kaid, 2001).

While some comparisons with prior presidential campaign years have been made throughout this analysis, the Bush and Gore videostyles can also be classified according to the overall style categories used for prior campaigns. Based on the categories adopted by Kaid and Johnston (2001), Bush's videostyle would be classified as "Direct-Logical-Positive." Only one other president merited this classification, Ronald Reagan in his 1980 campaign. Gore, on the other hand, fits best into the "Indirect-Emotional-Negative" classification, and in the company of Adlai Stevenson in 1952, Lyndon Johnson in 1964, Walter Mondale in 1984, Michael Dukakis in 1988, Bill Clinton in 1992 and 1996, and Bob Dole in 1996.

NOTES

The author would like to thank Mary Banwart, Ken Brown, and Kristen Landreville for their assistance with coding and analysis for this project.

1. This portion of the research was partially funded by the National Science Foundation under Awards # SBR-9729450 and SBR-9412925.

2. The formula used to compute reliability is a formula given by North, Holsti, Zaninovich, and Zinnes (1963). It is given for two coders and can be modified for any number of coders.

$$R = \frac{2(C_{1,2})}{C_1 + C_2}$$

where
$C_{1,2}$ = # of category assignments both coders agree on and
$C_1 + C_2$ = total category assignments made by both coders.

3. The spots used in the experimental sessions, in the order of their appearance, were: (1) a positive Bush spot titled "Trust" in which Bush talks about trusting America and renewing America's purpose; (2) a positive Gore ad, "College," in which Gore's college tuition tax deduction for middle-class families is featured; (3) a negative Bush ad, "Gore-Guantuan," that attacks Gore's spending plan and says it will wipe out the surplus and increase governmental spending; (4) a Gore ad titled "Down" that uses a graphic of a dissolving dollar bill to attack Bush's tax cut plan, ending with the message that Gore will pay down the debt, protect Social Security, and give a tax deduction for college tuition; (5) a Bush ad titled "Education Recession" that suggests there is a Clinton/Gore education recession, that Bush raised education standards in Texas, and tells the viewer how to obtain the "Bush blueprint for education" that features accountability, high standards, and local control; (6) a Gore ad titled "Apron" that attacks Bush on the minimum wage in Texas and promotes the "Al Gore plan" of increasing the minimum wage, investing in education, middle-class tax cuts, and a secure retirement; (7) a Bush ad called "Big Relief vs. Big Spending" that compares Bush's tax cut plan with Gore's spending plan, stating Gore's spending plan threatens America's prosperity; and (8) a negative Gore ad called "Needle" that opens with a foggy Houston skyline, attacks Bush on his environmental policies in Texas, and ends with a foggy Seattle skyline, asking the viewer to "imagine Bush's Texas-style environmental regulations" in Seattle.

REFERENCES

Burgoon, J.K., D.B. Buller, and W. Gill Woodall. 1989. *Nonverbal Communication: The Unspoken Dialogue*. New York: Harper & Row.

Devlin, L.P. 2001. "Contrasts in Presidential Campaign Commercials of 2000." *American Behavioral Scientist*, 44(12), 2338–2369.

Goffman, E. 1959. *The Presentation of Self in Everyday Life*. New York: Doubleday Anchor Books.

Kaid, L.L. 1994. "Political Advertising in the 1992 Campaign." In R.E. Denton, Jr., ed., *The 1992 Presidential Campaign: A Communication Perspective*. Westport, CT: Praeger, 111–127.

Kaid, L.L. 1996. "Technology and Political Advertising: The Application of Ethical Standards to the 1992 Spots." *Communication Research Reports*, 13(2), 129–137.

Kaid, L.L. 1997. "Effects of the Television Spots on Images of Dole and Clinton." *American Behavioral Scientist*, 40(2), 1085–1094.

Kaid, L.L. 1998. "Videostyle and the Effects of the 1996 Presidential Campaign Advertising." In R.E. Denton, Jr., ed., *The 1996 Presidential Campaign: A Communication Perspective*. Westport, CT: Praeger, 143–159.

Kaid, L.L. 1999. "Political Advertising: A Summary of Research Findings." In B.I. Newman, ed., *The Handbook of Political Marketing*. Thousand Oaks, CA: Sage Publications, 423–438.

Kaid, L.L. 2000. "Ethics and Political Advertising." In R.E. Denton, Jr., ed., *Political Communication Ethics: An Oxymoron?* Westport, CT: Praeger, 147–177.

Kaid, L.L. 2001. "TechnoDistortions and Effects of the 2000 Political Advertising." *American Behavioral Scientist*, 44(12), 2370–2379.

Kaid, L.L. and M. Chanslor. 1995. "Changing Candidate Images: The Effects of Television Advertising." In K. Hacker, ed., *Candidate Images in Presidential Election Campaigns*. Westport, CT: Praeger, 83–97.

Kaid, L.L. and J. Davidson. 1986. "Elements of Videostyle: Candidate Presentation through Television Advertising." In L.L. Kaid, D. Nimmo, and K.R. Sanders, eds., *New Perspectives on Political Advertising*. Carbondale: Southern Illinois University Press, 184–209.

Kaid, L.L. and A. Johnston. 2001. *Videostyle in Presidential Campaigns: Style and Content of Television Political Advertising*. Westport, CT: Praeger.

Kaid, L.L., C. Leland, and S. Whitney. 1992. "The Impact of of Televised Political Ads: Evoking Viewer Responses in the 1988 Presidential Campaign." *Southern Communication Journal*, 57, 285–295.

Kaid, L.L., Y. Lin, and G. Noggle. 1999. "The Effects of Technological Distortions on Voter Reactions to the Televised Political Advertising." In L.L. Kaid and D.G. Bystrom, eds., *The Electronic Election: Perspectives on the 1996 Campaign Communication*. Mahwah, NJ: Lawrence Erlbaum, 247–256.

Kaid, L.L., M. McKinney, and J. Tedesco. 2000. *Civic Dialogue in the 1996 Campaign: Candidate, Media, and Public Voices*. Cresskill, NJ: Hampton Press.

Kaid, L.L. and G. Noggle. 1998. "Televised Political Advertising in the 1992 and 1996 Elections: Using Technology to Manipulate Voters." *Southeastern Political Review*, 26, 889–906.

Kaid, L.L. and J. Tedesco. 1999. "Tracking Voter Reactions to the Television Advertising." In L.L. Kaid and D.G. Bystrom, Eds., *The Electronic Election: Perspectives on the 1996 Campaign Communication*. Mahwah, NJ: Lawrence Erlbaum, 233–245.

North, R.C., O. Holsti, M.G. Zaninovich, and D.A. Zinnes. 1963. *Content Analysis: A Handbook with Applications for the Study of International Crisis*. Evanston, IL: Northwestern University Press.

Trent, J.S. and R.V. Friedenberg. 1983. *Political Campaign Communication: Principles and Practices*. New York: Praeger.

Chapter 9

Network News Coverage of Campaign 2000: The Public Voice in Context

John C. Tedesco

Often termed the fourth estate, media are assumed to play guardian of American democracy and watchdog for public defense. Without a doubt, media play an important role in U.S. politics. Bennett (1996) argues that by controlling "democracy's most important product: political information" (p. xii), media play not only an important role but also a very powerful role. As guardian of democracy, perhaps no role is more significant for media than assisting citizens by providing reasoned and responsible candidate and platform coverage during election campaigns. In fact, political campaigns offer citizens and academics an "excellent benchmark" for assessing media's role as the facilitator of political campaign dialogue (Kaid, McKinney, and Tedesco, 2000). Although candidate, media, and public voices play out our campaign dialogue through a variety of media, television news is the primary source of political campaign information for a large portion of the American public. Unfortunately, by most accounts, television media reporting of presidential elections is not highly regarded by academics or citizens. This chapter assesses network news presentation of campaign 2000 by exploring a rarely examined component in the news: the public voice.

LITERATURE REVIEW

Public Assessment of News

In *Civic Dialogue* (Kaid, McKinney, and Tedesco, 2000) and *Crosstalk* (Just et al., 1996), political campaigns are treated as a dialogue between candidate, media, and public voices. Quantitative results and focus group comments from the 1996 campaign show that large numbers of Americans are disengaged from the political process (Kaid, McKinney, and Tedesco, 2000). Public and scholarly reports of media performance during political campaigns are similar in that both forms of analysis are largely disapproving. For example, public reaction to 1996 network news coverage demonstrated a marked feeling of frustration and cynicism (Kaid, McKinney, and Tedesco, 2000; Murphy, 1998). It appears that the public was also displeased with media coverage of the 2000 presidential campaign. Reports from voter analysis of media campaign coverage from the Pew Center for the People and the Press demonstrate a general feeling of media impartiality and overall poor reporting. Despite the general negative trends over the past four elections, evidence from Pew shows that public opinion regarding media impartiality may be waning. Pew's 2000 study reveals that large percentages of the public felt that media treated Al Gore and George Bush fairly, 74 percent for Gore and 65 percent for Bush ("Media Seen as Fair," 2000).

Conversely, the Pew study indicates that objectivity may be jeopardized by political preferences of journalists. For example, voters were twice as likely to perceive that journalists were Gore supporters as compared to Bush supporters. Despite this large divide in perceptions of political preference among journalists, the differences reported by Pew in previous years were larger. Journalists were perceived to support Bill Clinton by a 59 to 17 percent margin over Bob Dole in 1996 and a 52 to 17 percent margin over George Bush in 1992. However, the differences in perception of political preference are still very large regardless of the reduced ratio of divide in 2000. What makes the media gap in political preference significant is the fact that nearly 60 percent of respondents in the Pew study believed that political coverage was influenced by journalists' political preferences.

Media Criticism

While public criticism of media generally focuses on journalistic bias, media criticism among academics is widespread. Election news descriptions usually offer several encompassing categories of political journalism, including trivial information, issue information, strategy or horse race coverage, and candidate information (e.g., Graber, 1993; Jamieson, 1992; Patterson, 1993). These election news categories are typical objects of scholarly criticism of political journalism. For example, scholars argue that an overwhelming coverage of political campaigns focuses on "horse race" aspects of campaign strategy and opinion polling to the detriment of both in-depth analysis of policy positions (Patterson, 1993; Robinson and Sheehan, 1983) and civic education (Joslyn, 1990).

Additional media criticism alleges journalistic differences in use of tone, balance, and type of candidate information (Hanson, 1992; Patterson, 1993, 1994; Lichter, Noyes, and Kaid, 1999). Scholars also question media's social responsibility in regard to accuracy, fairness, and commentary in response to coverage of candidate ads (Jamieson, 1992; Kaid et al. 1999; Tedesco, McKinnon, and Kaid, 1996) and policy issues (Kaid, McKinney, and Tedesco, 2000). Yet further disapproval has focused on the "journalist centered," interpretive nature of political reporting that features more of the journalists' voice than the candidates' voice (Kerbel, 1999; Lichter and Noyes, 1995; Patterson, 1993). In fact, the average candidate sound bite in 1996 network news shrunk to an estimated 8.2 seconds (Lichter, Noyes, and Kaid, 1999).

The most recent criticism of U.S. political journalism evolves from a trace of the historical trends in campaign coverage. In fact, scholars identified a shift in political journalism around 1972, which is documented by a swing in coverage emphasis from policy issues to campaign strategy (Cappella and Jamieson, 1997; Jamieson, 1992; Kerbel, 1999; Patterson, 1993). The move from issues to strategy as the dominant focus of campaign coverage resulted in a transfer from candidates to journalists as the central voice in political journalism. More recently, since 1988, a shift toward "metacoverage" appears to dominate campaign reporting (Esser, Reinemann, and Fan, 2001; Kerbel, 1998). As defined by Esser and colleagues, metacoverage is "self-referential reflections on the nature of the interplay between political public relations and political journalism" (2001, 17). The stages of political journalism have restructured the dominant sources in news from candidates prior to 1972, journalists until 1988, and spin-doctors since 1988 (Esser, Reinemann, and Fan, 2001). Thus, it is argued that public relations efforts from political organizations and campaign staffs have assumed greater influence on the news.

Public Voice

The public voice is by far the least represented, the least understood, the least involved, and the least clear in our civic dialogue (Kaid, McKinney, and Tedesco, 2000; Larson, 1999). As DeRosa and Tedesco (1999, 66) argue, despite the theoretical representation of the public voice that occurs through public opinion polling, such polling "no longer features the citizen voice." In fact, "polls are personified by the reporter, the candidate, the campaign staff, or the academic researcher, who interpret with brief comments the results of hundreds or thousands of people polled" (DeRosa and Tedesco, 1999, 66–67). Some of the strongest critics of polls indicate that media polls constitute little more than "enterprise journalism" that does little for the public good and lots for the dramatic, horse race nature of political reporting (Lavrakas and Bauman, 1995, 35). In fact, the increased reliance on polls as expression of public opinion further disenfranchises citizens from the political process by limiting public expression and public debate (Herbst 1993, 1994; Salmon and Glasser, 1995).

Despite the enormous efforts by campaigns and media organizations to gather public opinion and appeal to audiences, public engagement in civic affairs continues to dissipate. The disenfranchisement or disengagement of the U.S. public has raised concern about the state of our civic condition, with a number of scholars indicating that the large numbers of disengaged or apathetic voters should be viewed with alarm (e.g., Elshtain, 1995; Fishkin, 1995; Putnam, 1995a, 1995b). The stifling effects that polling may have on public conversation and political debate certainly threatens essential elements of a rational, informed decision-making public that democratic theorists agree is a crucial requirement for self-governance (Berelson, 1966; Habermas, 1989; Kelly, 1960). Furthermore, Patterson (1993) and Sabato (1993) contend that the pack mentality of journalists works to erode public respect of politicians and the political process.

However, representation of the public voice in politics may not be so absent as critics of horse race coverage or polling contend. For years candidates have been using personal stories of citizens as examples to color and enhance their policy arguments. The strategy of "personalizing" or "exemplifying" is also a standard practice media use to enhance the "human interest" aspect of news (Bennett, 1996). Despite the relatively low incidence of public voices in network evening news during the 1996 campaign (Kaid, McKinney, and Tedesco, 2000), Larson (1999) contends that the diversity and quality of public comment aired by the networks constituted a genuine public sphere.

However, it is argued that a difference exists between exhibiting a diverse demographic set of characters within "human interest" reports and genuinely attempting to represent the public voice. For example, using a personal story or individual case to enhance political argument or color a news story is far different from investigating issues of public concern. In the former example, the candidate agenda and/or the media agenda take precedent over the public agenda. In fact, Iorio and Huxman (1996, 112) argue that what is needed is " 'bottom up' investigating and reporting to discover and voice the full range of citizens' common problems." Through such "bottom up" efforts, it is argued that the trend toward increased alienation of the public from the political process may be reversed (Iorio and Huxman, 1996). Interestingly, "civic journalism" was developed with optimism and heralded for its mission to provide citizens the possibility to voice their concerns to media through community focus groups and/or town hall meetings. However, analysis of civic journalism within television network coverage of political campaigns has not received specific scholarly attention. Currently, it appears as though civic journalism is challenged by the shift toward meta-coverage of political public relations and political journalism. Thus, it is interesting to investigate the role of the public in a political media environment that is paradoxically influenced as never before by political public relations yet striving toward a goal of public journalism.

Using a blend of content analysis and descriptive analysis, this study aims to investigate network news coverage of campaign 2000, with particular attention to the public voice. Since much media criticism focuses on horse race aspects and lack of policy discussion, public voice will be analyzed in relation to these campaign elements. Additionally, as researchers identify a new shift in political journalism that focuses on political public relations and spin, target audiences will also be assessed through mention of audience descriptors.

METHOD

Network News Transcripts

Network news transcripts of the 2000 U.S. presidential campaign were collected from Labor Day (September 4, 2000) through Election Day (November 7, 2000) using Lexis-Nexis transcripts of ABC, CBS, and NBC network evening newscasts. Two methods of locating stories were used. As an initial strategy, the Lexis-Nexis database for television transcripts was searched using the Boolean technique of keywords "Bush," "Gore," "Cheney," or "Lieberman" to identify all stories on each network that at least mentioned one of the two major presidential or vice presidential candidates. In addition, the story log produced from Lexis-Nexis was compared to the online version of the Vanderbilt Television News Index and Abstracts to validate that all campaign stories located on the abstracts were identified through the Lexis-Nexis search.

Lexis-Nexis presents stories in segmented reports and often presents leads and sign-offs as separate news items, particularly as provided by CBS. Thus, the number of stories reported for the Lexis-Nexis search is not identical to the number of stories identified by the Vanderbilt Television News Abstracts. All leads at the beginning of the newscasts, transitions before commercial breaks, summaries, sign-offs, and/or teasers at the close of the news program that mention Gore or Bush were also included in this analysis since these small segments often mentioned the candidates in the context of a policy issue, campaign strategy, or target audience.

Each story was read to ensure that it addressed one of the political candidates. A number of stories were eliminated because they referred to former President Bush or Governor Jeb Bush of Florida without relation to the 2000 campaign. Stories that dealt solely with Tipper Gore or Laura Bush were maintained for the analysis since the frequency of such stories was minimal. Also, the stories including the candidates' wives supply important implications for issues and policies that may be of particular prominence for each woman's role as first lady.

The Lexis-Nexis archive was used because it provides complete transcripts of the network news programs. The search produced 417 network news stories from Labor Day to Election Day. As noted previously, CBS was more likely than ABC or NBC to report their leads and sign-offs as separate news items in their transcripts for the Lexis-Nexis database. As a result, the number of news stories available from CBS was 173, followed by 129 for NBC and 115 for ABC. The difference in story documentation will not skew results since frequency of overall issue and strategy frames will be the source of comparison.

Coding Procedures

The VBPro computer program for content analysis was used in order to accomplish coding for the 417 transcripts.[1] The VBPro computer content analysis program was used based on its demonstrated strength to analyze print (Miller, Andsager, and Riechert, 1998) and televised news transcripts (Tedesco, 2001). Each text file was formatted and submitted to a word-rank-order procedure. Word synonyms were generated for the 2000 campaign based on the key word ranks from the transcripts and previous word strings generated on election news (Miller, Andsager, and Riechert, 1998; Tedesco, 2001). In this study, the key words that contextualize the election coverage served as content frames for the overall policy issues, campaign processes, and audience segments.[2]

Additionally, ABC, NBC, and CBS network evening newscasts were recorded from Labor Day (September 5) through Election Day (November 7). Two field study students were assigned to code various aspects of the network news, including representation of the public voice.[3] Patterns of usage for public voice and characterization of the public are presented in the descriptive section of the results.

RESULTS

Content Analysis

Campaign issues. As Table 9.1 shows, education was the leading policy issue represented on each of the major networks during the general election. Although the issue rank orders are a little different between the networks, education, taxes, Social Security, economy, and the oil/gas crisis were among the top six issues for each network, which demonstrates a high degree of policy issue convergence. While not a policy

Table 9.1
Network News Issue Rankings and Issue Mentions during the 2000 General Election[a]

ABC (*n* = 115)	CBS (*n* = 173)	NBC (*n* = 129)
1) Education (155)	1) Education (110)	1) Education (166)
2) Tax (94)	2) Social Security (104)	2) Tax (139)
3) Family Values (69)	3) Tax (84)	3) Family Values (102)
4) Oil/Gas (68)	4) Economy (81)	4) Economy (79)
5) Economy (59)	5) Oil/Gas (76)	5) Social Security (77)
6) Social Security (55)	6) Military (61)	6) Oil/Gas (72)
7) Prescription Drugs (51)	7) Family Values (51)	7) Health Care (51)
8) Crime (50)	8) Health Care (41)	8) Drugs (43)
9) Medicare (42)	9) Prescription Drugs (32)	9) Prescription Drugs (40)
10) Health Care (33)	10) Environment (30)	10) Balanced Budget (33)
11) Environment (20)	11) Medicare (25)	11) Medicare (28)
12) Drugs (17)	12) Crime (24)	12.5) Abortion (26)
13.5) Military (12)	13.5) Foreign Policy (20)	12.5) Environment (26)
13.5) Balanced Budget (12)	13.5) Balanced Budget (20)	14) Crime (17)
15) Foreign Policy (7)	15) Drugs (17)	15) Foreign Policy (12)
16) Tobacco (5)	16) Abortion (16)	16) Military (8)
17) Welfare (4)	17) Campaign Finance (9)	17) Welfare (3)
18) Agriculture (3)	18) Agriculture (7)	18) Agriculture (2)
19) Abortion (2)	19) Welfare (4)	20) Tobacco (1)
20) Campaign Finance (1)	20.5) Tobacco (1)	20) Campaign Finance (1)
21.5) Affirmative Action (0)	20.5) Affirmative Action (1)	20) Affirmative Action (1)
21.5) Immigration (0)	22) Immigration (0)	22) Immigration (0)

[a]The number in parenthesis represents frequencies for mentions from the key words content analysis.

issue per se, "family values" was a hot issue of the campaign, as it ranked third among ABC and NBC and seventh among CBS. Interestingly, CBS devoted much more coverage than either ABC or NBC to military issues, as military ranked sixth on CBS and a distant tie for thirteenth on ABC and sixteenth on NBC.

Although Social Security, Medicare, and prescription drugs were coded separately, and distinct from health care, the cumulative issue mentions for these three issues were similar for the networks, with ABC tallying a cumulative 148 mentions, compared to 161 for CBS and 145

Table 9.2
Network Relationships for Policy Issue Rankings and Frequencies

	Pearson Correlations for Issue Frequencies		
	ABC	**CBS**	**NBC**
ABC	1.000	.835***	.926***
CBS		1.000	.860***
NBC			1.000
	Spearman rho Rank Order Correlations		
	ABC	**CBS**	**NBC**
ABC	1.000	.901***	.911***
CBS		1.000	.871***
NBC			1.000

***Correlation results significant at the $p \leq .001$ level.

for NBC. Since many of the issues regarding Social Security, health care, Medicare, and prescriptions drugs were linked in news reports, the cumulative effects of these four issues combined would make them the number-one focus of each of the networks, with a total of 181 issues mentions for ABC, 202 for CBS, and 196 for NBC.

Two methods of analysis were used to determine the relationship between media coverage of the 22 issue frames analyzed through the key word content analysis. Pearson product moment correlations on issue frequencies demonstrate high to very high correlations with marked and very dependable relationships between each network. As Table 9.2 shows, Pearson correlations for issue mentions measured +.835 between ABC and CBS, +.926 between ABC and NBC, and +.860 between CBS and NBC. Similarly, Table 9.2 shows that Spearman rho rank-order correlations for the 22 issues were also very strong. Spearman rho correlations measured +.901 for ABC and CBS, +.911 for ABC and NBC, and +.871 between CBS and NBC. All correlations were significant at the $p \leq .001$ level.

In addition to the relationship between issues mentioned and the salience of issues as presented by the networks, overall totals for the 22 issues in this study were cumulated. While each network had the same opportunity to present a wide array of issues important to the public and the political campaigns, NBC led in this category with 947 references to one of the 22 issues analyzed. NBC was followed by 814 issue references from CBS and 759 from ABC.

Table 9.3
Issue, Strategy, and Audience Mentions by Network

	ABC	CBS	NBC	Total
Issue Mentions (22 Issues)	759	814	947	2,520
Process Mentions (9 Processes)	748	860	860	2,468
Audience Mentions (14 Audiences)	473	528	400	1,401

Campaign processes. It is clear from the findings of the content analysis that a large number of policy issue references were made throughout the general election. However, comparison between the respective frequencies for policy issues and campaign processes are necessary to get a sense of how these two categories represent campaign coverage. Although the analysis here identified only nine major campaign processes, the process results were nearly as prominent as all 22 issues. Table 9.3 indicates that there were 2,520 issue references compared to 2,468 process mentions. Analysis by network reveals a greater disparity between issues and processes for NBC than for CBS or ABC. However, policy issue frequencies were higher for both NBC and ABC, while process frequencies were higher for CBS.

A closer comparison of specific issue mentions and processes shows that processes were much more likely to be the dominant content of news stories. Table 9.4 shows the frequencies for the top five category mentions, which demonstrate the prominence of strategy over issue. A closer look at the frequencies by story shows very few incidences where a policy issue exceeds reference to political processes. As Table 9.4 demonstrates, polls, ads, and debates encompass a large share of network campaign coverage.

Audience descriptors. In an attempt to identify explicit appeals to specific audience groups and/or representation of specific groups in the campaign coverage, a wide array of audience descriptors were analyzed (see note 2 for a complete listing of audience categories). Of particular remark, NBC was the only network in which women's descriptors were more prominent than men's descriptors. Although NBC mentioned women (and/or women's concerns) slightly more than men, ABC was more than twice as likely to address men, and CBS was nearly 50 percent more likely to mention men. Appeals to the elderly were very broad across networks, particularly on NBC, where elderly descriptors exceeded those for either men or women. The networks also made significant reference to children and children's issues, particularly in regard to education. In fact, ABC presented slightly more references to children than to elderly.

Table 9.4
Prominence of Issues and Campaign Processes in Network News (frequencies)[a]

ABC	CBS	NBC
1. Voting (268)	1. Voting (318)	1. Voting (363)
2. Education (155)	2. Debates (162)	2. Education (166)
3. Debates (151)	3. Polls (146)	3. Polls (139)
4. Ads (107)	4. Ads (129)	4. Debates (137)
5. Polls (95)	5. Education (110)	5. Ads (98)

[a]Frequencies counts based on the key word content categories.

One additional interesting finding worth mention is the general absence of descriptors used to identify minorities and young voters. The largely disenfranchised young and minority audiences appeared generally disregarded by the networks. Despite the newsworthy nature of the first Jewish vice presidential candidate, religion and/or religious issues were also largely avoided during the campaign. Surprisingly, despite some coverage of union get-out-the-vote campaigns and other public relations campaign strategies, labor issues failed to play a dominant role in the news. Table 9.3 shows that audience descriptors were much less prominent than policy or process frequencies despite inclusion of such general party descriptors as "Republican," "Democrat," and "Independent."

Describing Public Voices

The public voice was present in 70 of the 417 campaign stories analyzed: 28 for ABC, 19 for CBS, and 23 for NBC. Despite the variation in the number of campaign stories that include public comment, treatment of the public was very similar across networks. For example, the networks primarily used public voice(s) to color a story with a personal example or demonstration of public reaction. Rarely did inclusion of the public voice demonstrate clear and purposeful public debate on issues. Rather, public voice was used to colorize journalistic horse race tendencies, particularly in regard to which candidate was likely to sway undecided voters in particular battleground states. The undecided voter appeared as a gross overrepresentation of the American public, especially through NBC's special collection of reports focused on the undecided voter. Seniors also received a large percentage of the public voice, mostly through stories where their emotional examples of the need for reform in Medicare and Social Security gave the news stories a dramatic element. In fact, use of the public voice was usually framed by despair, conflict, or disillusionment. Examples from Medicare, Social Security, education, and the undecided voters provide the best representation of the public voice.

Medicare/prescription drugs. Early on in the campaign it became apparent that Medicare was a big issue for the public. For example, a September 5 *CBS Evening News* story presented Esther and David Welsh as a couple that spends more than 20 percent of their monthly income on prescription drugs for Esther's cancer treatment and David's high blood pressure. The couple's comments are used to characterize the despair felt by senior citizens who are scared about the rising cost of prescription drugs:

Mr. Welsh: We need help from somebody.

Mrs. Welsh: Somebody better help us.

Mr. Welsh: If it continues at this rate, nobody will be able to afford medication.

Public despair over Medicare and prescription drugs was also prominent on ABC and NBC. For example, Sue Kling, a woman who spends more than $6,000 a year on prescription drugs, was used to exemplify the real choices citizens need to make in regard to affordability of prescription drugs (*ABC World News Tonight*, September 5):

Ms. Kling: How can we afford it? We can't. We'll have to decide which ones we can take and which ones we can't.

Additionally, *ABC World News Tonight* (September 25) framed a story of Bush campaigning in Florida around the hopelessness of Mr. and Mrs. Jack Tilton, cancer patients in fear that they will not find an insurance carrier due to their illness.

However, public despair about Medicare and prescriptions drugs extended beyond senior citizens. On October 15, *CBS Evening News* painted prescription drug reform as a central issue in the battleground state of Pennsylvania, where the young uninsured were represented:

Ms. Karen Chronister (Fitness Instructor): I hear fear. I have a lot of people in the class who are diabetic, who have pre-existing heart conditions, who have high—high blood pressure. When they started off taking their heart medication, it was $50 for a month, and now it's $80 for a month. And pretty soon it's probably going to be $100 a month.

Ms. Chronister is one of the 44 million Americans with no medical insurance, and she recently hurt a disk in her back.

Ms. Chronister: Just like that, I went from being a very healthy person with no prescriptions to paying close to $200 a month for myself just for prescription costs.

Another woman in the story nearly died in a car accident some eight years ago. In order to deal with the injuries suffered in the car accident, Ms. Caroline DaCosta must spend more than $4,000 a year on medication.

Ms. DaCosta (Uninsured Patient): So you just said, "Well, I just won't take this, you know. I should be OK. I'm feeling fine. I'll just cut this out for a week." And every time I did that, I got into big problems.

At the end of the story, the women were asked to share on camera their perception of which candidate would do more to help curtail their medical expenses. Not surprisingly, the story presented two women that shared similar circumstances but were divided on which candidate would help them get insurance and ease their situation.

However, of all the public voices heard on the networks during the general election, Winifred Skinner's story is perhaps the most compelling. Ms. Skinner made her story public in a town hall meeting, in full view of the three major networks. While all networks carried Ms. Skinner's story, this excerpt is drawn from *CBS Evening News* (September 27):

John Roberts (reporting): It was one of those rare moments when an ordinary citizen can convey the importance of an election-year issue better than any candidate ever could.

Ms. Skinner (Senior Citizen): My name is Winifred Skinner. I walk an hour and a half to two and a half hours, sometimes three hours, seven days a week, and I pick up cans. And that's what puts the food on my table. If they could lower the price of prescription drugs, then I could make it. There was a fellow that came along in a pickup truck and I was picking up cans, and—and he yelled at me, "Get a life," and that hurt.

Clearly, the networks captured the despair surrounding Medicare and prescription drugs and presented personal examples to add a dramatic flair to the news.

Social Security. Although a large number of the public voices represented on the issue of Medicare and prescription drugs were elderly, the networks did a good job balancing the generational divide on the issue of Social Security. On October 22, *CBS Evening News* presented an interesting comparison of a generational divide in regard to the Social Security plans for Gore and Bush. The story was based on citizens from Florida.

Ms. Velma Cazares (Senior, Social Security recipient): Social Security for seniors will always be there if we take care of it as we should and have in the past. The young people need to know how important Social Security and Medicare can be, unless they have a crystal ball and know what is down in their future.

Ms. Cazares's response was presented opposite that of Mr. Craig Patrick, a 28-year-old public relations executive:

Mr. Craig Patrick: Even the most optimistic projections I've seen have Social Security going bankrupt by the year 2037. Well, that's the same year, exact same year that Suzanna and I would turn 65.

In reaction to the plan proposed by Bush to take some money and put it into investment plans, Colonel Gabriel Cazares and his wife decided to vote for Gore.

Colonel Gabriel Cazares (Social Security Recipient): The stock market can go up. But as a former stock broker, I can tell you it can go down and it's terrible when it does.

Thus, there appears to be conflicting opinion on the issue of Social Security between younger and older generations. *ABC World News Tonight* (October 31) captured the Social Security conflict through voices of a father and son:

Mr. William Blumer, Jr. (Machinist): I could do with it what I want. If I make a bad decision, then it falls back on me, and I don't have to complain about anybody else messing my money up.

Mr. William Blumer, Sr. (Machinist): It's retirement money. It's Social Security money and if you lose it, it's gone.

Blumler, Sr. did not seem as comfortable with the risk that his son wanted to take with investments from Social Security money. In the same story, voices of a 29-year-old and a retiree were used to demonstrate further the conflicting views on this issue:

Mr. Mike Dubis (29-Year-Old Father of Three): If I give all that money to Uncle Sam to make his two percent on it or me turning around making 27 to 30 percent on it, I'd have to go that way.

Mr. Roscoe Farmer (Retired Machinist): I don't think nobody has the option to take my Social Security and invest it in nothing. It's mine.

In general, the young appear optimistic that they can make their money grow, while their elder counterparts appeared fearful that their lifelong security was in jeopardy.

Education. Education, particularly vouchers, was also a hot issue for public comment. *CBS Evening News* (September 23) presented Terrance Davis, a private school student who indicated that he received grades of F and unsatisfactory while a student in public schools. Once his mother placed him into a private Christian school, his grades increased dramatically. Now Terrance gets grades of As and Bs. A very similar story aired on *ABC World News Tonight* (September 20) involving a sixth-grade student named Jacey. Jacey's recent enrollment in a downtown Washington, D.C. Catholic school also improved his grades to As and Bs. Jacey's and Terrance's cases offered public testimony to the effectiveness of school vouchers.

In Michigan, the issue of school vouchers was also central to the electoral votes in that state (*CBS Evening News*, October 29). Mr. Art Luna felt that the public schools needed additional support, whereas Mr. Fuqua indicated that failing schools needed immediate attention and suggested that vouchers are the immediate solution:

Mr. Luna: Public schools are the foundation of all of our small communities. And it's important that we don't tear them down; we build them up.

Mr. Fuqua: I am for the vouchers. Those that say no are saying, "If a child is in a failing district, give us the time, give us the money and we will fix the problem." If that school is failing the students, then it is failing its purpose. It has no reason to be there. The only purpose that that school serves is to educate.

Mr. Luna: The difference between—in my opinion—between George Bush's plan and Al Gore's plan is he says, "Kids first. Kids first for this, kids first for that." Al—Al Gore says, "All kids first."

Mr. Fuqua: And so what Governor Bush proposed is that the accountability level will be raised. And if you fail to meet it, you're out. And that's the way that it should be.

Similar to the CBS report, ABC and NBC played out the conflict and divide that this issue produced among the public. Like CBS's voucher examples from Washington, D.C.'s inner city, *ABC World News Tonight* (October 17) focused on public response to vouchers from within a major metropolitan inner city. ABC was particularly effective in presenting this public issue in the larger context of the conflict it produced within competing religious groups:

ADAM Cardinal Maida (Roman Catholic Archbishop of Detroit): Give me $3,000, and I can take a kid and give him a—a good life. I mean, it's a fair bet.

Rev. Nicholas Hood (Plymouth United Church of Christ): With, you know, all due respect to the Catholic church, the—the church really is just, I think, trying to find a means to support its—its educational system.

Unidentified sources in the story show competing voices in respect to level of hope vouchers offer in rural areas as well. Considering that there are limited options for private and/or parochial education in many rural areas, vouchers would have a very small impact on the schools attended by students in rural areas. Nevertheless, the voucher issue resulted in divide among citizens in rural areas:

Unidentified Man #1: But we can't give people a false hope. If the schools aren't willing to accept their child, if the parents are not even that interested, then you're giving them a false hope.

Unidentified Man #2: Right now they have no hope. With a voucher, there's a possibility!

What was clear from the public comment on education and vouchers is that there are very real differences in perceptions of education solutions. However, the similarity exists in that the stories captured the immediacy of this issue (*NBC Nightly News*, September 8):

Ms. Melanie Brown (Harrisburg, PA): I don't want to see Harrisburg schools fail. But in the meantime, we won't be able to get our children four or five years back if they fail and don't get it right.

However, Ms. Brown's comments are presented against Ms. Hawkins's support for Al Gore's plans to try to fix the current system:

Ms. Jill Hawkins (Steelton, PA): Funding for more teachers would definitely help. I like his [Gore's] proposals because I feel like he wants to fix the system that's there.

Thus, particularly for education and Social Security, public voice was used to support conflict frames. However, undecided voters (particularly in swing or battleground states) received an enormous amount of media attention.

Undecided voters. By September 8, *CBS Evening News* reported that an estimated 90 percent of voters had decided on a candidate and that the battle for the White House would come down to a million or so voters in key states. However, the use of the undecided voter in campaign news did little more than express the confusion and disillusionment for the less than 10 percent of voters that had yet to select a candidate.

In fact, CBS and NBC were particularly interested in giving voice to the undecided voters throughout the general election campaign. NBC dedicated a large portion of its campaign coverage to the undecided voter through their special series, "The Undecided." Early on in NBC's general election coverage, Tom Brokaw informed views about the importance of the undecided voter in campaign 2000 (*NBC Nightly News*, September 5):

Tom Brokaw (Anchor): According to the polls, undecided voters in less than a dozen battleground states, mostly in the industrial East and Midwest, will be the tipping point for who wins the White House in November. We're going to be following these sought-after voters, "The Undecided," in a special series of reports until November 7th.

NBC's first undecided voter report demonstrated discontent with candidate choice (*NBC Nightly News*, September 5):

Tori Nygren: This year I don't feel like either one of the candidates are very strong candidates. I don't particularly like either one of their—either of their characters.

The dissatisfaction expressed by Ms. Nygren is echoed by a number of other undecided voters used as sources across the networks. Interestingly, a very passive example of the decision-making process for an undecided voter was presented on *CBS Evening News* (September 8):

Unidentified Man: I'm going to be watching TV one night, and somebody's going to say something that I agree with, and that's going to make my mind right then and there. And that's the person I'm going to go with.

Although not explicitly stated as a way to help decision making for undecided voters, CBS commissioned a number of focus groups to better understand undecided voter reactions to the presidential debates. After the first presidential debate, focus group respondents were presented with a scenario in which they were asked to write headlines for a hypothetical story about the debate (*CBS Evening News*, October 4):

Unidentified Man: No One Scores Big in Presidential Debate.

Ms. Peggy St. James (Retiree): A Lot of Garbage.

Unidentified Woman #2: The Debate's a Draw.

CBS also aired focus group reaction to debater style and content. Reaction to the debate was also a source of public voice on ABC. However, respondents to the debate on ABC gave it low marks for clarity. The public, representing the swing state of Pennsylvania, reacted as follows when asked whether the numbers Bush and Gore used were helpful in clarifying their policy differences (*ABC World News Tonight*, October 4):

Ms. Megan Dowd: Confuse me.

Reverend Ray Martin: I think people are going to get more confused. The elderly are going to get confused. The middle-income people are going to get confused. Probably the only ones who won't get confused will be the wealthy 1 percent.

Unidentified Man #1: I learned that there is such a thing as fuzzy math. I think they spent a great deal of time talking about helping the elderly, which is great. But they weren't more informative on what would be available for younger people and married couples.

The report ended with reporter John Cochran expressing the general recommendation from undecided Pennsylvania voters to the candidates for the next debate: "Keep it simple!" So the first presidential debate did not appear to assist the undecided voter.

Even after the conclusion of the debates, the expressed mood from the undecided voter did not appear to change much from the beginning of September. For example, *NBC Nightly News* (October 21) reported the displeasure of an unidentified man:

Unidentified Man: Neither one of the candidates interest me much.

Two evenings later, NBC's national correspondent Jim Avila appeared perplexed that voters were still undecided (*NBC Nightly News*, October 23):

Jim Avila: Two weeks to the election, 229 network news stories, nearly 400 minutes of air time since Labor Day. Three presidential debates, 4½ hours of the candidates side by side. And still, critical millions of voters cannot make a choice for president.

Maria Frances: I am currently completely undecided. . . . I probably will not know until the moment I step through the voting booth.

NBC also reported that Ms. Frances fit the typical profile for undecided voters:

Avila: More suburban than city, mostly women under 50 with incomes below $50,000 a year. More liberal than conservative, registered Independent, and leaning [toward] Gore.

NBC continued its coverage of the undecided throughout the election and maintained that a number of states were still in play based on the large number of undecided voters, like decidedly unenthusiastic Vera DiPauli (*NBC Nightly News*, October 28):

Vera DiPauli (Missouri Resident): Neither one of them impress me as presidents. I don't know why.

Certainly, beyond the network news stories, newspaper articles, and debates, not to mention Internet, radio, and additional campaign news, undecided voters in swing states during the last two weeks of the campaign were given the opportunity to digest the last-minute advertising barrage. Interestingly, the enormous amount of information available to the undecided voter did not appear to make candidate selection easy. In fact, NBC's Lisa Myers caught Detroit's Kevin Tulley in the middle of "ground-zero" Michigan during the last week of the campaign. Mr. Tulley expressed reaction to the candidate advertising (*NBC Nightly News*, November 2):

Kevin Tulley: You're seeing maybe three ads for one candidate, and then the next break you're seeing two or three for his opponent. It's a little much.

Throughout the campaign, public comment from undecided voters characterized a significant portion of the population with enormous power to swing the election yet struggling with mechanisms to tame the information tide.

Beyond the scope of the public voice presented above, additional comment from the public focused on reaction to Ralph Nader's candidacy. Supporters of Nader were given opportunity to demonstrate the reasons they rallied behind their candidate, particularly during the closing weeks of the campaign when it became apparent that Nader's bid might lose the presidency for Gore. Despite the threat of vaulting Bush to the White House, *ABC World News Tonight* (October 17) demonstrated that Nader supporters had a purpose:

Unidentified Woman: I want to see my vote as a statement that I will no longer compromise.

Continued support for Nader was demonstrated through a story that echoed ABC's October 17 report. The response from the Nader supporter indicated that the true Nader followers were not going to budge despite pressure from pundits that a vote for Nader was a vote for Bush (*ABC World News Tonight*, November 1):

Unidentified Man: We've got to make a statement, and we're going to have to lose something in order to gain something.

DISCUSSION

The content analysis findings demonstrate that there is a blend of issue and process information available to viewers of the major network evening newscasts during the general election campaign. Although the findings indicate that a wide range of issues were presented by the networks, the concentration of the issue frames for specific issues was not nearly as dense as discussion of candidate advertisements, political polls, presidential debates, or voting (particularly voter choice). The content analysis findings support previous research that demonstrates that political journalism focuses on the horse race aspects of campaign strategy and opinion polling (Patterson, 1993). Like previous investigation of the public voice in network news, this descriptive analysis reveals a great deal of consonance (Larson, 1999) in terms of the issues networks use to attach a public voice and the themes/comments presented by the public. In fact, the extremely high, significant issue correlations between the networks offer support to the arguments of pack mentality in campaign reporting (Patterson, 1993; Sabato, 1993).

Although election campaigns in the televised age have always been high speed, the ever emerging and expanded cable news media and additional nontraditional political sources and strategies make reporting political campaigns increasingly difficult. However, the focus on campaign processes and strategies in advertising, debates, and through polling draws the reporter closer to the campaign strategist and further from the citizen. As a result, political journalism appears to be influenced more by the campaign strategist and less by the candidate or the public. The intensity of process coverage by the networks supports research that detects a turn toward metacoverage in political campaigns in that much of the process coverage discussed appeal strategies in candidate advertisements and debates (Esser, Reinemann, and Fan, 2001). Furthermore, network news coverage of campaign 2000 demonstrated clearly that reliance on horse race and process aspects works to the detriment of civic education (Joslyn, 1990). For example, there were many missed opportunities for the media to assist undecided voters throughout the campaign.

Certainly the networks identified distinctions in the major policy issue proposals advanced by the candidates, especially education, Medicare, Social Security, prescription drugs, and taxes. In fact, to focus solely on criticism overlooks scholarly support that television news serves to convey important candidate issue and image information (e.g. Chaffee, Zhao, and Leshner, 1994; Zhao and Chaffee, 1995). However, the focus here is on increasing the level of information in such a way as to assist undecided voters in making reasoned and rational political choices. In only a few of the cases where citizens were used to provide "color" or human interest did reports go as far as to demonstrate outcome assessments for the citizens used in the story. Outcome-based models of political reporting are advocated as a way to enhance civic education, particularly for the undecided voter.

Figure 9.1 demonstrates an *NBC Nightly News* report that could serve as a model for future campaign reports that include a citizen example.

Figure 9.1
Sample Outcome Assessment Comparison from *NBC Nightly News,* October 2

TOM BROKAW, anchor: NBC News IN DEPTH tonight, the family and an issue where the two presidential candidates have starkly different positions, tax cuts. Governor Bush favors a sweeping tax cut, including a total overhaul of the tax code. Vice President Gore is for targeted tax cuts that he says will help the middle class more. With a look at how two American families would fare under these plans, NBC's Lisa Myers tonight IN DEPTH.

LISA MYERS reporting: The middle class suburbs of St. Louis. Heart of middle America, where pocketbook issues are a top priority for some families like Ron and Laura Holtz. She stays at home to care for their three children. He makes about $42,000 as manager of a fast food restaurant, and resents that so much of his hard-earned money goes for taxes.

Mr. RON HOLTZ (St. Louis, Missouri): As a taxpayer, I'd love to have some of my money back. That way, I know what—where it is and what it's being spent on.

MYERS: Last year, Holtz paid $1,500 in income taxes. Under Bush's tax plan, he'd save all that, owe no federal incomes taxes at all. Under Gore, he'd get only a small tax cut.

TEXT: 1999—Paid $1,504; Bush Plan—Owe No Taxes

Mr. HOLTZ: You know, that's a difference of $1,500. That's quite a bit of food on the table and clothes on our backs and things every year. Over a lifetime, that's quite a bit.

MYERS: Specifically, Bush would cut tax rates across the board, reducing the top rate from 39 percent to 33 percent, the bottom rate from 15 to 10 percent, double the child tax credit to $1,000 per child, and reduce the so-called "marriage penalty."

Mr. CLINT STRETCH (Deloitte & Touche): Everybody's going to get at least a 10 percent tax cut under the Bush plan.

MYERS: What would all this mean to your family? Experts say because Bush's $1.6 trillion tax cut is three times the size of Gore's, most families would get a bigger tax cut under Bush. Those who pay the most taxes now get the most. Al Gore says that's unfair.

Vice President AL GORE: The other side has proposed a giant tax cut for the—for—mainly for the wealthy. Forty-one percent of all their tax cut would go to the wealthiest 1 percent.

MYERS: Instead, Gore targets almost all his tax relief to families he calls the neediest, those earning less than $100,000, like Tom and Nancy Pettit. They have two kids in college and two more at home and oppose a big tax cut.

Mr. TOM PETTIT (St. Louis, Missouri): I would rather see money used in education and health care than any across-the-board tax cut.

MYERS: The Pettits earn $70,000, and spend almost $30,000 a year on college, so they like Gore's expanded tax break for tuition, up to $10,000. How helpful would that be?

Ms. NANCY PETTIT (St. Louis, Missouri): I can see that buying two semesters worth of books.

MYERS: Gore's plan, all-targeted tax cuts, would also reduce the marriage penalty for some couples, expand tax credits for child care and establish new retirement savings to help families like the Pettits build nest eggs. Under Gore's plan their tax cut would be $2,070, considerably more than under Bush.

Mr. STRETCH: Gore's trying, with his targeting, to keep the size of the tax cut down while helping people that he thinks need help.

Governor GEORGE W. BUSH: It is so targeted that it misses the target. Fifty million Americans get no tax relief under my opponent's plan.

MYERS: Tomorrow night both candidates will try to persuade voters that they hit the right target, for the economy and for families. Lisa Myers, NBC News, St. Louis.

In this sample story, Lisa Myers presents the policy issue differences between the candidates, provides "human interest" through personal stories, and delivers outcome assessments as to how the policy proposals will affect the citizens in the story. Such reporting style should serve as a mechanism for audience members in similar situations to identify how the policies might impact their lives. It is argued that this type of reporting would assist audiences by demonstrating a sample case on methods of interpreting policy implications.

Although political campaign reporting is an enormously high-speed endeavor, media could better serve the public through greater efforts to identify public information needs rather than chasing the campaign maneuvers. However, the overwhelming number of stories that provide in-depth detail about policy issues do little to translate how the candidate proposals affect typical audience members. Additionally, public reaction to the first presidential debate demonstrated that some citizens felt that it focused too heavily on seniors and alienated large portions of young and middle-aged audience members. Unfortunately, the audience descriptors in this study indicated that seniors also received the greatest attention from the network news. Since seniors comprise a major audience for network news, this result may demonstrate a strength of network news rather than a weakness. For example, in an effort to provide quality information to the public, the networks reported heavily on information of particular relevance to its typical viewer. Furthermore, some of the most prominent issues on candidate and public agendas (Social Security, Medicare, and prescription drugs) carried more consequences for seniors.

Although many of NBC's "In Depth" stories on the undecided voter provided a revealing study of this segment of the public, the reports appeared to approach the undecided voter from the wrong perspective. Rather than place the undecided voter under a microscope with occasional opportunities provided to voice frustration, the bottom-up strategy promoted by Iorio and Huxman (1996) could have served the media and the public well. Rather than frame coverage of a "mind-boggling" undecided voter, networks had a huge opportunity to assist undecided citizens by providing campaign information that was functional and manageable. Considering that the media has firsthand accounts from focus groups and "man-on-the-street" interviews that campaign information and policy proposals were complex and confusing, inclusion of personal examples provided opportunities not only to personalize issues but also to supply outcome models. For example, rather than focusing on the fact that nearly 400 minutes of coverage did not help voters make a candidate choice, focus groups of undecided voters commissioned to uncover public questions and/or information needs could be more fertile. Since the networks understood that the undecided voters had difficulty taming campaign information, felt overwhelmed by the statistics and competing allegations from the candidates debates and ads, the NBC reporting prototype provided in Figure 9.1 appears likely to make clear not only the candidates' differences but also the way the differences translate to a typical family or individual.

Iorio and Huxman's (1996) call for a bottom-up form of civic journalism is instructive for another purpose as well. Considering that the combination of Social Security, Medicare, and prescription drugs constituted the largest frequency of policy issue discussion—particularly relevant to seniors—it is reasonable to question what agenda items relevant to young voters and minorities missed the media radar screens. Although it is clear from the debates that Social Security, Medicare, prescription drugs, education, taxes, and foreign policy were central issues of debate in the campaign, foreign policy was not heavily covered on network evening news. Furthermore, the strong possibility that the winning candidate would make appointments to the Supreme Court did not receive wide coverage on the networks, despite the strongly held abortion beliefs carried by many individuals. In this case, to better understand ways to communicate information that undecided voters can process and employ in decision making, media should employ focus group– or town hall–style civic journalism.

Although some undecided voters were having difficulty weighing the advantages and disadvantages of a wide range of candidate policy and personal characteristics, other undecided voters obviously did not understand how to process the campaign information into a rational voting decision. In this case, media could offer voters an instructive mechanism, such as a campaign scorecard, for weighing the information presented throughout the campaign. It appears that a number of undecided would have benefited from an instructive model to help them weigh the costs and benefits of candidate policy and character dimensions.

As a final note, the predominant presentation of "public" as undecided, discontent voters undermines the political process. While it is interesting that a small portion of the population has the opportunity to swing an election, the reasoned and rational comment from strong partisans or decidedly independent voters was all but absent from the networks. Although committed voters did not constitute "news," such voters could serve as a positive reminder that aspects of the candidates' issue positions and personalities were widely respected and motivating to a large portion of the public.

NOTES

1. The VBPro computer content analysis program was designed by M. Mark Miller (University of Tennessee) for educational and scholarly research purposes.

Information about the program is available at http://excellent.com.utk.edu/~mmmiller/vbpro.html.

2. Issue frames were selected through the use of the following headers with the key terms in parentheses: Foreign Policy/Trade (foreign trade, trade, foreign policy, international policy, international trade, foreign affairs, international affairs, foreign relations, international relations); Military (military, defense, Army, Navy, Air Force, Marines, missile, missiles, weapons, armed forces); Economy (economically, economics, economic, economy, economy's, economies, economist, economists, job, jobs, unemployment, employment); Balanced Budget (budget, budgets, deficit); Crime/Guns (crime, crimes, violence, offenders, offender, death penalty, gun, guns, handgun, handguns, firearms); drugs (drugs, drug); Prescription Drugs (prescription drug, prescription drugs, prescriptions)—this category was compared to "drugs" to determine whether the discussion was about medical drugs or illegal drugs; Social Security (social security); Medicare (Medicare); Abortion (abortion, abortions, pro-choice, pro-life); Environment (environment, environmental, environmentalist, environmentally, pollution, pollutant, pollutants, nature, natural resources); Health Care (health, healthcare, medical, patient, patients, patient's); Tobacco (tobacco, smoking, cigarette, cigarettes, smoker, smokers); Tax (flat tax, mortgage, mortgages, overtaxed, tax, taxable, taxation, taxed, taxes, taxing, taxpayer, taxpayers, taxpayer's); Welfare (Medicaid, welfare, poverty); Education (educate, education, school, school's schools, schoolbooks, schoolchildren, schoolhouse, schooling, teacher, teachers, teacher's, voucher, vouchers); Affirmative (affirmative action, equal opportunity); Immigration (immigrant, immigrants, immigration, protectionism, protectionist, isolationist, foreign workers, migrant workers, alien, aliens); Campaign Finance Reform (campaign finance, finance reform, campaign contribution, campaign contributions, campaign loopholes, soft money, election contributions, spending limits, third party contributions, third party contribution, campaign limits); Family Values (family, parent, parents, parent's, families, family's, values, morals, morality, moral); Agriculture (agriculture, agricultural, farm, farms, farmer, farmer's, farmers, farmland).

Strategy and audience frames were selected based on the following key words that appeared frequently in context with one another: Business (small business, corporation, corporation's, corporation, businessmen, businessman); Labor (labor, labor union, unions); Ads/TV (ad, ads, advertisement, advertisements, advertising, television, TV, campaign commercials); Polls (poll, polling, polls); Debate (debates, debate, joint appearances, joint appearance); Speech (speech, rally, campaign stop, campaign trail); Endorse (endorse, endorsed, endorsement, endorsements, endorsers, endorses, endorsing); Voting (votes, voters, voting, vote); Cynicism (cynicism, cynical, disenfranchised, disenfranchisement, disengaged, alienated, detached, disconnected); Conservatism (conservatism, conservative, conservatives); Liberal (liberalism, liberal, liberals); Independent (Independent, Reform party, Reform party's); Republican (Republican); Democrat (Democrat, Democratic); Religion (religion, religions, religious, religiously, Christian, Christians, Jews, Jewish, Jew); Elderly (elderly, seniors, senior citizens); Young (youth, young, next generation); Children (children, children's, child, child's); Minorities (minorities, minority, African Americans, African American, Hispanic, Hispanics, Black); Women (women, women's, woman's, woman); Homosexual (homosexual, homosexuality, homosexuals, gay, gays, lesbian, lesbians); Experience (experience, experienced, experiences, leader, leadership).

3. Intercoder reliability for identification of public voice achieved a +.97 level of agreement. The author acknowledges the assistance of coders Kendra Beach and Carrie Mosser.

REFERENCES

Bennett, W.L. 1996. *News: The Politics of Illusion* (3rd ed.). New York: Longman.

Berelson, B. 1966. "Democratic Theory and Public Opinion." In B. Berelson and M. Janowitz, eds., *Reader in Public Opinion and Communication*. New York: Free Press, 489–504.

Cappella, J.N. and K.H. Jamieson. 1997. *Spiral of Cynicism: The Press and the Public Good*. New York: Oxford University Press.

Chaffee, S.H., X. Zhao, and G. Leshner. 1994. "Political Knowledge and the Campaign Media of 1992." *Communication Research*, 21, 305–324.

DeRosa, K.L. and J.C. Tedesco. 1999. "Surveying the Spin: Interpretation of the 1996 Presidential Polls." In L.L. Kaid and D. Bystrom, eds., *The Electronic Election*. Mahway, NJ: Lawrence Erlbaum, 65–80.

Elshtain, J.B. 1995. *Democracy on Trial*. New York: Basic Books.

Esser, F., C. Reinemann, and D. Fan. 2001. "Spin Doctors in the United States, Great Britain, and Germany: Metacommunication about Media Manipulation." *Harvard International Journal of Press/Politics*, 6(1), 16–45.

Fishkin, J.S. 1995. *The Voice of the People: Public Opinion and Democracy*. New Haven, CT: Yale University Press.

Graber, D. 1993. *Mass Media and American Politics* (4th ed.). Washington, DC: CQ Press.

Habermas, J. 1989. *The Structural Transformation of the Public Sphere: An Inquiry into a Category of Bourgeois Society*. Trans. T. Burger. Cambridge, MA: MIT Press.

Hanson, C. 1992. "Media Bashing: The Media's Alleged Political Bias." *Columbia Journalism Review*, 31(4), 52–55.

Herbst, S. 1993. *Numbered Voices: How Opinion Polling Has Shaped American Politics*. Chicago: University of Chicago Press.

Herbst, S. 1994. *Politics at the Margins: Historical Studies of Public Expression Outside the Mainstream*. Cambridge: Cambridge University Press.

Iorio, S.H. and S.S. Huxman. 1996. "Media Coverage of Political Issues and the Framing of Personal Concerns." *Journal of Communication*, 46(4), 97–115.

Jamieson, K.H. 1992. *Dirty Politics: Deceptions, Distraction, and Democracy*. London: Oxford University Press.

Joslyn, R.A. 1990. "Election Campaigns as Occasions for Civic Education." In D. Swanson and D. Nimmo, eds., *New Directions in Political Communication*. Newbury Park, CA: Sage Publications, 86–119.

Just, M.R., A.N. Crigler, D.E. Alger, T.E. Cook, M. Kern, and D.M. West. 1996. *Crosstalk: Citizens, Candidates, and the Media in a Presidential Campaign*. Chicago: University of Chicago Press.

Kaid, L.L., M. McKinney, and J. Tedesco. 2000. *Civic Dialogue in the 1996 Presi-*

dential Campaign: Candidate, Media, and Public Voices. Cresskill, NJ: Hampton Press.

Kaid, L.L., M.S. McKinney, J.C. Tedesco, and K. Gaddie. 1999. "Journalistic Responsibility and Political Advertising: A Content Analysis of State and Local Newspaper and Television Adwatches." *Communication Studies*, 50(4), 279–293.

Kelley, S., Jr. 1960. *Political Campaigning: Problems in Creating an Informed Electorate*. Washington, DC: Brookings Institution.

Kerbel, M. 1998. *Edited for Television: CNN, ABC, and American Presidential Elections* (2nd ed.). Boulder, CO: Westview Press.

Kerbel, M. 1999. *Remote and Controlled: Media Politics in a Cynical Age* (2nd ed.). Boulder, CO: Westview Press.

Larson, S.G. 1999. "Public Opinion in Television Election News: Beyond Polls." *Political Communication*, 16, 133–145.

Lavrakas, P.J. and S.L. Bauman. 1995. "Page One Use of Presidential Pre-election Polls: 1980–1992." In P.J. Lavrakas, M.W. Traugott, and P.V. Miller, eds., *Presidential Polls and the News Media*. Boulder, CO: Westview Press, 35–49.

Lichter, R.S. and R.E. Noyes. 1995. *Good Intentions Make Bad News*. Lanham, MD: Rowman & Littlefield.

Lichter, R.S., R.E. Noyes, and L.L. Kaid. 1999. "Negative News or No News: How the Networks Nixed the '96 Campaign." In L.L. Kaid and D.G. Bystrom, eds., *The Electronic Election: Perspectives on the 1996 Campaign Communication*. Mahwah, NJ: Lawrence Erlbaum, 3–13.

"Media Seen as Fair, But Tilting to Gore." 2000. Washington, DC: Pew Research Center for the People and the Press, October 15.

Miller, M.M., J.L. Andsager, and B.P. Riechert. 1998. "Framing the Candidates in Presidential Primaries: Issues and Images in Press Releases and News Coverage." *Journalism and Mass Communication Quarterly*, 75(2), 312–324.

Murphy, J. 1998. "An Analysis of Political Bias in Evening Network News during the 1996 Presidential Campaigns." Doctoral dissertation, University of Oklahoma.

Patterson, T. 1993. *Out of Order*. New York: Alfred Knopf.

Patterson, T. 1994. "Legitimate Beef—the Presidency and a Carnivorous Press." *Media Studies Journal*, 8(2), 21–27.

Putnam, R.D. 1995a. "Bowling Alone: America's Declining Social Capital." *Journal of Democracy*, 6 (January), 65–78.

Putnam, R.D. 1995b. "Tuning in, Tuning out: The Strange Disappearance of Social Capital in America." *PS: Political Science and Politics*, 28, 664–683.

Robinson, M. and M. Sheehan. 1983. *Over the Wire and on TV*. New York: Russell Sage Foundation.

Sabato, L.J. 1993. *Feeding Frenzy: How Attack Journalism Has Transformed American Politics*. New York: Free Press.

Salmon, C.T. and T.L. Glasser. 1995. "The Politics of Polling and the Limits of Consent." In T.L. Glasser and C.T. Salmon, eds., *Public Opinion and the Communication of Consent*. New York: Guilford Press, 437–458.

Tedesco, J.C. 2001. "Issue and Strategy Agenda-Setting in the 2000 Presidential Primaries." *American Behavioral Scientist*, 44(12), 2049–2068.

Tedesco, J.C. L.M. McKinnon, and L.L. Kaid. 1996. "Advertising Watchdogs: A

Content Analysis of Print and Broadcast Ad Watches." *Harvard International Journal of Press/Politics*, 1(4), 76–93.

Zhao, X. and S.H. Chaffee. 1995. "Campaign Advertisements versus Television News as Sources of Political Issue Information." *Public Opinion Quarterly*, 59, 41–65.

Chapter 10

Explaining the Vote in a Divided Country: The Presidential Election of 2000

Henry C. Kenski, Brooks Aylor, and Kate Kenski

> "Probably because of Clinton," she said. "Gore should have been stronger. He could have distanced himself. A lot of people in Tennessee feel that way."
>
> —A preelection statement by Diane Wright, a 52-year-old Humbolt, Tennessee, homemaker and voter who liked Gore's anti-HMO rhetoric but still felt she might vote for Bush (Harris, 2000)

The 2000 election was exciting and a sharp contrast with the lackluster contest of 1996. It was the closest presidential popular vote since the Kennedy-Nixon matchup in 1960 and the smallest margin in the electoral college since the 1876 clash between Hayes and Tilden. In the final tally, Gore won the popular vote by 449,898, with a 48.4 percent to 47.7 percent advantage. Bush won the electoral college vote 271 to 266, as one Gore elector from the District of Columbia abstained ("2000 Election Data," 2001). The battle for control of Congress was equally competitive, as the Democrats picked up five Senate seats for a 50–50 tie and two House seats to narrow the Republican majority to 221 to 212, with two independent House winners.

Michael Barone has labeled the United States at the end of the twentieth century as the "49% nation" and notes that "in three straight presidential elections and three straight House elections, neither party has won 50 percent of the vote" (Barone, 2001). Both political parties believed they could create a majority coalition by 2000, and both were unable to do so. In the election of 2000, neither a Reagan-Bush coalition nor a Clinton-Gore coalition proved dominant.

This study of political campaign communication focuses on the messengers, the messages, the channels of communication (print, radio, television, etc.), the audience, and the effects. The purpose of this chapter is to look at the final phase of the communication process in the 2000 presidential contest and to explain the vote. We analyze the messengers and their messages, campaign strategies, the vote in the electoral college, and the demographic base for the presidential vote. We then examine the role of gender in 2000, issues cited, candidate traits selected by voters as reasons for their vote, and perceptions of presidential job performance and character in the election outcome.

THE MESSENGERS AND THE MESSAGES

The political messengers and their traits, messages, and issue positions are at the heart of every campaign communication. Although analysts sometimes draw a strong line between issues and personality/character in campaigns, the reality is that American elections have always been image oriented/issue involved. The two concepts are like overlapping concentric circles. Candidates use issues, for example, to demonstrate personal qualities like knowledge, competence, leadership, vision, trust, and empathy. Voters may lack detailed issue knowledge themselves, but they can observe campaign behavior and assess how candidates fare on important personal traits. Alternately, voters may focus on the issues identified by the candidate to assess if he or she really cares about people like themselves or is biased toward other groups (Popkin, 1994). In some elections and for some candidates, voters may look for honesty and trust and feel that if they pick a good person, the individual will make sound decisions on the issues that affect them. More than two centuries ago in *Federalist paper No. 10,* James Madison argued that when elections are free, the people "will be more likely to center on men who possess the most attractive merit and the most diffusive and established characters" (Madison, Hamilton, and Jay in Kramnick, 1987, 27). From the very beginning, American voters have been concerned with personal traits and character as well as the issue positions of candidates running for public office.

The election of 2000 was no different, and once again voters expressed concern about both candidate traits and issues. Two of the authors had the opportunity to attend the University of Pennsylvania Annenberg School of Communication Election Debriefing on February 10, 2001, featuring the top campaign personnel from both the Bush and Gore campaigns.[1] Listening to the comments and discussion, we could not help but feel that Bush and Gore were probably the strongest candidates in their respective parties and that both campaigns, despite occasional blunders, were highly professional in delivering messages and targeting states and demographic groups. In this section we draw upon this and other material presented to explain the messages and the messengers.

Both campaigns were concerned about the messenger and the message, but the Republicans expressed more concern about the messenger as well as the messages than did the Democrats. Matthew Dowd, Bush's campaign director of polling and media planning, noted that issues and personality traits are not mutually exclusive. Personality, he argued, signals broader values and traits such as leadership and empathy (Dowd, 2001). Alex Castellanos, of National Media and a veteran presidential consultant who worked for Bush, stressed that elections are not only about issues but also about the people who are running. In 2000 Bush fared well because it was hard for the Democrats to demonize him (Castellanos, 2001). Karl Rove, top Bush campaign strategist and now assistant to the president and senior adviser, stated that the Bush campaign from the beginning believed that value and character would prove most important. The campaign continued to believe this even when they were hit in the final week by an attack about a DUI (driving under the influence) conviction that candidate Bush had never mentioned. Rove felt that this attack had cost them the state of Maine, where the story originated, and perhaps 5 percent in the national polls. He suggested that a compelling message for Bush, however, stressed that Gore was too political and would say anything to become president. Rove argued that the Bush campaign anticipated the Gore "attack dog style" of communication so evident from 1992 where Gore defined his opponents and not himself and prepared for the expected Gore attempt to make the campaign about us or what he wants us to be (Rove, 2001). Thus Rove thought it was essential for Bush to question Gore's credibility. In dealing with Gore, he noted that it helped that two of the campaign's top staff, Matthew Dowd and Mark McKinnon, were Democrats before joining Bush.

Like Karl Rove, Mark McKinnon, Bush's media director, conceded that Bush should never have won given the historic models that underscore the near impossibility of defeating an incumbent or an incumbent party candidate if the country was experiencing economic prosperity and was in a period of peace (McKinnon, 2001). Overcoming these two factors, he noted, was a tough hill to climb that was made even more difficult by the fact that issues like education, health care, and Social Security favored the Democrats. The Bush strategy and approach was to stress leadership, shared values, honesty, and trust and to contend that now was the time not to be too political and to do hard things. The campaign had to show that Bush was not only a leader but a different kind of leader who would address issues that Republicans often tend to ignore. Selection and framing of issues were critical to communication and persuasion. Thus Bush put forth his educational proposals with accountability standards to address the fact that 58 percent of our fourth graders could not read at their grade level, a plan to strengthen Social Security by partial privatization, an HMO (health maintenance organization) reform proposal, and a tax cut for all Americans.

It is not within the parameters of this chapter to assess the relative merits or demerits of the respective Bush and Gore proposals. It is within our purview to note, however, that the Bush approach to the concepts of messenger and messages fundamentally changed the pattern of campaign discourse that was more prevalent in past presidential campaigns. Ann Lewis (2001), senior adviser to the Hillary Clinton campaign and a participant on a panel on congressional races at the Annenberg Election Debriefing, noted that in more traditional campaign discourse one candidate proposes something and the other opposes. For example, one candidate might propose more federal spending on education, while the other argues against it. In 2000, she observed, it was more difficult for voters to assess not only the presidential candidates but also congressional candidates because almost everyone was for education, health care reform, and so on, but offered different solutions. Since it is more difficult to assess competing plans than a pro-con single-issue proposal, voters were more cross-pressured than they would have been with more traditional campaign rhetoric.

As to the messages, Bush finally found a way in early October to pump life into and to bring his tax cut proposal to center stage by using specifiers or actual families to illustrate how his proposal works (Mitchell, 2000a). Mark McKinnon (2001) pointed out that the presidential debates were critical not only to establish character traits but to advance Bush issues like the tax cut as well. Bush found some effective phrasing that also led to reinforcing campaign ads that were run during the October debate period. These included having George Bush say "I trust you but Gore trusts the government" and having him stress that under the Gore tax cut proposal 50 million people would be left out. In the final weeks of the campaign Bush messages included an attack ad that took a swipe at Gore's reputation for embellishing his experiences and achievements (Marks, 2000) and a message that Clinton and Gore have let the country be "undefended against missile attacks" (Mitchell and Bruni, 2000). Bush also gave rebuttal speeches and produced ads that asked the elderly to reject Gore's scare tactics that claimed that Bush would harm Social Security (Mitchell, 2000b). Finally, Bush in a concluding message argued that integrity made him the right man for the job (Bruni and Mitchell, 2000).

The Democrats who headed Gore's campaign placed a very heavy emphasis on messages and claimed Gore dominated the issue messages in 2000. Bob Shrum (2001) and Carter Eskew (2001b) from the firm of

Shrum, Devine, and Donilan, both felt that Gore really won. They noted that he won the popular vote, won more votes than any Democratic presidential candidate in history, and did better among African Americans, labor union household members, and voters making $100,000 a year or more than did the Clinton-Gore tickets in 1992 and 1996. Shrum said that Gore's favorite messages were contained in two ads produced during the nomination contest. One was a spontaneous commentary by Gore on the job of a president, and the other was the theme of "he's fighting for us," which portrayed him as saving Medicare, Medicaid, and Social Security and protecting seniors and working families.

All of Gore's campaign consultants stressed the central dilemma of their campaign, which was that their polling and focus group research showed that voters gave Gore very little credit for the good economy. All took strong exception to critics who alleged after the election that Gore was an inept candidate who failed to ask the voters for credit for a good economy. The bottom line in 2000 was that voters were skeptical and not very generous in their credit giving. Shrum (2001) said the campaign had to stress the importance of building on a strong economy and then focus on the economic future and promoting prosperity for all. Carter Eskew (2001b) described their message strategy as centrist and populist and building on Clinton's accomplishments by extending prosperity to all. In addition, Gore offered a value agenda that embraced individual responsibility, the next generation of welfare reform, and accountability in schools while taking on the powerful interests in such areas as HMO health care reform and prescription drugs for seniors. Shrum (2001) added that their campaign believed Gore had a stronger bio than Bush and was better prepared for the presidency. Also, the protection of Social Security was a strong and persuasive message for Gore. Critical to the overall Gore message strategy were strong messages, along with comparable advertising from the Democratic National Campaign Committee attacking Bush proposals on health care reform, Social Security, education, the environment, his Texas record, and the tax cut.

Stanley Greenberg (2001), Gore's pollster, also reported that a vast amount of polling data indicated that the Gore campaign would get little political mileage by crediting-claiming on the economy. Like Shrum and Eskew, he contended that voters liked Gore's policies and his view of the role of government better than Bush's. The Gore message, he argued, dominated on not squandering the prosperity, opposing big interests, pushing middle-class tax cuts, and embracing prosperity for all. The other side of the message strategy raised doubts about Bush by attacking his so-called risky plans, his position on the right to choose on abortion, his favoritism toward the wealthy, his inexperience, and his policy record as governor of Texas. Greenberg also explained that voters felt that Clinton did a good job as president but that many did not like him for his personal qualities. This was particularly true of younger males and rural voters in many of the strongly contested battleground states. This was why the Gore campaign did not bring Clinton into the campaign. In states where they needed help the most, Bill Clinton was a political liability.

Bill Knapp, another Gore campaign strategist and a media consultant from the firm of Squire, Knapp, and Dunn, reiterated the difficulty of using the economic credit-claiming message (Knapp, 2001). He also emphasized that the Gore campaign had tested 538 different ads during the course of the campaign in an effort to present the strongest possible messages. He claimed that they did get some voter traction, especially at the end with the attacks on Bush's Texas record and Social Security reform proposal and on Bush's readiness for the presidency.

In the final phase of the campaign, Gore attacked a Bush gaffe on Social Security by proclaiming: "Do you want to entrust the Oval Office to someone who doesn't even know that Social Security is a federal program?" Katherine Seelye of the *New York Times* observed that "the vice-president never allowed that Mr. Bush's comment might have been a mistake or a poorly worded thought, instead milking the idea that it was just plain dumb—and that it was further evidence that Mr. Bush is blank on basics and not equipped to be president" (Seelye, 2000a, A1). At the campaign's end Gore resurrected the name of Bill Clinton and called for a strong economy and progressive policies (Seeyle, 2000b). He invoked broad themes and sought to energize his black and labor electoral base (Sack, 2000). One of Gore's final ads was the most negative of the campaign and was a summary of attacks on whether George Bush had what it takes to be president. Peter Marks, a *New York Times* media analyst, noted the accusation that Bush's tax cuts was class warfare on behalf of billionaires was especially harsh. He contrasted the Bush attack ad on Gore embellishments with Gore's attack on Bush's fitness to be president and said: "But while the Bush spot was playfully nasty, the new Gore spot is intense and harsh, and seems intent on unnerving the voter" (Marks, 2000, A22).

The messenger/message contrast was dramatic and was conducted by two strong campaign teams. At the Annenberg School Debriefing on February 10, 2001, all of Gore's consultants noted that the execution of their message strategy was constrained by the Bush campaign tactic of reducing the policy differences between the two candidates by offering alternative policy proposals. It was patent that the Gore team would have preferred an opponent who simply opposed educational spending, health care reform, and Social Security reform. Voters had to choose, however, not only between the different traits of both Gore and Bush but also between different policies to address problems. Bill Knapp (2001) of the Gore campaign contended that the Bush campaign made very few efforts to rebut the Gore attack on Bush's Texas record. Karl Rove noted, however, that a similar attack by the senior George Bush on Clinton's Arkansas record in 1992 proved ineffective and that voters simply did not buy the Democratic efforts to demonize the younger Bush (Rove, 2001). Matthew Dowd, Bush's polling director, responded further by noting that their campaign did reply, but by counterargument and not rebuttal. Reminding voters of Gore's track record of embellishments, he argued, questioned Gore's credibility and was more effective than rebutting the Democratic attack point by point (Dowd, 2001). This exchange captured nicely the differences in approach from two very professional campaigns, with one relying more heavily on the issues and the messages and the other giving more attention to the messengers.

THE ELECTORAL COLLEGE AND THE POPULAR VOTE

Of course, Americans do not vote directly for president but instead cast their ballots for a slate of electors committed to a presidential ticket. Each state has a number of electoral votes equal to its representation in Congress. California, for example, has 52 representatives and 2 senators and therefore has 54 electoral votes. A small state like Dick Cheney's Wyoming has only 1 House member and 2 senators, for 3 electoral votes. The District of Columbia (D.C.) has 3 electoral votes as a result of a constitutional amendment. There are 538 total electoral votes. These votes in most states are based on "winner take all," and the ticket winning the state's popular vote receives all the state's electoral votes. There are two exceptions. Maine (4 electoral votes) and Nebraska (5 electoral votes) both award the ticket winning the state's popular vote 2 electoral votes and then give 1 electoral vote for each of the state's congressional districts. It takes a majority or 270 electoral votes to win the presidency.

Presidential candidates and their running mates frequently spend disproportionate time campaigning in the largest states with the most electoral votes and reach voters in other states through surrogates and advertising. In 2000, ten states together has 257 electoral votes. The big prizes in the East were New York (33), Pennsylvania (23), and New Jersey (15). In the South there were Texas (32), Florida (25), and North Carolina (14). In the Midwest, Illinois (22), Ohio (21), and Michigan (18) offered the most electoral votes, while California had 54 electoral votes in the West. Hypothetically, a presidential ticket that carried these ten states would have needed only the 13 electoral votes of Georgia or Virginia to have an electoral majority.

Campaign decisions are based on the likelihood that a ticket might carry the state. The demographic groups residing in the state and their numerical weight are important considerations in the allocation of campaign time. It would be difficult for a Republican in most elections to carry Massachusetts or for a Democrat to carry Texas. Each election is different, and the candidates and the political mood of the time are factors in campaign decisions. In some elections, it may be more profitable for a ticket to campaign in select medium and small states if there is a chance to win them and they are needed for an electoral majority. This was the situation in the election of 2000, as particular circumstances indicated that at minimum eight small or medium states were very competitive in early October and could have been won by either Bush or Gore. These included West Virginia, New Hampshire, Arkansas, Iowa, Wisconsin, New Mexico, Oregon, and Washington (Balz, 2000b). As the campaign continued, others would be added to the list. The focus on these states meant that the Democrat Gore, for example, would allocate little time in large, safe states like New York, Massachusetts, and California, while the Republican Bush would spend little time in Texas or North Carolina.

In presidential elections, Democrats are consistently strong in the East and the Pacific West, while the Republicans have an edge in the South, Mountain West, and rural Midwest. The larger Midwest states are usually competitive and are battleground states for both party tickets (Barone, 1990). If the Democrat is a southerner, like Carter in 1976 or Clinton in 1992 and 1996, inroads in the South are politically possible. Although Al Gore ran for the Democratic nomination in 1988 as a "son of the South" and regional candidate, his personal style and questionable past fund-raising endeavors created political problems for 2000. His recent issue stands (on the environment, abortion, and gun control), and his association with Clinton also made him a less attractive candidate in the more conservative South.

Prior to 1992, conventional wisdom posited that Republicans had an advantage in electoral college vote due to the fact that there were more safe Republican states than safe Democratic states at the start of a new presidential contest. Prior to Bill Clinton's victory in 1992, Republicans won every presidential election since 1968, except for Carter's close victory in 1976. Moreover, all of the Republican wins were decisive except for 1968, and two were landslides (1972 and 1984). In 1972 and 1984, the Republican tickets captured every state in the South and the West. In 1980, Reagan won the entire South, save for Jimmy Carter's Georgia, and the West, except for Hawaii (Barone, 1990). In 1988, Bush swept the South but slipped in winning 10 of 13 states in the West and experienced losses in Oregon and Washington as well as traditionally Democratic Hawaii (Pomper, 1989). This suggested that the GOP electoral lock might not be as secure as some analysts believed. The lone Democratic victory from 1968 to 1992 was Carter's narrow 1976 win, as he carried 11 of the 13 southern states with the help of an extraordinary African American vote and much of the East and Midwest. In the West, Carter's sole victory was Hawaii (Pomper, 1977).

The Democratic tide rolled in with the 1992 election as Bill Clinton won a three-way race with 43 percent of the popular vote, compared to 38 percent for Bush and 19 percent for Perot. He was victorious in 32 states and D.C. for a total of 370 electoral votes, while Bush carried 18 states with 168 electoral votes and Perot captured none. Clinton swept the East, winning all 13 states, and carried 7 of 12 Midwestern states with 100 electoral votes, including Illinois, Michigan, and Ohio, compared to Bush's 5 states and only 29 electoral votes. Clinton did well in the West, winning 8 states, including California, compared to Bush's 5 states and 23 electoral votes. The West was Perot's best region, and he ran ahead of his 19 percent national average in 11 of the 13 western states. His strength in Colorado and Montana hurt Bush and pushed these two states into the Democratic column. Bush's base was the South where he won 8 states and 120 electoral votes, but even here Clinton picked the Republican electoral lock by taking 5 states with 43 electoral votes. Clinton's 1992 popular vote was only 43 percent, but his electoral college total was 69 percent, and he carried 8 of the largest 10 states, including California, while losing only Florida and Texas (Barnes, 1992).

Clinton's political skills were evident in the presidential election of 1996. He preempted the Republicans on the traditional GOP issues of crime and welfare reform and embraced targeted tax cuts and proposed his own balanced budget formulation to reduce the edge that Republicans had on these issues. His pollster, Dick Morris, labeled the approach a "triangulation strategy" that placed Clinton between the more conservative congressional Republicans and the liberal congressional Democrats in his party (Morris, 1997). It proved quite successful as Clinton added Florida and Arizona to the Democratic column, while Dole recaptured Georgia, Colorado, and Montana for the Republicans. In Florida, Republican support (largely Cuban) declined dramatically, and Dole suffered erosion in GOP support from seniors, women, and younger voters. An increase in female, young, and Hispanic voters resulted in a dramatic upset in Arizona, a state that had not voted Democratic since Truman's victory in 1948 (Kenski, Chang, and Aylor, 1998). Overall, the Republicans won 1 more state and ended up with 19 states to Clinton's 31 and D.C. Clinton's vote in the electoral college, however, increased from 370 to 379, while the GOP proportion declined from 168 to 159. Clinton swept the East and carried 9 of the 10 largest states, losing only Texas. By contrast, the Republican 1996 ticket was confined to 8 states in the South, 5 small rural Midwest states, and 6 small Mountain states in the West. The so-called Republican electoral lock had been broken.

Our analysis of the electoral college vote and strategies for 2000 begins with the Republicans and is outlined in Table 10.1. The Bush team started

Table 10.1
Electoral College and Presidential Popular Vote in 2000: The Performance of Republican[a] and Lean Republican States[b]

State	Number of Electoral Votes	Number of Democratic Wins	1996 Winner	2000 % Gore	2000 % Bush	2000 % Nader[c]
Indiana	12	0	R	41	57	1
Kansas	6	0	R	37	58	3
Nebraska	5	0	R	33	62	4
N. Dakota	3	0	R	33	61	3
S. Dakota	3	0	R	38	60	
Alabama	9	0	R	42	56	1
Mississippi	7	0	R	41	57	1
N. Carolina	14	0	R	43	56	
Oklahoma	8	0	R	38	60	
S. Carolina	8	0	R	41	57	2
Texas	32	0	R	38	59	2
Virginia	13	0	R	44	52	2
Alaska	3	0	R	28	59	10
Idaho	4	0	R	28	67	
Utah	5	0	R	26	67	5
Wyoming	3	0	R	28	68	2
Florida[d]	25	1	D	49	49	2
Georgia	13	1	R	43	55	1
Arizona	8	1	D	45	51	3
Colorado	8	1	R	42	51	5
Montana	3	1	R	34	58	6

[a]State did not vote Democratic in 1988, 1992, and 1996.
[b]State voted Democratic only once out of three elections in 1988, 1992, and 1996.
[c]Only major party and Nader percentages listed. Blank space under Nader means that he was not on the ballot in that state.
[d]Bush wins the state.

Sources: 1996 electoral data from Kenski, Chang, and Aylor, 1998; 2000 data from "2000 Election Data," 2001.

with the 19 states carried by Dole in 1996, and these were small- to medium-sized states in the South, Midwest, and Mountain West. Sixteen of the states were in the Republican column during the last three elections. Three other states, Georgia, Colorado, and Montana, voted Republican twice and defected in 1992 because of the Perot factor. To this the Bush team added Florida and Arizona, hoping that their 1996 Clinton victories were aberrations. As the data in the table indicate, Bush carried all 21 of the Republican and Lean Republican states. In 18 of the states Bush won with 56 percent or more of the vote. Florida, of course, was a razor-close victory, while the election outcomes were a little closer in Arizona (51–45) and Colorado (51–42). These core Republican states yielded 192 electoral votes, and Bush had to go into Democrat and Lean Democratic territory to build an electoral vote majority.

An examination of the Poll Track ad collection ("Ad Spotlight," 2000) for the Bush campaign, the Gore campaign, and the two party organizations, (the Republication National Committee [RNC] and the Democratic National Committee [DNC] revealed that there were the same initial 17 battleground states on each of their advertising lists. The states included Delaware, Maine, and Pennsylvania in the East; Arkansas, Florida, Georgia, Kentucky, and Louisiana in the South; Illinois, Iowa, Michigan, Missouri, Ohio, and Wisconsin in the Midwest; and New Mexico, Oregon, and Washington in the West. On the battleground list, it was critical for Bush to pick up all the southern states and then add states from the other regions. After Labor Day, the campaigns kicked into high gear, and some of the battleground states began to fade for the two tickets. The Bush campaign did not invest as much time and money in Delaware and Illinois, while the Gore campaign found it desirable to cut back in Georgia, Kentucky, and Louisiana. As the campaign moved to October, the Bush campaign devoted campaign and advertising resources to West Virginia, New Hampshire, Tennessee, Minnesota, and California. Matthew Dowd of the Bush campaign claimed that West Virginia and Tennessee were always on the Bush list, while states like New Jersey were not (Dowd, 2001). Karl Rove said that the Bush campaign put money into West Virginia because of Gore's environmental, gun control, and coal positions. The campaign set up 25 headquarters, as well as phones, direct mail, yard signs, bumper stickers, volunteer organizations, and the recruitment of marshals (Rove, 2001). The Bush campaign felt that Gore's home state of Tennessee was a possible pickup and went into Minnesota in the latter part of October because of an encouraging private poll, hoping that Nader might do well enough to tip the Gopher State into the GOP column (Balz, 2000c). Gore was ahead in California throughout, but the large number of electoral votes at stake made it too tempting to leave off the GOP list. In fact, Bush spent 30 days in California since June 1999, while Gore spent little time in the state (Purdam, 2000). Bush spent considerable money, while Gore adviser Bob Shrum emphasized that his candidate spent nothing at all in California (Shrum, 2001).

Table 10.2 identifies the Democrat and Lean Democrat states that the Gore campaign coveted. The list included 10 states and D.C. that voted Democratic in the past three elections, including New York with 33 electoral votes. The remainder of the list consisted of 19 states that voted for

Table 10.2
Electoral College and Presidential Popular Vote in 2000: The Performance of Democratic[a] and Lean Democratic States[b]

State	Number of Electoral Votes	Number of Democratic Wins	1996 Winner	2000 %		
				Gore[c]	Bush	Nader[d]
D.C.	3	3	D	85	9	5
Mass.	12	3	D	60	33	6
N.Y.	33	3	D	60	35	4
R.I.	4	3	D	61	32	6
W.Va.	**5**	**3**	**D**	**46**	**52**	**2**
Iowa	7	3	D	49	48	2
Minn.	10	3	D	48	46	5
Wis.[c]	11	3	D	48	48	4
Hawaii	4	3	D	56	38	6
Ore.[c]	7	3	D	47	47	5
Wash.	11	3	D	50	45	4
Conn.	8	2	D	56	39	4
Del.	3	2	D	55	42	3
Maine	4	2	D	49	44	6
Md.	10	2	D	57	40	3
N.H.	**4**	**2**	**D**	**47**	**48**	**4**
N.J.	15	2	D	56	40	3
Pa.	23	2	D	51	47	2
Vt.	3	2	D	51	41	7
Ark.	**6**	**2**	**D**	**46**	**51**	**2**
Ky.	**8**	**2**	**D**	**41**	**57**	**2**
La.	**9**	**2**	**D**	**45**	**53**	**1**
Tenn.	**11**	**2**	**D**	**47**	**51**	**1**
Ill.	22	2	D	55	43	2
Mich.	18	2	D	51	46	2
Mo.	**11**	**2**	**D**	**47**	**50**	**2**
Ohio	**21**	**2**	**D**	**46**	**50**	**3**
Calif.	54	2	D	53	42	4
Nev.	**4**	**2**	**D**	**46**	**50**	**2**
N.M.[c]	5	2	D	48	48	4

*Boldface indicates shift to Republican in 2000.
[a]State voted Democratic in 1988, 1992, and 1996.
[b]State voted Democratic in 1992 and 1996 elections but not in 1988.
[c]Gore wins the state.
[d]Only major party and Nader percentages listed, not other minor parties or candidates.

Sources: 1996 electoral data from Kenski, Chang, and Aylor, 1998; 2000 data from "2000 Election Data," 2001.

the Clinton-Gore ticket twice. These included the prize electoral jewel, California, with 54 electoral votes, Illinois (22), Ohio (21), and Michigan (18) in the Midwest, and Pennsylvania (23) and New Jersey (15) in the East. In the top 10 big state electoral showdown, Democrats had the edge in 8 of the states. On the battleground list of 17 states, previously mentioned, 15 tilted Democrat, all but Georgia and Florida. At one point in the fall of 2000, the Gore campaign pumped some money into Nevada as an offset to the southern battleground states that had moved into the Bush column. In short, the Democrats had more to defend than did the Republicans. As the data in the table illustrate, Gore won all of the Democratic states except for Bush's surprise upset in West Virginia. Among the Lean Democratic states that voted for Clinton-Gore twice, he lost New Hampshire in the East; Arkansas, Kentucky, Louisiana, and Tennessee in the South; Missouri and Ohio in the Midwest; and Nevada in the West. In short, he lost 9 of the 29 states on the Democratic list, and with them the electoral vote 271–266. A victory in any one of these states would have given Gore the electoral majority and the presidency.

THE DEMOGRAPHICS OF THE 1996 AND 2000 PRESIDENTIAL VOTES

Explaining the vote requires an analysis of voter support demographics for both level of support (percentage of the vote) and the percentage changes from the previous election. Most demographic groups do not divide evenly for the two parties but have historic tendencies to favor either the Democratic or Republican ticket (Barone, 1990; Kenski and Sigelman, 1993). A key demographic variable is party identification, which today is still the single strongest predictor of the vote. If a Republican ticket cannot draw 90 percent or more of its identifiers in a two-party race or 85 percent in a three- or four-party race, it is not a strong slate. Since Democrats historically are less likely to vote and more likely to defect, a strong Democratic ticket needs at least 85 percent in a two-party race and at least 80 percent in a three-way contest.

In any given election, more voters are likely to identify themselves as Democrats than as Republicans. In the national exit survey in 2000, for example, 39 percent of the voters identified themselves as Democrats, 35 percent as Republicans, and 27 percent as Independents (Connelly, 2000). Both party tickets have to consolidate their partisan base before seeking crossover votes or support from Independents. The latter are meaningless if the partisan base is not intact. The highest presidential defection for Republicans was 1964 when 20 percent voted for Lyndon Johnson. The highest defection rate for Democrats was 1972, when 33 percent cast their ballots for Richard Nixon. The historical record also shows that the Republican candidate usually receives a majority of the Independent vote

(Stanley and Niemi, 1994, 105–106). The only exceptions since 1952 were 1964, with Independents favoring Johnson, and 1992 and 1996, when Bill Clinton won by pluralities (39 percent to 30 percent and 43 percent to 35 percent) in three-way races with Ross Perot (Kenski, Chang, and Aylor, 1998).

With this background, we now examine select demographic groups for 1996 and 2000. The data are reproduced in Table 10.3. Overall, there was a dramatic change with Gore winning a close popular vote margin by 48.4 percent to 47.9 percent, compared to Clinton's 49 percent to 41 percent margin in 1996. Third-party tickets were the big losers, capturing 10 percent of the vote in 1996 but only half as much or a minuscule 4.7 percent in 2000. In 1996, the Clinton-Gore ticket won in all four geographic regions. In 2000, Gore continued the strong Democratic dominance of the East and also led in the West, although by a smaller margin than 1996. Dramatic change occurred in the South, where Bush led 55 percent to 43 percent, compared to parity in 1996. Equally important for Republicans was that Bush-Cheney led in the Midwest or heartland 49 percent to 48 percent, whereas Clinton-Gore dominated 48 percent to 41 percent. What both elections underscore is that the Democrats have a clear edge in the East, the Republicans the South, while the Midwest and West (although divided by Pacific versus Mountain) are becoming more competitive.

The geographical area demographic data show that Gore dominated and outperformed Clinton in both large- (over 500,000) and medium-sized cities (50,000 to 500,000). Bush registered a better showing than Dole by winning the small towns (population 10,000 to 50,000) that Dole lost and improving the narrow edge that Dole had in rural areas from 46 percent to 44 percent to a very substantial 59 percent to 37 percent. Equally dramatic was Bush's narrow 49 percent to 47 percent margin in the suburbs, an area lost by Dole 47 percent to 42 percent in 1996.

Scholars and the media have long been concerned about gender gaps in the political arena (H. Kenski, 1988; Edsall and Morin, 1996; Kenski and Jamieson, 2000, 2001). The gender gap, or the differences in how men and women vote, is often viewed too simplistically and will be explored in more detail later. At this point, however, we simply note that an overall gap existed in both elections, with Dole carrying men narrowly, while Clinton won decisively with women 54 percent to 38 percent. In 2000, Gore had a smaller but clear 54 percent to 43 percent edge with women, while Bush registered a larger 53 percent to 42 percent advantage with men. The marital gap persisted in both elections, with the GOP capturing married voters narrowly by 2 percent in 1996 and improving the margin to 53 percent to 44 percent in 2000.

The data on race and ethnicity show whites supporting the Republican ticket by a slim 46 percent to 43 percent in 1996 and by a more sizable

54 percent to 42 percent differential in 2000. The black or African American vote is solidly Democratic, as blacks voted overwhelming for Clinton-Gore 84 percent to 12 percent and by a stunning 90 percent to 8 percent margin for Gore-Lieberman. The Hispanic vote was Democratic in both elections, but Bush improved on the GOP percentage by garnering 31 percent to Dole's 21 percent. Asians went for the Republican ticket in both elections, but by a larger 54 percent to 41 percent margin for Bush. The relative percentage proportion of the total vote for all race-ethnic groups was the same in 1996 and 2000 nationwide.

The vote by religious groups followed a familiar historical pattern. In both elections white Protestants voted Republican, but Bush increased Dole's 53 percent support to 63 percent. In both elections the Jewish vote was heavily Democratic, with 78 percent for Clinton in 1996 and 79 percent for Gore in 2000. The Democratic-leaning Catholic vote went for Clinton 53 percent to 37 percent, but narrowly for Gore by a 49 percent to 47 percent margin. In 1996, all four age groups voted Democratic. In 2000 the vote was competitive within every age group, with Gore registering a narrow 48 percent to 46 percent advantage with younger voters (18 to 29 years) and a slightly larger 51 percent to 47 percent edge with seniors (60 years or older). Conversely, Bush carried both the 30 to 44 and the 45 to 59 age groups 49 percent to 48 percent.

Both major party tickets delivered their partisans in both elections, with the Democrats doing slightly better (84 percent to 10 percent) than the Republicans in 1996 (80 percent to 13 percent). The 1996 outcome was atypical for presidential elections going back to 1952, as slightly more Republicans defected than did Democrats. Both the Bush and Gore campaigns reached their partisans in 2000, with the Bush team doing slightly better (91 percent to 8 percent compared to 86 percent to 11 percent for Gore). The key group was Independents, approximately 27 percent of the electorate in 2000, as they gave a slight 47 percent to 45 percent edge to Bush and 6 percent to Ralph Nader. The Clinton-Gore ticket had carried Independents 43 percent to 35 percent in 1996, with Perot siphoning off 17 percent of the vote. Union household members favored the Democrats in both elections, by 59 percent to 30 percent in 1996 and 59 percent to 37 percent in 2000. Although most media and political analysts emphasize Gore's success in capturing the labor vote, we believe that what is equally important is that the Democratic percentage of the union vote was comparable in 1996 and 2000 (59 percent). The Bush campaign should be given more credit for increasing the GOP share of the labor electoral pie from 30 percent to 37 percent by capturing union members who voted for Perot in 1996.

Another demographic category is ideological identification. In past presidential campaigns, self-identified liberals have been disproportionately Democratic, and conservatives lopsidedly Republican. Moderates

Table 10.3
The Demographic Base of the 1996 and 2000 Presidential Vote (in percent)

% of 2000		1996 %			2000 %		
Total Vote	Category	Clinton	Dole	Perot	Gore	Bush	Nader
	Total Vote	49	41	8	48	48	2
23	East	55	34	9	56	39	3
26	Midwest	48	41	10	48	49	2
31	South	46	46	7	43	55	1
21	West	48	40	8	48	46	4
9	Population over 500K	68	25	6	71	26	3
20	Population 50K to 500K	50	39	8	57	40	2
43	Suburbs	47	42	8	47	49	3
5	Population 10K to 50K	48	41	9	38	59	2
23	Rural Areas	44	46	10	37	59	2
48	Men	43	44	10	42	53	3
52	Women	54	38	7	54	43	2
65	Married	44	46	9	44	53	2
35	Unmarried	57	31	9	57	38	4

82	White	43	46	9	42	54	3
10	Black	84	12	4	90	8	1
4	Hispanic	72	21	6	67	31	2
2	Asian	43	48	8	54	41	4
47	White Protestant	36	53	10	34	63	2
26	Catholic	53	37	9	49	47	2
4	Jewish	78	16	3	79	19	1
17	18 to 29 Years	53	34	10	48	46	5
33	30 to 44 Years	48	41	9	48	49	2
28	45 to 59 Years	48	41	9	48	49	2
22	60 Years Plus	48	44	7	51	47	2
35	Republicans	13	80	6	8	91	1
27	Independents	43	35	17	45	47	6
39	Democrats	84	10	5	86	11	2
26	Union Household	59	30	9	59	37	3
20	Liberal	78	11	7	80	13	6
50	Moderate	57	33	9	52	44	2
29	Conservative	20	71	8	17	81	1

Source: 1996 and 2000 Voter News Service exit polls reported by Connelly, 2000.

have been a swing vote. This pattern held up in both elections. The liberals voted for Clinton 78 percent to 11 percent, with 7 percent for Perot, and then went for Gore 80 percent to 13 percent, with 6 percent for Nader. Conservatives supported Dole 71 percent to 20 percent, with 8 percent for Perot and voted for Bush 81 percent to 17 percent, with only 1 percent for Nader. Bush benefited from the fact that there was no Perot as a third-party candidate to encourage conservative defections in 2000.

In a 2000 postelection analysis, Thomas Edsall of the *Washington Post* noted that George W. Bush made it a close contest by cutting into Democratic constituencies like poor and moderate income voters, Hispanics, Catholics, suburbanites, the young, as well as the 1996 supporters of Ross Perot. Critical to Bush's win, he argues, was his success with "three target groups at the center of his strategy: Catholics, suburbanites, and Hispanics" (2000a, A29). Barone states that the demographic factor that divides the country more than any other is religion (2001). Historically Protestants have favored the Republicans, while Jews, non-Christian religion practitioners, and those with no religious preference the Democrats. Catholics have leaned Democratic historically but have been more of a swing vote during the past three decades.

In any social science or media analysis, aggregates reveal but also conceal (H. Kenski, 1996). An overall generalization may be true, but disaggregating the subgroups could suggest other political realities. Such is the case for both Catholics and suburbanites. On the subject of religion, Barone emphasizes that it is not only religious identification but also church or synagogue attendance that makes for political differences. Those who attend religious services weekly or more often, approximately 42 percent of the electorate, voted for Bush by a 59 percent to 39 percent margin. Those who attend religious services seldom or never, also 42 percent of the electorate, favored Gore 56 percent to 39 percent. The remaining 14 percent, or the middle group, cast a 51 percent to 46 percent margin for Gore. In Barone's analysis, more observant Catholics supported Bush 57 percent to 43 percent, whereas less observant Catholic identifiers went for Gore 59 percent to 41 percent (Barone, 2001). Although the national exit survey demonstrates that Gore edged Bush 49 percent to 47 percent with the one-quarter of voters who identified themselves as Catholic, it also showed that Bush carried white Catholics 52 percent to 45 percent (Exit Polls: National, 2000).

As the data in Table 10.3 illustrate, Bush carried the suburban vote 49 percent to 47 percent while Dole lost it 47 percent to 42 percent. What the nationwide percentage does not capture is the marked geographical division in the suburban vote. Barnes notes that Gore did strikingly well by running well in some suburban areas. Gore ran ahead of Clinton, for example, in the Cook County suburbs of Chicago, in Long Island and the New York City suburbs, the suburban counties north of Detroit, and the suburbs in the Midwest with more elderly populations. Bush, by contrast, was successful in the suburbs in the South and West, particularly those with prosperous and young professionals (Barnes, 2000). Although Bush did much to improve his party's appeal to suburban voters, Gore made it competitive. Republican pollster Bill McInturff notes that "Bush lost the Philadelphia suburbs by 55,000 votes and went on to lose the state, while Bush's father won those same suburbs by a 250,000-vote margin and carried the state" (Edsall, 2000b, A37).

Barone contends that geography matters and divides the country. This division, he suggests, is captured by an examination of the election returns in the major metropolitan areas (Barone, 2001). The top seven major metro areas (New York, Los Angeles, Chicago, San Francisco, Philadelphia, Detroit, and Washington) went decisively for Gore by a 60 percent to 37 percent margin, while in 1988 they were at parity with Dukakis receiving 49.8 percent and Bush 49.5 percent. Crime and welfare were salient issues in 1988, and as they faded in importance, so did the GOP appeal. These metro areas are the most affluent parts of the country, with income gains, high housing values, and widespread stock ownership. Opposition to tax increases helped the senior Bush here in 1988, but the tax cuts proposed by the younger Bush in 2000 had relatively little appeal in the 7 top metro areas. The next 16 major areas overall went from a 52 percent to 47 percent Republican advantage in 1988 to a 51 percent to 45 percent edge for Al Gore in 2000. Barone suggests the importance of disaggregating the data, however, which shows that some of these areas (Atlanta, Baltimore, Boston, Miami, Phoenix, San Diego, and Tampa-Orlando) experienced Democratic gains from 1988 that paralleled the top 7 major metro areas. In others, however, the Democrats only gained from 1 percent to 4 percent (Cleveland, Seattle, and St. Louis). In 6 of these areas (Dallas, Denver, Houston, Minneapolis, Pittsburgh, and Portland), Gore actually had a lower percentage of the vote than Dukakis. Barone also notes "that all but one of these last five are in states in which Bush in 2000 ran ahead of his father" (Barone, 2001). There is little doubt that the metro areas are Democratic. Data disaggregation reveals, however, that some are more Democratic than others. In some metro areas a Republican candidate might minimize the Democratic advantage and offset it with Republican votes in the rural areas or elsewhere to make a state competitive.

The national exit survey data reveal that Bush improved the Republican percentage of the Hispanic vote from 21 percent to 31 percent (Connelly, 2000). The election, of course, is not decided by the national popular vote but by the electoral college vote that depends on popular majorities in 50 states and the District of Columbia. We looked at the race-ethnic vote in more detail by analyzing the individual exit polls for all the 50 states and D.C. (Exit Polls: States, 2000). In 9 states the Hispanic subsample was large enough to record Hispanic vote preferences. The top 4 states in the Hispanic proportion of all voters were New Mexico (28 percent), Texas (16 percent), Florida (12 percent), and California (11 percent). The other 5 were Colorado (9 percent), Arizona (8 percent), New York (7 percent), New Jersey (4 percent), and Nevada (3 percent). Gore won the Hispanic vote in 8 of the 9 states ranging from an 80 percent to 18 percent in New York to a smaller 58 percent to 38 percent margin in New Jersey. Bush's Latino popularity was evident in Texas as he drew 43 percent of their vote compared to Gore's 54 percent. Bush won the Hispanic vote in only 1 state, but it was the decisive state of Florida where he edged Gore 49 percent to 48 percent. On the other hand, Gore won New Mexico by the narrowest of margins because of the Hispanic vote, as the 28 percent of New Mexico voters who were Hispanic favored him decisively by 66 percent to 32 percent, while the 59 percent of voters who were white voted for Bush 58 percent to 37 percent.

The African American vote was an extraordinary 90 percent to 8 percent endorsement of Gore nationally (Connelly, 2000), and this was duplicated in the exit polls in 22 states and D.C., where the subsamples were large enough for reliable generalizations (Exit Polls: States, 2000). In 18 states, black voters were 10 percent or more of the total vote, with the largest proportion being 63 percent of the vote in D.C., and the lowest proportion of the 22 states being 7 percent in California, Indiana, and Pennsylvania. The largest Democratic African American percentages were in D.C., with Gore 93 percent to 6 percent over Bush and in Florida with Gore up 93 percent to 7 percent. The lowest was still a healthy 84 percent to 14 percent lead for Gore in Virginia. In 15 states the Democratic proportion of the African American vote was 90 percent or more. One limitation on the electoral influence of the African American vote is that a number of the states with the largest proportion of black voters are in the South, which has approximately half of the black vote. The states include Mississippi (30 percent), Louisiana (29 percent), Alabama (25 percent), and Georgia (25 percent), where a heavily Democratic vote is largely wasted in Republican-oriented states.

At the national level Bush captured the non-Hispanic white vote 54 percent to 42 percent, a definite improvement from Dole's 46 percent to 43 percent margin (Connelly, 2000). Our analysis of the 50 states (Exit Polls: States, 2000) shows that the proportion of the non-Hispanic white vote, while 82 percent nationally, ranged from highs in Maine (98 percent), New Hampshire (97 percent), Vermont (97 percent), Iowa (97 percent), and Utah (96 percent) to lows in New Mexico (59 percent), Hawaii (34 percent), and D.C. (29 percent). Bush won this group in 41 states and Gore in 9 and D.C. Bush picked up 70 percent or more of the non-

Hispanic white vote in 7 states including Texas, Alabama, Louisiana, Georgia, South Carolina, Idaho, and Wyoming, with his home state Texas leading the pack with 73 percent. Gore won a majority of the non-Hispanic white vote in 6 states in the East and D.C., with D.C. leading with 67 percent and followed by Rhode Island (60 percent), Massachusetts (57 percent), Maine (54 percent), New York (53 percent), New Jersey (51 percent) and Vermont (51 percent). He also registered narrow plurality advantages with non-Hispanic white voters in Minnesota, Hawaii, and Washington.

Hammering away with attack messages on Social Security, Medicare drug prescription coverage, and health care reform, Gore won the senior vote (those 60 years and older) 51 percent to 47 percent (Connelly, 2000). Seniors 60 years or older constitute 22 percent of the national vote, with 14 percent of all voters 65 years older or more. The highest proportions of senior voters (65 years or older) live in Kansas, California, Arkansas, Florida, North Dakota, Pennsylvania, Nebraska, and Oregon. Our analysis of the 65 years of age or more senior vote for the individual states shows Gore carried 26 and Bush 23. The subsamples were too small to generalize for Alaska and D.C. Gore captured the senior vote in 10 of the 12 states of the East, 4 of 13 states in the South, 5 of 12 in the Midwest, and 5 of the 12 in the West, where data were available. While Gore won the senior vote overall, Bush did well with seniors in the South and was competitive in the Midwest. Gore's best percentage showings with seniors over age 65 were in Hawaii (65–32), Rhode Island (64–31), Maryland (60–38), and the important battleground state Pennsylvania (60–38). In fact, our analysis shows that Gore's 3-to-2 ratio with the 19 percent of Pennsylvania seniors 65 years of age or more coupled with the vote from labor union households were the two most important voter demographic factors in his winning the Keystone state. On the other hand, Bush's best senior percentages were in South Carolina (67–29), Mississippi (64–36), North Carolina (63–37), Nebraska (61–34), Indiana (61–39), and Montana (60–37). To illustrate the diversity in the senior vote, Florida went narrowly for Bush, in part because he carried seniors 52 percent to 46 percent, as did Missouri, with its seniors favoring Bush 52 percent to 47 percent. On the other hand, Bush managed to win Ohio narrowly, although Gore captured the Buckeye seniors 53 percent to 46 percent.

Voters who live in households with a labor union member are a core Democratic constituency that Gore won 59 percent to 37 percent (Connelly, 2000). The state exit polls (Exit Polls: States, 2000) asked the labor union household question in 16 states but ended up dropping Texas because the sample was too small. The largest union member household percentages were in Michigan (43 percent), New York (39 percent), and Rhode Island (38 percent). The face of unionism has changed the past quarter century, and many union members are in white-collar unions like those of governmental employees and teachers. Gore dominated the union vote in the 15 states, with his strongest percentage showings in New York (65–30), Pennsylvania (65–32), and Maryland (65–33). His weakest union percentages were in West Virginia (51–47) and Nevada (51–43). The West Virginia exit poll also disaggregated the union question for the 33 percent labor voters as to whether the voter was actually a union member (16 percent) or simply lived in a household with a union member (17 percent). Gore's weakness in losing Democratic West Virginia is captured by the fact that union members themselves favored Bush 50 percent to 48 percent, while other household members endorsed Gore 54 percent to 44 percent. The importance of the labor vote to the Democrats is illustrated by the fact that labor delivered good margins for Gore in the battleground states of Minnesota, Michigan, Wisconsin, and even in Oregon and Washington where 22 percent and 27 percent of the voters, respectively, were union members.

We look now at the important predictor variable party identification. In the national exit survey, both Gore and Bush carried their respective party bases. Gore dominated the Democrats 86 percent to 11 percent and Bush the Republicans 91 percent to 8 percent, with the Independents splitting for Bush 47 percent to 45 percent (Connelly, 2000). We analyzed the state exit surveys (Exit Polls: States, 2000) to identify high rates of defection that could have influenced the state's popular vote. Gore carried the Democrats in all 50 states and D.C. and won 90 percent of the Democrats or more in D.C. and 6 states, including New Hampshire, New Jersey, Virginia, New York, Missouri, and California. In 9 states, however, Gore experienced Democratic defections to Bush of 20 percent or more, including Oklahoma, Kentucky, West Virginia, Louisiana, Idaho, Colorado, Wyoming, North Dakota, and South Dakota. Oklahoma had the highest percentage of defectors at 27 percent. Gore's losses in the southern battleground states of Kentucky and Louisiana and his surprise loss in West Virginia can be attributed in part to his failure to consolidate his Democratic base. Bush, by contrast, did not have any state with 20 percent or more Republican defections to Gore. His four worst states were New York (19 percent), Pennsylvania, (16 percent), Connecticut (15 percent), and West Virginia (15 percent). The only major weakness in the GOP partisan base was Pennsylvania because the 16 percent defection rate occurred in a battleground state that Bush had an outside chance to win.

While the 27 percent Independent vote went 47 percent to 45 percent nationally for Bush (Connelly, 2000), Gore managed to carry the Independent vote in 19 states and D.C. (Exit Polls: States, 2000). He won 10 of 12 states and D.C. in the East, all but Maryland and West Virginia. His loss of Independents to Bush (50 percent to 42 percent) in West Virginia, of course, proved fatal. Gore won the Independent vote in only

1 of 13 southern states (Florida, but only by a 47 percent to 46 percent margin, not enough to offset Bush's numbers with Republicans). In the Midwest, Gore captured the Independent vote in 4 of 12 states (Iowa, Illinois, Michigan, and Minnesota). His margins with Independents in Iowa and Minnesota helped him to carry these states. In the West, Gore registered Independent majorities in only 4 of the 13 states (Nevada, New Mexico, California, and Washington). His Independent percentages helped him win close races in New Mexico and Washington. The state exit survey data underscore that Independents were important for Bush and helped him solidify his southern base, as well as capture important competitive races in West Virginia, Missouri, and Ohio. Without Independents and a more inclusive coalition, he would never have won the presidency.

A major irony in the presidential election of 2000 is that Gore emphasized prosperity and populism but did better with upper-income, higher-educated, and upscale voters. Bush, by contrast, campaigned for smaller government and a tax cut for all but did better with less educated and lower-income voters and not as well as expected with upscale voters. "Voters who do not have college-degrees—a constituency targeted by both campaigns—moved in a strongly Republican direction" (Edsall, 2000a, A29). Clinton had dominated this constituency 51 percent to 37 percent in 1996, but Bush edged Gore by a slim 49 percent to 48 percent. In 1988, the senior Bush controlled voters making $50,000 or more by 25 points, 62 percent to 37 percent, while in 2000 the younger Bush struggled to carry them, 53 percent to 43 percent. Edsall observes that "some of the nation's best educated and highest income countries have become Democratic bastions, and some of the nation's poorest white counties—especially in the southern border states—have turned into GOP strongholds" (Edsall, 2001, A29). In 2000 17 out of 25 of the nation's most affluent counties, with high percentages of people with advanced degrees, went solidly for Gore, sometimes by more than 70 percent. Alternately, 9 of the 10 poorest counties in Kentucky, areas with no tradition of voting Republican, shifted to Bush. Stan Greenberg, Gore's pollster, summed it up and said: "We lost it downscale and gained it upscale" (Edsall, 2001, A29).

Finally, in pursuing communication and persuasion in the presidential campaign 2000, Gore dominated down the stretch with a stronger finish. Historically, the undecided vote usually breaks against the incumbent or the incumbent party. If voters have not committed to the incumbent or incumbent party, it means that they have reservations that will benefit the opposition when the ballots are cast. The 2000 election was the first election since Truman's upset win in 1948 in which the incumbent party's candidate won the undecided vote. The 11 percent who decided the last three days favored Gore 48 percent to 46 percent, as did those 6 percent who decided the last week by a 48 percent to 44 percent margin (Exit Polls: National, 2000).

GENDER IN THE 2000 ELECTION

Although the aforementioned demographic variables are important to explain the vote in 2000, special attention is given to the important variable gender. Gender has attracted media and scholarly attention since the election of Ronald Reagan in 1980 (Delli Carpini and Fuchs, 1993; H. Kenski, 1998; Kenski and Jamieson, 2000, 2001; Wirl, 1986). Beginning in 1980, differences seemed more apparent between men and women on party identification, presidential job approval, political knowledge, issues, and candidate choice. The category of gender, of course, is a broad one, but analysts have been struck by the tendency of men overall to be more Republican and women more Democratic. On issues, women are less inclined to use force in foreign policy and to express more support for domestic issues like education, health care, support for the poor, and the environment. In presidential elections, men are more supportive of Republican candidates than are women. There is much that is true in these observations, but they are too sweeping and at times even misleading. Political reality looks more complex if one disaggregates the gender data to control for race-ethnicity, party identification, and marital status (Kenski, Chang, and Aylor, 1998).

We begin our analysis with a historical overview, presented in Table 10.4. These data demonstrate that the differences between how men and women voted from 1952 to 1976 are minimal. Of interest, however, is that both sexes voted Republican in 1952, 1956, and 1972. Despite media emphasis on Kennedy's youthful image and physical attractiveness, women nevertheless preferred Nixon in 1960 (51 percent to 49 percent), while men favored Kennedy (52 percent to 48 percent). In 1968 women supported Humphrey (45 percent to 43 percent) and men Nixon (43 percent to 41 percent). In 1976 females leaned toward Ford (51 percent to 48 percent), while men opted for Carter (53 percent to 45 percent). Although these differences were different in the latter three elections, the margins of difference were not great.

Larger percentage differences emerged in 1980 and were labeled in mass media as the gender gap. The data in Table 10.4 confirm the existence of a gap, but the more significant point is that the Republican candidates were preferred by both sexes, although more so by men. In 1980 Reagan had a 15 percent advantage with men and a 5 percent edge with women, while in 1984 his male margin was a striking 28 percent and 10 percent with women. In 1988 Bush led among men by 12 percent and among women by 4 percent. There was a gap in these three elections, but it did not threaten the Republican presidential ticket since it was

Table 10.4
Gender and the Presidential Vote: 1952–2000 (% vote by gender)

	Males			Females		
Year	Democrats	Republicans	Independents	Democrats	Republicans	Independents
1952	47	53	0	42	58	0
1956	45	55	0	39	61	0
1960	52	48	0	49	51	0
1964	60	40	0	62	38	0
1968	41	43	16	45	43	12
1972	37	63	0	38	62	0
1976	53	45	1	48	51	0
1980	38	53	7	44	49	6
1984	36	64	0	45	55	0
1988	44	56	0	48	52	0
1992	41	37	22	46	38	16
1996	43	44	10	54	38	7
2000	42	53	3	54	43	2

Sources: Gallup polls from 1952 to 1992 in Stanley and Niemi, 1994, 105–108; 1996 and 2000 Voter News Service exit polls reported by Connelly, 2000.

favored by both sexes. In 1992, there was a gap, but Clinton surpassed Dole with both men (4 percent) and women (8 percent).

Clinton's campaign strategy in 1996 sought to capture both sexes and to win as many white males as possible. This election, however, recorded the largest gender gap in U.S. history as men favored Dole by a slim 1 percent and the women Clinton by a striking 16 percent advantage. Clinton exploited the gender gap, emphasizing issues women favored more than men, including the family Medical Leave Act, the Violence against Women Act, tough enforcement of child support laws, the assault weapons ban, and the V-chip, designed to screen out the objectionable television programs. The Clinton strategy made him almost even with males, but it gave him overwhelming approval from women (Kenski, Chang, and Aylor, 1998). In 2000, Bush was able to increase the Republican male advantage from 1 percent to 11 percent, while Gore experienced a drop in the Democratic female edge from 16 percent to 11 percent. Looking at these large gender aggregates, the gender gap was alive and well in 2000.

To test the scope and strength of the gender gap pattern, we examine the national exit survey data and control for race, age, marital status, party identification, and suburban residence. The data appear in Table 10.5. Large aggregates like male and female may overshadow or conceal subgroup differentiations. Since African Americans and Hispanics, for

Table 10.5
Gender and the Presidential Vote in 1996 and 2000 by Race, Age, Marital Status, and Party Identification

% of 2000		1996 %			2000 %		
Total Vote	Category	Clinton	Dole	Perot	Gore	Bush	Nader
	Total Vote	49	41	8	48	48	2
39	White Men	38	49	11	36	60	3
43	White Women	48	43	8	48	49	2
4	Black Men	78	15	5	85	12	1
6	Black Women	89	8	2	94	6	0
8	Men 18 to 29	47	38	12	41	51	6
9	Women 18 to 29	58	31	9	53	42	4
16	Men 30 to 44	41	46	10	42	54	2
17	Women 30 to 44	54	37	7	53	45	2
13	Men 45 to 59	44	43	10	41	55	2
15	Women 45 to 59	52	40	7	53	44	2
10	Men 60 Plus	43	48	8	44	53	2
11	Women 60 Plus	53	41	5	56	42	2
32	Married Men	40	48	10	38	58	2
33	Married Women	48	43	7	48	49	2
16	Unmarried Men	49	35	12	48	46	4
19	Unmarried Women	62	28	7	63	32	3
18	Republican Men	11	81	6	7	92	1
17	Republican Women	15	79	5	9	90	1
14	Independent Men	38	37	21	39	51	7
13	Independent Women	49	34	14	51	42	5
15	Democratic Men	82	11	6	85	12	2
23	Democratic Women	85	9	4	87	11	1
20	Suburban Men	41	47	10	41	55	3
23	Suburban Women	53	39	7	52	45	2

Source: 1996 and 2000 Voter News Service exit polls reported by Connelly, 2000.

example, are quite Democratic, the overall gender results may conceal, for example, if white females are also Democratic. The data shows that Clinton dominated three of the race-gender categories and was particularly popular with black women and black men, but especially black women. He did win white women 48 percent to 43 percent, but Dole had a 49 percent to 38 percent edge with white men. Gore's percentages were even more lopsided with black women (94 percent to 6 percent) and black men (85 percent to 12 percent) than Clinton's. The major change in 2000 was Bush's ability to increase the GOP advantage with white men (60 percent to 36 percent and to win white women by 1 percent (49 percent to 48 percent). Thus the overall gender percentages conceal that there was parity in the white female vote in 2000.

Clinton carried six of the eight age-gender categories, winning all four for women and losing only males 30 to 44 and older males over 60. Gore likewise led in all four age-gender categories for women and even improved on Clinton's percentage (53 percent to 41 percent) with women over 60 (56 percent to 42 percent). Unlike Clinton, however, Gore lost all four male categories, and his best male showing was a 53 percent to 44 percent loss to Bush with older men. Contrary to much newspaper reporting, the gender gap not only involves a Democratic advantage with females but a Republican advantage with males as well.

An important aspect in gender analysis is marital status. Republicans traditionally fare better with married voters, while Democrats are more attractive to the unmarried. In 1996, Clinton was especially strong with unmarried women, a very economically vulnerable group, and topped Dole 62 percent to 28 percent. He also led with unmarried men (49 percent to 35 percent) and married women (48 percent to 43 percent). Dole won among married men (48 percent to 40 percent). Gore did not fare as well save for unmarried women, where he buried Bush (63 percent to 32 percent). It is likely that his messages on health care prescription drugs, Social Security, education, and tax cut resonated well with this group. Gore carried unmarried men, but his margin (48 percent to 46 percent) was lower than Clinton's (49 percent to 35 percent). Gore's pollster Matthew Dowd (2001) noted that the Bush campaign really concentrated on married women. He said that this was a difficult group to persuade. It paid off, as Bush won married women by a razor-thin 49 percent to 48 percent, while increasing the GOP margin with married males to a solid 58 percent to 38 percent.

Both party tickets carried their partisans in 1996 and 2000. In both elections, Democratic women were a little more supportive of their party's candidate than Democratic men. Conversely, in both contests Republican men were slightly more supportive of Dole and Bush than GOP women. In 1996, Clinton won Independent women by a comfortable margin of 49 percent to 34 percent and Independent men by 1 percent (38 percent to 37 percent). Perot received 21 percent of the Independent male vote and 14 percent from Independent women. In 2000 Bush won Independent men (51 percent to 39 percent), while Gore won Independent women (51 percent to 42 percent). The suburban residence variable was comparable in both elections, with suburban men tilting Republican and suburban women Democratic. Bush did increase Dole's percentages with suburban men (47 percent to 55 percent) and suburban women (39 percent to 45 percent).

ISSUES IN THE 1996 AND 2000 ELECTIONS

The data in Table 10.6 capture the issues as both the 1996 and 2000 election exit polls asked respondents to identify the issue that mattered the most in their presidential vote and their views on the economy. The data indicate that voters rewarded Clinton if they felt the economy was excellent (4 percent) or good (52 percent), as he dominated Dole 78 percent to 18 percent and 62 percent to 31 percent with these voters. Those who believed that the economy was not so good or poor tended to support Dole (52 percent to 34 percent and 50 percent to 23 percent, respectively). Although the media constantly mentioned economic prosperity in 2000, voters were harsher in their assessments. The 28 percent who assessed the economy as excellent, however, favored Gore (53 percent to 46 percent). The 12 percent who said the economy was good supported Bush (53 percent to 38 percent), while those who saw the economy as not so good (57 percent) opted narrowly for Bush (49 percent to 47 percent). In 2000 seven times as many voters rated the national economy excellent but favored Gore by only 7 percent, compared to the 1996 voters who said excellent and gave Clinton a 60 percent margin. It should be noted that the 2000 exit survey showed that 50 percent of voters believed that they personally were better off than four years ago, 38 percent thought they were in the same situation, and only 11 percent thought they were worse off (Exit Polls: National, 2000). In the past, however, the best indicator of electorally relevant voter feelings on prosperity has been voter evaluation of the condition of the national economy rather than their own family's financial situation. Contrary to much media and political pundit analysis, we contend that Gore was hurt on the issue of the economy on two counts. First, voters were optimistic about their personal financial situations but more negative on the condition of the national economy. Second, voters were far less generous in giving the incumbent party candidate credit for an excellent or good economy.

The data in Table 10.6 underscore that Clinton had the edge on three of the four top issues—the economy, Medicare/Social Security, and education—and he did so by decisive margins. Dole had an advantage on the deficit, taxes, crime/drugs, and foreign policy. The tax cut strategy was viewed as the centerpiece of Dole's strategy (Kenski, Chang, and Aylor, 1998), and he captured 73 percent of the voters who chose it as their top concern. The 2000 data support the claim of Gore's issue dominance. Gore registered decisive percentage advantages over Bush on the

Table 10.6
Issue Reasons for the Presidential Vote in 1996 and 2000 (in percent)

	1996 %		
	Clinton	Dole	Perot
Which issues mattered most in deciding how you voted?			
Economy, Jobs (21%)	61	27	10
Medicare, Social Security (15%)	67	26	6
Budget Deficit (12%)	28	52	19
Education (12%)	78	15	4
Taxes (11%)	19	73	7
Crime, Drugs (7%)	41	50	8
Foreign Policy (4%)	35	55	8
Is the condition of the economy . . . ?			
Excellent (4%)	78	18	3
Good (52%)	62	31	5
Not So Good (36%)	34	52	12
Poor (7%)	23	50	21
		2000 %	
	Gore	Bush	Nader
Which issues mattered most?			
Economy, Jobs (18%)	59	37	2
Education (15%)	52	44	3
Social Security (14%)	58	40	1
Taxes (14%)	17	80	2
World Affairs (12%)	40	54	4
Health Care (8%)	64	33	3
Medicare, Rx Drugs (7%)	60	39	1
National economy?			
Excellent (28%)	53	46	1
Good (12%)	38	53	6
Not So Good (57%)	47	49	3

Sources: 1996 Voter News Service exit poll data in Kenski, Chang, and Aylor, 1998; 2000 Voter News Service exit poll data in Exit Polls: National, 2000.

top issue of the economy, as well as Social Security, health care, Medicare/Rx Drugs, and also by a smaller margin on education. Bush had a big edge on taxes and a closer margin on world affairs. Gore had the edge on five of the seven issues. Bush did better than Dole, however, and was competitive on education (44 percent to Gore's 52 percent), whereas Clinton overwhelmed Dole 78 percent to 15 percent. Some 14 percent chose tax as the top issue in 2000, 3 percent more than in 1996, and Bush increased the GOP percentage from 73 percent to 80 percent. He was also more competitive on Social Security, trailing 58 percent to 40 percent compared to Clinton's Medicare/Social Security 67 percent to 26 percent dominance. Finally, it is interesting that only 4 percent mentioned foreign policy in 1996, and this tripled to 12 percent in 2000 for foreign affairs, as Bush edged Gore 54 percent to 40 percent. Overall, Gore maintained the advantage on issues, but Bush did capitalize on the tax cut and foreign affairs and was able to improve the GOP percentages on the other domestic issues, enough to establish his image as a different kind of Republican leader.

The national exit survey data tap the main issues in the campaign as covered in the media and as reflected in the mass advertising of the campaigns. Other issues, however, were also important, such as abortion, guns, and the environment, and were used in personal campaigning, radio, and phone banking in hotly contested states like Arkansas, Tennessee, and West Virginia (Barone, 2001). Their importance is also confirmed in a national postelection survey conducted on November 10–12, 2000 (Pew Research Center, 2000). This survey used an open-ended question to ask voters what they liked most about the candidate they voted for. The data are a little surprising in that some 57 percent of Bush voters cited issues compared to only 42 percent of the Gore voters. Moreover, the study concluded that "abortion proved to be the sleeper issue of Campaign 2000—it was volunteered as a decisive issue most often by Bush voters who said issues mattered most. It rated less important, but still highly, among Gore voters. For the vice-president's supporters, abortion was ranked nearly as important as the environment, and not much below Social Security and education." (1). The top priorities for the issue-oriented Bush voters were abortion (28 percent), taxes (25 percent), Social Security (17 percent), gun control (14 percent), and education (13 percent). The top priorities for the issue-oriented Gore voters were Social Security (25 percent), education (24 percent), environment (20 percent), abortion (13 percent), and health care (13 percent). Among the issue voters there are partisan differences, as Democrats include the environment and health care as top priorities but not Republicans, while GOP respondents emphasize taxes and gun control but not the Democrats.

Table 10.7
Candidate Trait Reasons for the Presidential Vote in 1996 and 2000 (in percent)

		1996 %	
	Clinton	Dole	Perot
Which candidate quality mattered most in deciding how you voted?			
Is honest and trustworthy (20%)	9	84	7
Shares my view of government (20%)	42	45	10
Has a vision for the future (16%)	77	13	9
Stands up for what he believes (12%)	42	40	15
Cares about people like me (10%)	72	17	9
Is in touch with the 1990s (10%)	89	8	4
		2000 %	
	Gore	Bush	Nader
Which quality mattered most?			
Honest, trustworthy (24%)	15	80	3
Has experience (15%)	82	17	1
Strong leader (14%)	34	64	1
Good judgment (13%)	48	50	1
Understands issues (13%)	75	19	4
Cares about people (12%)	63	31	5
Likeable (2%)	38	59	2

Sources: 1996 Voter News Service exit poll in Kenski, Chang, and Aylor, 1998; 2000 Voter News Service exit poll in Exit Polls: National, 2000.

CANDIDATE TRAITS IN 1996 AND 2000

Another important factor in the vote is the qualities that people observe in candidates (Aylor, 2000). Table 10.7 summarizes the data from 1996 and 2000. As the data demonstrate, no single trait dominated in 1996, although Dole captured the 20 percent of voters selecting honesty and trust and had a very slim edge with the 20 percent who selected "shares my view of government." Clinton had a slight advantage with the 12 percent who said that he "stands up for what he believes in." He then ran up substantial and lopsided margins on the traits where 10 percent selected empathy ("cares about people like me"), the 16 percent who said "has vision for the future," and the 10 percent who mentioned "is in touch with the 1990s." The situational context of each campaign is a little different, and so are the qualities that candidates emphasize in their advertising and what the professional media decide is most important. Thus only two of the qualities tested in 2000 also appeared on the 1996 list (honesty, trustworthy, and cares about people). In 2000, Bush had an edge on candidate qualities and led on four of the seven traits mentioned. His strongest suit was honest, trustworthy, where he led Gore 80 percent to 15 percent among the 24 percent citing this quality. He also dominated the 14 percent mentioning strong leader (64 percent to 34 percent) and the minuscule 2 percent selecting likeable (59 percent to 38 percent) and prevailed narrowly with the 13 percent citing good judgment (50 percent to 48 percent). Gore won decisively the 15 percent citing experience (82 percent to 17 percent), the 13 percent saying understands issues (75 percent to 19 percent), and the 12 percent cares about people (63 percent to 31 percent). While Gore had an edge on issues, Bush had the advantage on candidate qualities.

THE ELEPHANT IN THE LIVING ROOM AND THE REST OF THE STORY

In past presidential elections, an important predictor variable has been the job performance of the president. A high job approval rating and a strong economy were the top ingredients to assure reelection or to help elect the incumbent party nominee. In early September 2000 political analyst Bill Schneider (2000a) observed that "normally, people who approve of the President's performance vote for his party" (2834). It was not unusual to see 80 percent or more of those voters expressing positive job approval to vote for the president or his party's nominee. The 2000 election was an anomaly. The public approved the job Clinton was doing by a decisive 57 percent to 41 percent margin but also expressed an unfavorable view of him as a person by a 60 percent to 36 percent margin (Exit Poll: National, 2000). In past elections, high job approval ratings and high personal ratings went hand in hand, with only minor deviations. Thus the 2000 exit poll for the first time created a fourfold classification of job/approval and like/dislike. It found that 35 percent of the voters registered approve/like, while 39 percent recorded disapprove/dislike. Some 2 percent were barely on the political radar screen and disapproved the way Clinton performed the job but liked him personally. The swing vote in this election would prove to be the 20 percent who said approve/dislike. At the national level, those who said approve/like voted for Gore (85 percent to 12 percent), while those who said disapprove/dislike favored Bush (89 percent to 7 percent). The minuscule 2 percent indicating disapprove/like chose Bush (50 percent to 43 percent), while the one-fifth of voters registering approve/dislike cast their ballots for Gore (63 percent to 33 percent), a much smaller margin than one would have expected for positive job approval (Exit Poll: National, 2000). Much depends, of course, on how the public assesses character (Aylor, 2000). In 2000, it appeared that a significant percentage thought it was important enough to offset positive job approval, and it worked to Bush's advantage.

Bob Shrum (2001) and Carter Eskew (2001a), two of Gore's top campaign advisers, have argued that without the legacy of scandal and the subsequent increase in the percentage of voters who disliked President Clinton's personal behavior, Gore would have been elected president. Shrum stressed that a prosperous economy, a country at peace, and a decisive Democratic edge on many of the issues gave Gore a strong edge over Bush. The legacy of scandal, however, provided a counterweight to Gore's advantages. Eskew reiterates this claim and argues that "our tracking polls consistently showed the Gore-Lieberman message on the role of government beat the Bush-Cheney message. And, indeed, on Election Day, exit polling showed that the voters preferred Al Gore's approach on most of the major issues facing the country" (2001a, A17). He goes on to say that the argument that the election was gift wrapped because of a great economy "leaves out a big fact—one might say the elephant in the living room. Al Gore not only inherited a great economy, but also inherited voters' deep dissatisfaction and anger over the scandals in Washington" (A17). He concludes by noting that the election was about restoring "honor and integrity" to the White House. The Gore campaign knew the power of this phrase and failed in the end: "We didn't do enough to reassure voters about what is true: Al Gore is a man of strong values and bedrock integrity" (A17).

We agree that the Clinton legacy of scandals hurt Gore, and the critical defections came from those who registered presidential job approval but dislike for Clinton's personal behavior. To support our claim we present data in Table 10.8 that compares the presidential vote in the 23 states that at one time or another were on the battleground list for one or both tickets by the three voting groups of approve/dislike, approve/like, and approve/dislike. The percentage of voters in each of these categories in all 23 states is also printed. The data underscore that voters who registered disapprove/dislike voted for Bush by sizable margins ranging from 92 percent to 4 percent in Clinton's home state of Arkansas to a low of 84 percent to 12 percent in Iowa. Conversely, those who both approved of and liked Clinton cast a strong vote for Gore that ran from a high of 90 percent to 8 percent in Gore's Tennessee to a low of 76 percent to 23 percent in West Virginia. Some 18 of the 23 states' approve/like voters registered 80 percent or more support for Gore. Gore lost the election with the approve/dislike voters, all of whom cast Gore majorities but by much lower percentages than the hoped-for 80 percent vote for positive job approval. In 12 of these 23 states, Gore was able to offset and overcome the lower-than-expected vote from these voters and car-

Table 10.8
Combined Impact of Clinton Job Approval/Disapproval and Personal Like/Dislike on the 2000 Presidential Vote[a] in Initial and Final Phase Battleground States

	Disapprove/Dislike			Approve/Like			Approve/Dislike		
State	% Total	% Gore	% Bush	% Total	% Gore	% Bush	% Total	% Gore	% Bush
Maine	34	11	83	33	79	16	26	58	32
Del.	32	9	86	40	88	10	21	61	35
Pa.	37	9	88	33	87	12	22	62	33
Ark.	42	4	92	33	87	8	18	62	35
Fla.	37	5	91	37	84	13	18	57	38
Ga.	43	5	92	34	89	10	15	53	44
Ky.	46	6	92	30	81	16	18	57	40
La.	41	7	90	34	77	20	13	55	42
Ill.	31	7	90	41	89	9	21	64	33
Iowa	41	12	84	33	85	13	22	60	37
Mich.	37	9	87	35	87	12	20	64	34
Mo.	38	8	90	33	87	11	20	56	42
Ohio	39	7	90	34	84	13	21	62	32
Wis.	40	9	85	32	85	13	23	66	30
N.M.	43	5	90	35	88	10	15	69	26
Ore.	36	9	85	31	81	14	21	58	37
Wash.	36	8	86	34	82	12	21	61	34
W.Va.	38	13	85	31	76	23	24	63	34
N.H.	40	8	86	29	82	11	25	65	32
Tenn.	45	10	88	33	90	8	16	59	37
Minn.	33	11	85	35	76	16	27	56	36
Calif.	33	7	88	40	84	12	20	62	32
Nev.	38	9	86	36	79	18	19	50	42

[a]State exit survey data for the 50 states and Washington, D.C. appear in Exit Polls: States (2000).

ried their states. In 11, however, this voter group was central to Gore's losing. A victory in any of them like Florida, West Virginia, New Hampshire, or Tennessee would have won the presidency for Gore.

Although much media commentary focused on the possibility of third-party candidate Ralph Nader picking up enough of the vote in Maine, Minnesota, Wisconsin, Oregon, and Washington to give these states to Bush, Gore did win all of the so-called Nader-vulnerable states. Ironically, Nader may have pulled enough votes in two other states, however, Florida and New Hampshire, to give their electoral votes to Bush (Kaiser, 2001). As the radio commentator Paul Harvey would note, it is a good practice to hear the rest of the story. Although Clinton's character was a drag on Gore, the vice president also did things that hurt his campaign and damaged his credibility. Al Gore trailed George Bush throughout most of 1999 and 2000 but finally pulled ahead after the Democratic convention in August. He continued to gain momentum while Bush stumbled and pulled even or slightly ahead on many of the personality and character traits. In early September a *Washington Post*–ABC News poll found Gore to be the equal of Bush. It discovered that a majority of Americans say that both Bush and Gore are honest and trustworthy and have high moral and ethical standards. "Gore even has an advantage on which candidate could best change the tone in Washington" (Balz, 2000a, A1). A few days later a *New York Times*/CBS poll conducted on September 9–11, 2000, reported that Gore had overcome voter concerns on likeability and character and was "as highly regarded as Gov. George W. Bush on matters of character, leadership, and overall personal popularity" (Berke and Elder, 2000,). *National Journal* analyst Bill Schneider proclaimed that Gore had turned the corner, had a 7 percent lead, had unshackled himself from Clinton, and had demonstrated his commitment to family values (2000b, 3006). In short, the evidence for the late August through almost three weeks of September was that Gore had the edge on issues and was at least even with Bush on character.

He was unable to maintain the lead he had opened and made campaign errors that allowed the personality and character factor to shift again to Bush's advantage. Top aides in both campaigns believe that Gore made a costly blunder on September 20 "when he publicly urged President Clinton to release a portion of the Strategic Petroleum Reserve to help hold down heating-oil prices" (Babington, 2001). It was a risky request because the reserves were created for national security and not consumer comfort, and it made Gore look very political. Bush pollster Matthew Dowd said that it was the first positive step to get the Bush campaign back on track because it took away from the "new Gore" (Babington, 2001). Stan Greenberg (2001), Gore's pollster, conceded that Gore dropped 4 percentage points in their own poll after this event.

The other campaign error involved Gore's conduct during the presidential debates, especially the first one where he was criticized by both the media and the Bush campaign for exaggeration and embellishment. *Congressional Quarterly*'s Ron Elving (2000) called the debates Bush's October surprise. Gore's tendency to interrupt, sigh audibly, and embellish a little detracted from the positive image he had been so successful in establishing in August and the first part of September. Elving observes that "while Gore may have been the winner on 'points' in two of the three presidential debates, Bush seemed to come off as the more likeable and trustworthy." The debates helped the Republican ticket. Its impact was even reflected in the late night television shows. Elving observes and asks: "After one debate, NBC's Jay Leno said the two candidates worked well together because whenever Bush couldn't think of a fact, Gore would make one up for him. Which candidate comes out ahead on that exchange?" (Elving, 2000).

Political columnists Germond and Witcover (2000) observe that while the Gore campaign managers were justified in pointing out that Clinton hurt Gore in critical states "other Democrats point out, however, that Gore didn't help himself by so emphatically embracing Clinton after the impeachment" (3632). Diane Wright, a 52-year-old Humbolt, Tennessee, homemaker, heard Gore speak in October 2000 and liked his anti-HMO rhetoric. She nevertheless felt that she might vote for Bush. When asked why she said: "Probably because of Clinton. Gore should have been stronger. He could have distanced himself. A lot of people in Tennessee feel that way" (Harris, 2000). And that, my friends, as Paul Harvey would say, is the rest of the story.

NOTE

1. Henry Kenski and Kate Kenski express their appreciation to Dean Kathleen Hall Jamieson of the Annenberg School of Communication for inviting them to be observers at the Presidential Election Debriefing 2000 at the Annenberg Public Policy Center in Philadelphia on February 10, 2001. Our use of comments by participants is based on our own notes of the debriefing. A video has been made of some of the proceedings and is available by contacting the Annenberg Public Policy Center of the University of Pennsylvania, 3620 Walnut Street, Philadelphia, PA 19104 or by calling (215) 898–7041. The University of Pennsylvania Press will publish a book form of the debriefing, *Electing the President 2000*, to be available in 2002.

REFERENCES

"Ad Spotlight." 2000. A submenu at http://nationaljournal.com

Aylor, Brooks. 2000. "Source Credibility and Presidential Candidates in 1996: The Changing Nature of Character and Empathy." *Communication Research Reports*, 16(3) 296–304.

Babington, Charles. 2001. "Rats Ad, Oil Story: More Footnotes from Election 2000." *Washington Post*, August 13. www.washingtonpost.com

Balz, Dan. 2000a. "GOP Split on Best Strategy for Bush." *Washington Post*, September 10. www.washingtonpost.com

Balz, Dan. 2000b. "Smaller States Play a Big Role." *Washington Post*, October 9. www.washingtonpost.com

Balz, Dan. 2000c. "Gore to Attack Bush in Ads on Social Security." *Washington Post*, October 22. www.washingtonpost.com

Barnes, James A. 1992. "Tainted Triumph?" *National Journal*, 24(45) (November 7), 2537–2541.

Barnes, James A. 1996. "Planting the Seeds." *National Journal*, 28(45) (November 9), 2400–2405.

Barnes, James A. 2000. "The GOP's Shifting Terrain." *National Journal*, 32(46) (November 11), 3609–3610.

Barone, Michael. 1990. *Our Country: The Shaping of America from Roosevelt to Reagan*. New York: Free Press.

Barone, Michael. 2001. "The 49 Percent Nation." http://www.nationaljournal.com, June 8.

Berke, Richard L. and Janet Elder. 2000. "Poll Shows Gore Overcoming Voter Concerns on Likeability." *New York Times*, September 13, A1, A16.

Bruni, Frank and Alison Mitchell. 2000. "Bush Says Integrity Makes Him Right for Job." *New York Times*, November 5, A1, A32.

Castellanos, Alex. 2001. "Comments at the Annenberg School of Communication Election Debriefing," University of Pennsylvania, February 10.

Connelly, Marjorie. 2000. "Who Voted: A Portrait of American Politics, 1976–2000." *New York Times*, November 12, sec. 4, 12.

Delli Carpini, Michael X. and Ester R. Fuchs. 1993. "The Year of the Women? Candidates, Voters, and the 1992 Election." *Political Science Quarterly*, 108(1), 29–36.

Dowd, Matthew. 2001. "Comments at the Annenberg School of Communication Election Debriefing," University of Pennsylvania, February 10.

Edsall, Thomas B. 2000a. "Analysis: Bush Cut into Democratic Coalition." *Washington Post*, November 8, A29.

Edsall, Thomas B. 2000b. "Political Party Is No Longer Dictated by Class Status." *Washington Post*, November 9, A37.

Edsall, Thomas. 2001. "Voter Values Determine Political Affiliation." *Washington Post*, March 26, 1–4. www.washingtonpost.com

Edsall, Thomas B. and Richard Morin. 1996. "Clinton Benefited from Huge Gender Gap." *Washington Post*, November 6, B7.

Elving, Ronald. 2000. "Bush Gets Pleasant 'October Surprise.'" *Congressional Quarterly*, October 25. www.washingtonpost.com

Eskew, Carter. 2001a. "The Lessons of 2000." *Washington Post*, January 30, A17.

Eskew, Carter. 2001b. "Comments at the Annenberg School of Communication Election Debriefing," University of Pennsylvania, February 10.

Exit Polls: National. 2000. www.cnn.com/Election/2000/epolls/US/P000.html

Exit Polls: States. 2000. Individual states cited (for example, New Jersey as NJ) at www.cnn.com/Election/200/epolls/state/P000.html

Germond, Jack and Jules Witcover. 2000. "The Blame Games." *National Journal*, 32(46) (November 11), 3632.

Greenberg, Stan. 2001. "Comments at the Annenberg School of Communication Election Debriefing," University of Pennsylvania, February 10.

Harris, John F. 2000. "In Full Roar, Gore Tries to Rally His Tennessee." *Washington Post*, October 26. www.washingtonpost.com

Kaiser, Robert G. 2001. "Political Scientists Offer Mea Culpas for Predicting Gore Win." *Washington Post*, February 9, A10.

Kenski, Henry C. 1988. "The Gender Gap in a Changing Electorate." In Carol Mueller, ed., *The Politics of the Gender Gap: The Social Construction of Political Influence*. Newbury Park, CA: Sage Publications, 38–60.

Kenski, Henry C. 1996. "From Agenda Setting to Priming and Framing: Reflections on Theory and Method." In Mary E. Stuckey, ed., *The Theory and Practice of Political Communication*. Albany: State University of New York Press, 67–83.

Kenski, Henry, Carol Chang, and Brooks Aylor. 1998. "Explaining the Vote: The Presidential Election of 1996." In Robert E. Denton, Jr., ed., *The 1996 Presidential Campaign: A Communication Perspective*. Westport, CT: Praeger, 263–284.

Kenski, Henry C. and Lee Sigelman. 1993. "Where the Votes Come From: Group Components of the 1988 Senate Vote." *Legislative Studies Quarterly*, 28(3), 367–390.

Kenski, Kate. 2000. "The Gender Gap in Political Knowledge: Are Women Less Knowledgeable Than Men about Politics?" In Kathleen Hall Jamieson, ed., *Everything You Think You Know about Politics . . . and Why You're Wrong*. New York: Basic Books, 83–89.

Kenski, Kate and Kathleen Hall Jamieson. 2001. "The 2000 Presidential Campaign and Differential Growths in Knowledge: Does the 'Knowledge Gap' Hypothesis Apply to Gender as Well as Education?" Paper presented at the Annual Meeting of the American Political Science Association in San Francisco, August 30–September 2.

Knapp, Bill. 2001. "Comments at the Annenberg School of Communication Election Debriefing," University of Pennsylvania, February 10.

Kramnick, Isaac, ed. 1987. *The Federalist Papers*. London: Penguin Books. Citing James Madison, Alexander Hamilton, and John Jay.

Lewis, Ann. 2001. "Comments at the Annenberg School of Communication Election Debriefing," University of Pennsylvania, February 10.

Marks, Peter. 2000. "Commercial Attacking Bush Is Most Hostile of Campaign." *New York Times*, November 3, A22.

McKinnon, Mark. 2001. "Comments at the Annenberg School of Communication Election Debriefing," University of Pennsylvania, February 10.

Mitchell, Alison. 2000a. "Bush Returning Tax-Cut Plan to Center Stage." *New York Times*, October 2, A1, A23.

Mitchell, Alison. 2000b. "Bush Hits Florida." *New York Times*, November 6, A1, A21.

Mitchell, Alison and Frank Bruni. 2000. "Bush's Message Focuses on Military Themes." *New York Times*, November 6, A1, A12.

Morris, Dick. 1997. *Behind the Oval Office: Winning the Presidency in the Nineties*. New York: Random House.

Pew Research Center for the People and the Press. 2000. "Endnotes on Campaign 2000: Some Final Observations on Voter Opinions." December 21, 1–2. http://www.people-Press.org/endnote00rpt.htm

Pomper, Gerald. 1977. "The Presidential Election." In Gerald Pomper et al., eds., *The Election of 1976: Reports and Interpretations*. New York: David McKay, 54–82.

Pomper, Gerald. 1989. "The Presidential Election." In Gerald Pomper et al., eds., *The Elections of 1988: Reports and Interpretations*. Chatham, NJ: Chatham House, 129–152.

Popkin, Samuel L. 1994. *The Reasoning Voter: Communication and Persuasion in Presidential Campaigns*. Chicago: University of Chicago Press.

Purdam, Todd S. 2000. "Efforts by Bush Showing Results across California." *New York Times*, October 26, A1, A24.

Rove, Karl. 2001. "Comments at the Annenberg School of Communication Election Debriefing," University of Pennsylvania, February 10.

Sack, Kevin. 2000. "Gore Urges Votes of Black and Labor Base." *New York Times*, November 5, A1, A32.

Schneider, William. 2000a. "Clinton: Just Doing His Job." *National Journal*, 32(37) (September 9), 2834.

Schneider, William. 2000b. "How Al Turned the Corner." *National Journal*, 32(39) (September 23), 3006.

Seelye, Katharine Q. 2000a. "Gore Describes Texan as Not Up to the Job." *New York Times*, November 4, A1, A13.

Seelye, Katharine. 2000b. "Gore Rallies Base." *New York Times*, November 6, A1, A20.

Shrum, Bob. 2001. "Comments at the Annenberg School of Communication Election Debriefing," University of Pennsylvania, February 10.

Stanley, Harold W. and Richard G. Niemi. 1994. *Vital Statistics on American Politics* (4th ed.). Washington, DC: CQ Press.

"2000 Election Data." 2001. http://www.uselectionatlas.org/USPRESIDENT/GENERAL/pe2000data.html

Wirl, Daniel. 1986. "Reinterpreting the Gender Gap." *Public Opinion Quarterly*, 50, 316–330.

Selected Bibliography

Aylor, Brooks. 2000. "Source Credibility and Presidential Candidates in 1996: The Changing Nature of Character and Empathy." *Communication Research Reports*, 16(3), 296–304.

Bennett, W. Lance. 1996. *News: The Politics of Illusion* (3rd ed.). New York: Longman.

Blumenthal, Sidney. 1982. *The Permanent Campaign*. New York: Simon and Schuster.

Boyle, Richard P. and Richard M. Coughlin. 1994. "Conceptualizing and Operationalizing Cultural Theory." In Dennis J. Coyle and Richard J. Ellis, eds., *Politics, Policy, and Culture*. Boulder, CO: Westview Press, 191–218.

Cappella, Joseph and Kathleen Hall Jamieson. 1997. *Spiral of Cynicism: The Press and the Public Good*. New York: Oxford University Press.

Ceaser, James and Andrew Busch. 2001. *The Perfect Tie: The True Story of the 2000 Presidential Election*. Lanham, MD: Rowman & Littlefield.

Crotty, William, ed. 2001. *America's Choice 2000*. Boulder, CO: Westview Press.

Delli Carpini, Michael X. and Ester R. Fuchs. 1993. "The Year of the Women? Candidates, Voters, and the 1992 Election." *Political Science Quarterly*, 108(1): 29–36.

Denton, Robert E., Jr. 1998. *The 1996 Presidential Campaign: A Communication Perspective* Westport, CT: Praeger.

Devlin, Patrick. 2001. "Contrasts in Presidential Campaign Commercials of 2000." *American Behavioral Scientist*, 44(12), 2338–2369.

Douglas, Mary. 1982. *In the Active Voice*. London: Routledge and Kegan Paul.

Ellis, Richard J. 1993. *American Political Cultures*. New York: Oxford University Press.

Ellis, Richard J. 1998. *The Dark Side of the Left: Illiberal Egalitarianism in America*. Lawrence: University Press of Kansas.

Fishkin, James S. 1995. *The Voice of the People: Public Opinion and Democracy*. New Haven, CT: Yale University Press.

Friedenberg, Robert. 1997. *Rhetorical Studies of National Political Debates—1996*. Westport, CT: Praeger.

Jacobson, Gary. 2001. *The 2000 Elections and Beyond*. Washington, DC: Congressional Quarterly Press.

Kaid, Lynda L. 1994. "Political Advertising in the 1992 Campaign." In Robert E. Denton, Jr., ed., *The 1992 Presidential Campaign: A Communication Perspective*. Westport, CT: Praeger, 111–127.

Kaid, Lynda L. 1996. "Technology and Political Advertising: The Application of Ethical Standards to the 1992 Spots." *Communication Research Reports*, 13(2), 129–137.

Kaid, Lynda L. 1997. "Effects of the Television Spots on Images of Dole and Clinton." *American Behavioral Scientist*, 40(8), 1085–1094.

Kaid, Lynda L. 1998. "Videostyle and the Effects of the 1996 Presidential Campaign Advertising." In Robert E. Denton, Jr., ed., *The 1996 Presidential Campaign: A Communication Perspective*. Westport, CT: Praeger, 143–159.

Kaid, Lynda L. 1999. "Political Advertising: A Summary of Research Findings." In Bruce I. Newman, ed., *The Handbook of Political Marketing*. Thousand Oaks, CA: Sage Publications, 423–438.

Kaid, Lynda L. 2000. "Ethics and Political Advertising." In Robert E. Denton, Jr., ed., *Political Communication Ethics: An Oxymoron?* Westport, CT: Praeger, 147–177.

Kaid, Lynda L. 2001. "TechnoDistortions and Effects of the 2000 Political Advertising." *American Behavioral Scientist*, 44(12), 2370–2379.

Kaid, Lynda L. and Anne Johnston. 2001. *Videostyle in Presidential Campaigns: Style and Content of Televised Political Advertising*. Westport, CT: Praeger.

Kaid, Lynda L., Michael McKinney, and John Tedesco. 2000. *Civic Dialogue in the 1996 Campaign: Candidate, Media, and Public Voices*. Cresskill, NJ: Hampton Press.

Kaid, Lynda L. and John Tedesco. 1999. "Tracking Voter Reactions to the Television Advertising." In Lynda L. Kaid and Dianne G. Bystrom, eds., *The Electronic Election: Perspectives on the 1996 Campaign Communication*. Mahwah, NJ: Lawrence Erlbaum, 233–245.

Kendall, Kathleen E. 2000. *Communication in the Presidential Primaries: Candidates and the Media, 1912–2000*. Westport, CT: Praeger.

Kenski, Henry C. 1988. "The Gender Gap: in a Changing Electorate." In Carol Muellen, ed., *The Politics of the Gender Gap: The Social Construction of Political Influence*. Newbury Park, CA: Sage Publications, 38–60.

Kenski, Henry C. 1996. "From Agenda Setting to Priming and Farming: Reflections on Theory and Method." In Mary E. Stuckey, ed., *The Theory and Practice of Political Communication*. Albany: State University of New York Press, 67–83.

Kenski, Henry, Carol Chang, and Brooks Aylor. 1998. "Explaining the Vote: The Presidential Election of 1996." In Robert E. Denton, Jr., ed., *The 1996 Presidential Campaign: A Communication Perspective*. Westport, CT: Praeger, 263–284.

Kenski, Henry C. and Lee Sigelman. 1993. "Where the Votes Come From: Group

Components of the 1988 Senate Vote." *Legislative Studies Quarterly*, 28(3), 367–390.

Kenski, Kate. 2000. "The Gender Gap in Political Knowledge: Are Women Less Knowledgeable Than Men About Politics?" In Kathleen Hall Jamieson, ed., *Everything You Think You Know About Politics . . . and Why You're Wrong*. New York: Basic Books, 83–89.

Kerbel, Matthew. 1998. *Edited for Television: CNN, ABC, and American Presidential Elections* (2nd ed.). Boulder, CO: Westview Press.

Kerbel, Matthew. 1999. *Remote and Controlled: Media Politics in a Cynical Age* (2nd ed.). Boulder, CO: Westview Press.

Leichty, Greg and Ede Warner. 2000. "Cultural Topoi: Implications for Public Relations." In Robert L. Heath, ed., *Handbook of Public Relations*. Thousand Oaks, CA: Sage Publications, 61–74.

Morris, Dick. 1997. *Behind the Oval Office: Winning the Presidency in the Nineties*. New York: Random House.

Nelson, Michael. 2001. *The Elections of 2000*. Washington, DC: Congressional Quarterly Press.

Patterson, Thomas. 1993. *Out of Order* New York: Alfred Knopf.

Pavlik, John V. 1997. *New Media Technology: Cultural and Commercial Perspectives* (2nd ed.). New York: Allyn and Bacon Press.

Pew Center for Civic Journalism. 2001. "James K. Batten Award for Excellence in Civic Journalism." *American Journalism Review*, 23(4), 8–9.

Pomper, Gerald. 2001. *The Election of 2000*. New York: Chatham House.

Popkin, Samuel L. 1994. *The Reasoning Voter: Communication and Persuasion in Presidential Campaigns*. Chicago: University of Chicago Press.

Putnam, Robert D. 1995. "Bowling Alone: America's Declining Social Capital." *Journal of Democracy*, 6 (January), 65–78.

Sabato, Larry J. 1993. *Feeding Frenzy: How Attack Journalism Has Transformed American Politics*. New York: Free Press.

Stephanopoulos, George. 1999. *All Too Human: A Political Education*. Boston: Little, Brown.

Tedesco, John C. 2001. "Issue and Strategy Agenda-Setting in the 2000 Presidential Primaries." *American Behavioral Scientist*, 44(12), 2049–2068.

Thompson, Michael, Richard Ellis, and Aaron Wildavsky. 1990. *Cultural Theory*. Boulder, CO: Westview Press.

Trent, Judith S. and Robert V. Friedenberg. 2000. *Political Campaign Communication: Principles and Practices* (4th ed.). Westport, CT: Praeger.

Wayne, Stephen. 2000. *The Road to the White House 2000*. Boston: Bedford/St. Martin's Press.

Wildavsky, Aaron. 1989. "Choosing Preferences by Constructing Institutions: A Cultural Theory of Preference Formation." In Arthur Asa Berger, ed., *Political Culture and Public Opinion*. New Brunswick, NJ: Transaction Publishers, 21–48.

Wolfe, Alan. 1998. *One Nation, After All*. New York: Penguin Books.

Index

About the Contributors

BROOKS AYLOR is an Assistant Professor at LaSalle University. He has degrees from Arkansas State University and the University of Arizona. While at Arkansas and Arizona he helped direct nationally competitive debate programs and public speaking programs. Aylor teaches a variety of graduate and undergraduate human communication courses, and his interest areas are communication theory, interpersonal communication, and political communication. His current research focus is on relational maintenance processes in long-distance relationships. He has authored and coauthored several essays and book chapters.

ROBERT E. DENTON, JR. holds the W. Thomas Rice Chair of Leadership Studies and serves as Director of the Virginia Tech Corps of Cadets Center for Leader Development at Virginia Polytechnic Institute and State University. He has degrees in political science and communication studies from Wake Forest University and Purdue University. In addition to numerous articles, essays, and book chapters, he is author, coauthor, or editor of 12 books. His most recent titles are *Political Communication Ethics: An Oxymoron?* (Praeger, 2000) and the forthcoming *The Symbolic Crisis of the American Presidency: The Case of William Jefferson Clinton*. Denton serves as editor for the Praeger Series in Political Communication and Presidential Studies.

ROBERT V. FRIEDENBERG is Professor of Communication at Miami (Ohio) University. In addition to numerous articles and book chapters, he is the author, coauthor, or editor of five books. Recent titles include *Rhetorical Studies of National Political Debates: 1960–1996* (Praeger, 1997),

Communication Consultants in Political Campaigns (Praeger, 1997), and *Political Campaign Communication: Principles and Practices* (4th ed.) (with Judith Trent) (Praeger, 2000). In 1989 he received the "Outstanding Book of the Year Award" from the Religious Speech Communication Association for *"Hear O Israel": The History of American Jewish Preaching 1654–1970.* He has served as a communication consultant for the Republican National Committee and has been involved in over 80 political campaigns.

RACHEL L. HOLLOWAY is an Associate Professor of Communication Studies at Virginia Polytechnic Institute and State University. She has degrees from Morehead State University and Purdue University. She teaches courses in public affairs and issue management. In addition to numerous articles and book chapters, she is author of *In the Matter of J. Robert Oppenheimer: Politics, Rhetoric, and Self-Defense* (Praeger, 1993) and coeditor of *The Clinton Presidency: Images, Issues, and Communication Strategies* (Praeger, 1996) (with Robert E. Denton, Jr.).

LYNDA LEE KAID is Professor of Telecommunications and Associate Dean of the College of Journalism and Communications at the University of Florida. She received her Ph.D. degree from Southern Illinois University. She previously served as the Director of the Political Communication Center and supervised the Political Archive at the University of Oklahoma. Her research specialties include political advertising and news coverage of political events. She is the author, coauthor, or editor of 14 books, including *Videostyle in Presidential Campaigns* (Praeger, 2001), *The Electronic Election* (1999), *Civic Dialogue in the 1996 Campaign* (2000), *Mediated Politics in Two Cultures* (Praeger, 1991), and *Political Advertising in Western Democracies* (1995). She has also written over 100 journal articles and book chapters and over 100 convention papers on various aspects of political communication. Dr. Kaid is a former Chair of the Political Communication Divisions of the International Communication Association and the National Communication Association, and has also served in leadership roles in the American Political Science Association and the Association for Education in Journalism and Mass Communication.

HENRY C. KENSKI is a Professor holding joint appointments in the Communication and Political Science Departments at the University of Arizona. His areas of interest and publication include public opinion, campaigns, and elections, Congress, the presidency, political communication, and political leadership. He is the author of *Saving the Hidden Treasure: The Evolution of Ground Water Policy* (1990) and coauthor of *Attack Politics: Strategy and Defense* (Praeger, 1990). In addition to various articles and book chapters, his work has been published in the *Journal of Politics, American Politics Quarterly, Public Opinion Quarterly,* and *Social Science Quarterly,* to name a few. In the applied realm, he is a partner in the firm of Arizona Opinion and Political Research, having been involved in more than 100 political campaigns, and also works with Arizona U.S. Senator Jon Kyl.

KATE KENSKI is a doctoral graduate student at the Annenberg School of Communication at the University of Pennsylvania. Her research interests are political communication, political advertising, and political campaigns.

NEIL MANSHARAMANI is a doctoral graduate student in the Department of Communication at Wayne State University. His research interests are public communication, political campaigns, and the politics of the presidency.

CRAIG ALLEN SMITH is Professor and Chair of the Department of Communication at Wayne State University. He teaches courses in political communication, rhetorical criticism, and speechwriting. In addition to numerous articles and book chapters, he is the author, coauthor, or editor of *Political Communication* (1990), *Persuasion and Social Movements* (4th ed.) (2001), *The President and the Public* (1985), and *The White House Speaks* (Praeger, 1994).

JOHN C. TEDESCO is an Assistant Professor in the Department of Communication Studies at Virginia Tech. He has degrees from the University at Albany, State University of New York, and the University of Oklahoma. His research specialties include political advertising, campaign communication, news coverage of political events, and political public relations. Dr. Tedesco is published in *American Behavioral Scientist, Communication Studies, Harvard International Journal of Press/Politics, Journal of Broadcasting and Electronic Media, Argumentation and Advocacy, Journal of Communication Studies,* and the *Handbook of Public Relations.* He is coauthor of *Civic Dialogue in the 1996 Presidential Campaign* (2000) and contributor to *The Electronic Election* (1999), *The Lynching of Language* (Praeger, 2000), and *The Clinton Presidency* (Praeger, 1996).

JUDITH S. TRENT is Professor of Communication at the University of Cincinnati. She is the author of numerous books and book chapters including "The Beginning and the Early End" in *The 1996 Presidential Campaign: A Communication Perspective* (Praeger, 1998), "The Early Campaign of 1992: The Reluctant Candidates" in *The 1992 Presidential Campaign: A Communication Perspective* (Praeger, 1994) and, with Robert Friedenberg,

Political Campaign Communication: Principles and Practices (4th ed.) (Praeger, 2000). In 1997 she served as President of the National Communication Association.

DAVID E. WHILLOCK is Dean of the College of Communication at Texas Christian University. He has written numerous articles on media images in journals such as *Literature and Film Quarterly* and *Journal of American Culture*. In addition, he has contributed chapters to several books on American Vietnam War films. He has also produced and directed a number of artistic films.

RITA KIRK WHILLOCK is the Meadows Distinguished Teaching Professor at Southern Methodist University. She has degrees in communication and political science from the University of Arkansas and the University of Missouri. Whillock is the author of several award-winning books and articles, including *Political Empiricism: Communications Strategies in State and Regional Elections* (Praeger, 1991) and *Hate Speech* (coeditor David Slayden) (1998). Whillock has more than 15 years of experience as a strategist for city council, mayoral, state, U.S. representative, and gubernatorial races. In addition to her political consulting, she has served as a communications consultant to several national and multinational corporations on public policy matters.